371.95
St8

140405

DATE DUE			

Strategies for
Educational Change

Strategies for Educational Change:

Recognizing the Gifts and Talents of All Children

Walter L. Marks

Raphael O. Nystrand

Editors

Macmillan Publishing Co., Inc.
New York
Collier Macmillan Publishers
London

Copyright © 1981. Board of Education, Montclair, New Jersey

Printed in the United States of America

Macmillan Publishing Co., Inc.
866 Third Avenue, New York, New York 10022

Collier Macmillan Canada, Ltd.

Library of Congress Cataloging in Publication Data
Main entry under title:

Strategies for educational change
Bibliography: p.
Includes index.
1. Gifted children—Education—Addresses, essays, lectures. 2. Education, Urban—Addresses, essays, lectures. I. Marks, Walter L. II. Nystrand, Raphael O.
LC3993.A33   371.9'5   79-19378
ISBN 0-02-376180-6

Printing: 1 2 3 4 5 6 7 8   Year: 1 2 3 4 5 6 7

Acknowledgements

To acknowledge all who have aided in the production of this book would require more space than we have available. However, there are some special groups and individuals whose contributons should be noted here.

We are indebted to the citizens—especially the parents and students of The Montclair Public Schools—for their support in accepting the many innovations to their school system. Acknowledgement is further given to the Montclair Board of Education for its support and commitment to the concept of educational alternatives and choices for students, parents, and teachers.

We express our appreciation to the many authors whose ideas and expertise give breadth to the theories and implementation strategies for the various curriculum ideas illustrated in this book on educational change.

A very special acknowledgement is given to the staff of The Montclair Public Schools for their assistance in the creation of the gifted and talented program, the modifications to it, and the consistent educational work to make it bear fruit. A final word of thanks is given to Edna Harris and Elizabeth Burton for their critical reading of, coordination of, and final touches to the manuscript, as well as to Gwen Pines and Rosemarie Noback for countless hours of typing and patient coping with revisions.

W.L.M.
R.O.N.

Contents

The Authors

James A. Adams is superintendent of the Winston-Salem/Forsyth County Public Schools. He attended Morehead State University for his undergraduate work and master's degree and completed the Ph.D. in educational administration at Ohio State University. He has been an elementary and a junior high school teacher. He has served as an elementary school principal, a junior high school principal, an administrative assistant to the superintendent, a research associate, an assistant superintendent, and a superintendent in Montclair, N.J., and Grosse Pointe, Mich. He has published various articles in the field of education and frequently addresses groups on public education in today's world.

Louise M. Berman is a professor in the Department of Administration, Supervision and Curriculum and associate dean in the College of Education, University of Maryland, College Park. Possessing an Ed.D. in curriculum and teaching from Teachers College, Columbia University, she has major interest in curriculum theory and development. She is active in the World Council for Curriculum and Instruction, Professors of Curriculum, and Association for Supervision and Curriculum Development. She has authored, coauthored, and edited a number of books and articles, two of which are *New Priorities in the Curriculum* (Merrill) and, with Jessie Roderick, *Curriculum: Teaching the What, How and Why of Living* (Merrill). Prior to her university work, she taught in the public schools and continues consultative work with a variety of school systems.

Yvonne L. Blanchard is assistant director for the National Council for Accreditation of Teacher Education; former assistant superintendent for administrative services in the Montclair Public Schools (N.J.); selected as an Educational Policy Fellow, George Washington University, Washington, D.C. She also served as special assistant to the associate commissioner for Equal Education Opportunity Programs, U.S. Office of Education. Dr. Blanchard received her B.A. from Fisk University, M.Ed. from Loyola, and Ed.D. from the University of Masssachusetts. She was the 1977 recipient of the Distinguished Educator Award (Magna Kappa Mu) and the 1976 Bi-Centennial Woman of the Year in Public School Education in New Jersey (National Council of Negro Women, Inc.). Among her writings is *A Study to*

Examine Learner Efficiency and Institutional Effectiveness as Measured by Perceived Self-Concepts and Locus of Control of Black Students in Segregated vs. Desegregated Schools.

Louis Clerico is a reading specialist and advisory specialist for Learning Centers in Montclair, N.J. He received his bachelor of arts and master's degrees from Jersey City State College. He has served as coordinator of a "storefront" academy in Jersey City, N.J.; reading specialist in the Jackson Public Schools, Jackson, N.J.; media and curriculum specialist for a special federal program for educable mentally retarded children at Yeshiva University, N.Y.; and special consultant to the University of Colorado special project for mentally retarded children in Boulder, Colo.

Elliot W. Eisner, professor of education and art at Stanford University, received his bachelor's degree from Roosevelt University in Chicago, a master of science degree in education from the Illinois Institute of Technology, and the master of arts and doctor of philosophy degrees from the University of Chicago. Professor Eisner has done extensive work in the fields of art education, curriculum, and educational evaluation. His research interests include the study of children's artistic development and the use of art criticism as a means for evaluating educational practice. He has served on the editorial board of professional journals, and his writings include several books and numerous articles. His most recent book is *The Educational Imagination.* He is recipient of the Palmer O. Johnson Memorial Award and the Manuel Barkan Memorial Award. He delivered the John Dewey Lecture in 1976 at the University of Chicago, and once again in 1979 he was invited to deliver the John Dewey Lecture by the John Dewey Society. He is past-president of the National Art Education Association. In 1978 he served as Senior Fulbright Scholar in Australia.

Mario D. Fantini, professor and dean of education at the University of Massachusetts, has also served as the dean of the Faculty of Education at SUNY at New Paltz. With a doctorate from Harvard, he has taught at all levels, from the elementary to graduate, and has wide experience in public school administration. Often referred to as the architect of New York City's school decentralization plan, which he worked on while serving with the Ford Foundation, he has been deeply involved in many other movements designed to improve American education. Dr. Fantini is an active speaker and author and coauthor of many books, including *Community Control and the Urban School* (with Marilyn Gittell and Richard Magat); *Toward Humanistic Education* (with Gerald Weinstein); *Decentralization: Achieving Reform* (with Marilyn Gittell); *Disadvantaged: Challenge to Education* (with

Gerald Weinstein); *Public Schools of Choice: A Plan for the Reform of American Education;* and *Alternative Education: A Source Book for Parents, Teachers, Students and Administrators.*

Ward J. Ghory is associate director of the Urban Education Pilot Project for Cincinnati Public Schools. He holds a B.A. from Yale University and M.Ed. and Ed.D. from the University of Massachusetts. The founder of an alternative school program, he has teaching experience at various levels from kindergarten through high school. Trained at Stanford University in effective teaching practices, his interests lie in research and curriculum development for marginal learners particularly in urban settings.

Jerome D. Kaplan is professor of education at Seton Hall University. He received his B.S., Phi Beta Kappa, from Rutgers University in mathematics, his M.A. from Cornell in mathematics, and his doctorate from Columbia University's Teachers College in mathematics education. He has had a long and deep interest in applying learning theory to curriculum design. He is the senior author of *High Intensity Learning Systems—Mathematics,* a management system for individualizing instruction, and a coauthor of *Scoring High in Mathematics,* both published by Random House. He has written widely in the areas of individualized instruction, management systems and testing. A former elementary and secondary school teacher, Dr. Kaplan was an associate professor at Teachers College, Columbia University, prior to his present position.

Stanton Leggett is president of Stanton Leggett and Associates, an educational consulting firm with offices in Martha's Vineyard and Chicago. His company specializes in working in the United States and abroad with public school systems, independent schools, and colleges in the areas of educational management and educational facilities planning. He holds a B.A. from Columbia College and M.A. and Ph.D. from Columbia University. For many years he was a partner in the educational consulting firm of Engelhardt, Engelhardt and Leggett. His most recent book, of which he was senior author with three others, is *Planning Flexible Learning Places,* published by McGraw-Hill in 1977.

Bethene LeMahieu is director of Gifted/Talented and Futuristics for the Montclair (N.J.) Public Schools and was director of elementary education during the planning and implementing of Montclair's Gifted and Talented Program. She is completing her doctoral studies in administration at Rutgers University.

James Macdonald is presently Distinguished Professor in the School of Education at the University of North Carolina (Greensboro). He spent 16 years teaching at the University of Wisconsin, during which time he was also visiting professor of the University of London (Goldsmith College). At various times he has served as director of school research, director of the laboratory school, director of doctoral studies, and chairman of the Department of Curriculum and Instruction. He is a member of AAUP, AERA, and ASCD and has held a number of offices both locally and nationally. He has published well over 80 articles including research studies and chapters in books. His major emphasis is curriculum design and theory and society in education.

Walter L. Marks is superintendent of schools in Montclair, N.J. His interest in alternative methods of education led to establishment of numerous options for students in the Montclair schools. A member of the University Council of Educational Administration, he is a former teacher, principal, college administrator, and assistant superintendent. Dr. Marks is the author and coauthor of numerous articles and papers that have appeared in educational journals or been delivered at national workshops and conferences. He holds a B.A. from Glenville State College, a master's degree from Kent State University, and a Ph.D. in Educational Administration from Ohio State University. He is the 1979 recipient of the Second Annual Human Rights Award for outstanding contributions in the field of education from the Desegregation Institute of Rider College (N.J.).

Alice Miel is a professor of education emerita, Teachers College, Columbia University. Following her retirement in 1971, she worked for eighteen months in the Ministry of Education, Kabul, Afghanistan, as a social studies consultant for the Curriculum and Textbook Project. For the next four years she served as executive secretary of the World Council for Curriculum and Instruction. Her writings include *Changing the Curriculum—A Social Process* (1946), *Cooperative Procedures in Learning* (1952), *More Than Social Studies* (with Peggy Brogan), (1957), *Creativity in Teaching* (1961), and *Supervision for Improved Instruction* (with Arthur J. Lewis) (1972).

Harry Morgan is professor of education at Syracuse University. He has taught graduate and undergraduate courses at Bank Street College, Brooklyn College, the University of New Hampshire, and Ohio University. He was involved in the initial planning stages of Project Headstart and served as the northeast regional director for New York, New Jersey, and the New England states. Dr. Morgan's on-going research activity is lifespan oriented and involves workshops on infancy, early childhood, adolescence, and gerontology, for care-giving professionals. A graduate of the University of Wisconsin with an M.A. in social work, he received an Ed.D. from the University of Massachusetts. His most recent writings have appeared in *The New York Times* and a textbook, *The Learning Community.*

Candace Nattland is a former elementary school teacher in the Gifted and Talented Program in Montclair, N.J. An elementary school teacher for eight years, she is presently teaching in Spartanburg, S.C., District #7. She holds a master of science degree from Bank Street College of Education.

Raphael O. Nystrand is professor and dean of the School of Education at the University of Louisville. Formerly professor and chairperson of the Academic Faculty of Educational Administration at Ohio State University, he is author, coauthor, and editor of several articles and books in the area of educational administration. Dr. Nystrand has taught in public schools and holds degrees from Cornell College (Iowa), Johns Hopkins University, and Northwestern University.

Robert H. Parker is a program director at Educational Testing Service, Princeton, N.J. His professional background includes organizing and directing programs in adult education, continuing education, minority assessment concerns, urban education, and organizational management. he is a retired USAF colonel who holds a B.S., and M.S. in education and a Ph.D. in adult and continuing education. His experiences include addressing educational concerns within elementary schools, secondary schools, and institutions of higher education.

William C. Parker is a program director in the Office of Minority Studies at Educational Testing Service, Princeton, N.J. Formerly a teacher and principal in inner-city schools, he has also had experience as a professor in Oberlin, Ohio, and at the University of Ghana. His areas of expertise are urban education, minority assessment, and the development of assertive learning systems for minority youngsters. Mr. Parker holds a B.S. and M.S. in education and will receive his Ph.D. in urban education in June 1980.

Jessie A. Roderick is professor of education at the University of Maryland, College Park. She holds degrees from Wilkes College, Teachers College of Columbia University, and Temple University. Her professional areas of interest are curriculum and communication, which are reflected in her writing and research. In addition to teaching preschool, elementary, and college students, Professor Roderick was associate director of the Center for

Young Children at the University of Maryland. A recent text coauthored with Louise M. Berman is *Curriculum: Teaching the What, How and Why of Living.*

Robert L. Sinclair is professor of education and director of the Center for Curriculum Studies at the University of Massachusetts. He received his Ed.D. in curriculum and instruction from the University of California at Los Angeles. Dr. Sinclair is primarily interested in developing schools consisting of multienvironments that are responsive to the academic and personal strengths and weaknesses of learners. Toward this end, he has consulted with schools and school systems throughout the United States and in England about curriculum decision making and the influence of educational environments on human behavior. His research and writing centers on the practical problems teachers and administrators face when implementing curriculum change, theoretical issues about systems for curriculum decision making, and measurement of student perceptions of learning conditions.

Warren Singer is math/science coordinator for gifted and talented education in Montclair, N.J. He holds an M.A. in advanced specialization in elementary education. He has served as a math/science specialist and as a curriculum writer on Montclair's adjunct staff during the planning and development of the Gifted and Talented Program. He has recently been inducted into the Phi Kappa Phi National Honor Society.

Tonnes Stave went through the New York City public schools, attended Wagner College, the University of Nebraska, Rutgers University, and Montclair State College, with majors in Asian, European, and American history. He has been a high school teacher and an assistant principal of a high school. Since 1970 he has been the principal of Montclair (N.J.) High School.

Dorothy S. Strickland is professor of reading and language arts in the Early Childhood Department of Kean College of New Jersey. A former classroom teacher, reading consultant, and learning disability specialist, she has had considerable experience teaching and studying children. Her publications include numerous articles in major educational journals and chapters in books concerning language arts and reading instruction. She is a major contributor to the Allyn and Bacon Reading Program, *Pathfinder*, and coauthor of a forthcoming text on language arts instruction. An active researcher, she was recipient of a national research award in 1972. She has held elected office in both the National Council of Teachers of English and the International Reading Association in which she served as president, 1978-79.

Daniel L. Stufflebeam is director of the Evaluation Center and professor of education at Western Michigan University. He holds a bachelor's degree from the University of Iowa and master's and Ph.D. degrees from Purdue University. He has served as teacher, test developer, researcher, evaluator, administrator, and author and has held offices in the National Council on Measurements in Education and the American Educational Research Association. He chaired the committee that wrote the book *Educational Evaluation and Decision Making*, and his CIPP Model has been widely used in the United States and a number of foreign countries. Currently, he is the chairman of the Joint Committee of Standards for Educational Evaluation.

E. Paul Torrance is Alumni Foundation Distinguished Professor of Educational Psychology at the University of Georgia. A major interest of his 43-year professional career has been concern with the education of gifted and talented children and the search for indicators of giftedness and talent. He is the author of 26 books and over 1,000 journal articles, monographs, chapters in books, and other publications. His latest book is *The Search for Satori and Creativity* (Creative Education Foundation). A major career contribution has been the development of the Future Problem Solving Program into a national curriculum and interscholastic competition project.

M. Jerry Weiss is Distinguished Service Professor of Communications at Jersey City State College, New Jersey. He holds a B.A. from the University of North Carolina and M.A. and Ed.D. from Teachers College, Columbia University. Dr. Weiss has taught in secondary schools and colleges and served as a consultant to school systems across the nation. Recipient of the Elliott Landau Award in 1977 as outstanding teacher in the field of children's and adolescent literature, he has been an editor and advisor to numerous publishers of literature for children and adolescents. His most recent publication is *The American Way of Laughing*, published by Bantam Books, 1977.

RAPHAEL O. NYSTRAND, University of Louisville

Introduction

The primary purpose of this book is to help others develop and implement programs for young people who have special gifts and talents. Written by professors and practitioners, it deals with both theoretical and operational concerns. It provides general and specific suggestions for curriculum design from early childhood through grade 12 and offers analysis and discussion regarding such issues as the identification of student needs and capabilities, the acceptance of minority cultures, leadership strategies, the relationship of schools to their surrounding community as well as new roles for parents in planning educational programs for their children.

The tone of these chapters is optimistic. The material in the book is developed from the viewpoint that all young people have special gifts and talents. We live at a time when it is commonplace to criticize schools and educators. Problems associated with teaching and learning are well-known and widely publicized by public as well as professional media. Indeed, the level of criticism regarding education has reached the point in some areas that people despair about the possibility of improvement. The people who wrote the following chapters are not so pessimistic. They suggest strategies to improve school programs that are workable and that in some instances have already been implemented with satisfactory results. This book illustrates some new methods of organizing schools, their curriculum and instructional methodologies, in ways that provide some new answers to the old problems of achievement, motivation, parent participation, school organization, and so forth.

The origins of this book can be traced to the educational program in Montclair, New Jersey. Montclair is a city of approximately 50,000 persons that is twenty-five minutes from New York City. The city is characterized by diversity; of the more than six thousand pupils in the public schools, 41 per cent are black, 55 per cent are Anglo, and 4 per cent come from a wide variety of countries. Children enrolled in the English as a second language program in 1978 spoke more than twenty different native languages.

A few years ago, the Montclair Public Schools began an alternative schools program. At least part of the motivation for this program was the desire to find a strategy for school desegregation that would be acceptable to the public. Desegregation had been a consistent, if controversial, objective of the school system for several years. Earlier plans that depended on forced busing, changes in attendance areas, and school closings had been resisted.

It can now be reported that Montclair has successfully desegregated its schools by implementing the alternative schools program. However, this is but part of the program's success. Of greater interest and long-range significance is that the school system has provided children with new and expanded educational opportunities that are satisfying to them, their parents, and their teachers. Alternatives exist at middle and high school levels, but the range of alternatives available to students at the elementary school level is most graphic. Options offered include a neighborhood school with either a self-contained classroom or an open, multi-aged, team-taught class; a fundamental school; a futures school; or a gifted and talented magnet school. It is the last option that is unique and that provided the intellectual stimulus for this book.

The central premise of the Montclair Gifted/ Talented Program is that *all* children are gifted and talented and that it is the responsibility of the school to recognize and nurture the individual gifts of each child. This orientation contrasts with the traditional view of giftedness, which emphasizes intellectual ability. Notwithstanding the widely noted 1972 report of the U.S. Commissioner of Education, which established six categories of giftedness and talent (general intellectual ability, specific academic aptitude, creative or productive thinking, leadership ability, visual and performing arts, psychomotor ability),[1] most school programming for gifted/talented

---

[1] Sidney P. Marland, Jr., *Education of the Gifted and Talented*, Vol. I, Report to the Congress of the United States by the U.S. Commissioner of Education (Washington, D.C.: U.S. Government Printing Office, 1972), p. 2.

children focuses on serving small numbers of children. Zettel[2] reports that most states employ a definition that is more restrictive than these six categories in an effort to identify gifted/talented children and that general intellectual ability is the most prominent criterion. Moreover, specific procedures for identifying gifts or aptitudes are often highly restrictive. For example, intellectual or academic giftedness is often determined by performance at the 95th or 98th percentile on standardized tests.

The chapters that follow call into question the desirability of defining giftedness in such limited terms. They also challenge traditional notions about curriculum design, individualized instruction, educational planning, and urban education. They were prepared for a symposium on educating the gifted/talented that was held in Montclair in the spring of 1978.

Some of the chapter authors and symposium participants are teachers or administrators who helped to create and provide the gifted/talented program in Montclair. Others are persons outside the system who consulted with Montclair officials as they designed the program. Still others are persons with general interest and knowledge about school programming who were invited to share their perspectives at the symposium. All participants were invited to visit the Montclair schools and discuss their prospective chapter before the symposium. Thus everyone began with some understanding of the Montclair program, and some initial effort was made to reduce overlap among the various chapters.

The purposes of the symposium were to explore the concept of giftedness, to demonstrate the Montclair approach to identifying and teaching gifted/talented children to an audience of educational leaders from across the country, and to stimulate dialogue about approaches to teaching the gifted, particularly in urban settings. This book was a planned outcome of the symposium. Participants were selected because of their willingness and ability to consider new approaches to educating children in urban areas in ways that give special attention to their individual gifts and talents. Each was asked to write a paper for publication and to bring it to the symposium. Unlike most conferences, however, this was not a session where authors made formal presentations to large audiences. The papers were presented instead to small discussion groups, which met in the homes of community residents. Discussion was encouraged and authors were provided opportunity to revise their papers on the basis of this discussion.

The chapters that follow are presented in five sections. Part I presents

---

[2] Jeffrey Zettel, "State Provisions for Educating the Gifted and Talented," in A. Harry Passow (Ed.), *The Gifted and Talented: Their Education and Development*, The 78th Yearbook of the National Society for the Study of Education, Part I (Chicago: University of Chicago Press, 1979), pp. 63-74.

general perspectives regarding the nature of the gifts and talents among children and the responsibilities and opportunities for educators who teach them. Part II addresses general concerns related to curriculum development responsive to individual needs of all children's gifts and talents. Part III deals with developing curricula for children in different age groups, i.e., early childhood through early elementary, the middle years and the high school years. Part IV discusses curricula for gifted children in typical school-content areas., i.e., math, language arts, science, social studies, arts, and so forth. In the final section, suggestions are presented regarding administrative concerns of evaluation, finance, and facilities for gifted/talented programs.

PART ONE **General Perspectives**

The question of "Who is gifted?" is one of the most persistent queries encountered by those who study and/or teach gifted children. E. Paul Torrance addresses this question in the initial chapter. He begins with a series of poignant vignettes about giftedness in children and then reviews a number of models for identifying giftedness. The chapter concludes with a set of guidelines for identifying gifted children and developing programs for them.

The role of educators in shaping society has been debated for many years. During the last decade much of the argument about this subject has shifted from the question of what role educators should play to whether they actually have any impact. Raphael O. Nystrand reviews some of the literature surrounding these issues, examines expectations for schools, and concludes that educators have substantial impact on young people and society and that they should view their responsibility to the community from this perspective.

Mario D. Fantini traces the development of alternative schools as they emerged first outside and subsequently within public school systems. He notes that in the most recent phase of the alternative movement the difference between schooling and education has become more important. Schools are increasingly called on to share the responsibility for achieving educational goals and to coordinate the activities of other agencies to that end. He identifies the Montclair program as one that "starts us on the road from schooling to education."

The chapter by Robert H. Parker and William C. Parker addresses the issue of accepting minority cultures within majority institutions such as school systems. They point out that in contrast to European and Western culture, which is primarily "lettered," Afro-American culture emerges from an oral tradition. This distinction results in different lifestyles, thought processes, behavioral learning patterns,

5

concepts of time versus perception, value systems, communications, and assessment procedures. The authors write that educators must be mindful of these differences in order to recognize and build on the strengths of minority students.

1

E. PAUL TORRANCE, University of Georgia

Who Is Gifted?

Who indeed is gifted? This is one of the most important educational questions today. How we define giftedness makes an enormous difference in the way we treat children, the ways we teach them, how a community organizes its school system, and how children learn, grow, and achieve. In observing some children, we may help answer and define the question, "Are they gifted?"

Wally was 11 years old, deaf, and assigned to a class for mentally retarded children. His powerful drawing, "Shout in Silence," attracted the attention of Rawley Silver, an art teacher.[1] She found that his talent and art works were truly outstanding. She also discovered that his ability to solve spatial problems was equally outstanding, betraying a level of intelligence never shown on intelligence tests. His scores on the *Torrance Tests of Creative Thinking*[2] (Figural Form) would place him in the upper 1 per cent of almost any educational group. Was Wally gifted? What would the consequences be if Wally, provided with appropriate opportunities, had been defined as gifted in art and problem solving? What would be the

[1] R. A. Silver, *Shout in Silence: Visual Arts and the Deaf* (New York: Metropolitan Museum of Art, 1976).

[2] E. P. Torrance, *The Torrance Tests of Creative Thinking: Norms—Technical Manual* (Lexington, Mass.: Personnel Press/Ginn and Co., 1966, Revised edition, 1974).

consequences if he were defined as mentally retarded (and deaf) and educated as such? Which would be better for Wally? Which would best serve the needs of society?

John was a strong, energetic 12-year-old sixth grader who had never learned to read.[3] He was known as the school's vandal, although no one could ever prove that he and his friends made a shambles of the school each weekend. Because he had been a problem to teachers almost from the first day of his schooling, no one thought he could learn—except his sixth grade teacher, who thought he was gifted. Being a veritable mechanical genius, he could repair any mechanical or audiovisual equipment. He was charismatic; he could attract other boys, organize them, and lead them in almost anything. His art was also superior.

John's teacher encouraged the student council to appoint him as head of the lunch room committee to help arrange the school cafeteria and keep things functioning. John recruited other boys to help, and this initiated many other leadership activities aimed at improving the school. School vandalism ceased. John learned to read about as well as almost any sixth grader and actually enjoyed school. Was John gifted? Was it better to treat John as gifted in psychomotor and leadership areas or as a retarded nonreader and a behavior disorder case? Which was in John's best interest? Which was in society's best interest?

Bob's classroom behavior was almost the opposite of that of John.[4] He was not a troublemaker. He sat through classes sadly and quietly. He was withdrawn and rarely spoke to anyone. He was a brilliant basketball player, but in the ninth grade he no longer played. Nor could he read. However, his art teacher thought that he was gifted as an artist and had an intelligence not betrayed by his scores on reading and intelligence tests. She was also his English teacher but could not get him to respond even orally to her tests in literature. In desperation she asked Bob to illustrate the poems and stories the class had read while the rest of the class took the tests of the material. The depth of understanding displayed through his drawings amazed both teacher and classmates. Through Bob's drawings they became aware of deeper meanings and new insights into what they had been reading. Their appreciation of the thoughts and emotions communicated through his art made a difference in the way Bob felt about himself. He learned to read, excelled in basketball again, and "rejoined society." Was Bob gifted? Would it be better to define Bob as gifted in art and basketball or as emotionally disturbed and retarded in reading? Which served Bob's and society's interest better?

[3] E. P. Torrance and R. E. Myers, *Creative Learning and Teaching* (New York: Harper & Row, 1970).

[4] E. P. Torrance, *Guiding Creative Talent* (Englewood Cliffs, N.J.: Prentice-Hall, 1962).

Eva was an 8-year-old third grader, although she had not achieved well in the first or second grade. She lacked confidence and was very quiet and inarticulate. Her third grade teacher said that she was gifted. Her art work was excellent and showed an advanced level of thinking. Her performance on the figural form of the *Torrance Tests of Creative Thinking*[5] placed her in the upper 1 per cent on national norms for her age and grade. Her science fair project reflected her artistic talent, aesthetic sensitivity, originality, attention to fine details, motivation, and persistence. It was selected by a panel of judges as the school's best project. When the school principal learned that Eva's project had been selected for the science fair, he assumed something was wrong; such work could not come from a child raised by a "no good" family—a family who could not even speak English. He questioned Eva in his office to support his conclusion that she had not done the project herself. Almost mute and unable to explain what she had done, she was scolded and the award was given to someone else. The teacher knew Eva had done the work herself but she was not permitted to defend Eva. The child was of course crushed by this experience, despite the teacher's efforts to console her. Again, was Eva gifted and talented? Would it be better to define Eva as an inarticulate, slow-learning, Mexican-American child or as a gifted artist, a self-directed learner, a persistent and tireless creative child?

Maria had come to the United States from Puerto Rico.[6] She was a charming child, loved her teacher, worked tirelessly, and scored 100 on almost every arithmetic or spelling paper. By almost any criterion of achievement she was the best student in Mrs. Olive Decker's fifth grade class. Even on a standardized reading test she ranked second in the group of 30 "normal" children in the class. When Maria was assigned to a class for children with retarded mental development, Mrs. Decker was shocked; she protested the decision unsuccessfully. The school principal's explanation to Mrs. Decker reads:

> I can see the extent of your interest and the nature of your relationship with this charming child. This is precisely what the psychologist called attention to, namely, that a very cordial feeling between pupil and teacher has helped the pupil to perform above her level on the basis of her willingness to please her teacher. It is not uncommon for a child with a high desire to please, to function above her "equipment" in many school areas.[7]

Although he could not bring himself to say it, the principal recognized that Maria was highly motivated. It had perhaps never occurred to him that the

[5] Torrance, *Torrance Tests.*

[6] H. Black, *They Shall Not Pass* (New York: Morrow, 1963).

[7] Ibid., p. 158.

ability to become motivated is one of mankind's most valuable gifts. A definition of giftedness that does not include motivation for excellence is unimaginable. Would it have been better to define Maria as gifted in motivation and achievement—or as a child with retarded mental development?

Louella was a black 6-year-old in a residential retardation center. I learned about Louella from a doctoral student in one of my classes. He was doing laboratory practice in an evening recreation and arts program at the center. He discovered the most gifted child he had ever seen with the ability to empathize with other children. This child was a genius at detecting when other children were in trouble and then going to their rescue. He had never seen anything like it. Should Louella be defined and taught as empathically and emotional gifted or as retarded? Who can deny the value of human empathy and emotional communication? In helping professions such as medicine, social work, psychology, and the like, the skill to awaken and develop these characteristics is prized. Who can say that such giftedness is not among the mentally retarded?

A familiar 1930 Iowa study found two children, identified by a psychologist as mentally retarded, living on a ward populated by retarded adolescent girls because of crowded conditions.[8] On return, the psychologist noted that these two children were alert and bright. He retested them and found that they were functioning at a normal level. He then arranged an experiment in which a larger number of retarded children were placed with these retarded adolescent girls, and a matched control group was given regular institutional care. Within a few years the IQ of the children placed with the retarded adolescents increased by about 25 points whereas that of the control group decreased on equal degree. Subsequently both groups were placed in foster homes and followed up in 1965 (35 years later). Almost every member of the experimental group had succeeded in life—holding jobs, completing a considerable amount of schooling, maintaining families, and the like. Almost every member of the control group had spent almost all of his/her life in some institution. The cost to taxpayers had been enormous. The cost in the loss of human talent was more so.

One could continue almost endlessly with descriptions of children such as Wally, John, Bob, Eva, Maria, and Louella. One would never find any of them in programs for identified gifted/talented children. I doubt that they would gain very much in gifted/talented programs as they are known today. Yet no one can deny their giftedness or the value of their particular kinds of giftedness to society. Surely schools should be flexible enough to nurture the kinds of giftedness that they represent.

[8] H. M. Skeels, *Adult Status of Children with Contrasting Early Life Experiences* (Chicago: Society for Research in Child Development, University of Chicago Press, 1966).

Search for a Model of Giftedness

The fuzzy model of giftedness that I have presented through these individual cases is quite unsatisfactory. People want specific standards. Psychologists and educators want models that can be expressed concretely with well-defined criteria. Such models have been advanced and these have helped in broadening our definition of giftedness; some, which I shall identify, will be examined briefly for their potential contributions.

Six Categories of the USOE

A landmark in the history of gifted/talented education was the 1972 report of the United States Commissioner of Education to the Congress of the United States.[9] This influential report embodies a broadened concept of giftedness and talent. Six types of giftedness were identified as meriting special attention:

- General intellectual ability.

- Specific academic aptitude.

- Creative and productive thinking.

- Leadership ability.

- Visual and performing arts.

- Psychomotor abilities.

This report, furthermore, accepts as gifted all children whose outstanding abilities require differentiated educational programs and/or services beyond those normally provided by the regular school program in order to realize their contributions to self and society.

Whereas many states and specific school systems have doggedly limited their definition of giftedness to the first of the six categories identified in the USOE report, a number of states and school systems have moved in the direction of the six-category definition. In doing so, they have helped to move us away from the elitist concept of giftedness. Almost no minority/disadvantaged children have been included in programs for the intellectually or academically gifted. As schools create programs in the other five areas, more and more such children are included.

Minority/disadvantaged children will probably have only a slightly better chance of being included if schools use as criteria indicators of specific academic aptitudes. However, instruments for identifying some specific

[9] *Education of the Gifted and Talented: Report to the Congress of the United States by the U.S. Commissioner of Education* (Washington, D.C.: U.S. Government Printing Office, 1972).

academic aptitudes are more attuned to the strengths of minority/disadvan-
taged children than are measures of general intellectual aptitude. For
example, such children may have unusually high aptitudes for mathematics
despite the fact that their language skills are rather poor. Others may have
unusual giftedness in languages and be quite deficient in mathematics.

There are already a few programs for creatively gifted children and
these include a considerable proportion of minority and disadvantaged
children. The *Torrance Test of Creative Thinking* (previously cited) and the
Creativity Scale of the *Alpha Biographical Inventory*[10] seem to have little or
no racial or socioeconomic bias. Classical twin-type studies of heritability
have consistently shown that creativity as assessed by existing tests has little
or no heritability.[11] Also, studies have consistently shown that there is an
overlap of roughly 30 per cent between groups identified as intellectually
gifted and groups identified as creatively gifted.[12]

Programs in the visual and performing arts also include high proportions
of minority/disadvantaged children. Identification in such programs has
usually been on the basis of performance and achievements in music, dance,
drama, painting, sculpture, photography, creative writing, and the like.
However, I think more attention should be given to the development and
use of talent tests in these areas to identify potentialities that may not have
been noted and developed because of poverty and minority group restrictions. I am convinced that such tests administered in elementary schools
would make teachers, psychologists, parents, and children aware of important talents that might otherwise go unnoted.

Not much has yet happened in the development of programs in
leadership and psychomotor categories. If developed, both of these areas
would include rather large proportions of minority/disadvantaged children.
There seems to be especially strong resistance to programs in the psychomotor area. Most people seem to associate this area with sports, where strong
programs of identification and development exist. The psychomotor area,
however, should be defined more broadly to include, for example, those
gifted in mechanical manipulation (the mechanical geniuses) and talented
gymnasts and dancers.

---

[10] C. W. Taylor and R. L. Ellison, *Alpha Biographical Inventory* (Salt Lake City: Institute for
Behavioral Research in Creativity, 1968).

[11] T. R. Pezzullo, E. E. Thorsen, and G. F. Madaus, The Heritability of Jensen's Level I and
Level II and Divergent Thinking, *American Educational Research Journal*, 1972, 9, 539-546.

[12] E. P. Torrance, *Guiding Creative Talent* (Englewood Cliffs, N.J.: Prentice-Hall, 1962).

Other Aptitude Models

An earlier and influential model of human abilities was J. P. Guilford's Structure of Intellect Model.[13,14] The model is represented by a cube. One set of dimensions represents five ways by which the human mind processes information: cognition, memory, convergent production, divergent production, and evaluation. Each dimension operates on four kinds of content (figural, semantic, symbolic, and behavioral) and six kinds of products (units, classes, relations, systems, transformations, and implications). Theoretically, this gives 120 different abilities. The model is complex, and although it has been very influential, it has not been satisfactory and acceptable for gifted/talented education. People have searched for simpler, more manageable models.

One of these is Calvin W. Taylor's Multiple Talents Model.[15] Taylor has represented his model by a series of six totem poles, each ranking the children in a class or group on each of the talents in the model. These talents are academic, creative, planning, communicating, forecasting, and decision making. In gifted programs based on this model, an instructor teaches six of these talents and increases the chances that a larger number of children will emerge as gifted in performance. A sizable number of school systems have adopted this model and developed assessment procedures and program materials to implement it. At the present time, it is difficult and perhaps premature to evelute these programs. However, evaluations are in progress.

A New Kind of Model of Multiple Criteria

All the models just described are ability or aptitude models. In practice, there have been operating a variety of multiple criteria models. However, most of them have not been conceptualized clearly and have generally been dominated by measures of intelligence or academic ability. Multiple criteria have included measures of achievement, teacher grades, teacher nominations, parent nominations, self-nominations, creativity test scores, peer nomination, and the like. Just how these multiple criteria are used has rarely been specified. After research, it appears that the program administrator's only criterion that has much influence is the intelligence or aptitude score. Ann Lamkins of the New York State Department of Education has recently suggested a model that will be useful in dealing with issues of multiple

---

[13] J. P. Guilford, *The Nature of Human Intelligence* (Buffalo, N.Y.: Creative Education Foundation, 1977).

[14] M. N. Meeker, *The Structure of Intellect and Its Interpretation and Use* (Columbus, O.: Merrill, 1969).

[15] C. W. Taylor and R. L. Ellison, Predictors and Criteria of Creativity, in C. W. Taylor (Ed.), *Climate for Creativity* (New York: Pergamon Press, 1972).

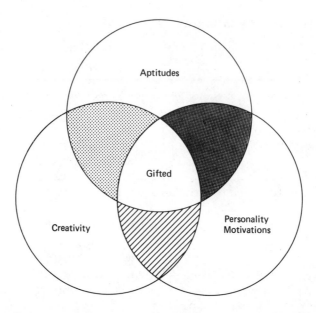

FIGURE 1-1. General model of giftedness by Ann Lamkins (1977).

identification criteria and thereby reduce some of the existing confusion about who is gifted.[16]

Her model considers three sets of variables: aptitude, creativity, and personality/motivation. The model can be conceptualized by drawing three intersecting circles, one representing each of these three sets of variables.

In Lamkins's model the identification program would consider the aptitude or aptitudes relevant to the specific program (e.g., vocal music, instrumental music, drama, mathematics, leadership, mechanical manipulation) rather than several kinds of aptitude for selection into a single program. To be considered truly gifted a child must, in addition to the relevant aptitude, be creative and possess the personality characteristics and motivations required for giftedness in the specific program. The truly gifted would be high in all three criteria. These children would be represented by the area where all three circles overlap. The potentially gifted would be those who are high in two of these sets of criteria. Considering criteria of giftedness in this way, there would be useful clues for guidance and meaningful programming. Such an analysis would help in assisting a child high in aptitude but lacking in creativity, personality characteristics, and motivation; the child

---

[16] A. Lamkins, *A Model: Planning, Designing and Evaluating Identification and Instructional Programs for Gifted, Talented and/or Potentially Gifted Children* (Albany, N.Y.: New York State Department of Education, 1977).

high in creativity but lacking in personality characteristics, motivation, and aptitude; and the one high in personality characteristics and motivation but lacking in the other criteria.

Creativity as a Common Factor in Giftedness

Lamkins's model assigns an important role to creativity in all areas of giftedness. This concurs with my longstanding conviction that creativity is a distinguishing characteristic of giftedness in every area of human activity. Creativity has long been recognized as essential in medical and scientific advances, invention, and excellence in the arts. I have insisted that it is also essential in excellence in human relations, leadership, parenting, teaching, and all other human affairs.

Motivation as Another Common Factor

It is equally obvious that motivation is another common factor in gifted behavior. A person may have the aptitudes for greatness in a particular endeavor and even be highly creative. Yet if this person is not motivated to use his/her aptitudes and creativity, gifted behavior will not occur. Generally, however, people are motivated to do the things that they do best. Thus there is a high correlation between aptitude and motivation, but there are many forces that destroy motivation—lack of opportunity, pressures to overconformity, derogation of excellence, to name a few.

The research of Calvin Taylor and Robert Ellison,[17] Donald Mac-Kinnon,[18] and Frank Barron[19] strongly supports the importance of personality characteristics and motivation in outstanding creative achievement. In another study there is one partial validation of the Lamkins's model.[20] The difficulty of longitudinal study in predicting the adult creative achievement of women was more fully examined. By combining scores on the *Torrance Tests of Creative Thinking* with scores on the Creativity Scale of the *Alpha Biographical Inventory*, the predictability of adult creative achievement increased tremendously.

---

[17] C. W. Taylor and R. L. Ellison, Moving Toward Working Models in Creativity: Utah Creativity Experiences and Insights, in I. A. Taylor and J. W. Getzels (Eds.), *Perspectives in Creativity* (Chicago: Aldine, 1975).

[18] D. W. MacKinnon, IPAR's Contribution to the Conceptualization and Study of Creativity, in I. A. Taylor and J. W. Getzels (Eds.), *Perspectives in Creativity* (Chicago: Aldine, 1975).

[19] F. Barron, The Solitariness of Self and Its Mitigation Through Creative Imagination, in I. A. Taylor and J. W. Getzels (Eds.), *Perspectives in Creativity* (Chicago: Aldine, 1975).

[20] E. P. Torrance, C. B. Bruch, and J. A. Morse, Improving Predictions of the Adult Creative Achievement of Gifted Girls by Using Autobiographical Information, *Gifted Child Quarterly*, 1973, *17*, 91-95.

Conclusion

The following is a summation of my views on a set of tentative guidelines for identification and programming:[21]

1. Evaluate, identify, develop, and reward many different kinds of excellence—all those kinds of giftedness and talent that our society needs and that members of our society need for health and self-fulfillment.

2. For a particular program (such as a magnet school), the criteria used in identification and evaluation should be those that are relevant to the purposes of the program.

3. Although emphasis may be placed on the aptitudes relevant to the program under consideration, attention should also be given to personality characteristics, motivation, and creativity.

4. In programs designed to encourage excellence, one variable that should be consistently evaluated and encouraged is creativity.

5. In evaluating excellence and searching for giftedness and talents among racial and ethnic minorities, especially disadvantaged groups, it is important to give attention to those kinds of giftedness or excellence that are encouraged and valued by the particular culture to which the person belongs.

6. Just as there are an almost infinite number of ways of attaining excellence, there are also an almost infinite number of ways in which a person can behave creatively. Thus, to evaluate creative excellence or potentiality for such excellence, there must be a reasonable sampling of possible ways of behaving creatively. Using a single task to assess creative abilities should be carefully avoided.

7. Schools should be concerned about all kinds of giftedness and talent that, if given a chance, would result in excellence and that can be modified through educational experiences.

8. Evaluations of giftedness and excellence should not be limited to competitive activities or their rarity. A major criterion should be useful to the society and to the individual.

9. In evaluating giftedness and excellence, freedom from imperfections should not be a criterion. Too frequently, imperfections irrelevant to the evaluation prevent us from becoming aware of those gifted qualities that are highly relevant.

10. One fundamental quality in all evaluation of excellence is an aesthetic quality. The gifted person's behavior is "beautiful" and makes others aware of the beauty and excitement about them.

[21] E. P. Torrance, Broadening Concepts of Giftedness in the 70's, *Gifted Child Quarterly*, 1970, *14*, 199-208.

11. A fundamental quality of excellence evaluation is to be found in perspective: the ability of the person, his ideas, his products to make others see the world in a different and better perspective—to maintain its beauty and its excellence under changing perspectives. Perhaps the evaluator—the identifier—must also assume different perspectives to even become aware of giftedness, talent, and excellence.

12. Another fundamental quality underlying excellence and giftedness is that of constancy: endurance, predictability, and perseverance in always being there and being actively involved.

13. Yet another fundamental quality is emotional responsiveness— genuine caring, love, working for the good of others. It is a mainspring of energy and creativity that compensates for a variety of imperfections.

14. Above all, each child's individuality must be respected and she/he must be aided in achieving a strong, healthy sense of identity. Rather than honoring the cultural assumption that "the good child is a modest child," the fact should be stressed that recognition and acceptance of positive characteristics are necessary for self-realization.

15. Children must be taught from an early age about their individuality. This will enable children to become aware of, accept, and develop their giftedness and talents—and increase chances of avoiding being misfits.

16. Educational programs must be made open ended so that giftedness can emerge and be guided in healthy ways.

2

RAPHAEL O. NYSTRAND, University of Louisville

Educators as Social Architects

The title of this chapter connotes a view of the world in which educators, individually and/or as a profession, have a plan for the future of society—programs are designed, resources allocated, and children taught. Educators not only prepare young people for the future but, by virtue of their decisions and subsequent actions, also determine what that future will be. Although it usually is not stated so directly, this perspective is not altogether uncommon among educators and the general public.

Many people believe that education and educators not only influence the future for young people but also should do so. Some of us in the profession believe that we should do this but feel that we lack the power required to be effective. Others note what they believe to be the great influence of the schools and express fear and/or resentment of the effects educators' decisions may have for the future. In short, the concept of educators as social architects provokes controversy because it begs questions about the future of society and suggests that educators have a special role in determining that future.

Our purpose here is to examine the extent to which this concept is realistic or illusory and to consider its implications for educational leadership in the future. The inquiry will be guided by several general questions: What is the impact of schooling and school policy decisions on society in the near

19

and long term? How do educators participate in these decisions? What is the impact of schooling on individuals in the near and long term? How do educators contribute to this impact?

Development of the Architectural Perspective

American schools were established on the premise that an educated citizenry was essential. The initial impetus for public education was partly religious; the founding fathers were concerned that children be taught to read the Bible and worship properly. However, secular concerns were also present. The Massachusetts law of 1647 required all towns to appoint a teacher of reading and writing and, if the town included one hundred or more families, a teacher of Latin grammar.[1] Koenig[2] observes that the motivation for this legislation was more the welfare of the Massachusetts Bay Colony than the benefit of the children. It was believed even at that early date that a citizenry that could read and write would be better able to sustain itself economically and maintain its political and religious autonomy.[3]

Although the principle of need for an educated citizenry was established in colonial times, free compulsory education did not become reality until the nineteenth century. As new states were established, responsibility and authority to establish educational systems were incorporated in their constitutions and implemented through subsequent statutes. Local school committees, which until this time had employed teachers and established curricula, were established as agents of the respective states and required to implement state purposes and minimum standards through local school control. The first state compulsory education law was enacted in 1852, and other states followed. The establishment of free compulsory education testified to the public belief that an educated citizenry serves all society and that education can be the basis for personal growth and development. The adamance with which legislators and others opposed religious teaching in schools (lest young people become unduly influenced by alien orthodoxy) was further proof of society's belief in education's impact.

As America became more heavily industrialized and urban, schools took

---

[1] R. Freeman Butts, Search for Freedom—The Story of American Education, in Emanuel Hurwitz, Jr., and Robert Maidment (Eds.), *Criticism, Conflict and Chance* (New York: Dodd, Mead and Co., 1970), p. 4.

[2] Robert A. Koenig, The Law and Education in Historical Perspective, in *The Courts and Education*, Clifford P. Hooker (Ed.), The Seventy-seventh Yearbook of the National Society for the Study of Education, Part I (Chicago: The Society, 1978), p. 10.

[3] Ibid. Also see Richard Pratte, *The Public School Movement: A Critical Study* (New York: David McKay Co., 1973).

on even greater importance. The emerging complexities of urban life, characterized by its impersonal messages, placed increasing premium on abilities to read in order to understand and respond. By 1900 the curriculum of the elementary school had expanded to include literature, geography, history, nature study, physical training, manual training, and other subjects.[4] More important in the present context is the fact that society assigned to the schools at this time a large part of the responsibility to integrate into our society the many immigrants who came to the United States. Schools were expected to teach newcomers the customs, traditions, institutions, and, in many cases, the language they would need to know in their new country. Both the magnitude and "architectural" orientation of this expectation are apparent in the remarks of a New England educator quoted by Katz:

> A very large proportion of the pupils in our cities and populous towns come from homes utterly destitute of culture, and of the means and the spirit of culture, where a book is never seen, and reading is with the adult members a lost art, or one never acquired. There are schools in which four-fifths or more of the children are in this class. I at one time had under my supervision a school in which ninety-nine percent of the children were of foreign parentage, and hardly one of the whole from a home level with the lowest status of native-born intelligence. In such minds a sunken foundation must be laid by months or years of unpromising toil, before any portion of the work begins to appear above the surface. It seems almost impossible to give them a conception of either the uses or the pleasures of knowledge, or to lead them to that primal exercise of judgment by which two ideas are compared or combined. Even the simplest object-lessons are often unintelligible to them. Instruction can hardly be conveyed to them in terms which they can understand, and in what they attempt to learn, memory derives no assistance from association. A person of exceptional skill and patience might hope out of a single such block in the lapse of years to carve a statue; but what shall we think of the sculptor who is compelled every day to make some strokes of the chisel on forty or fifty of them?[5]

As Katz makes clear, the quotation indicates the strong bias that some teachers manifested toward immigrant children. Indeed, the school life of immigrant children was often unpleasaant and short.[6] Nevertheless, there was a generalized expectation that the schools would somehow help these children fit into future society. At times the school and the industrial and

---

[4] George Beauchamp, *The Curriculum of the Elementary School* (Boston: Allyn and Bacon, 1964).

[5] Michael B. Katz, *Class, Bureaucracy, and Schools* (New York: Praeger Publishers, 1971), p. 41.

[6] For example, see David B. Tyack, *The One Best System* (Cambridge, Mass.: Harvard University Press, 1974).

cultural values it espoused were in conflict with the preindustrial values of rural and immigrant Americans.[7]

Efforts to cope with these differences expanded the schools' mission at the turn of the century. According to Lazerson,

> They underlay reformer demands that schools act as moral stewards, that education overcome the baneful effects of family life, and that schooling become the mechanism to create a sober and deferential workforce. They fueled the periodic outbursts of Americanization, as well as the movements to centralize, bureaucratize, and professionalize school systems.[8]

So successful were the schools in conveying the values and teaching the skills required for success in the modern economy that young people, as well as their parents, came to view education as a means to economic and social mobility. This view and condition have persisted throughout the twentieth century. As a society we have become well indoctrinated about the instrumental importance of schooling. We send our children to college—or even to a particular college or preparatory school—with the view that such an education will make it easier for them to climb a professional or corporate ladder in the future.

Equality of Opportunity as an Architectural Problem

A unique feature of the evolution of the American education system was the precept that all children would attend the same school system and therefore have the same educational opportunity. The exceptions to this generalization of course were the relatively small number of students who elected private schools and black segregation in states with dual school systems. The heterogeneous neighborhood school was an essential component to this view of equality. Accordingly, such schools would not only provide equal access to educational resources but, by integrating children from different backgrounds, also promote cultural assimilation and interpersonal understanding and acceptance. The importance of such experiences was particularly underscored by those who argued that schools instilled democratic values.

It is important to note now that whatever success schools may have had in instilling such values was often achieved in spite of rather than because of neighborhood schools. Neighborhoods and their schools have become in-

---

[7] Marvin Lazerson, Consensus and Conflict in American Education Historical Perspectives, in James S. Coleman et al., *Parents, Teachers, and Children: Prospects for Choice in American Education* (San Francisco: Institute for Contemporary Studies, 1977), p. 21.

[8] Ibid., p. 23.

creasingly homogeneous. This is attributable to the growing sprawl of suburbs that cater to various economic lifestyles and transportation systems that make it possible for individuals to reside far from their places of employment.[9] Conditions for equal educational opportunity are even more strained by the fact that school communities vary in their ability to pay for education.

Another educational factor historically important is that American education is a state function administered through local district officials. However, this system also permits, at times, the articulation and implementation of broad national purposes through the schools. This may be achieved through professional pronouncement, as it was with the enunciation of the Seven Cardinal Principles.[10] National purposes may also be achieved through the enactment of federal legislation; among the important examples here are vocational education legislation and the emphasis on science and mathematics brought about through the National Defense Education Act. It is also clear that recurring expressions of public sentiment can give voice to national purposes. For example, most educators today are personally aware of national concern for "Back to Basics," although there has been no clarion professional pronouncement or federal legislation regarding this theme.

We have suggested until now that the development of public schools in America has been based on the premise that they will perpetuate core values in the society and prepare young people for the future. Former Commissioner of Education Sterling McMurrin typified the grand nature of this expectation when he wrote, "The proper function of schools . . . is to be the chief agents of progress, whether it is the advancement of knowledge, improvement in the arts, technology or the social conscience, in institutional organizations and administration, or in the attainment of those large visions of the future which are the prime movers of history.[11]

As we shift from the consideration of the schools' impact on society to their impact on the individual student, the concept of equal educational opportunity arises. For many years, this concept was thought to be relatively simple and to include the following elements:

- Providing a *free* education up to a given level that constituted the principal entry point to the labor force.

- Providing a *common curriculum* for all children regardless of background.

[9] James S. Coleman, Choice in American Education, in Coleman et al., *Parents, Teachers and Children* (San Francisco: Institute for Contemporary Studies, 1977).

[10] National Education Association, *Seven Cardinal Principles of Education*, U.S. Bureau of Education, Bulletin No. 35 (Washington, D.C.: U.S. Government Printing Office, 1918).

[11] Sterling M. McMurrin, What Tasks for the School? in Hurwitz and Maidment (Eds.), op. cit., p. 49.

- Providing that children from diverse backgrounds attend *the same school* partly by design and low population density.

- Providing equality within a given *locality*, since local taxes provided the source of support for schools.[12]

More recently, however, this concept has been seen as problematic and limited. For example, it has been generally accepted that the best interests of all children are not served through a common curriculum. Currently, the concept of equal educational opportunity is both complex and controversial. Some would continue to argue that it is defined adequately by the aforementioned four points. Others, however, are inclined to view it in terms of the effects of school programs on individual students despite differences in backgrounds. From this perspective, providing equal educational opportunities to individuals means providing them with those school experiences most likely to help them achieve their full potential given their aptitude, background, and surrounding environment.[13] Weintraub and Abeson have stated this view as "providing individuals with equal access to differing resources for differing objectives."[14]

This definition of equal educational opportunity places great responsibility with educators. At the very least it calls for them to define the procedures through which objectives will be defined and corresponding resources made available to particular individuals. It is a definition consistent with the concept of social architecture. Those who work in this area, however, must be mindful that important challenges have been directed to the effectiveness of the educational system in providing equal educational opportunity.

Challenges to School Effectiveness

Some of the most fundamental challenges to school effectiveness in providing equal opportunities have come through the courts. The basic case is *Brown v. Board of Education*, in which the Supreme Court declared dual school systems unconstitutional:

> Today, education is perhaps the single most important function of state and local governments. Compulsory school attendance laws and the great expendi-

[12] James S. Coleman, The Concept of Equality of Educational Opportunity, *Harvard Educational Review*, 1968, 38, Winter, p. 11.

[13] Ibid. For further discussion of this concept, see William Tayler, *The Sociology of Inequality* (London: Methuen and Co., 1977).

[14] Frederick J. Weintraub and Alan Abeson, Appropriate Education for All Handicapped Children: A Growing Issue, *Syracuse Law Review* 1972, 23, (4), 1056. Cited in Jeffrey J. Zittell and Alan Abeson, The Right to Free Appropriate Public Education, in *The Courts and Education*, op. cit., p. 192.

tures for education both demonstrate our recognition of the importance of
education to our democratic society. It is required in the performance of our
most basic public responsibilities. . . . It is the very foundation of good
citizenship . . . . the principal instrument in awakening the child to cultural
values, in preparing him for later professional training, and in helping him to
adjust normally to his environment.[15]

More recent decisions have struck at school failures to provide suitable
opportunities for mentally retarded and other handicapped children.[16] These
decisions provided impetus to federal and state legislation designed to
expand educational opportunities for handicapped children, including the
right to individualized programs in the least restrictive educational environments.[17] In another important case that required school districts to expand
educational options, the Supreme Court ruled that failure to provide some
1,800 non-English-speaking Chinese students with education in their native
language violated provisions of the 1964 Civil Rights Act.[18]

Other important challenges to school effectiveness have come from the
academic community. The first and best known of these was the 1966
Equality of Educational Opportunity survey by Coleman and his associates.
Widely interpreted to mean that schools have little impact on student
achievement, Coleman did find that differences in school facilities, curricula,
and teacher characteristics had little effect on student achievement on
standardized tests. He also found that although there were differences in the
schools attended by black and white students, these were not sufficient to
explain the differences in achievement by black and white students, a
difference that increases over the twelve years of school.[19]

A subsequent study by Christopher Jencks and associates reanalyzed
data from the Coleman study and others.[20] Jencks concluded that there is
little relationship between the quality of schooling and development of
individual cognitive skills or subsequent economic success.[21] Yet another
important study was a comprehensive literature review done by the Rand

[15] 347 U.S. 483 at 493. (1954).

[16] See *Pennsylvania Association of Retarded Children v. Pennsylvania* 343 F. Supp. 279 (E.D.
Pa., 1972) and *Mills v. Board of Education of D.C.* 348 F. Supp., 866 (D.D.C., 1972).

[17] For discussion of this litigation, see Jeffrey J. Zettel and Alan Abeson, The Right to Free
Appropriate Public Education, in *The Courts and Education*, op. cit.

[18] *Lau v. Nichols*, 414 U.S. 563 (1974).

[19] James S. Coleman et al., *Equality of Educational Opportunity* (Washington, D.C.: U.S.
Government Printing Office, 1966). For discussion, see Donald M. Levine and Mary Jo Bane
(Eds.), *The "Inequality" Controversy* (New York: Basic Books, 1975).

[20] Christopher Jencks et al., *Inequality: A Reassessment of the Effects of Family and Schooling
in America* (New York: Basic Books, 1972). Also see Levine and Bane (Eds.), op. cit.

[21] Ibid.

Corporation that concluded among other things that no single educational practice is consistently related to students' educational outcomes, that increasing educational expenditures for traditional practices is not likely to produce substantial improvements in achievement, and that educational expenditures could probably be reduced or redirected without seriously affecting educational outcomes.[22] The cumulative effect of these studies has been to challenge the conventional wisdom that increasing expenditures will improve education, thus providing a rationale for legislators and others who seek to reduce educational expenditures.

Another kind of study that bears on the social architecture theme has asked, "Who does benefit from the educational system?" Some revisionist historians argue that the real effects of the American educational system have enhanced the capitalist system by training workers and instilling work-oriented norms, advancing cultural homogeneity, and maintaining social class distinctions while controlling social discrimination and income differentials.[23] Another contemporary theory is that the primary beneficiaries of school decisions are persons employed by the schools.[24] Adherents of this view note that increases in educational expenditures go primarily to higher professional salaries and that the professionalization of education has reduced the participation of laymen in educational decisions to the benefit of professionals. A different perspective has emphasized the social consequences of contemporary school decisions. For example, it is asserted that school desegregation causes white flight and upheaval in the real estate market, that bond issues benefit the construction industry and textbook decisions provoke community conflict.

Challenges regarding the impact and effectiveness of schools have also been apparent in citizen protests and political actions. The widely noted disruptions in Boston, Louisville, and Kanawha County were citizen messages of dissatisfaction with the perceived impact of schooling upon the social fabric. The persistent defeat of tax levies has been likewise interpreted. The pressure for minimum competency examinations, which to date have

[22] See Harvey A. Averch et al., "How Effective Is Schooling? A Critical Synthesis and Review of Research Findings." This is abstracted from Stephen J. Carroll et al., *How Effective Is Schooling? A Critical Review of Research* (Englewood Cliffs, N.J.: Educational Technology Publications, 1974), in Levine and Bane (Eds.). The Levine and Bane volume is an excellent resource, which also contains the Coleman article and the Moynihan article cited in this chapter.

[23] For example, see Michael B. Katz, op. cit., Samuel Bowles and Herbert Gintis, *Schooling in Capitalist America* (New York: Basic Books, 1976), and Joel H. Spring, *Education and the Rise of the Corporate State* (Boston: Beacon Press, 1972).

[24] For example, see Daniel P. Moynihan, Equalizing Education: In Whose Benefit? *The Public Interest*, 1972, No. 29, 69-89, and L. Harmon Ziegler and M. Kent Jennings, *Governing American Schools* (North Scituate, Mass.: Duxbury Press, 1974).

received legislative consideration in at least thirty-seven states, reflects citizen dissatisfaction, as does the growth of private alternative schools.

In many cases concerns about the effectiveness of school decisions have prompted doubt about the representativeness of school decision makers and even the legitimacy of prevailing decision structures.[25] One manifestation of this has been greater competition for positions on boards of education. More radical proposals have been to restructure school governance arrangements; these began as cries for decentralization from the ghetto but have now shifted to demands for building level policy/advisory bodies from the suburb and state legislatures. A noteworthy aspect of these movements is that they reflect continued citizen commitment to the view that schools have important impact on society. It is citizen desire to influence this impact that motivates their participation.

The debate over school effects and educational equality does not lead to the conclusion that schools are unimportant to individuals or society. The research does suggest, however, that no single educational strategy is appropriate for all children, that the education of children is influenced by more than school factors, and that the impact of schools transcends their immediate effects on children. Partly because the outcomes of schooling are less easily taken for granted than they once were and because citizens are increasingly aware of the social consequences of educational decisions and hold different values regarding them, educational decisions are often controversial. In short, educational decisions are perceived as having social implications, and the complexity of the environment in which they are made is such that easy answers are often not readily apparent.

Coping with Environmental Complexity

The rhetoric and ideology of school policy making have been that local boards of education make policy decisions on behalf of the community and that professionals carry out these decisions. However, there is substantial evidence that this view overstates the power of school boards and understates the influence of school professionals.[26] Policy decisions have been made primarily on the basis of professional advice that takes into account the anticipated response by board of education members to administrative proposals.[27] Implementing decisions have been made by professionals. This

[25] The relationship between concerns about effectiveness and legitimacy is discussed by Leonard J. Fein, *The Ecology of the Public Schools* (New York: Pegasus, 1971).

[26] Ziegler and Jennings, *Governing American Schools*, op. cit.

[27] William L. Boyd, The Public, The Professionals and Educational Policy Making: Who Governs? *Teachers College Record*, 1976, 77, No. 4.

pattern has led to the institutionalization of education where school personnel have a vested interest in system-wide policies and curricula, standard operating procedures, and a plethora of rules and regulations.

A corollary to this institutional development has been the strengthening—some would say rigidifying—of organizational boundaries that limit both adaptiveness to environmental changes and cooperation with other institutions. Schools have too often seen their policy and operating preferences as "The One Best System"[28] and have required clients and constituents to deal with them only on their terms. The public dissatisfaction discussed above has come at least partly because schools have taken this posture. The timing of such protests has been given impetus by certain societal trends that press for more options in school policies and programs and greater adaptability in curriculum and policy-making processes.

The most basic trend is what Daniel Griffiths defines as "the collapse of consensus" regarding American institutions and values.[29] The 1960s and early 1970s were a period of social revolution in the United States. The visible extremes of this movement—urban rioters, flower children, and campus protesters—have all but disappeared. However, a populace remains that is less committed to core values and institutions than twenty years ago. Esteem for and confidence in public officials have declined. We are cynical about the motives of elected officials; and we doubt the competence and industriousness of civil servants. We are open in our criticism of government agencies and reluctant to support them financially. California citizens no longer just refuse to vote additional taxes; they have achieved repeal of some already in place. This movement is spreading and may lead to basic changes in government activities. Robert Nisbet refers to our time as a "twilight of politics" and observes, "It is the fate of all civilizations to outgrow the system of power that binds them. This, quite clearly, is happening in the West today, not least in the United States. I believe the waning of the political order . . . is a fact of highest significance, and far too little noted."[30]

Government is not the only institution in which traditional values and practices have changed. The church, the family, and the workplace have all been affected. Church membership is down, divorce rates are up, and business and industry confront growing work alienation. Underlying these developments is an emerging set of values that deemphasizes personal feelings of guilt and commitment and stresses openness and personal

[28] See the book of this title by David Tyack.

[29] Daniel E. Griffiths, Preparation Programs for Administrators, in Luvern L. Cunningham, Walter G. Hack, and Raphael O. Nystrand (Eds.), *Educational Administration: The Developing Decades* (Berkeley, Calif.: McCutchan Publishing Corp., 1977), p. 402.

[30] The Decline of Academic Nationalism, *Change*, 1974, *26*, quoted in Griffiths, Preparation Programs for Administrators, p. 402.

satisfaction. We are urged to get over our hangups, escape our constraints, and pursue self-fulfillment. The implications of these changes are far-reaching. Yankelovich, for example, asserts that business and industry must find ways to modify their incentive systems to respond to this change in values or accept the loss of industrial supremacy in the world.[31]

It must be emphasized that the situation described here is not necessarily a gloomy one. The emergence of pluralism has paralleled the collapse of consensus. The most prominent outcome of the 1960s revolution has been the growing integration of minorities and women into American institutions. Their views and presence are increasingly seen in government, civic activities, and the workplace. In striving for this integration, we have learned that the old consensus was false in some respects. The challenge for the 1980s is to build a new consensus rooted in openness, acceptance, and mutual commitment.

Schools are strategic institutions in this context. They have suffered from the same disillusionment, alienation, and lack of support that have affected other agencies. Moreover, the ambiguity surrounding goals, which has always characterized education, has been heightened by the identification of "new" social problems and an expanded set of claimants. The result has been great pressure on schools to be all things to all people. The progress of schools has thus become an indicator of the extent to which society is actually becoming more accepting of pluralistic values. In some areas various segments of the public will support the schools as long as they do only what they want. In other areas citizens will support schools that do what others wish if the schools also do what they want. The schools will reflect the new and desired consensus when they can shift from serving publics on this quid pro quo basis to one in which the general public recognizes the common benefit in differentiated programs. Building and implementing this consensus is a process of social architecture.

There are presently at least three significant barriers to achieving such consensus: conflicts among citizens, conflicts between citizens and professionals, and the lack of evidence of school effectiveness itself. Differences among citizens have produced some spectacular school-related conflicts on desegregation, sex education, and textbook selection. Citizen−professional conflict has already been discussed, but it is worth noting that it has escalated into public confrontations in some settings.[32] It has also contributed

---

[31] Daniel Yankelovich, The New Psychological Contracts at Work, *Psychology Today*, 1978, *11*, (*12*), 46-50. Also see Rosabeth Moss Kanter, Work in a New America, *Daedalus*, 1978, 107 (*1*), 47-48.

[32] The best-known example was Ocean Hill−Brownsville, but such conflict has also occurred in suburbs and small towns.

to interest group proposals to alter educational governance procedures to their own benefit.[33]

The problem of evidence was discussed earlier from a macro or national perspective. More important to local citizens and educators is the difficulty of ascertaining the effects of local policy decisions and school practices. It would be helpful to know more than we do about the effects of social policy decisions on local economic, demographic, and civic factors. Most of us believe there is a relationship. For example, one superintendent recently explained his practice of maintaining close contact with local realtors; he believes that local property values are an important barometer of community satisfaction with schooling.

The question of the effect of teachers or particular programs is more perplexing. Most educators are aware of the arguments regarding the difficulty of measuring these effects. The major ones are based on (1) the difficulty of specifying objectives that reflect general goals in a comprehensive way and toward which progress can be measured and (2) the confounding effects of developmental, home, and environmental variables. In the absence of such evidence parents and teachers have been prone to blame the shortcomings of students on one another. Conversely, student progress and good teaching become largely a matter of faith: because we like what is happening in the classroom now, Johnny or Mary will be "successful" in the future.

A recent study addresses the question of teacher effectiveness in a new and remarkable way. It is a longitudinal study of the effects of first grade teachers on the subsequent adult status of their pupils.[34] The study reports "a positive correlaton between one first grade teacher and the adult success of children from a disadvantaged neighborhood. More importantly the findings suggest that an effective first-grade teacher can influence social mobility.[35] The study affirms the importance of high teacher expectation in shaping students' self-concept and achievement, thereby providing a basis for subsequent success in life.

Although it would be improper to overgeneralize from this one study, the findings are an important indicator to teachers that their individual efforts can have long-term effects. For those of us who want to believe that schooling can make a difference in the lives of young people, this is cause for optimism. It is also further reason to reflect on our roles as social architects and to consider the strategies available to educators.

[33] Examples include professional practice boards and building level policy boards.

[34] Eigel Pedersen, Therese Annell Faucher, with William W. Eaton, A New Perspective on the Effects of First-Grade Teachers on Children's Subsequent Adult Status, *Harvard Educational Review*, 1978, *48*, (*1*), 1-31.

[35] Ibid., p. 29.

Conclusion

In conclusion, some implications for educational leaders can be noted of the societal conditions previously discussed. First, it is important to acknowledge the potential long-range significance of school-related decisions. The decision-making process can be thought of as social architecture because the results can alter the social fabric of the community. Thus it is important for educators to think in future terms and be sensitive to the fact that others in the community are doing so as well.

A related point is that educational leaders can help the community make decisions about education. The stereotype of an architect is that of a person with an eyeshade, pencil, and T-square atop a high chair who spends long hours developing blueprints. Although attention to technical detail is important for architects, their starting point for any project is to learn what their client wants. With such interaction, skillful architects help clients expand their vision and understand possibilities not previously contemplated. So it can be with educators. In the final analysis, educators must provide the educational system that their constituents desire. Like skillful architects, however, they can seek and use opportunities with constituents to heighten their understanding of what educational opportunity means and how to provide it.

The contemporary educational architect will help the community clarify its educational goals and see its broader relationship to the public and the world. Sensitive to changes in values, resources, issues, and opportunities, he will help the community remain abreast of such developments and consider their implications for educational goals and programs. Central to such efforts is clear understanding of one's own values for making decisions about the future, along with willingness and ability to share these values with others. Despite our contention that the social architect will help the community make decisions rather than act unilaterally, he will have significant impact on these decisions by virtue of his strategic position and persuasiveness.[36] Rather than deny or withdraw from this role, he should acknowledge it, explicitly stating his own values.

The complexity and interdependence of modern society require the educator-architect to view education in a systems perspective. Schools are not the only educative institutions in the community. Parents, business and industry, the media, social and welfare agencies, and others make important contributions to the education of young people. This is fact. It remains for us to redesign educational systems to take advantage of the opportunities presented. The initial steps in this direction will be to communicate more

[36] Harlan Cleveland, *The Future Executive* (New York: Harper & Row, 1972).

often and effectively across the professional boundaries we have helped to create. Successful development of community educational systems will likely call for school personnel to serve as diagnosticians, planners, coordinators, and evaluators of educational opportunities that exist in other agencies as well as schools.

Implicitly stated thus far is that a single monolithic program cannot adequately serve the educational needs of a modern community. Variations in student goals, interests, weaknesses, and strengths call for programs which contain multiple options. The present "Back to Basics" movement protects against widescale educational weakness. Equally important for the future is the need to develop idiosyncratic strengths in children; progress calls for individualized options within educational programs. Such programs are feasible where educators and concerned citizens will unite to convince others of their importance.

3

MARIO D. FANTINI, University of Massachusetts

Options/Alternatives and Gifted/Talented

Introduction and Historical Background

American education is proceeding through an important transition. As the needs of our advanced industrial society become more complex, the means by which we respond to these needs will have to undergo a basic alteration. This means in part that the institution called the school, established to respond to societal needs, has to be updated to more effectively meet the demands of our changing society.

One promising means by which we can reform our public schools is through expanding the number of options and choices available in education. My purpose in this chapter will be to examine the movement that has developed toward increased options and choices in the public sphere. I will also propose that this trend toward variety is only the initial phase of a much broader transition in the evolution of public education in the United States. Current experiments in alternative education represent only one step in the conversion that is now under way from our outdated *school* system to a more responsive and comprehensive *educational* system. An educational system is characterized not only by increased options and choices but also by fuller utilization of the learner's talent as the basis for creating more personalized

33

learning environments, as well as by the comprehensive use of community resources. Specific attention will be given to the Montclair Public School experience, which in many ways represents an example of the most contemporary stage of development for educational alternatives. I predict that many of the principles on which the Montclair experience is based will become foundations for future educational systems.

Public school systems in this country have traditionally developed in response to community or societal needs. From colonial days when public schools were first instituted through postindustrial society, the school, as a basic institution of our society, has attempted to keep pace with the needs of the American populace. Until the first half of this century the primary way the school system kept pace with new needs had been through the adoption of compensatory programs, known as "add-ons." Each time a new need was identified, the schools would "add on" a responsibility (usually through a system of appendages) to a basic structure established in the nineteenth century. With the school-age population growing and the economic system based on increasing growth, the system of add-ons appeared to make sense—viewed from within the school system by those trying to make it work and from without by the recipients of this service. However, the revolutions that have taken place over the past century in science, technology, economics, and communications have transformed our society so extensively as to alter the needs of a significant portion of the population.

Educational Needs of Today's Society: Why Alternatives Are Necessary

Today the educational consumer needs a quality education to survive economically and politically. Over the past decades, stimulated by the civil rights movement of the 1950s and 1960s, greater equality of opportunity is being sought by women, senior citizens, the handicapped, and so on—all demanding a new responsiveness from the institutions that were established to serve their needs. The new movement toward diversification has been in direct response to the pluralism and growing power of the educational consumer. However, although the public position toward education has changed, life inside the public school remains relatively unchanged—except in two important ways. First, educators have responded to the new demands by adding layers to the basic educational system. For example, they have added vocational education, adult education, special education, compensatory education, and the like to the standard curriculum. These additions have attempted to update the schools—to make them more responsive to diversity. Unfortunately, appendages, although somewhat helpful, cannot deal with fundamental problems of institutional reform. These efforts have at best improved an outmoded system of public education; we now have an improved outdated system, not a reformed one.

Moreover, in the face of a tightening economy the citizen through his/her elected officials has called for a new public accountability. In June 1978 the passage of Proposition 13 in California appeared to be a "taxpayer revolt." Educational issues have become linked to the citizen's pocketbook, and the average citizen has now begun to question the effectiveness of programs on which his/her taxes are spent. Are the federally and state supported programs in education working? Have the financial investments of the 1960s been justified?

Field reports on programs such as Title I of the Elementary and Secondary Education Act of 1965 have been far from promising. Desegregation efforts appear fraught with problems and controversy. With this new demand for public accountability is the growing awareness that the "add-on," or "compensatory" approach to school improvement actually results in more money being spent in the same old ways—the very ways that have been subjected to increased criticism by growing numbers of students and parents (the educated consumers themselves). Forced cutbacks coupled with declining school enrollments place the schools in double jeopardy. How can they move forward to respond to the changing needs of the society with diminishing resources and an electorate which is losing confidence in the institution itself?

Given this situation, it is not surprising that the movement of Back to Basics should surface. If we have limited resources—as one group of citizens reasons—devote them to developing the traditional validated basic skills such as the 3 R's and establish minimal competency testing; why try to spread the school's program responsibilities too thin? At the same time another group of citizens pushes for more opportunities in the school program. Thus a tug of war results among competing citizen groups over the desired direction for these school programs. Such groups become increasingly political, placing pressure on school officials and becoming active in school board elections. These community pressures in turn cause political reaction from professional educators who feel threatened by what they perceive to be unreasonable demands. The entire school environment turns into an arena of power politics: school boards are split 4 to 3 in key issues, chief school officers become scapegoats in these institutional conflicts and their contracts are terminated prematurely.

This scenario is being repeated around the nation, eroding the bonds between community and school and citizen and professional. Meanwhile, such a dysfunctional climate hardly has a salutary effect on the learners themselves. The deepening politicization of our school system is also, in part, a key symptom of the need for reform. Given this situation, if our institutions are not updated, we can expect that the public will increasingly seek political and/or legal means of redress.

The problem before us is to modernize our public schools so that they can provide universal quality education for a pluralistic society. This must be done without giving up on our public schools and without compromising the rights of students, parents, taxpayers, or professionals—in short, without scrapping the good things that are presently going on in our schools. Thus providing a pluralistic, technologically advanced society with universal quality education continues to be a problem that requires a basic reform of our educational institutions. Because quality education has an important survival value in today's world, its absence increasingly becomes urgent. Although getting their children a quality education has become an important priority for most American families, it is difficult, if not impossible, for a monolithic system of public education to respond to the different conceptions of quality education held by a pluralistic society; consequently, these differences have resulted in increased confrontations between parents and educators. Hence the advent of alternative schools and the public quest for such plans as vouchers and tax credit arrangements.

Alternatives to Public Schools

The beginnings of the American alternatives movement took place *outside* the public schools; these schools provided an "alternative" to the public school system (from a certain point of view, all private schools fit this category). Thus, if one were affluent and felt strongly enough about a particular kind of school (because it was spiritually oriented or academically superior), a whole range of private schools, academies, and Montessori schools was available. Although the masses continued to attend standardized public schools, the first alternative schools created in the 1960s clearly surfaced as reactions to the constraints of the public school system. By providing a standardized structure the public schools attempted to respond to societal demands for bringing diverse subcultures into mainstream American life; they sought to establish equality for all. Indeed, this standardization process has accomplished a great deal. However, our public schools have recently begun to feel the strain of the universal demands for a quality education.

During the 1960s these "alternative" or "free" schools responded to the aspirations of countercultures or lifestyles groups. For the most part these schools were freer in form and substance than their public school counterparts. Their philosophy was heavily based on the writings of A. S. Neill and the Summerhill model and on the "romantic" public school critics of that period: Holt, Goodman, Kohl, Dennison, Herndon, Kozol, and so on.

One main branch in the free schools movement promoted the "freedom works" philosophy of A. S. Neill, whereas the other emphasized "freedom" as liberation of the oppressed. The former group of free schools provided settings in which the learner was in complete charge of his/her own learning; i.e., what is learned, when, where, why, how, and with whom. The latter group of freedom schools based much of its curriculum on the liberation struggle, the evils of a capitalist economy and political system.

In his celebrated book *Free the Children* Allen Graubard studied these alternatives to the public school and outlined (rightly as it turned out) that they would be declining significantly in number by the early 1970s.[1] Their diminishing number was largely due to the more limited resources that characterize our greatly weakened economy in the 1970s—this in sharp contrast to the period of expansion that occurred in the 1960s. A handful of dedicated teachers working around the clock on substandard wages trying to run a school on a shoestring cannot last indefinitely. However, these alternatives did make the public schools aware that other ways of education were possible.

During the 1960s the civil rights movement had also contributed to the promotion of alternative schools. At times school boycotts protesting segregation resulted in the establishment of temporary alternative schools in such hitherto unikely settings as teachers' apartments or church basements. These were staffed by community persons who developed formats different from those in the public schools. Whereas the curriculum in these community schools dealt with the 3 R's, it also included such things as black history (including the civil rights movement) and discussion of how schools could be tied to community needs.

In the late 1960s and early 1970s some of these alterantive schools became established as more permanent structures—like the street academies associated with the Urban League. Harlem Prep, which first existed outside the public school system, getting its support from foundations, business, and industry, later went on to become one of New York City's public schools. In this period some independent private school alternatives became places that catered to "disruptive" students, often with public school support in the form of tuition payments.

Another development serving to promote alternatives that emerged during this same time was the "open classroom" experiment. During this period the British experience with "informal classroom and integrated day"

---

[1] Allen Graubard, *Free the Children: Radical Reform and the Free School Movement* (New York: Pantheon Books, 1972).

stirred some interest in the United States. Silberman's *Crisis in the Classroom*, a widely read book of the time, was instrumental in promoting the use of these types of classrooms.

The impact of all these activities was to bring to the attention of concerned citizens and professionals the need for variety in education—especially in public education. Thus alternative private schools played an important role in bringing the concept of options to the public eye.

Simultaneously, a proposal for the utilization of a system of educational vouchers was given widespread public attention. Based on the theories of such prominent economists as Milton Friedman, educators proposed that public education should be considered a free marketplace with the learners and families as consumers; each family should then be provided with a voucher redeemable at a school of its own choosing. The competition resulting from consumers' shopping around for the school that best satisfied their needs would result in an increased choice of educational goods. This method of school financing was also viewed by its proponents as a means of equalizing opportunities for the poor.

With federal government support, a number of planning grants were made available to the districts considering implementation of voucher systems. Many of these planning efforts were viewed as highly controversial by professional educators and, therefore, were never operationalized. Others were implemented—the most notable being Alum Rock, California, which still remains operational.

Options Within the Public Schools: First and Second Phases

Schools first considered the possibility of introducing options into public education about 1970. In the first phase the alternatives introduced were primarily adaptations of "free schools" within "the system." These sub-schools were usually separated from the main school, in settings more flexible than those found in the main school. The teachers and students attracted to these alternative schools were usually middle-class whites, perceived as "bright and intellectual" but rejecting the more formal conventional structure of the public schools. Nontraditional in appearance, they were labeled "hippie" schools. With mainstream America still oriented to more familiar approaches in education, such perceptions and labels contributed to a negative image of these early alternatives.

Other alternatives in this first phase involved separate schools for dropouts, unwed mothers, disruptives, and so on. These were perceived by the general public as "dumping grounds" for problem students in public schools. In short, they were viewed as special places for learners who were "turned off" or who did not belong in the regular schools.

The other major sector of this first phase of alternatives focused on urban school districts. Varied patterns of schooling surfaced in an attempt to deal with the massive failures of poor children. Berkeley, California, became one of the first city school districts to embark on a full-scale alternative schools program. With the assistance of foundation and federal funds the Berkeley public school system mounted over twenty school options in its elementary and secondary schools. Besides basic skills centers, these included multicultural school settings, commercially oriented learning, environmentally oriented programs, independent contract curriculum, and the like.[2]

Assisted by the Urban Coalition, New York City's Harlem High School (the site of the motion picture *Up the Down Staircase*) was subdivided into smaller units that could foster more personalized relationships. The Parkway Project in Philadelphia moved away from the schoolhouse and claimed the city and its resources as "the school." The school without walls attracted a diverse student population, thus promoting integration by socioeconomic and racial groups. Philadelphia also established an Office of Alternative Education to oversee the more than fifty alternative schools in the city system. In Cincinnati a major effort to develop alternatives resulted in a wide range of options—including that of Montessori education, which had previously been limited to private schools. Minneapolis mounted an alternative experiment in the southeast section of that city. With the assistance of federal monies, four different schools were formed: (1) the contemporary format—a traditional approach; (2) the open format—based on informal classroom design; (3) the continuous progress format—an upgraded program; and (4) the free fromat—in which the individual directs his own learning. The experience with this project was so positive that it led to a systemwide policy promoting alternatives.

This first phase of options introduced the notion to the public schools. That they were perceived as focusing on "special" cases had a twofold effect. First, the public schools were eager to find some solution to the nagging problems that faced them. Alternative schools appeared to be the latest and most effective way of dealing with such problems as those posed by middle-class students who were turned off, who were about to drop out, or who were acting out deeper frustrations—those not achieving academically. Through the adoption of alternatives within the public school system, educators were

---

[2] John Bremer and Michael Von Moschzisker, *The School Without Walls: Philadelphia Parkway Program* (New York: Holt, Rinehart and Winston, 1971).

able to voice their continuing concern with these issues. Second, establishing possible solutions to these problems through alternatives served to educate the mainstream by acquainting it with the concept of alternative education.

It must be emphasized that in this period the public still viewed alternative education as something for the problem kids, having little to do with the other students. In fact, when alternatives were on occasion proposed for regular students, people questioned what possible value this could have. After all, alternatives were for those who were not really normal!

However, despite this temporary impasse the seeds for the second phase of alternative schools were also being sown during this period. From 1972 to 1976 new options moved into the mainstream schools of the middle class in the suburbs and other affluent areas. In Brookline, Massachusetts, a wealthy suburb of Boston, the high school offered over a dozen options in an attempt to update the concept of "comprehensive" high school. Quincy II High School in Quincy, Illinois, a typical middle-American community, undertook a process of cooperative planning involving parents, teachers, and students that resulted in a school within a school: 1,500 students and eighty teachers were divided into five subschools (traditional, flexible, individual, fine arts, and career), each offering a distinctive program. This Quincy Education by Choice Model has since won national acclaim. In Pasadena, California, two alternatives—one an open high school, the other a fundamental school emphasizing a return to basics and to more traditional values—brought the idea of a range of options to the public eye.

In addition, alternatives began to appear in many of America's suburbs and rural schools, involving semester options, classroom options, or schools within schools. Usually, they were also introduced through cooperative planning by administration, teachers, parents, and students. The influence of options spread to the state level. Illinois and New York created offices for alternative schools, whereas in California an alternative school assembly bill was passed (Assembly Bill No. 1052, introduced by Assemblymen Dunlop, Dixon, and Vasconcellos, April 3, 1973). Some higher education institutions were involved from the beginning. Indiana University developed a Center for Options in Public Education, as did the University of Massachusetts/ Amherst with its Center for Alternative Schools. The Indiana Group also helped form the International Consortium for Options in Public Education.

These and other developments have begun to point to emergence of alternatives as a serious reform effort in American education. Politically, the American mainstream does play gatekeeper in public education, and thus the surfacing of options within middle-class schools represents an important development in the alternatives movement. Because any major educational reform has to be acceptable to the mainstream if it is to be seriously undertaken by the public schools, this development represents a legitimizing of the concept of alternatives. This support has been an outgrowth of our experience with the second phase of options.

Magnet School Alternatives: The Third and Fourth Phases

The concept of alternatives has also been used in an attempt to solve the longstanding problem of desegregation. Because alternative learning environments involve distinctive features that can be attractive to different learners, why not have them serve as one means of promoting desegregation: as a magnet? Such "magnets" started in places like Philadelphia with science-rich schools, arts-oriented schools, and the like, and then slowly began to tap community resources; these latter were called schools without walls.

The move from the *magnet as schoolhouse* to the *magnet as a community-based center* is very important. Education is historically perceived as occurring in special buildings with school teachers and a standardized curriculum. This has led most laymen to conceive a "good" school as one that "good" students attend, and this usually means middle-class children. The socioeconomic composition of the student body and the neighborhood from which they come—not the quality of the programs offered in the school—has often been the determining factor in influencing public opinion on this subject.

The pioneering efforts of Montclair, Dallas, and Houston have paved the way for a new conception of quality public education. In order to set the stage for the third and fourth phases of options, an introduction to the philosophy underlying these approaches may be useful.

Alternative schools have called attention to differences in programs—rather than social class or race. Because "status" and "prestige" are important contributions to our perceptions of "good" and "quality," the move toward community-based options has capitalized on these values. Art centers, museums, insurance companies, banks, medical schools, government offices, doctors, lawyers, musicians, and sculptors (all with prestigious connotations) have begun to join school personnel as teachers in such schools.

Thus the seeds of a third and a fourth phase of alternatives are already planted. If properly nurtured, these seeds can yield fruits that will significantly alter the form and shape of American public education and the role of professional educators as well. Third and fourth phase options will have to build on the cumulative wisdom of the past to form the new context of education for the next century. Our vision of converting a school system to an educational system depends on how we deal with these alternatives, and how carefully and fully we link the school to other community resources that must be tapped if a comprehensive delivery of services to all learners is to be realized.

Ultimately the transformation of a school system into an educational system will involve tapping the network of learning resources that exists in the community, from art museums to the expertise of government, business, and industry. Rather than duplicate these potential educational environments the competencies already available in these diverse settings will be utilized by the schools. It will be the responsibility of the artistic community, not the schools, to teach aesthetic literacy, of the medical profession to teach drug and sex education, of the business community to teach career preparation, of the legal profession to teach legal rights.

By sharing the responsibility for the accomplishment of educational objectives with these various community resource groups, the school will still deal with the basics, as it has done historically; it will also assume a crucial new role as orchestrator and coordinator of the entire educational system.

It should now be obvious that the difference between schooling and education is of critical importance. Whereas basic literacy, general knowledge of the disciplines, and vocational training are the primary goals of the former, the latter stresses personal psychosocial development, the cultivation of talent, and the development of competencies in performing societal roles such as consumer, parent, and citizen. The educational curriculum would include such issues as communications, health, law, global survival, war and peace, social justice, and the development of compassion, trust, dignity, and human potential.

Such a system would encourage the expression and development of the highest values of a free and open society. As a result, in addition to being literate and talented, the educated person of the twenty-first century (the graduates of an educational system) will have a disciplined sense of caring for others and be actively involved in transforming such negative milieus as those fostered by poverty, prejudice, and illiteracy into a social environment marked by dignity, equality, and the promotion of human growth. Internationally, educated persons of good will and vision will strive to maintain world peace and an ecological balance and to eliminate starvation from the globe.

The trend toward increased options and choice for parents, teachers, students, and administrators has legitimized variety within the public school system. People are now coming to accept and sometimes even embrace the idea that there are many roads to learning and to quality education. The threat of imposing formats on those who do not identify with the approach is thereby largely removed, for the single greatest strength of options is that they can provide a style of education that is compatible with the philosophies of educational conservatives, moderates, liberals, and radicals alike. Given our political and economic diversity, this introduction of options with emphasis on personal choice tends to reduce potential conflict between educators and parents. In short, options can provide us with this much valued diversity while they enable us to become unified by a common commitment to quality education—we are tied together by our ends and by our right to the means most compatible with these ends.

However, the task of identifying the common ingredients for good education remains. In an era when receiving a quality education is a basic necessity (i.e., essential to survival) this task becomes critical; such an educaton is no longer a privilege but a civil right. Guaranteeing each person quality education will necessitate an updated system of public education— not a school system but an educational system. In order to get us thinking about alternatives and their role in the development of a modernized system of public education, it may be useful to sketch a definition of quality education so that our destinations are established once and for all. We can then move on to new alternative configurations for increasing the opportunity for every learner to attain these ends, so that he/she may be a fully educated person in the twenty-first century.

The universal demand for quality education includes the following set of common objectives:

- *The New Basics:* In addition to reading, writing, and arithmetic, and learning how to learn, new basic competencies in language, legal, economic, social, cultural, and visual literacy are necessary in our society.

- *The Identification and Cultivation of Talent:* It must be recognized that every person can develop a talent and that this talent can potentially lead to careers that are financially and psychologically rewarding.

- *Adult Social Competencies:* Every educated person should be able to perform the roles of citizen, consumer, parent, and so on in the larger social arena.

- *Personal Validation:* Through education, a person should become aware of his/her own self-worth. By feeling good about themselves, people are more likely to achieve to their fullest potential.[3]

These objectives are tied to the person's sense of *fate-control*—one of

---

[3] Mario D. Fantini, Alternative Learning Environments Based on Community Resources, paper presented at Conference at Texas A & M, Spring 1976.

the most powerful motivators known. When a person possesses the skills, concepts, and attitudes that promote a sense of control over his/her own destiny, the educational process has been a success. Thus, if a person cannot read or write, he/she is more likely to be dependent, more likely to be oppressed. Similarly, a person who has not had an opportunity to develop a talent feels less fulfilled, less educated.

These objectives are too important to be left to chance. Some societal agency must assume responsibility (and accountability) for ensuring that every citizen has the opportunity to be educated. Because of the unique role they play in helping people to meet their aspirations, our educational institutions must assume this responsibility.

The school and educational systems can be represented as shown in Figure 3-1.[4]

The Montclair Experience

The Montclair approach to alternatives and choices is important and unique on several counts. Whereas others in this anthology will report on the specific Montclair plan, it will be my purpose to look at the underlying assumptions that contributed greatly to the success of the Montclair program.

A unique part of the Montclair program is its attitude toward the learner, its recognition of talent as a basic ingredient in motivation and learning, and its further recognition that every learner has the capacity to develop a talent and utilize it as an important vehicle for improved learning and self-development. If the cornerstone of a school system was the 3 R's, then the cornerstone of the emergence of an educational system will be *talent*.

The Montclair schools have, in addition, significantly redefined what constitutes "giftedness." They have established a view of every child as gifted, as having some talent worthy of development. This attitude has begun to erode earlier conceptions that viewed giftedness as a characteristic pertaining to a special few. These conceptions were definitions limited to such things as IQ and intellectual didactic functioning. By keeping pace with new findings presented by such scholars as Torrance, the Montclair conception has broadened and clarified the definition of giftedness.

The old view was that there were certain people who were gifted (the winners) and others who were not (the losers); the human potential of the learner was pretty well determined by this classification. In brief, if one were

---

[4] Adapted from *Design for Change* (Staff Bulletin, The Public Schools of New York City, May 15, 1972).

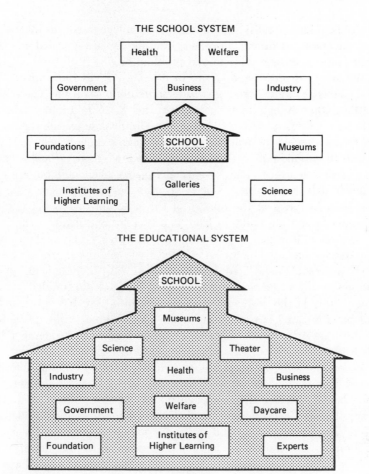

THE SCHOOL SYSTEM

| Health | Welfare |

| Government | Business | Industry |

| Foundations | SCHOOL | Museums |

| Institutes of Higher Learning | Galleries | Science |

THE EDUCATIONAL SYSTEM

SCHOOL

Museums

Science   Theater

Industry   Health   Business

Government   Welfare   Daycare

Foundation   Institutes of Higher Learning   Experts

FIGURE 3-1

gifted, there was an *expectation* of one's performing up to his/her potential, whereas if one were merely normal or below normal, the expectations were different and lower. By applying the earlier conception of giftedness we would have overlooked such talents as Einstein, Tolstoy, Poe, Edison, Dickens, and Buckminster Fuller. Montclair's conception that all learners are in some way talented effectively eliminates the winner and loser syndrome. Education is thus defined as a process in which the conditions that promote the achievement of a person's potential are generated.

It must be underscored that this approach does not discount the earlier definition but views it as one type of giftedness. There are those who are talented in an academic sense *and* those who are talented in human relations, in technology, in empathy, in organizational management, in futuristics, in communications, in humor, in music, in athletics, in the visual arts, in the culinary arts, in crisis resolution and problem solving, in future's design, in architecture, in science, and so on. In other words, as Buckminster Fuller puts it, *"every child is born a genius in something."* It is the search for this something that is extremely important and basic to quality education. Furthermore, if every child is talented, the Montclair approach suggests that talent is not affected by such factors as race, class, sex, and age.

Still the public's general perception is that a "good" school is one that "good" children attend. These are usually places where children are viewed as intellectually more able. "Good" is often defined in social class terms rather than in terms of the quality of the program that is being offered. Consequently, busing children from one social-class school to another has been viewed with suspicion. However, the Montclair experiment emphasizes quality education based on the recognized status and prestige of the program offered and people associated with it. In Montclair the judgment "good" is based not on the social class composition of the students enrolled but rather on the quality of the program being offered. Montclair has developed such talent-based magnet environments as the Fundamental Magnet, the School of Performing Arts, and the Gifted/Talented Magnet, all attracting a diverse student population.

Whereas earlier conceptions of what constituted being gifted and talented were biased in favor of a certain social class of students, those involved here conceive the best educational system as providing maximum opportunities for every learner to seek an environment that is compatible with his/her learning style and particular talent. By shifting the focus on education to the individual learner's talent and to the quality of the environment that can promote that talent, the ground rules have been altered. This change has gradually affected the community's perception of the schools. In Montclair parents are now responding to the new definitions of talent and of a quality education as including the cultivation of talents through the promotion of different environments that acknowledge them. In so doing, the system is not ignoring the basics, which remain among the objectives central to their definition of quality education. Skill in the basics is included as a kind of talent that needs to be cultivated as part of a quality education. Instead of having one format to which all youngsters must adjust (which in the past has tended to create situations favoring those who might be more gifted in academic pursuits), they have created a talent-based alternative learning environment.

Moreover, by focusing on the individual's talent the school can concentrate on the learner's strengths, rather than on weaknesses. Again, the effect is to validate the person, to assume that he/she is a valuable individual who has a talent, and to cultivate that talent as a means of access to the basic educational goals that all people need to function at an optimum level in our society. The individual student is thereby more likely to become all he/she is capable of becoming.

Thus the Montclair approach to alternatives starts us on the road from schooling to education. This is not a conversion that will or can take place in one fell swoop. Importantly, Montclair's plan is the emerging philosophy of education that characterizes every facet of education. It begins by valuing each learner and his/her family. Whereas diversity has often been viewed as an unfortunate barrier to homogeneity and, therefore, as an impediment to learning in the public schools, diversity here is seen as a fact that should be made the most of. Diversity is supported through options, and personalized learning is the norm rather than the exception. Being encouraged to pursue one's talent—whatever it is—has a positive psychological effect on the learner that ultimately strengthens his/her sense of identity and self-worth. The opportunity to express and develop a talent allows human energy to be expended in a way that is personally satisfying and consequently regenerative and motivational.

The Montclair plan of recognizing each student as talented will, over time, establish a new and progressive "psychology of expectation" for the child and his/her parents. For the student the realization that he/she is gifted in some way and that this area of talent is viewed as important by the school is enormously beneficial; this psychological boost has the effect of increasing his/her motivation to learn. For the family this psychology presents a view of their son or daughter as a gifted or talented person who is considered important by school officials. For teachers and other professionals the view of each child as a winner can begin to help operationalize the long-held professional ideal of making every learner central to the educational process; educators are thereby justified in tailoring their approach to fit each child's individual needs.

The Montclair alternative program justly replaces the view that academic competition is the sole path to success and recognition. By extending the conception of giftedness to include all learners, it facilitates a situation in which each child considers him/herself to be an integral part of the school. In fact, for many youngsters talent can become the vehicle that will not only increase their motivation to learn the basics but also will link these basics with the talent that they love. We have all been witness to young people who, when asked to speak or write about something that they are good at or interested in, really excel. This same principle can be applied in a planned interaction of basic skill and talent development.

By designing optional learning environments based on talent areas, the Montclair model begins to signal to all parties that it is the quality of the educational program that is central to improved performance and not some preconceived definition of intellectual giftedness. If a rich learning environment can be structured that will enable each child not only to learn the basics but also to develop a talent, then *where* this takes place is less important than the fact that it actually *does* take place. Beginning at the formal school classroom and extending into the community, the Montclair philosophy broadens the conception of teaching and learning. Learners are able to take sabbaticals so that they may travel with their parents as an integral part of the new education system.

Conclusion

The worth of the Montclair Plan is already in evidence. In the 1960s and 1970s, the history of desegregation in Montclair, as in many other places, witnessed an exodus of families from that city. However, in recent years with the implementation of the alternative schools based on talent, it is reported that families have moved back into the town, property values have increased, and housing is difficult to find. Much of this can be traced to the careful planning and sound educational philosophy of men and women who guided the development of this unique program.

The framework I use for evaluating any kind of social change involves determining whether it is justified educationally, economically, politically, and legally; Montclair receives high marks when evaluated from all of these points of view. *Educationally*, the program is sound because it elevates the concept of the learner and personalizes the learning process while emphasizing the quality of the program as important. In addition, by using talent as a motivating force it provides individualized options for parents, students, and teachers alike. *Economically*, it makes good sense in these inflationary times because it uses available resources more efficiently. By tapping hitherto ignored community resources, it reduces duplication at the same time that it improves the facilities that are available in the education process. *Politically*, it continues to promote quality desegregated education without imposing one view of learning on the learner, thereby placing a high value on individual choice and on the self-worth of every individual. *Legally*, it begins to tailor programs that are the least restrictive for the learner. In this way, the spirit of Public Law 94-142 is not only complied with but also embodied in Montclair.

Not only is desegregated quality education taking place in Montclair but also its success is increasingly serving as an example for other school districts seeking help. As such, the Montclair Public Schools are providing a useful national model for developing quality education. In so doing, they are a sign that the conversion of a school system to an educational system is, indeed, taking place.

ROBERT H. PARKER

WILLIAM C. PARKER

Educational Testing Service Princeton, New Jersey

4

"I Ain't No Group, I'm Me"

We have reached the point where minority-group students are an integral part of our educational system. For many years the educational system in this country relegated practically anything connected with the education of minority people to the status of "separate." The popular compensatory programs are the most obvious product of this attitude. More recently, the education of minorities has come to be associated with the term *special* (witness the many "special" programs that were established as a result of the pressures of the Civil Rights Movement of the 1960s).

Educators must abandon the age-old premise of addressing the educational needs of minorities within the context of an appendage, or as an afterthought. Educational programs that are developed in blindness to the genuine interests and needs of minorities are of suspicious origin and are often intentionally targeted for early obsolescence. To effectively address the needs of minorities, educators must understand and be sensitive to the students' deep-seated cultural and social differences. In addressing these heretofore unmet educational needs of our gifted and talented minority students, we must stress the importance of recognizing that minority cultures are legitimate—that the influence of these cultures can (and often does) render minorities profoundly different from the majority and that these differences must be considered in our mandate to educate, assess, or counsel minority youth.

To be effective, our curricula must account for and address the

49

significant uniqueness of cultural, social, and moral forces. These forces
must transcend the traditional academic domains to encompass the students'
preacademic and sociopsychological needs. Effective incorporation of minor-
ity-oriented values into overall program goals, along with the development
of a supportive community base, cannot help but contribute significantly to
the reinforcement of assertive minority learning.

Minority educational concerns in any context must be approached, at
first, with an understanding of the cultural forces that affect the behavior,
values, attitudes, and lifestyles of minority youth. All too often, under the
guise of being "minority experts," educators and educational decision
makers have prostituted the notion of understanding into a dehumanizing
attitude toward minority education. Toward this unfortunate end, proponents of the deficit model operate on the premise that black cultural traits
and characteristics are to be eliminated during the educational process.
Hence many of our well-intentioned minority educational programs are
destined to fail because of an approach that stresses the need for ethnic
cultural purge. While most educators will *vocally* endorse the concept that
prideful learning must be additive, they dichotomously embrace purgative
modes of learning when dealing with the minority aspect of education.

Implicit in the deficit model premise are many common beliefs concerning black pathology, among them that black speech is a bastard form of
what majority Americans call Standard English.[1] To label black Americans
as verbal cripples, unexpressive, or linguistically incapable demonstrates an
uninformed, blindly arrogant posture of pseudosuperiority. Such a position
cannot but significantly contribute to the failure of minority educational
programs.

An alternative to the deficit model has begun to emerge within recent
years. The proponents of this alternate model recognize that black Afro-
American culture is different from the majority culture. This "difference
model"[2] appears to be gaining acceptance or endorsement by more and
more majority Americans, in that it is more socially acceptable to members
of both groups and is culturally less offensive than the blatant deficit model.
However, the main weakness of the difference model lies in its simplistic but
deep-rooted implications necessitating "special programs."

The very nature of the difference model perpetuates the age-old mind
set that to be different is to be deficient. Such ethnocentrism is extremely
difficult to combat because of its deep-rooted and enculturated development.

---

[1] Charles A. Valentine, It's Either Brain Damage or No Father, *Toward Social Change: A Handbook For Those Who Will* (New York: Harper & Row, 1976).

[2] Charles A. Valentine, Challenging the Myths: The Schools, The Blacks and The Poor, *Harvard Educational Review*, 1975, p. 4.

Because of psychological vanity (ego), the bearer is often totally unaware of the limitations imposed by such ethnocentric perceptions. An equally significant weakness of the difference model is the belief that different cultures present conflictual alternatives and that distinct cultural lifestyles can enter the human equation only as a mutually exclusive experience.[3] This "either-or" belief is often laden with a "better-than" value system that perpetrates low self-esteem among our black youth. Both the deficit and difference models impinge negatively on the minority youth's perception and feelings of self-worth. These models fail to address the actualities of polyculturation—that is, simultaneous enculturation into other distinct cultures without sacrificing personal worth.

Within the context of polyculturation, it is ironic to note that although blacks do demonstrate an acceptance and the practice of this concept on a daily basis, most majority members either misinterpret or elect not to understand this phenomenon. The ability of most blacks to move skillfully and with perceivable ease from one culture to another compounds this misunderstanding. To be oblivious of this ability to assume a cross-cultural posture is to discern no differences between the two cultures. Such monolithic cultural blindness is tantamount to the basic premises underlying the insensitive and dehumanizing aspects of the models previously mentioned.

The failure of the majority society to understand the phenomenon of polyculturation has been perpetuated, in part, by our conventional monolithic educational institutions. Traditionally, these institutions have contributed to this monocultural perspective through both omission and commission. From an educational point of view, we have traditionally and often intentionally omitted from our curricula the essence of a polycultural concept in an attempt to minimize differences. This is often done under the guise of attaining a utopian "melting pot." These conventional institutions have designed the pot, identified the ingredients, and dictated its consistency with little or no regard or input from the minority culture. Such a recipe has contributed significantly to the chronic persuasion that "to be different is to be deficient." Despite our pluralistic society, little or nothing has been done to foster ethnic pride within our schools. This flagrant and damaging omission virtually eliminates the minority youth from the benefits of those "noble" educational goals and objectives by which our schools justify their existence. Indeed, there lies much to be done to fill this educational void since no single or band-aid solution will suffice.

The complexity of educational problems stemming from questions and issues of human worth demands multifaceted approaches if meaningful solutions are to be achieved. Basic to any such approach that embraces the

[3] Ibid.

education of Afro-Americans is a need to understand the Afro-American youth from a cultural and historical perspective.

The influences of black culture render blacks significantly different from the majority culture in very important ways, and such differences must be considered in our attempt to educate, counsel, assess, or evaluate black youngsters. The case for black culture and the black experience must begin with those Africans who were transported to the new world as slaves. Contrary to the assertions of many historians and sociologists, the social and cultural heritage of Africans was not destroyed and replaced by a pathological imitation of social and cultural practices of the majority culture. Afro-American culture has a historical perspective that extends to Africa and has a contemporary importance that influences the lives of almost all black people in America.

From an Afro-American point of view, it is dehumanizing to be placed in positions of having to "legitimize" one's existence (culture) or raison d'etre. However, the educational mainstream of our society erodes this legitimacy on a sustained basis. Many sociologists contend that the legitimacy of a culture is based on ten basic criteria:

- *History:* Does your culture have a history? Are traditions handed down to younger generations?

- *Lifestyle:* Is there a predictable and structured lifestyle in the culture?

- *Society Within the Culture:* What is the importance of the good status? What is good? What is bad?

- *Communications:* Is there a distinct effective communications system within the culture?

- *Work Occupations:* Is there a relationship between worker and society? Are there rewards (both psychological and material) for work?

- *Sexism:* Are sexual roles compatible with the betterment of society?

- *Time:* Are there time indicators that promote societal unity?

- *Child-Rearing Procedure:* Is there a consistent and predictable child rearing mode?

- *Recreation:* Does the society have (both social and individual) emotional and physical outlets?

- *Protection:* Is there a protective mode within the society?

As can be readily seen, even in light of criteria established outside of the Afro-American culture, the essence of minority culture ceases to remain a question of legitimacy but emerges as a question of differences. For example, the differences in the communication process between blacks and members of the majority culture are sometimes obvious; however, most minority languages are often viewed from a deficit model perspective by the majority mainstream.

Oral Cultural Tradition

Historically, the basic foundations of the two cultures have diverse origins. European or Western culture is an offspring of lettered cultures, while Afro-American roots lie in an oral cultural tradition. The dominant culture of the Western world has failed to assess the values and effects of the oral culture, which demands different lifestyles, thought processes, behavioral learning patterns, concepts of time versus perceptions, value systems, communications, and assessment procedures.

As the European and the Afro-American came to this alien land (America), both brought specific and different cultural patterns. In spite of the assumed amalgamation of these cultures, separate lifestyle patterns have been nurtured through black social isolation. Sidran states that African culture has an oral rather than a literary or lettered base, thus making it possible to suggest a new method for examining the continuum of the Afro-American experience.[4] If Afro-Americans managed to perpetuate their oral culture and extend its base into the greater American society, then we must admit the existence of black culture with its own social and value structures and modes of perceptual orientation capable of supporting such structures. Because the two cultures have alternative views as to what constitutes relevant and practical information, they impose alternative modes of perception for gathering information.

Oral cultures use primarily the spoken word and its oral derivatives. The sounds of speech are tied to the time continuum, and the hearer must accept them as presented. Time is the current of the vocal stream. To paraphrase McLuhan, "the message becomes the medium."[5] The oral man thus has a unique approach to the phenomenon of time in general; he is forced to behave in a spontaneous manner, to act and react simultaneously. Oral man is, at all times, emotionally involved in, as opposed to intellectually detached from, his environment through the acts of communications. This can be called the basic "actionality" of the oral personality. McLuhan characterized this lack of intellectual detachment as contributing to a

[4] Ben Sidran, *Black Talk* (New York: Holt, Rinehart and Winston, 1971).

[5] Marshall McLuhan, *Understanding Media* (New York: Signet, 1964).

superior sense of community. When one functions beyond a constructed intellectual plane, his thoughts and action transcend restrictive mental and cultural barriers.

The advantages of the lettered culture are well demonstrated through the advances of modern technology and literature. The advantages of the oral mode become manifest in the ability to carry out improvised acts of a group nature. Sidran[6] states that oral man makes decisions, acts on them, and communicates the results through an intuitive approach to a phenomenon. The intuitive can respond in immediacy; this level of response freedom is maximally actualized at that moment of spontaneity—the moment when we are free to relate and act involving ourselves in both the dynamics and essence of our environment.

The lettered man's criteria of what constitute legitimate behavior, perceptions, and communications often shut out what constitute legitimate stimuli to the oral man. Sidran further asserts that in language the African tradition aims at using as few words as possible to convey a message.[7] Additionally, this tonal and lexical significance is thus carried into the communications process. Consequently, we have what scholars from the majority culture have negatively labeled "black English," the "black dialect," or "ghettoese." Black linguistic scholars have officially labeled the minority mode of communications *ebonics*, thereby eliminating the lexical implication that the black communication process is a deficit deviation of standard English.

Another general theory of an oral approach to time can be found in the examination of oral grammar. Werning's research discovered through the examination of West African grammar that "The African in traditional life is little concerned with time."[8] Time is merely a sequence of events taking place now or in the immediate future. Great cultural changes occurred in Western civilization when it was found possible to fix time as something that happens between two fixed points. Modularized time is a European notion. The rhythm of the body is human and will always be slightly different from (although related to) the metrical beat of time. Consequently, Spegler may have been more than merely ingenious in identifying the post-Christian obsession with time (as metrically exemplified in European music) with the decline of the West.[9] Time in the Western sense is a translation of motion through space. Time in the oral sense is a purer involvement with natural

[6] Sidran, op. cit.

[7] Sidran, op. cit.

[8] Painer Werning, Tribe Time, *International Times*, May 1968.

[9] Oswald Spegler, *Music in a New Found Land* (New York: Holt, Rinehart and Winston, 1970).

occurrences and perceptual phenomenon (an Afro-American phenomenon the authors call ethnoconceptualism). This pure involvement is manifested by the fact that black people do not listen to music, they *are* the music. Black singers do not sing to Afro-Americans, they sing *for* them. Blacks do not dance to music, they dance *the* music.

Much has been written about the expressive nature of black people. Research has ranged from a negative interpretation of this value[10] to a very sensitive analysis of it as found in the works of Jones[11] and Keil.[12] What we find is that black people have not abandoned their humanism—they are a feeling people, who express this feeling in various ways throughout the culture. The inner existence of black people is very closely related to their values of shared existence and their emphasis on the uniqueness of the individual. Black parents emphasize the right of the child to express himself, to show feelings of love and hate. No attempt is made to separate the two emotions. That is, one recognizes at an early age that he can both love and hate at the same time. He is taught diunital existence, as Dixon and Foster[13] define the phenomenon. Thus there is little need to repress feelings of love and hate. Family life is not sedentary; rather, the child is born into an exciting, active environment. Several things may be going on at the same time, and as the child matures, he learns how to tune-in at any given time on things that involve him.

One specific aspect of the expressive nature of black culture is seen in the use of language. The polylingual aspect of black expressions, the rhythm of the language, the efficient use of verbs, the body language, the inflections and intonations, and the contextual syntax are all examples of the expressive uses of language. The significance of this is seen in the number of times majority culture sociologists have missed the meaning of contextual expressions of black people, or the number of times they have not understood the subtle meaning of words. For example, Rainwater,[14] in describing a black mother's reaction to her child, missed the meaning of the expression when the mother said that her child was bad. Rainwater took this to mean that the mother hated or disliked her child, rather than the fact that the mother was characterizing a particular instance of the child's life—nothing was intended concerning her love or hate for the child.

[10] Lee Rainwater, Crucible of Identity, in Talcott Parsons and Kenneth Clark (Eds.), *The Negro American* (Boston: Beacon Press, 1966).

[11] LeRoi Jones, *Black Music* (New York: William Morrow, 1967), and *Blues People* (New York: William Morrow, 1963).

[12] Charles Keil, *Urban Blues* (Chicago: University of Chicago Press, 1966).

[13] Vernon J. Dixon and Badi Foster, *Beyond Black or White* (Boston: Little, Brown, 1971).

[14] Rainwater, op. cit. LeFrancis Rose, Communal Existentialism, unpublished transcript, 1970.

The expressive aspects of black culture may also be seen in music, dance, literature, religion, and social rituals. Jones's *Blues People*[15] and Keil's *Urban Blues*[16] are excellent analyses of the blues in relation to black expression. Dance is seen by many as being basic to the way black people express themselves. Herskowits[17] related that dance is the expressive way that blacks use their body. They walk in a unique manner, and part of this uniqueness is that each person strives for individuality. Likewise, black people show greater freedom in touching one another. This touching is not linked to sexual overtones as sociologists would have us believe, but rather there is no clear distinction between one body and another. Thus in conversation the social distance of blacks is closer than that for the majority culture—more gestures including physical contact are used.

In the black cognitive process there is no claim that self makes truth.[18] What is claimed, however, is that self is the medium and the only adequate medium through which truth or reality, in its total existential dimensions, is wholly and totally perceived and assimilated. Without the intervention of the self in the cognitive act, knowledge falls short of true knowledge, not only in comprehensiveness but also in in-depth intellective penetration of the life force or life pulse of reality. A mere abstract insertion of intellect into a subject disqualifies itself by definition from live contact with the living and operating principles in things. Mathews asserts that in that state of mental existence which we call knowledge, the self in the black cognitive process is seen as the intellectual mediator and not as the intellectual fabricator of the real. Self is also the complete assimilator and reverberator of truth in the black cognitive system. He contends that, in theory at least, self is not presented as a substitute for reality—nature is the norm.[19] Nature, then, is the controlling reality, and realism is an imperative for African thought in every form. This is the first principle.

Principle is one thing; practice is quite another. We must now ask what practical safeguards exist in the black cognitive process to prevent self from interfering with or prejudicing truth in thinking. What are the guarantees of objective validity in this methodology of thinking through feeling? Basically the black cognitive process sets up a dual control for objectivity through the use of symbolic imagery.

First, the collective experience of the group sanctions the participatory

[15] LeRoi Jones, *Blues People* (New York: William Morrow, 1963).

[16] Keil, op. cit.

[17] Melville Herskowits, *The Myth of the Negro Past* (New York: Harper, 1941).

[18] Basil Mathews, Symbolic Imagery and the Afro-American Experience, unpublished document, 1972.

[19] Ibid., and Robert Parker and William Parker, Cultural and Academic Stress Imposed on Afro-Americans, *With Bias Toward None* (University of Kentucky, 1975).

use of symbolic imagery by the individuals. The second control for objectivity is by appeal not to people but rather to the facts observed in nature or the environment. It is not relevant whether these facts were the subject of observation by the thinker himself or the subject of observation by the group over a period of time. Both forms of appeal operate as controls against the interference of self to prejudice truths in thinking.[20]

From this cursory look at a very small aspect of the Afro-American culture, we can now ask how can such understandings be utilized in the quest for an effective education of gifted/talented minority youth. Knowing that cultures are principally sets of value systems that directly influence our behavior and attitudes, we need an examination of self before attempting to relate to or teach others. To know that each of us carries our cultural baggage with us is to know that our daily attitudes, dislikes, and biases influence our perception of others. When relating to members of other cultures, this phenomenon is often acutely pronounced. Educators of minority youth must develop an awareness of the limitation of this personal enculturation on their perception. They must make a concerted effort to overcome their culture's imperatives of phenomenological absolutism. An important and often harmful social aspect of phenomenal absolutism[21] is the observer's assumption that all others perceive a situation as she/he does. The individual accepts the evidence of perception uncritically, ignoring the fact that perceptions are mediated by indirect systems, such as personal experiences and cultural exposure; if others respond differently, it is because of some deficiency rather than because they are acting on different perceptional data.

Anthropologists have recognized phenomenal absolutism in man's tendency to view other cultures in terms unconsciously based on his own but phenomenally experienced as absolute and universally applicable.[22] Because such naive enculturated beliefs are learned from or fostered by significant others, they are difficult to recognize and more difficult to set aside. However, this recognition is a *must*, especially when relating to or interacting with minorities from different cultures. Notwithstanding the difficulty, educators who must reach the minority youth must first understand how they perceive the world (themselves, their role, their students) and must know the limitations of their perceptions.[23] They must recognize how limitations are learned and, most important, gain skills for entering into the perceptions of others without placing a value on differences. The effective

[20] Mathews, op. cit.

[21] Edmund Portnoy, Phenomenological Absolutism as a Barrier to Social Problem Solving, unpublished paper, The Ohio State University, 1974.

[22] F. Boas, Some Traits of Primitive Cultures, *Journal of American Folklore*, 1904.

[23] William Wayson, Developing Student Self Discipline In Schools and Classrooms, unpublished document, 1976.

educator understands that minority youth come to the educational arena with set values and perceptions. This is essential to effective and prideful education of minorities.

One cannot adequately address minority educational concerns without addressing attendant identification and assessment issues. This is especially relevant in educational programs such as for the gifted/talented. The national cry for high-quality educational programs in our public schools resounds throughout our communities as educators, legislators, parents, and taxpayers are seeking solutions to the miseducation problems of today. Interwoven in this activity lies one basic problem that is prevalent in scope, often identified, and widely discussed. This problem area revolves around educational assessment and measurement issues in our schools. The overuse of standardized tests, the quest for culture-free tests, and the elimination of test bias are but a few of the issues that have caused both national and local organizations to press for a moratorium on conventional testing methodologies. Educational assessment and measurement procedures are generally attacked from three perspectives: (1) by those seeking indicators of accountability, (2) by those seeking data for improvement of instruction, and (3) by those who see a need to classify (track) students. It is naive to believe that such issues should not be addressed early in the planning phases of gifted and talented programs.

In addressing the totality of the assessment of minorities, educators must remain cognizant of the limitations and dangers imposed by overdependence on written instruments as the sole assessment and measurement methodology. Unobtrusive measures or nontest indicators are but a few of the nonreactive measures that must be utilized if effective programs are to be established. Such measures do not impinge negatively on minority test attitudes and do much to reinforce, encourage, and foster prideful learning. More emphasis must be placed on the assessment of the affective domain for cross-validation purposes. When test results are not compatible with expectations, professional teacher judgments, or actual unobtrusively observed performance, one should reexamine the written instrument rather than conclude (as is traditionally done) that the student has not learned. The identification and utilization of nontest indicators should provide a verification process for those who must rely principally on the written instrument. In attaining this end, educators must remain mindful of the delimitative roles of tests, questionnaires, and interviews. The validity of responses obtained through the sole reliance on such instruments must always remain suspect. When a student is presented with a written instrument, we are not only seeking a reaction but also creating a reaction. Role playing, test attitudes, health conditions, and interests are but a few of the significant factors that distort the results of the written instrument.

The ultimate goal of the educational process is change. That is, if a person assimilates a desired learning outcome, he/she is assumed to be capable of thinking, acting, or reacting differently from the person who has not learned the same thing. Nowhere in this accepted assumption do we find an addendum which in substance reflects " . . . and he/she must be able to reflect this knowledge on paper." It appears then that performance observed and assessed through unobtrusive measures should play a more dominant role than is now true in our conventional assessment and measurement repertoire.

From a human relations point of view, planners of educational programs (such as for the gifted/talented) must keep in mind the perceived negative implications geared toward those students and teachers who are not involved in the programs. Even when this noninvolvement is the result of a personal option, the perceived negative implications are still evidenced. Much talk and study have been generated over the identification of the gifted and talented. The selective process for denoting giftedness has run a wide gamut from the theory of absolute criteria demonstrated by advanced learners (as espoused by Martinson)[24] to that of measurement against individual ethnic culture (as set forth by Gallagher).[25] The latter asserts that giftedness reflects those dimensions the culture values. Implicit in the process of identification lies the notion of selectivity. The fundamental essence of a selective process necessarily must omit certain students who do not meet preestablished criteria. Regardless of reasons for nonparticipation, the perception of others toward those participating or not participating will have an impact on students, peers, and parents. This impact can be positive or negative depending on the nature of the program (i.e., gifted/talented versus compensatory programs).

Both types of programs can and do create both negative and positive reactive feelings, depending on whether a student is a participant or a nonparticipant. If such programs are established under the premise that all students have gifts and talents, then the identification process becomes a moot activity. Our quest then is to utilize the students' interests (albeit unconventional) as a springboard in the full development of their potential. It seems apparent that if a selection process can be eliminated, we ought to be about the business of doing so. For those programs where the identification/selection processes cannot be avoided (because of funding, societal mandates, and so on), educators must guard against establishing traditional restrictive criteria or areas to identify. We must remain aware of and strive

[24] Ruth J. Martinson, *Identification of the Gifted and Talented*, (Ventura, Calif.: Office of Ventura County Superintendent of Schools, 1974).

[25] James J. Gallagher, *Teaching the Gifted Child* (Boston: Allyn and Bacon, 1975).

to minimize one of the most dangerous imperatives inherent in the identification process—that is, as in the instance of a gifted/talented program, generally one must know what he/she is seeking to identify before it can be identified. The restrictive perils in this kind of process are obvious; hence early program planning must address this very real but often overlooked concern. Plans must be effected to minimize this negative impact while maximizing the positive elements of the program.

Conclusion

Education remains the primary vehicle by which the plight of minorities in this country can be controlled and changed. If minorities are to be pridefully taught and educated, it is imperative that educational methodology, processes, and procedures be utilized that will capitalize on the assets that are buried in the cultural aspects of one's being.

The promulgation of a prideful learning process, accompanied by the notion that all students have gifted potential, fosters appropriate attitudinal changes and coping techniques that enable minority youngsters to meet educational requirements with a realistic understanding of their value. Explicitly clear in this goal lies a fiat for educators to be able to recognize and nurture both traditional and nontraditional potential from a student self-motivational point of view. Supportive educational curricula and activities, therefore, must utilize minority cultural strengths as a fundamental sustaining force in the determination of areas of giftedness and the perpetuation of personal worth.

PART TWO Curriculum— Leadership, Philosophy, and Organizational Strategy

This section presents a number of viewpoints on essential features in developing curricula for gifted/talented students. In the first chapter of this section, Louise M. Berman and Walter L. Marks discuss curricular priorities in the context of social trends and the implications of these priorities for educational leadership.

James B. Macdonald presents a model for curriculum design that draws on the total environment to provide learning experiences for children. Organizing foci for these experiences include the community, shared governance, interdisciplinary inquiry, special interest areas, and person-to-person relationships.

The Montclair gifted/talented program model is explained in the chapter by Walter L. Marks. The program is interdisciplinary and based on the premise that all children have special gifts and talents which should be nurtured in school. The ABC's of the Montclair model are Aesthetics, Basics, and the Creative I. All students partake of curricular offerings in each of these areas.

To state that all children have gifts and talents is one thing; for the school to identify such gifts may be another. Jessie A. Roderick and Bethene LeMahieu suggest ways in which educators may do this. They note the importance of settings to such identification and provide an example of identifying compassion as a child's talent in various settings.

Relationships among home, school, and community can provide valuable support for gifted and talented programs. Yvonne L. Blanchard discusses the nature of these relationships and proposes guidelines for a supportive alliance among these parties. Key to this alliance is the acceptance of mutual responsibility for "defining school programs, giftedness, and curriculum planning."

Robert L. Sinclair and Ward J. Ghory address the critical role of teachers in identifying and responding to the special gifts and talents of each child. They indicate ways that teachers can develop such awareness of their students and discuss the implications of such an approach for instructional leadership in the classoom. It is important for teachers to understand their own styles and the kind of learning environment they provide for students. By so doing they can improve the interaction between the student and the learning environment.

Candice Nattland is a classroom teacher in the Montclair gifted/talented program. She writes about her day-to-day experiences in teaching a social studies unit to 8- and 9-year-olds. Her chapter demonstrates ways that children developed group skills and individual interests for further exploration as a result of this experience.

Harry Morgan discusses the relationship of sensorimotor development to learning potential. He suggests that an active learning environment is conducive to cognitive development, particularly among minority students. He then argues for diversity in learning environments and close contact between schools and parents about the nature of these environments and ways that families can support school activities.

5

LOUISE M. BERMAN, University of Maryland

WALTER L. MARKS, Montclair Public Schools

Educating Gifted/ Talented Youth: Perspectives on Curriculum and Leadership

What does it mean to grow up in the latter part of the twentieth century? What does it mean when teachers, parents, superintendents, curriculum directors, and the community at large believe that all children can develop gifts and talents? What kinds of setting can school provide so that the young can develop talents? What kind of networks or webs of relationships can be established in a community so that all segments of it feel a sense of responsibility toward its youth?

What can happen when the superintendent assumes the posture that his focus should be on the curriculum? What happens when he attempts to mobilize the community for the purpose of strengthening programs for children and youth?

The comments that follow are the perspective of two persons—a curriculum developer and a superintendent—on designing programs in which talent, individuality, and creativity can flourish.

A Curriculum Developer Speaks

The latter part of the twentieth century is an exciting time to be growing up. Many people have opportunities to make greater use of their own abilities, interests, and talents because of the advances that have been made in simplifying certain areas basic to living—cooking, care of clothing, transporting, and the like. If time is utilized wisely that was formerly given

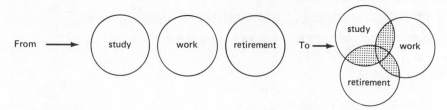

FIGURE 5-1

to areas in which little choice existed, then persons have more moments to develop interests and skills of choice.

As we look at what it means to grow up talented in the twentieth century, we first consider certain ideas that challenge previous conceptions of schooling. Then attention is given to our beliefs about curriculum and its development. Lastly, based on our beliefs, needed curriculum priorities are briefly discussed.

Ideas Inviting Fresh Ways of Thinking and Acting

In the past persons have ordinarily seen their lives as divided into three boxes: study, work, and retirement. Little overlap existed among these three aspects of life. Currently, with persons staying healthy longer, with knowledge developing at an ever faster rate, with different kinds of jobs appearing more frequently, and with persons realizing the need to be continuous learners, a need exists to rethink the concept of study, work, and retirement being three separate facets of life. We need to move toward interrelating and integrating these aspects (see Figure 5-1).

When we think about the overlapping nature of these dimensions of life, we realize that some persons may wish to study at intermittent periods throughout life, some persons may wish to begin work a little earlier, and some may wish to continue work longer than has been common practice. We realize some persons may wish interludes of retirement throughout life, tapering off their work experiences rather than ending them abruptly. We need to think about a core of understanding (shown in the shaded area of Figure 5-1) that helps persons decide the best utilization of life's moments.

Providing experiences to encourage reflection on how life shall be lived can be the functon of the school in collaboration with the family and other institutions. Networks of individuals and groups within the community can be formed to enrich the lives of all persons who tie into the network. For example, a 30-year-old might retool for a new career through an apprenticeship in the area he/she wishes to enter. Drawing early on a retirement plan sometimes can help finance the career shift. Another person might make a carer change by combining work in a known area with study in a new field.

Networking is a process by which close collaborative relationships may be formed among persons and institutions. Authority, information, and resources are shared.[1] Within the networking concept, talent involves the ability to form creative linkages among the three stages of life and among the various resources within the community. Talent may also involve being able to use available resources in order to live joyously and productively.

A second idea inviting a new look is the nature of occupations. In the past, persons frequently saw the professions or top managerial jobs as being appropriate for persons with talent. Now a dilemma exists in that an increase of persons obtaining higher education is evident, but a lack of new positions demanding professional and managerial skills exists.[2] For example, in 1975-1985 the proportion of workers who are college graduates will grow, but the percentage of professional-technical jobs will remain the same (15 per cent).[3] Within this context questions can be raised about the talent that is needed to be an innovative shopkeeper, a creative carpenter, a socially concerned policeman, a compassionate aide, a vital assemblyline worker. What kinds of networks are necessary to continue to foster talent in jobs that heretofore may not have been defined as being for the talented? How can linkages be formed among groups of people so that persons remain alive, vital, and learning in whatever line of work they choose? How can people expand their horizons so that they learn how to build a total shelter rather than just one small part of it, so that they learn the full operation of a bakery rather than just kneading the dough, so that they learn the total art of gardening rather than just grading? Flexibility among positions and preparation for a variety of jobs within a total system may evoke and sustain creative talent. All work must be seen as making it possible to put one's stamp on the activity rather than being stamped by the activity.[4]

A third concept inviting a fresh look has to do with the problem of fragmentation that characterizes people, nations, bodies of knowledge, and institutions. Consider the fact that about ninety nations are on the agenda of the United Nations for consideration for self-government and independence, but most of these have less than a hundred thousand inhabitants.[5] What kinds of talent in diplomatic skills do persons need so that networks may be established among nations?

[1] Seymour Sarason et al., *Human Services and Resource Networks* (San Francisco: Jossey-Bass, Publishers, 1977).

[2] Fred Best, Recycling People: Work-Sharing Through Flexible Life Scheduling, *The Futurist*, 1978, *12*, 10.

[3] Ibid.

[4] Seymour Sarason, *Work, Aging and Social Change* (New York: Free Press, 1977).

[5] Elmer Plischke, Microstates: Lilliputs in World Affairs, *The Futurist*, 1978, *12*, 20.

Consider the proliferation of knowledge in various fields. When insights from different disciplines are necessary in the solution to problems, such as the management of natural resources or the care of the dying, how can talent be utilized so that persons can work together productively on issues?

Consider towns that have high rates of unemployment. How can persons develop the talent to work out new arrangements among persons so that jobs are available and fewer are unemployed?

Dramatic changes in the latter part of the twentieth century call for new kinds of talent. Networks that cut across all segments of local and world settings can make possible the development of talent so necessary to dealing with the many complexities of living.

Beliefs Underlying Action

Any curriculum worker, or indeed any person, has a set of beliefs that implicitly or explicitly guide behavior. The more one reflects on beliefs and the more one considers practice in terms of beliefs, the more effective school programs will be for all. Frequently, instead of asking questions relative to the beauty, or the goodness, or the rightness, or the justice of the curriculum, we raise questions relative to efficiency or minimal standards. We sacrifice children to norms, complexity to simplicity, and creative action to regurgitation of insignificant facts.

If we accept the concept that all persons possess gifts and talents and that a community can consist of a network of relationships enhancing the people within the community, what are other assumptions that might underlie curriculum development and implementation?

- Gifts and talents can best be developed in settings that invite transactions, rather than reactions, to elements within the environment. In other words, individuals see themselves as possessing personal power to make decisions, rather than only having decisions made about them.

- A person can better develop his/her talents when significant others have faith in him/her and when the community provides a compassionate, responsive setting. The community needs to allow its young to search, to try (and even to fail), but then to have a fresh beginning.

- We all yearn for what we might be. Persons in the community welcome honest invitations to participate in the life of the school. Persons outside the school have as much need to grow as those within the school.[6] Community people wish to participate in what

[6] Seymour Sarason et al., op. cit., p.51.

they see as socially worthwhile, as something challenging and novel in their lives. When participation in the school "is presented and experienced as a mutually rewarding experience—not a ritualistic, one-way give-but-not-get opportunity"—significant community resources may become available.[7]

- The day of rugged individualism is over. Persons of all ages need to learn to live collaboratively and cooperatively with others.

- The school has the potential to be a meeting place for persons of all ages to develop talents that enable them to live more fully within the networks of the late twentieth century.

Curriculum Priorities

If those responsible for the education of the young are concerned with providing opportunities for young people to develop their gifts, then certain kinds of actions bear consideration. Two key ideas underlie the curriculum priorities that are discussed: (1) any learning opportunity must be seen as significant and meaningful by those undergoing it if it is to have impact, and (2) schools can reach out to communities to provide rich experiences for the young. This latter point is developed more fully as we suggest a few qualities that should be evoked by the educational experiences in which children and youth participate.

Perceiving Fully. If persons are to enlarge their ideas, to give them a new turn, and to utilize them to some end, they need to learn to see accurately and fully. Students need help in checking out how much they see like others and how much they see differently. Persons can increase their skill in seeing what others see but also seeing what others do not see.

In reaching out to the community, schools can call on artists and photographers to work with the young in seeing new designs and patterns in nature or architecture. Schools can call on theologians and philosophers to help children see conflicting values inherent in an ethical dilemma. Schools can call on carpenters to help children see the infinite varieties of ways a cabinet can be built.

The concept of perception can be introduced in many ways in school programs. Of prime importance is the notion that school administrators and teachers need opportunities to enlarge and to study their own modes of perceiving. Workshops, conferences, and retreats that require persons to examine phenomena in new ways are modes of enhancing perceptive skills. Taking unusual photographs helps to build aesthetic perceptiveness. Enlarging the circle of persons one enjoys and appreciates develops skill in social

[7] Ibid., pp. 109-110.

awareness. Teachers, administrators, parents, students, and other citizens can enlarge the vision of others. Persons can also extend their own skills to see so that they perceive what others see—but also what they do not.

Increasing Skill in Relationships. Perhaps one of the most critical areas in which talent is needed both now and in the future is in the area of human relationships. For example, persons need to be able to deal with the dynamics of relationships that are new and exploratory, as in the brief one-time encounter a person may have at a meeting. Persons need also to be able to deal with sustained relationships, those that have lost the explosive power of new friendship.

Schools can provide varieties of opportunities for students for encounters with persons both within and outside the peer group. For example, students might have work experiences in shops, restaurants, hospitals, nursing homes, museums, and churches for purposes of interacting with different kinds of persons over time. Students can then analyze their own feelings and thinking as they relate to different people. Included with these persons should be ones who may deviate from what is commonly considered normal behavior. Students can keep records of their gains in caring about a variety of people. It is imperative that those who work with the young examine their own gifts of compassion.

Valuing. Networks of persons can assist the young in seeing the various value schemes that may pervade the community. Students can work directly with individuals and groups who represent divergent points of view. For example, who are the individuals or groups who favor busing? Why? Which individuals or groups tend to help the "underdog"? Why? What values seem to surface in organizations or associations with different platforms?

As students gain experience in working within their community, they may feel tensions that democracy engenders. Surely students need to begin early to develop modes of attempting to deal with the dilemmas of competing ideologies. This skill can be more easily developed after students have been immersed in the marketplace of ideas and values. Students can then sort through their values and ascertain those that seem to surface in various situations. Students can consider whether they seem to have a core of values, whether and to what degree they are influenced by the values of others, and how they can plan for continuous growth in dealing with complex ethical issues.

Assessing Situations. Students need help in seeing how they (inwardly) assess situations and (outwardly) respond to them. For example, one high school girl was noted in five different classes, each of which had a different type of instructor and, consequently, a different climate. The student had an uncanny way of seeing what was appropriate behavior for that situation and demonstrating it. From poetry class, where she displayed a sensitive handling of the subject, to band, where she as an assistant spent much of her time trying to get her classmates to SHUT UP, she indicated an ability to assess the qualities of the situation and to respond in terms of her assessment.

The community provides unique opportunities for the young to be in a variety of settings and try on different modes of behavior in them. The task of the school then becomes that of helping students sort out their behaviors, in terms of those recurrent in a variety of situations and those appearing only in selected settings. Such an analysis helps a person answer the fundamental question: Who am I?

Composing Knowledge Creatively. One of the dominant themes of schooling is and has been to impart to the young the culture that the larger community deems important. However, the school has another task. It must provide settings where greater emphasis is given to helping the young compose what they know into new fresh patterns. Children and youth must deal with the process of knowing, as well as with learning the known.[8]

The community can provide settings where youth may test out, weigh, and compose afresh knowledge derived from planned school experiences. Youth need opportunities to see through the lenses of the different disciplines—mathematics, philosophy, literature, and biology—but then to compose their insights into visions and ideas that have unique meaning for them. For example, a young student of philosophy might apply philosophical analysis to certain problems that a park department faces in terms of allocation of resources. In his application of knowledge he may compose knowledge into a framework unique to him.

Becoming Rooted. In a day of mobility the place of identity must be in the self.[9] The more one finds one's own identity, the more one can reach out to others. Being rooted, knowing one's identity, allows persons to flower out into the community.

If schools help the young know themselves, then ultimately we can hope they will reach out, thus becoming part of the networks that influenced them. In the last analysis, talent involves intense use of intelligence and compassion for the common good. We are working on the premise that this end can be accomplished. Under the guidance of talented leaders schools that consider the total community as their setting can provide opportunities for the young to grow up talented.

If the establishment of networks among various agencies will provide

---

[8] Adapted from Walker Gibson, The Knowledge of Human Minds, *The Chronicle of Higher Education*, 1978, *16*, 48.

[9] Cornelis Verhoeven, *The Philosophy of Wonder*, Mary Foran, trans. (New York: Macmillan Publishing Co., Inc., 1972), p. 134.

new and better initial mechanisms for the clients of education, it is important to look at the type of leadership needed for the growth of these networks. If networks improve and establish community/student relationships and provide youth with skills to assess who they are in the total scheme of things, the public schools must be led by people who value these ideas.

Recent polls and other informal surveys have shown that the American public is not truly convinced that education is doing all that it should do to contribute to a better life for all. If new and exciting collaborative efforts can be formed by business, industry, parents, school systems, and professional organizations with fiscal help from federal, state, and local governments, as well as foundations, we may be able to design and implement programs geared toward the future instead of the past.

As stated earlier in this chapter, we believe that all youngsters have special gifts and talents and that educational programs must be designed toward these gifts and talents. It is our contention, however, that the most advantageous way to develop programs for the gifted and talented youth of our country is through networks providing both human and fiscal resources for enhancing schools. We further contend that to make these collaborative networks viable and sound, leadership in the public school sector must be redirected toward a future based on shared responsibility through a variety of networks. The question we deal with now is what characteristics must that public school leader develop, and what skills must he or she possess?

A Superintendent Speaks

There is a growing concern that public education, especially in urban school systems, is useless. Schools in urban communities are havens for the poor and powerless; people with political clout and money have purchased another education and have fled the public school systems. Many schools are employment agencies for adults; they are no longer institutions for learners. Many schools are organizations designed to further disenfranchise their clients—the young and their parents. There is growing consensus that schools should no longer be operated by local boards of education or by the educational establishment, but that the business of operating schools should be turned over to parents and to business and industry.

A more radical proposal is that a new model for teacher training be developed because the business of training teachers by universities is so ineffective. One model would give money to parents to buy commercially produced training materials with which they could learn how to teach their youngsters at home. The extension of this notion leads one to suggest that compulsory school attendance would be waived as long as the parent was conducting this activity in the home. A further extension of this idea, not at all novel, is that parents should be given an educational voucher to buy the kind of school, program, or teaching style they desire.

These ideas do not spell chaos; they spell new linkages and new power bases for education, especially for program development. Public schools and colleges of education (the traditional power bases and hence the locus of control) will be joined by at least two other strong partners, parents and the world of industry and business.

Curriculum Development—The Chief Function of the Superintendent

Curriculum development, i.e., commitment to the educational program, must be at the center for a school superintendent. Realization of quality instructional program through structure, schedules, teaching technology, roles, rules, and allocation of resources is the ultimate hazardous act of administrative leadership. Practitioners say of theoretical, professorial types: to conjure up notions of the new in the protected environment of the university is all very well; however, it is quite another matter for a superintendent to put status, career, and security on the line in support of change that touches intimately the present and future lives of children, the daily experience of teachers, and the expectations and hopes of parents.

Education is very important—yet it is an unclear process, universally pursued to determine the future social and economic success of tomorrow's adults. The curriculum, all the child's learning experiences, is value based. Its impact is long range; its effectiveness difficult to assess. Implementation of curriculum change is fraught with uncertainties. Rules and policies are artificial guides that cannot map a clear direction for the decision maker. Is it any wonder then that administrators have been slow to enact and support substantial curriculum change?

If the administrator is to commit himself to the effort of realizing curriculum change, he needs to be supported by a frame of reference, a model, a perspective that is enabling, that expands rather than constrains, and that fits the complexity of the task. Traditional theoretical efforts miss the mark. They do not address the central issue that concerns the practitioner: How do I fit myself to the task? How do I know when to advance, when to retreat, when to confront, when to compromise?

Today's administrative theories have developed from industrial and corporate models and from the behavioral sciences. Although we do not intend to analyze in detail those models that explain the role of the administrator, we do assert that the recurring complaint of the practitioner that theory has not been useful in the so-called real world is not simply a rejection of the insights of an alien academic world. Administrative theories have failed to illuminate the central factor determining the administrator's mastery of the special environment of the school, curriculum development and its implementation.

The scientific management view of administration emphasizes the role of the superintendent in coordinating the organization for efficiency; the bureaucratic model has chiefly focused on the distribution of power/authority through the structure of the organization. The natural systems perspective has tended to view the organization as a spontaneously maintained entity operating to achieve its own survival. More recent theorists observing the educational organization have noted the lack of linkage between bureaucratic structures and the central task of educating children. This linkage between the chief administrator and the central task of educating children is the development of curricula. Other contructs—for example, the use of conflict, political considerations, planning and management systems, and human relations techniques—are then strategies to create an instructional opportunity maximizing the full development of the young.

Goodlad reflects this belief when he states that the work for which superintendents will be held accountable "is to maintain, justify and articulate sound comprehensive programs of instruction for children and youth."[10] To accomplish this end, he suggests that discretionary time—as much as 25 per cent of one's work week—must be set aside for matters of curriculum.[11]

Assuming that the focus of the superintendent is curriculum and instruction, how then does he successfully negotiate the political waters that can unsettle the safety of the ship he captains? What about the pressures of interest groups? What about collective bargaining? What of the myriad of projects, tasks, and concerns that distract the superintendent from the central goal of curriculum development and instructional program? Concepts derived from management theory, sociology, and psychology do not teach the administrator to synthesize these learnings, do not enable him or her to satisfy the need of the moment or to meet the experiences of the real situation.

Beliefs About Leadership

The philosophy framing the beliefs and values of the individual is the long-ignored dimension that provides the synthesizing factor so that the superintendent can place curriculum in the center, see and seize opportunities, manage and create environments, recognize and select means, and dream and project futures. It is the individual's world view and understanding of self that finally enables a person to act. It is what the individual tells

[10] John I. Goodlad, Educational Leadership: Toward the Third Era, *Educational Leadership*, 1978, 35, 326.

[11] Ibid., p. 327.

himself about the world that allows risk taking. A positive view of self and others enables leadership. It is the full investment of the man or woman in existential terms that provides the synthesizing capacity, the symbolizing capacity, and the exploring capacity. It is the personal concept of freedom that gives power to effect change. This view supports Halpin's observation that it is the authenticity of the leader that has overriding influence on the climate of the school.[12]

The superintendent's impact in the decision-making process in curriculum development is primarily a product of his development. Administrators must discover what Charles Hampden-Turner termed the "radical man" in themselves if they are to be transformed from bureaucrats into educational leaders. In Hampden-Turner's view they must possess developed characteristics of radical vision:

> vision which can stare into the face of injustice and absurdity without yielding in determination to "balance" and make it just; of investment and commitment of self to others authentically and with intensity; of risking self by deliberately suspending assumptions and exposing the undefended self to friends and to forces of reaction. Further, as educational leaders, they must bridge the great distances to the deviant, the despised, the minority groups, and the "enemies" of his country, to make contact, to bring compassion, and to discover novel life; they must find self-confirmation and the new meanings invested must transcend the individual's own personality and enter into the consciousness of the community.[13]

Educational change is effected by leaders who dare to be the "radical man." This approach, however, does not suggest a return to the "great man" school of thought. Rather, the proposal is that effective leadership in curriculum development is not simply maintenance or controlling or organizing. Effective leadership is high-risk creative activity requiring the development of the affirming, integrated self.

But how does the superintendent achieve this worthy goal? What activities or behaviors nurture the creative self? How does the administrator structure real events in time and space to provide effective leadership? Some initial thoughts might be

- The leader must spend time dreaming about ways to seek out and design methods to find out what we do not know, instead of spending time refining and controlling what we already know. Dreaming is the fun part. Implementing the dream is fulfillment. Seeing it work is salvation.

[12] Andrew W. Halpin, *Theory and Research in Administration* (New York: Macmillan Publishing Co., Inc., 1966), pp. 192, 204-206.

[13] Charles Hampden-Turner, *Radical Man* (Garden City, N.Y.: Doubleday, 1971), p. 60.

- Superintendents must spend time conjecturing, probing, hypothesizing about how to make their environments do what they want them to. They cannot afford to believe that their environments control them or their actions. Passivity leads to apathy; involvement leads to action. The "we can't" syndrome must be replaced by "let's give it a try" enthusiasm.

- An effective superintendent realizes that most individuals have greater potential than is used. Some researchers say we seldom use more than 25 per cent of our potential. Therefore the educational leader, if concerned about leading into the future, must through involvement and earned ownership produce in himself and his staff the use of a fuller potential. An effective superintendent deals in the future, not in the present and not in the past.

- A crucial element in successful leadership is the inability of others to predict the behavior of the leader. Once classified as predictable (liberal, moderate, or conservative), the leader is ineffective. Instead, the leader should be impossible to classify. Leaders do what they believe is right, good, beautiful, and proper—not what society interprets as right, good, beautiful, and proper. As a result, the leader must be willing to take risks.

- Change is the expected. Great degrees of change yield as much conflict/controversy in education as do small degrees of change. When change is to occur, the moment must be grasped to create change that makes a difference for children. It is imperative that a superintendent have the ability to manipulate crisis, to reduce it, to use it effectively, and to stop it when desirable. Above all, he should expect conflict and be able to manage it in order to produce the desired results.

- To lead, one must have power and know how to use it constructively. Power to bring about positive change is earned through cooperation, intelligent and creative problem solving, involvement of all members of the team, and provision for everyone to experience some success each day. An effective leader believes that power comes from provision for individuals to succeed over institutions.

    The leader who deals with power successfully must be able to perceive the reaction of his ideas on audiences and individuals. He must be able to determine hard issues and soft issues. He must be able to exercise the art of compromise and to know what is compromisable. The effective leader has the ability to organize strong, convincing arguments and to think on his feet. The effective leader understands how to mobilize people to create events that move policy-making bodies, thus making possible the creation and implementation of curriculum. He must understand the notion that leadership is a phenomenon of opportunity—creating the right idea for the right place at the right moment. Problems are opportunities that can be cornerstones for leadership. Leaders grasp problems in an effort to move their ideas. Educational leaders must mix some Machiavellian notions with the idealism of Thoreau if they are to be successful in program development that runs against the mainstream of societal thinking. Finally, power comes *with* people, not over them. Power is kept by winning. Show me a good loser, and I will show you a loser.

- The single most important aspect of leadership is the personality of the leader. Through his actions and deeds he creates excitement, shares visions, sets leadership styles, rewards risk taking, prizes dreaming, sanctions crying, and develops the human side of the organization. From the humanism of the organization come commitment, hard work, optimism, and growth possibilities. The personality of the leader must not be so open as to eliminate the mystery about why he is an effective leader. The effective leader needs the Madison Avenue touch without the classification. He needs to project a jet-set enthusiasm, but refute the image. The aura of excitement, enjoyment, and the concept of discovery must surround the leader and his team. The personality of the leader must be intact enough to accept and understand that he will be loved, hated, and tolerated. He must know that he cannot be all things to all people. The leader must present himself as an educator—not a manager, a politician, or a jack-of-all-trades. He must be committed to the fact that for education to lead as a profession he must lead with style, mystery, and enthusiasm.

The Curriculum Developer and the Superintendent Speak

Attention has been given briefly to factors that necessitate reconceptualizations of curricula, to the importance of involving in a real way the community, and to the significance of stalwart and innovative leadership. Even though a community may be aware of societal trends with implications for its children and youth, even if fresh ideas are found in the curricula, and even if the leadership is energetic and wise, educational leaders are still confronted with unfinished business. Unfinished business means that schools, school systems, and communities must always press ahead to find solutions to new and old problems, to establish new directions, to throw out old practices that have outlived their usefulness, and to go about the business of creating and implementing fresh ideas with the potential for enhancing the quality of life for those affected.

Universities, public school people, business, industry, and citizens must together establish dream factories, or think tanks, which are constantly coming up with concepts worthy of further development, implementation, and testing. But how do persons in leadership positions evaluate the worth of ideas? On what bases do they decide which good ideas are worth trying out? Obviously, if we could answer these questions we would have utopian school systems—or at least almost utopian. As educational leaders continue to strive toward excellence in school systems, what guidelines should they consider? In other words, how does one consider and evaluate the worth of an educational idea? Let's think about these guidelines:

- Be prepared to deal with conflicting *good* ideas, rather than good and bad ideas. We need to assume that most people talk in terms of what makes sense to them. What makes sense may be good to the person(s) who developed the idea. People need to feel that their ideas are worthwhile even if not "good" or appropriate for a school or school system at a given moment in time.

- Prize complexity. One of the problems with education generally is that we are often likely to sacrifice basic human qualities for easy answers. People are full of contradictory but vital qualities. We must deal with people as they are, rather than how we wish them to be. The tendency of schools to utilize simplistic standardized tests or to develop competency-based programs, where competencies are linear and fail to take into account the complexity of persons, are examples of our failure to deal with and prize complexity.

- Allow ideas to be initiated in a variety of places and by a variety of persons. When people initiate and then see their ideas evolve into actuality, they feel some ownership of the ideas. Ownership begets the enthusiasm and excitement so necessary to any vital school system. As students develop and refine their ideas they are gaining a sense of ownership. Parents, students, teachers, central office personnel, board members, citizens, and others should know the procedures to initiate an idea. The more people in a system who feel that they have a sense of power, that they can make a difference, and that they count, the more likely a system is to be wholesome, healthy, and energetic.

- Value the capacity of each person in the system to make independent decisions of worth. This principle applies to the youngest child in the schools as well as veteran teachers and administrators. When a proposal is introduced that infringes unnecessarily on the right of each individual to be in control of his/ her own destiny, then that proposal should be carefully examined. We are not proposing anarchy, for we all know that a community involves rules, regulations, customs, and habits that are for the common good. Particularly in the area of curriculum development we are proposing, however, that people will be more enthusiastic about learning and teaching if they have had a part in decisions that affect their lives. For example, in the teaching of reading, teachers and youth may be victims of a reading system in which little choice exists for the individual teacher or student. For, within a framework of stated goals and objectives, individual teachers and students can determine alternative paths to unlocking the written word.

- Create images of direction before considering costs. "It's a time of recession or cutbacks; therefore we can't . . ." is too frequently the utterance of leadership personnel. Before worrying about paying for the implementation of a fresh idea, develop the idea fully. Then consideration can be given to resources. What new resources can be tapped? What program is obsolete and needs to be phased out?

- Consider all persons in the community—not just children and youth—as part of the educative process. Helping children grow up talented is not the task of the schools alone; it is the task of the family of persons with whom the child has contact. All people have something to give and to receive through intimate contact with the schools. Educate and prepare the media to portray as accurately and vividly as possible what is transpiring in the schools. Communicate dreams and visions as well as problems. Involve community people in projects to which they might give and/or receive. In this way networks incorporating people with different talents in the community can be established, and all persons stand to benefit.

- Engage in continuous dialogue with various sectors of the citizenry and professional community about images of persons and roles of the school. This statement may sound trite, but the trivia of schooling can become so overwhelming that we forget the whys of education. If our eyes are constantly focused on what people can become, new ideas will have a better chance of being thoughtfully evaluated.

- Try to implement some ideas which draw people together. A community needs a system of shared beliefs and values if individuality is to flourish. As ideas are evaluated, therefore, special attention should be given to those that seem to have a unifying power while simultaneously benefiting children.

Conclusion

In summary, leadership in the schools cannot be afraid of the ambiguous, of the difficult, or of the challenging. These realities of living must be acknowledged, but they should not be the stopping point. We mentioned earlier that much research on the human mind indicates that people use only a small percentage of their potential. If the community through its leaders is committed to developing a diversity of gifts and talents in its youth, how real and vital each individual can become. And who can tell what such people would ultimately contribute to self, the community, the nation, and indeed the world?

6

JAMES B. MACDONALD, University of North Carolina, Greensboro

Curriculum Design for a Gifted/Talented Program

A curriculum design is a plan or a set of specifications for the construction of a learning environment. As such it is a rational construction of a contrived environment that will, we hope, facilitate the learning of what the planners feel are worthwhile outcomes. Curriculum designing is thus both a rational and moral enterprise. Therefore, a curriculum design must be defensible and validated by both our data and our values. Central to any conceptualization of a curriculum design are our ideas of human nature and the role of the school in society.

The American school system has been predicated on the development of the democratic ideal. Realization of this ideal entails an education dedicated to rational processes of problem solving with the concomitant ethical principles. It also entails honoring those attitudes and values that facilitate the fulfillment of justice, equality, liberty, and brotherhood for all. Central to this doctrine is faith in the dignity and integrity of each human being and the resultant prizing of the necessary actions that facilitate the development of individual uniqueness and potential. The schools serve the youth of our society to the extent they help them become better democratic citizens and better individuals. According to this view, there is no separation between individual and society, for the needs of society require the development of committed individuals capable of functioning as participating members of a democratic society, and a participant democracy creates the very conditions that maximize the development of individuals. Thus individual human development and participant democracy are mutually supportive.

The idea of human nature that accompanies that school role rejects the vision of persons as machines or robots in a deterministic external set of circumstantial conditionings, as well as the image of humans as creatures who are buffeted and shaped by genes, instincts, and emotions. Instead, people are seen as creators, as free agents.

Human beings are creative actors who make over the world and are, in turn, made by it. People are free agents. Human existence is open ended rather than predetermined, and it is characterized by choice, contingency, and chance, rather than compulsion. To experience oneself as a free agent creates the awareness of self as active rather than reactive, and the experience of oneself as active creates the basis of self-respect and personal responsibility.

Further, this view of human nature perceives people as open rather than closed systems, self-determined rather than pre-determined, resourceful rather than reflexive. What is distinctive is the person's power to choose, the freedom to say "yes" or "no." Each individual is unique, both genetically and environmentally. Each person is an active agent in the affirmation and creation of self and the world, and each person possesses gifts and talents, potentialities and possibilities to be discovered and created in the process of choosing and creating.

Given these definitions of the role of the school and the nature of human beings, a curriculum design must reflect both ethically and rationally a constructed environment of learning experiences that will help realize these commitments.

Directions for a Curriculum Design

Life Values

All curricula have some desired directions, goals, or objectives that guide the construction of learning opportunities. The design proposed here for facilitating the development of giftedness and talent in all youngsters—compatible with our concept of human beings as freely choosing self agents in a participatory democracy—leads to the identification of goals that reflect the integrated wholeness of the person. These we call life values.

The curriculum, in other words, should be focused on facilitating the development of life values as integrated learnings in the individual. Life values are the outcome of experiences that have cognitive, affective, and action aspects to them. They have been internalized and integrated into the personal identity of the individual. Thus a value in this sense calls for cognitive discrimination(s), calls for affective response to it, and demands some action with it before it can be said to be internalized and integrated as a life value. This, of course, is in contrast to the traditionally narrow, specific, often trivial, and highly segmented statement of goals or objectives in most programs.

The conceptualization of goals or objectives is often overlooked in terms of its importance in a curriculum design. Different designs demand different definitions of the conceptions of end points. This is why, for example, a design working from a mechanistic model of human nature is most appropriately organized by behavioral objectives. For a program to reflect a free agent view of persons in relation to giftedness and talent, it is imperative that goals be broader and more flexible, reflecting an integrated wholeness in human learning: thus—life values.

Life values must be seen not only in the perspective of individual development and learning but also in terms of environmentally locatable experiences. What is necessary is a resource grid of the appropriate learning environments to help locate places and experiences that could foster the development of gifts and talents through emerging life values. This means looking for opportunities whereby learners may find experiences in encountering social, legal, scientific, technical, economic, political, aesthetic, religious, spiritual, physical, and interpersonal life values. The search for political resources will include the total environment: community, mass media, family, and school. All are appropriate.

Areas of Experience: The Umbrella

The curriculum design proposed here may be seen as an umbrella (Figure 6-1). That is, it is in some sense a shield from the negative rain of certain social pressures but also a rounded, opening environment for learning.

There are five experience organizers and locaters identified by the umbrella. Each of these (community, governance, person to person, interdisciplinary studies, and special interests) areas represents an aspect of the total local environment that has been utilized to provide learning experiences for youngsters. Each has its own unique potential contribution to make to a rich set of experiences that provide personal, social, and academic relevance to the design.

Community

The community may be utilized in many ways. Central to the design proposed here is the use of the community in two special ways: (1) as a series of places to encounter life values and (2) as a resource pool of persons to involve in schooling.

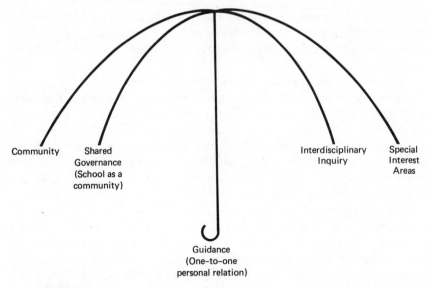

Community   Shared   Interdisciplinary   Special
             Governance   Inquiry   Interest
             (School as a   Areas
             community)

Guidance
(One-to-one
personal relation)

FIGURE 6-1

It is critical that the young be aware of the importance of knowledge and skill in the conduct of our lives in the community as consumers, workers, and citizens. The relevance of school can best be understood by learning in the community and through the community. Any concern for gifts and talents must have some connection with the communal meanings of the possibilities.

The community must be gridded to find learning network stations reflecting the range of potential life values. These need only responsive adults who like the young and are willing to include them as participant-observers in their own activity. There is no need to provide any formal teaching, only meaningful activity.

Furthermore, the potential contributions of older youngsters and adults to the development of life values, gifts, and talents are enormous in terms of coming into the school to display the possibilities of human learning and development in all possible areas. A design of this sort encourages a totally open door policy with located people who can be called on to come into the school for special purposes.

Shared Governance

The school not only must be in a community but also must be seen as a community. As such it should reflect a way of living together that represents an adequate response to a participant in democracy and a choosing, creative person. This strongly suggests a model of shared governance.

Shared governance is self-explanatory. It means literally that the power to make decisions that affect the activities and social lives of all people is shared in some meaningful way by all. This requires considerable ingenuity in meaningfully involving students and staff in a participant flow of decision making.

This aspect of the design is predicated on the assertion that learning democracy is achieved by living it—not studying about it, per se. Democracy is important, of course, for our form of government; but also it is the best political system to ensure the emergence of the ideal human nature accepted in this design. Thus shared governance is consistent with eliciting gifts and talents in social, political, and legal life values in all persons; it is necessary to ensure experiences in a total integrative perspective.

Interdisciplinary Inquiry

Discovering the potentialities and possibilities in gifts and talents is also facilitated by offering the opportunity of seeing and coping with social problems. This must be done on an interdisciplinary basis, because no social problem is solvable in terms of one academic discipline alone.

There are two important meanings for the learning environment found in interdisciplinary study. The first is the thematic study of areas such as violence (crime, war, and child abuse), pollution, communication, and so on from a team-teaching approach. The second is the organization of activity around inquiry or projects by individuals and small groups. This active research and inquiry are stimulated and developed in these thematic studies.

Special Interest Areas

Perhaps the most recognizable aspect of the design is the area of special interests. Here we offer the option of what are usually recognized as the disciplines or study areas. Thus a person may elect science, mathematics, art, music, or foreign language; or opt for skill development laboratory work; or propose, along with other persons, new interest areas for study.

It is important that there be a built-in way of adding short-term interest items as minicourses and that teachers feel free to introduce their specialities for students to elect. Gifts and talents must be encouraged to move in a variety of directions through the agency of special interests and needs.

Person-to-Person Relationships

Each youngster needs to have a feeling of belonging with a group of other youngsters and a close personal relationship, by mutual attraction, with a concerned adult. Thus emotional security and knowledge and experience of caring and helping must be a part of any curriculum design that embodies respect for people in its ideals.

What is envisioned here is a close personal relationship in a home base at school. Each student, perhaps in a 1-to-20 ratio, would have a home base with an adult. This would provide the guidance system for utilizing the curriculum design and the support system for close personal relationships.

Essentially this home base would have the following goals:

- Acquainting students with the alternative learning possibilities in the design.

- Providing opportunity for students to identify needs and interests and to clarify values.

- Providing experiences and opportunities for students to make decisions about what they wish to do.

- Providing a base and interactive setting for self-evaluation and reflection on experiences.

- Providing for reexamining, clarifying, making new choices, and entering new activities.

We can envision many ways of trying to achieve these ends. And such a pattern would involve individual students and an adult spending a great deal of time getting to know each other before leaving their home base for a broader learning environment. Later they return to their home base to share and to evaluate their experiences with other students.

Some General Conditions

There are general circumstances that all curriculum designs must respect and account for. Size is a good example. We have ample evidence to suggest that overpopulation only fosters grave difficulties. Under these circumstances no unit should exceed a rough figure of five hundred youngsters. It is important to keep instructional units under this total if at all possible.

Furthermore, it makes little sense to restrict learning environments to same age groups. Thus a curriculum design respecting individual gifts and talents would be organized to include the broadest possible age range of learners.

Conclusion

Thus a curriculum design for gifted/talented, reaching the potentialities and possibilities of all students and based on an image of human nature as a free, creative, and choosing self, begins to emerge. It involves the broad definition of directions in terms of life values and the provision of a broad and varied range of experiences in the community, as a community, in interdisciplinary inquiry and special interest areas; all based on a warm, caring, one-to-one relationship with an adult in a family or core interpersonal group situation.

In this way the best possible gifts and talents will emerge in the process of student-adult choosing, freedom and perseverence of strengths, interests, and needs.

7

WALTER L. MARKS, Montclair Public Schools

Reaching Out to All Children: A Gifted/Talented Program Model

Seemingly, educators and to a larger degree parents have accepted a very narrow definition of what public education is and should be. Often those individuals who have ventured to dream, to reshape, and to move ahead have not been highly prized by either the educational establishment or parents. Once again in the late 1970s, it seems there is a hue and cry for a return to the basics, although skill acquisition in all fields is surrounded by complexity. Those proponents of reading, writing, and arithmetic fail to recognize that the education of the future not only must deal with these 3 R's but also must deal with the complexity of our society and our future. Natural intelligence must seek ways to better utilize manmade intelligence.

Schools should be developed to teach young people to deal with the complex nature of our society. Programs that deal with philosophy, logic, foreign languages of the future, social institutions as they may be constructed, creativity, leadership skills, appreciation of the arts, and enhancement of leisure-time activities are all very basic to man's survival. Therefore, education for gifted/talented young people is to a great degree defined in the following model as an expansion of curriculum into lifevalue areas that deal very specifically with structured programs to affect youth in cognitive, affective, and psychomotor areas.

It is a curriculum design that is interdisciplinary and is aimed at giving parents, students, and teachers a choice model involving the community and its resources. It is a model for the gifted/talented aimed at enhancing relationships through shared governance to a common aim. It is a model predicated on the belief that everyone has special gifts and talents. Realizing that everyone is in some way special, it designs various curricula to meet special interest needs of parents, teachers, and students. The curriculum model advocated is a definition of what elementary and middle school education might be. It rejects the deficit model for young people—that is, to determine what is wrong with them and then try to address it. Instead, it advocates the notion that education should start with the idea of determining what is right with the young and build from that perspective. It is a curriculum model that embraces the idea that socioeconomically deprived youngsters must be provided with superior, not equal, educational opportunities in all school endeavors. The curriculum and instructional model proposed asks educational planners in public schools to challenge the following concepts:

> The organization of the school day or school year for young people—the scheduling of students—the role of students in choosing schools and programs—the amount of time spent in each subject area—the type of teachers needed—the number of teachers a youngster should have per day—who should teach our youth—the kind of training/certification necessary—the role of parents in choosing for their children—the role community resources play in program development.

In general, the curriculum model advocated is a choice model. It is future oriented. It provides options and alternatives, and it challenges many of the assumptions about how schools should be organized. It also makes a statement about a type of educational program that will allow all youngsters to celebrate their special gifts and talents no matter whether they are urban or suburban youngsters, whether they are poor or rich, whether they are academically talented, talented in the arts, or multiply talented. It speaks to a new priority for the education of youth.

Gifted in the minds of many is an elitist term. Similarly, programs for gifted all too often are expected to sort out the winners and the losers. Some individuals fear that this will be the case, whereas others fear that it won't be. The model presented in this chapter is organized along the lines and the belief that all children have talents, gifts, and/or special interests. This model presents the responsibility to students, parents, educators, and interested others working collaboratively to identify these talents and differentiate instruction for them. The program access is open, and all children are eligible. The program design must be sufficiently flexible to accommodate varying types of giftedness and to address either singly or in combination at least the following areas:

- General intellectual ability.

- Special academic aptitude.

- Creative or productive thinking.

- Leadership ability.

- Visual and performing arts.

- Psychomotor ability.

- Futuristic planning.

However, it is the parents alone who should decide whether a child will take part in a gifted/talented program. Children may be gifted in a variety of areas or in one of two; some may be gifted in multiple fields. Whatever the area of his/her talent, the gifted child is capable of high performance in that area because of outstanding ability. General intellectual ability, aptitude in specific academic subjects, creative or productive thinking, leadership ability, visual and performing arts, and physical arts skill are just a few areas in which a child may be gifted and talented.

This philosophy is realized through new instructional methodology and innovative curricular activities structured into three curricular components. These components are variations of traditional basic curricula, and they are formulated to arouse interest, stimulate learning, develop lalent talents, and ensure the development of basic skills. The three curricular components in this model are denoted as the ABC's of a gifted/talented program. A representing *Aesthetic* offerings, B representing the *Basic* program, and C representing the *Creative I* portion of the program.

The A (Aesthetics) portion of the program, the second level of the gifted/talented model, is exploratory in nature and incorporates new ideas into the elementary curriculum. It gives parents and/or their children many choices relative to the content of a student's education. In the B (Basic) component, the first level of the gifted/talented model, teachers prescribe content and students receive instruction in heterogeneously grouped core blocks of math/science and humanities (reading, language arts, and social studies). In the C (Creative I) portion, the third level of the gifted/talented model, outstanding performance or capability is nurtured, encouraged, and developed. A student who excels in academics, for example, can do in-depth study; a student with a passion for science will be able to pursue that interest further that is usually permitted in an elementary program. Another student who excels in the visual and/or performing arts will receive instruction appropriate to his/her talent, will be able to practice regularly, and will be able to recognize continued growth in an area of strength.

Classes in all three major components of the gifted/talented model can be multiaged or on grade level and can be based on the continuous progress model of learning. The amount of time students spend in any one component is based on student ability and need, designed and directed by students and teachers alike. In prekindergarten, kindergarten, and first and second grades a gifted/talented program is characterized as an awareness phase with different programs in various areas offering enrichment activities to broaden the primary curriculum. In third through eighth grades, students are grouped in houses or units of approximately 100—150 (multiaged or self contained) children with a team of four to six teachers working with each house. The program at these levels takes on scheduling, organizational, and operational methodology similar to that of a high school program. The program is individually tailored to fit each child, developing talents and strengthening weaknesses.

Teachers, parents, administrators, curriculum specialists, school psychologists, artists, musicians, and others all pool their information to develop a program for each child. Children are then scheduled into activities and lessons depending on their abilities, interests, and needs. Instruction can take place individually, in small groups of children with similar abilities and/or interests, and in self-contained classes of mixed abilities. Instruction for the total day then is divided into Aesthetics, Basics, and the Creative I.

Basics Component

All children receive instruction in the Basics component. This area includes the core of the elementary curriculum: science and math and the humanities (social studies, reading, and language arts). In addition, some students will be getting additional math and reading instruction in special programs, i.e., learning centers, Title I, and media center. Students who are classified as exceptional children will be receiving additional help through the resource centers and from supplemental tutors. The Basics education component is the core of the student's day, and it represents the sum of learning experiences common to most elementary schools. Students are expected to achieve conceptual and skill competency through this Basics education component. All students are grouped into the Basics component by teachers and administrators, who in turn prescribe content and instructional methodology in heterogeneously grouped classes. Variances in ability will determine the amount of time spent daily in the Basics curriculum, and this could range from 40 per cent to 80 per cent depending on the capabilities of the student. An average instructional time within this component would be somewhere between twelve and eighteen hours of direct skill instruction per week.

In this component students are structured into houses of 100–150 students with four to six teachers composing the team. The team would have two or three math/science teachers and two or three humanities teachers. There should be at least one instructional aide per house, a series of volunteers, and student teachers. The teachers are to be chosen based on their demonstrated competencies in teaching math/science or in teaching in the humanities block. In the Basics block, therefore, all students will have a minimum of two teachers—one from the humanities block and one from the math/science block—as their core teachers.

Aesthetics Component

Depending on the program design for the student and on parent/ student choice, students will be exposed to a wide range of experiences and subject areas beyond the basics in the Aesthetics component of this curriculum model. Figure 7-1 shows the content areas in which a child may do exploratory studies (Aesthetics) or in-depth accelerated study (Creative I). There could be, and should be, many other areas developed within the Aesthetics component because students will display gifts and talents in areas far beyond this list of curricular offerings.

Studies in the Aesthetics are designed to enhance a child's background and to allow him/her to develop new interests and knowledge. Each of these areas of curriculum must be developed in great depth in an effort to probe and to expand the young person's mind. A child should not have to show a special talent in order to be introduced to these areas, just a willingness to learn and to be exposed to new situations. The willingness to learn and be exposed to new situations should be the decision of the parent and the child as they choose among the variety of courses offered within the Aesthetics component.

The Aesthetics component of this curriculum should be composed of as many individual curricular activities as individuals can design, and they should permit children to probe and to explore a wider world of learning and to define themselves within it. The Aesthetics component should encourage students to apply basic skills and concepts in the pursuit of their knowledge. This component should be highly individualized, and it should address the child's need to know, for the Basics component will ensure that children learn those concepts and skills the culture demands and requires. Offerings within the Aesthetics component can be scheduled based on the amount of time necessary, as the teacher and student define it. Typically, two or three 45-minute periods per week on eleven-week cycles would accomplish what is needed in the Aesthetics areas; that is, the ability to expand one's horizons based on interest, motivation, and the desire to know. Exploration and

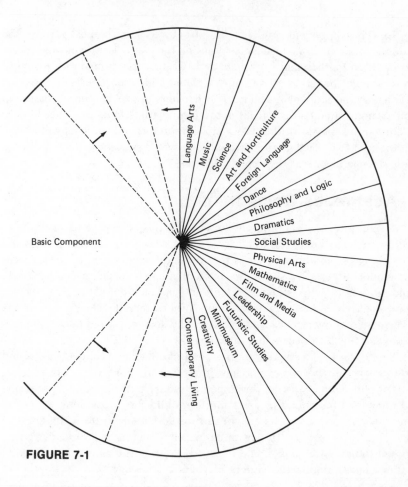

FIGURE 7-1

motivation are the keys to the Aesthetics component. This exploration by students and their ability to comprehend the exploration become the basis for the identification of those students who will pursue various areas within the Creative I component of this model. The Aesthetics component is the second level of the gifted/talented curriculum.

Creative I Component

The Creative I component, or third level, of the program prizes outstanding performance or capability, which is then nurtured, encouraged, and developed in depth. A child's particular strengths and talents determine what type of work he/she will pursue in the Creative I, for this is a highly individualized part of the curriculum. Through the staff of the gifted/ talented school, guidance will be given to students to assist them in private lessons, individual projects, small group activities, utilization of community resources, and work with adjunct or part-time staff on individual projects under independent study. A student. sabbatical could be designed for students who desire to travel with parents or grandparents, or to plan a special project with the teacher or community resource person.

The nature of Creative I participation depends entirely on individual interests and talents. This component encourages young people to put together what they have learned in the Basics and Aesthetics part of the curriculum, applying knowledge in new ways and pursuing ideas in greater depth and breadth.

In Creative I a student who excels in academics can do in-depth study or accelerated study to his fullest potential. A student with a passion for science will be able to pursue that interest to a greater extent than is usually permitted in elementary programs. Another student, for example, who excels in visual and/or performing arts, will receive instruction appropriate to his/ her talent. He/she could be a member of the orchestra, could be on the board of directors of the Mini-Museum, or could be a member of the Mime Time Players, the pantomine groups within the drama department.

It is crucial that the Creative I component be a very individualized instructional project to ensure the development of competencies and talents uncovered in the Aesthetics and Basics components of the educational program. Academically high-achieving as well as low-achieving students will participate in the program. Children who exhibit behavior problems, children who excel in one or two areas but are not well rounded, children who learn a great deal on their own but do not excel in school work, and children who are academically gifted will all participate in the program.

Scheduling in the Creative I will be as in the Aesthetics, e.g.,45-minute periods two or three times a week. Nearly half of a child's week is devoted to Aesthetics or Creative I. The amount of time devoted to Creative I is dependent on demonstrated excellence. Figure 7-2 is illustrative of the possible time spent on a weekly or yearly basis by a student in the gifted/ talented program.

Students participate in the Creative I on a yearly basis, as opposed to eleven-week cycles in the Aesthetics area. For example, if a youngster is pursuing Arabic as his foreign language, the continuity of that program over an extended period of time would be crucial; therefore, his program could be extended over many years of study. Likewise, if a youngster has chosen violin instruction, it is important that this continue and that skill development be extended over a number of years.

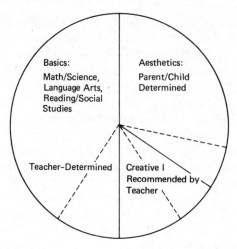

FIGURE 7-2

Rainbow Day

The Basics, Aesthetics, and Creative I programs are offered in time blocks that segment the school day into a set of eight periods. This time allocation allows for diversity of experiences but does not permit extended concentration in any single activity. The gifted child requires opportunity to pursue a project in depth, to persevere in a task, and to discover the rewards of continued commitment to a goal. To structure this opportunity, one school day entitled "Rainbow Day" is scheduled each week to allow children to specialize in the performing arts, visual arts, physical arts, futuristics, or academic areas. Students, with parent consent, select one of these five programs on a semester basis. Each program is composed of an elaborate array of experiences from which students choose. For example, the performing arts program includes

Dance Technique
Clowns, Character, and
Makeup
Music Theory
Creative Dramatics
Shakespeare for Children
Brass Choir
Eastern Stages

Concert Band
Puppet People
Theater—Then and Now
Dance Composition
Piano Ensemble
Choral Ensemble
Playwriting

A child with a high level of interest may devote Rainbow Day to music. He/she may work in the concert band, study music theory, and play in the brass choir. This same child may study instrumental music in the Aesthetics and Creative I program components during the remaining four days of the school week.

The richness and variety of activities in each of the five Rainbow Day programs are achieved through the participation of all teachers. For example, a language arts teacher who enjoys candle making, needlepoint, crafts, and so on will offer instruction in that specialty to students while receiving guidance and assistance from the visual arts leader, a professional art teacher. Another language arts teacher applies his/her skill to developing a sports newsletter with students in the physical arts. Although Rainbow Day allows children to explore a field of interest for an extended time period, it also provides staff a structure to develop new skills, to generate new ideas for the Aesthetics and Creative I programs in a supportive setting. Rainbow Day serves as a continuous and systematic enrichment to staff as well as students.

The following schedules illustrate the distribution of program components: Basics, Aesthetics, Creative I, and Rainbow Day for four students who vary in their interests, strengths, and educational needs.

The curriculum for the gifted/talented program is the key to its success. This is especially true in both the Aesthetics and Creative I components. Curriculum must be developed in depth in major new areas in order for a gifted/talented program to truly meet the needs of gifted/talented youngsters. Shown below are areas of study and some special courses for students age fourth grade through eighth grade that further define the ABC's of this gifted/talented curriculum model.

Schedule I—Sarah Martin

	MONDAY	TUESDAY	WEDNESDAY	THURSDAY	FRIDAY
	Homeroom	Homeroom	Homeroom	Homeroom	Homeroom
1	Basics	Basics	Basics	Academics	Basics
2	Basics	Basics	Basics		Basics
3	Printmaking	Printmaking	Lacrosse		Lacrosse
4	Cookbook to Culture	Cookbook to Culture	Creative I		Creative I
5	Creative I Humanities		Percussion		Percussion
6	Basics	Basics	Basics		Basics
7	Basics	Basics	Basics		Basics
8	Data Processing		Philosophy and Logic		Philosophy and Logic

Schedule III—John Rolf

	MONDAY	TUESDAY	WEDNESDAY	THURSDAY	FRIDAY
	Homeroom	Homeroom	Homeroom	Homeroom	Homeroom
1	Basics	Basics	Basics	Visual Arts	Basics
2	Basics	Basics	Basics		Basics
3	Kitchen Chemistry		Writers Workshop		Writers Workshop
4	Cinematography	Cinematography	Fact to Impact		Fact to Impact
5	Lunch		Creative I		Creative I
6	Basics	Basics	Basics		Basics
7	Basics	Basics	Basics		Basics
8	Rocks and Minerals		Reptile Study II		Reptile Study II

Schedule IV—Patricia Mack

	MONDAY	TUESDAY	WEDNESDAY	THURSDAY	FRIDAY
	Homeroom	Homeroom	Homeroom	Homeroom	Homeroom
1	Basics	Basics	Basics	Futuristics	Basics
2	Basics	Basics	Basics		Basics
3	Mind Benders		Horticulture		Horticulture
4	Sculpture		Lunch		Lunch
5	Lunch		Cookbook to Culture		Cookbook to Culture
6	Basics	Basics	Basics		Basics
7	Basics	Basics	Basics		Basics
8	Predicting the Weather		Softball		Softball

Schedule II—Robert Green

	MONDAY	TUESDAY	WEDNESDAY	THURSDAY	FRIDAY
	Homeroom	Homeroom	Homeroom	Homeroom	Homeroom
1	Basics	Basics Supplementary Instruction	Basics	Performing Arts	Basics
2	Basics	Basics	Basics		Basics
3	Golf	Golf	Bulls and Bears		Bulls and Bears
4	French	French	Lunch		Lunch
5	Lunch		Clay Workshop		Clay Workshop
6	Basics	Basics	Basics		Basics
7	Basics	Basics	Basics		Basics
8	Measurements		Gymnastics		Gymnastics

Basics
Science
Math
Humanities (reading, language arts, social studies)
Library
Learning Center (reading and mathematics)

Aesthetics

Art

Terrariums, Vivariums, and Rain
   Gardens
Gardening Under Lights
Bonsai Styling
Winter Activities in Horticulture
Fine Arts
Printmaking
Elements of Design
Cultural Art
Model Making

Scenic Paint
Environmental Art
Media Exploration
Crafts
Horticultural Art
Sculptures
Makeup and Costume Design
Mural Painting
Clay Workshop
Designing for the Theater

Contemporary arts

Recycling for New Products
Popular Mechanics
Experimental Cooking/Food for
   Astronauts

Chefs and Caterers
Cookbook to Culture
You Are What You Eat
Image Building

Science

Animal Care
Reptile Study
Introduction to Computers
Microgardening
Science Laboratory Explorations

Kitchen Chemistry
Rocks, Precious Gems, and
   Fossils
Data Processing
Man and the Environment

Math

The Year the Meter Took Over
The Numbers Game
Probability and Statistics
Numerology
Scientific Measure
Mathematical Logic
Getting into Shapes
Computer Math
I Hate Mathematics Workshop

The Machines of Math
Geometric Constructions
Introduction to Algebra
Statistics/Real Functions
Transformational Geometry I & II
Shape and Form
The Game's the Thing
Review of Basic Skills

Social studies

Foreign Language Intercultural
   Studies
Consumer Education
Debate
Your World
Geography Lab
Community Projects

Archeology
Nostalgia
Passage to Other Cultures I & II
Entrepreneurship: Free Enterprise
   at Its Best
Looking at Leaders
City Planning

Language arts

Versification: A way With Words
Sensational Signs
Whodunit?
Out of This World
Science Fiction
Poetry: Appreciation and Creation
Write On!

Journalism—A Simulation
Typing: Getting Your Fingers
   Together
Getting into Books
Learning to Read Through the
   Arts
So You Want to Be a Writer

Music

Family Involvement—Suzuki Style
Lift Every Voice and Sing
A Mixed Bag—Nontraditional
   Orchestra
Wonderful World of Music
Recorders Can Be Beautiful
Tuneup Time
I'd Rather Do It Myself
Getting Started

Concert Band
Rock Band
Orchestra
That's Take
Traditional Harmony
Vocal Techniques
Birth of a Song
Concert Choir
Keyboard Technique

Prelude/Beginning Band
Symphony of Strings-One

Strum and Sing

Dance
Social Dance
Folk, Ethnic, and Square Dance
Tap
Modern Dance
Modern Jazz
Creative Rhythms

Ballet
Space, Shape, and Movement in
    Your World
Dance Fever
Movement and Meditation

Drama
Creative Dramatics Workshop
Where There's a Will There's a
    Play
Harlequinade
Speak Out
Choral Speaking
Playing and Directing
Play Production
Acting I and II
Magic and All That
Poetry: Puppetry

All the World's a Stage: Gods and
    Goddesses
All the World's a Stage:
    Groundlings and Strutters
All the World's a Stage:
    Commedia Characters
All the World's a Stage:
    Melodrama to Soap Opera
So You Want to Be an Actress or
    Actor?

Physical arts
Gymnastics Workshop
Team Sports: Touch Football,
    Soccer, Track and Field,
    Lacrosse, Volleyball,
    Basketball, Softball
Physical Arts
Health

Individual and Dual Sports:
Tennis, Wrestling, Swimming, Ice
    Skating, Archery, Horseback
    Riding, Bowling, Fencing,
    Badminton, Hand Paddle Ball,
    Skiing, Fencing, and Golf

Foreign language
Instruction will be given in
    Mandarin Chinese, Russian,
    Hebrew, Arabic, Spanish, and
    French

Passport to Adventure

Media
Video Insights
Mixed Media Bag

The Photo Essay

Philosophy and logic
In this course the teaching of reasoning skills is done in a systematic way.
The curriculum combines philosophical discussion and rigorous exercise

in logical expression. The logic is applied to the problems the students have.

Leadership

This activity-centered program will include course offerings such as the following:

Looking at Leaders: Conductors, Directors, Mayors, Shamans, Gurus

Courts and Trials

Communication—Nonverbal and Verbal

Parliamentary Procedure

Encouraging Creativity in Problem Solving

Who Am I—Insights from Dance, Music, and Art

Leadership Functions in the School

Futuristics

What is it? What of it? What to do about it?

These basic questions guide a study of the future. Students will participate in "fact-to-impact" learning experiences, i.e., they may write a book, produce it, and send it to publishing houses. Or they may make a file and market it. Course offerings will include

Life in the Undersea World

Life in Outer Space

Advertising U.S.A.

Environmental Studies

Pollution and Controls

The Future and the Environment

Mini-Museum

The Mini-Museum is a project designed by students for other students as well as for their families, friends, and the community. Once the museums are designed and built, the students will be able to apply for jobs. The museum will display student work, art prints, borrowed collections, and special exhibits. The Mini-Museum will sponsor special events, lectures, field trips, and programs. Mini-Museum course offerings will include

Museum Workshop

Architecture/Interior Space Design

Research of Special Program

Mini-Museum Employment

Contemporary living

American institutions will be studied in this course:

The Family

Law and a Free Society

The Church, etc.

Course offerings will include

Future Autobiographies

Discovering Changing Lifestyles

The Developing Megalopolis

Getting into the Picture

Film Making

Media Messages

Creativity

Teaching the perception of the arts as an aesthetic experience will be the focus of these offerings. Students will find that they can sharpen their perceptions and make critical judgments. Course offerings will include

Little Red Riding Hood in a Variety of Media

Music—Beethoven to The Captain and Tennille

I Can Make You Different

Creative I

Foreign languages
Russian
Chinese
Arabic
Hebrew
Spanish
French

Mathematics

Humanities
Reading
Social Studies
Writing

Dance

Drama

Physical arts

Music
Orchestra
Vocal

Gymnastics

Futuristics

Art

Science

An elementary or middle school master schedule is included in this chapter (Table 7-1). From this comprehensive listing of possibilities a student's schedule is constructed based on student/parent desire (Aesthetics), staff assignment (Basics), and Creative I (by nomination).

TABLE 7-1. Gifted and Talented Master Schedule (Cycle I—11 Weeks) (This Schedule is for grades 3, 4, 5.)

Period 1–2 Mon, Tues, Wed, Fri	Basics (Math/Science Core and/or Humanities Core)
Period 3 Mon,Tues	Curious Creatures IA, IB; Debating; Hillside Gazette; Whodunit; French IA (4 days); French IB (4 days); Spanish II; Games the Thing—Eng.; Linguistics; Writers Workshop I and II; Learning Center; Museum Workshop; Cookbook to Culture; Creative Problem Solving; Kings and Queens IB; Philosophy and Logic II; Bulls and Bears;

Constructo Math; Data Processing; Games the Thing—
Math; I Hate Math Workshop; Mind Benders; Insect
Study; Kitchen Chemistry; Microgardening; Reptile Study
I; Fine Arts; Printmaking; Puppetry; Weaving/Stitchery;
World of Plastics; Ballet IB; Creative Dramatics; Your
Own Radio Show; Flute; Trumpet/Trombone; Piano;
Archery/Badminton; Fencing.

Period 3
Wed, Fri

Curious Creatures IA; World Power; French IA, IB (4 days
each); Spanish II; STAR; Under the Sea; Games the
Thing—Eng; Literature Study; Writers Workshop I and II;
Library Research; Learning Center; Museum Workshop;
Cookbook to Culture; Cradle Civilization; Great Inventors;
Kings and Queens IA; Philosophy and Logic I; Bulls and
Bears; Casino Math; Data Processing; Games the
Thing—Math; I Hate Math Workshop; Electricity; Insect
Study; Kitchen Chemistry; Rocks and Minerals; Crafts
Horticulture; Weaving/Stitchery; World of Plastics; Ballet
IA; Creative Dramatics; Cinematography; Drum Corps;
Drill Team; Flute; Piano; Archery/Fencing; Volleyball.

Period 4
Mon, Tues

French IA, IB (4 days each); Spanish; Learning Center;
Architecture; Cookbook to Culture; Crafts; Sculpture;
Theater Arts; Fact to Impact; Ballet IA; Play Production
(also 5th period); Cinematography; Percussion; Piano;
Gymnastics; Ice Skating/Bowling (also 5th period); Team
Sports.

Period 4
Wed, Fri

French IA, IB (4 days each); Spanish I (4 days); Learning
Center; Cookbook to Culture; Clay Workshop; Crafts;
Sculpture; Weaving/Stitchery; Fact to Impact; Ballet IB;
Harlequinade; Getting into Picture; Strings; Trumpet/
Trombone; Piano; Gymnastics; Ice Skating/Bowling (also
5th period); Basketball.

Period 5
Mon, Tues

French IB (4 days); Spanish IB (4 days); Writers Workshop
I; Learning Center; Museum Workshop; Architecture;
Cookbook to Culture; Fine Arts; Theater Arts; Fact to
Impact; Play Production (also 4th period); Clarinet;
Percussion; Gymnastics; Ice Skating/Bowling (also 4th
period); Volleyball.

Period 5
Wed, Fri

Sign Language; French IB (4 days); Spanish IB (4 days);
Games the Thing—Eng; Learning Center; Cookbook to
Culture; Clay Workshop; Fine Arts; Weaving/Stitchery;
Fact to Impact; Modern Dance IB; Creative Dramatics;
Rhythmic Recorders; Clarinet; Percussion; Gymnastics;
Wrestling; Ice Skating/Bowling (also 4th period).

Period 6—7 Mon, Tues, Wed, Fri	Basics (Math/Science Core and/or Humanities Core)
Period 8 Mon, Tues	Curious Creatures IA; Word Power; French II; Spanish I (4 days); Luna City; Under the Sea; Games the Thing—Eng; Literature Study; Super Stars; Learning Center; Museum Workshop; Cookbook to Culture; Diverse Cultures; Casino Math; Constructo Math; Data Processing; Games the Thing—Math; I Hate Math Workshop; Measurements; Mind Benders; Insect Study; Predicting the Weather; Reptile Study I; Rocks and Minerals; Fine Arts; Weaving/Stitchery; Modern Dance IA; Creative Dramatics; Lift Every Voice; Orchestra; Percussion; Tennis; Basketball.
Period 8 Wed, Fri	Curious Creatures; Debating; Sensational Sagas; Whodunit; Word Power; French II; Spanish I (4 days); Luna City; Games the Thing—Eng; Linguistics; Literature Study; Super Stars; Writers Workshop I; Learning Center; Museum Workshop; Cookbook to Culture; Cradle Civilization; Philosophy and Logic; Constructo Math; Data Processing; Games the Thing—Math; Measuremetrics; Mind Benders; Insect Study; Microgardening; Reptile Study II; Crafts; Fine Arts; Printmaking; Puppetry; Modern Dance IA; Choral Speaking; Lift Every Voice; Jazz Band; Strings; Basketball; Team Sports.

The gifted/talented program advocated in this chapter requires new roles for teachers, parents, students, and administrators, and hence for the community. Those roles are discussed in depth in other chapters in this book and are keyed very closely to this curriculum model. In addition, the Roderick/LeMahieu chapter in this book, which deals with selection criteria for the gifted/talented, emphasizes the methods by which students can select themselves, be nominated by parents, or be nominated by teachers and interested others.

There are many modifications that can be made to the model described in this chapter. It is hoped that with an atypical program administrators, teachers, parents, and young people could dream and design further futuristic thrusts for those youngsters who are certainly gifted and talented in many ways. It is the responsibility of all who work with young people to design a curriculum that meets the overall needs of each person, while enhancing the development of his/her special talent.

8

JESSIE A. RODERICK, University of Maryland

BETHENE LeMAHIEU, Montclair Public Schools

Identifying Gifts and Talents in All Children: Focus on Newness

No action, no proposal for action, and no feelings about actions occur within a vacuum. Likewise, the proposals for new ways of identifying gifts and talents of children and youth presented here are not without a context. That the term *context* is derived from weaving is significant, because it connotes interacting facets or components that together form patterns and textures. So, too, the contexts in which these proposals are made consist of a complex of interacting, interdependent facets. One aspect of this complexity is a rethinking of ideas and practices related to providing educational experiences for children and youth possessing a variety of gifts and talents. This aspect of context is a driving force behind the proposals, but an even stronger force is a commitment to identifying talents and gifts in a diverse population such as that found in an urban setting. The discussion that follows explicates the latter aspect of the context in which new proposals for identifying gifts and talents are made.

Although seemingly paradoxical, educational experiences for children in a community characterized by diversity must make it possible for this diversity to increase at the same time a sense of community increases, for it is only when these conditions are met that there can be equal access to opportunities—opportunities for all children in the setting to be individuals, different one from another and at the same time members of a group that encompasses and values the diversity. Increasing diversity means that a broader range of talents and gifts is identified and expressed within more diverse educational contexts or offerings. Increasing diversity also means that more people contribute to schooling in the community and that these individuals bring diverse insights and employ more varied problem-solving techniques to concerns related to educating all children. When diversity so conceived is valued, input from people with a variety of experiences, ideals and interests is automatic. Without such input as a basis for decision making, the principle of equal access to opportunities is violated, and the value of the individual's contribution negated. Without respect for diversity, talents and gifts not yet identified in children and youth may go unnoticed, and as a result some children are denied opportunities that are rightfully theirs.

How can diversity be increased at the same time a sense of community is increased? Essentially there is no paradox when a sense of community is defined as persons in the process of embracing diversity and working together to give it form and direction. Community is seen as individuals together valuing diversity, transacting as opposed to reacting, and sharing concerns. Community is also viewed as a means of sharing experiences, ideas, and feelings and making every effort to see that visions are not lost in negotiations. This view of community builds on diversity, but at the same time gives opportunities for all to collaborate on procedures that incorporate diverse elements in ways to benefit all persons in the community. It is important that the community look at new kinds of gifts and new procedures for identifying them. The next section proposes possible ways of dealing with this task.

Identifying Talents in Settings

The task of identifying talents and gifts possessed by all children is fraught with complexities. Emanating from these complexities are questions related to the variety of ways the talents can be identified and encouraged. Which children have talents that have not been identified? Which children have gifts that have not yet been realized? Are children whose talents have not yet been identified those who do not perform well on paper-and-pencil tests? Is it possible that these children have not had appropriate occasions for realizing their talents? Or, if an occasion has presented itself, has the child missed the opportunity to reflect on the experience in such a way as to gain insight into the nature of the talents he/she possesses? Or is it possible that the range of talents recognized and encouraged is so limited that some talents, and therefore the children who possess them, are left unnoticed and underdeveloped in certain areas?

In order to increase the likelihood that the whole range of talents, including those noted in the previous section, is realized, another approach to identifying talents is proposed. This proposal involves identifying or designing settings that highlight or encourage the use of talents. Settings or contexts are composed of materials, people, ideas, time, and space interacting. It is hoped that children and youth see within settings opportunities for using and building on the talents they possess. Settings that are seen as having the potential to highlight and encourage different talents and to provide children with opportunities to reflect on their interactions with these settings are more than chance occurrences. Careful thought must be given as to how interactions with these settings must encourage expression of talents. Thought should also be given to how children and youth can analyze and reflect on their experiences in selected settings, either alone or with a significant other. When children are given opportunities to interact with such settings and to reflect on these interactions, expression of talents and gifts is more apt to occur.

The notion of identifying and designing contexts or settings that highlight and encourage talents in given areas is based on several assumptions about individuals and contexts. It is assumed that no person can be considered apart from the contexts or environments with which he interacts. Hobbs expresses this idea when discussing the "ecological system of which the child is an integral part."[1] The individual is part of a complex system or synergy whose parts impact one on the other. For example, how a child interacts with other children and adults is influenced by space, materials, and time constraints of the environment. Likewise, no concern or issue can be viewed apart from its broader context. The hunger problem facing the world cannot be viewed from an economic perspective only. Political, social, and technological considerations are but a few elements composing the complex context in which the problem must be examined.

If persons need to be viewed within contexts, then it seems logical to assume that talents possessed by persons be viewed within the contexts in which the talents develop and are expressed. A child's interests and skills in painting cannot be considered apart from the social, physical, and ideational contexts in which he/she lives and plays. The nature of the support, encouragement, and criticism a child receives from significant others, as well as how time, space, and ideas are structured, either by him/her or others, influences artistic expressions.

A second assumption on which the proposal to identify talents within settings is based is that not all children have had opportunities to interact with contexts that encourage a range of talents. Therefore, talents that have not emerged in some children might become evident when these children interact with settings that offer opportunities to express the latent or yet undiscovered talents. Support for this assumption is found in Weick's

[1] Nicholas Hobbs, *The Futures of Children* (San Francisco: Jossey-Bass, 1975), pp. 113-114.

discussion of ways in which settings can be modified to bring forth behaviors that are not known to be part of a person's repertoire. In addition, Weick proposes techniques for highlighting or amplifying known responses, thereby making them more apparent.[2] This assumption implies that settings can encourage children who are not self-starters. It also implies that so-called latent talents are more apt to emerge when certain settings are made available to children.

The last assumption underlying the notion of identifying talents within contexts relates to the nature of talents other than the more traditional academic ones. It is assumed that certain talents—such as compassion, the valuing of surprises in life, and social vision—are best expressed and consequently more readily identified in contexts that encourage action commensurate with these talents.

Potentials of Settings

Individuals who assume responsibility for the kinds of settings in which children interact need to consider the range of possible settings and the nature of these settings in terms of the potentials they hold for encouraging the surfacing of talents. The range of settings is broad, extending from a school classroom to an experience in a foreign country. A learning center within a classroom, a community museum, a neighborhood factory, a nearby research facility, a historic battlefield, a construction site, a legislative session, and a distant metropolitan area are a few of the settings that can be utilized. This variety of settings includes those that can be designed and those that are a vital part of the community beyond the school but that at the same time envelop the school.[3]

Characteristics of settings that highlight and encourage the surfacing of talents can be viewed from three perspectives: (1) the nature of talents and gifts, (2) the opportunities for significant choices among and within settings, and (3) the potentials for acting on and taking from settings. How individuals perceive talents such as those named in this proposal influences which settings are selected or designed to encourage talents. The discussion of the talent of compassion later in this chapter illustrates the possible relationships

---

[2] Karl E. Weick, Systematic Observational Methods, in Gardner Lindzey and Elliot Aronsen (Eds.), *The Handbook of Social Psychology, Second Edition*, Volume Two (Reading, Mass.: Addison-Wesley, 1968), pp. 357-451, 376-380.

[3] For specific ideas on designing settings in classrooms and for utilizing settings in the broader community, see Louise M. Berman and Jessie A. Roderick, *Curriculum: Teaching the What, How and Why of Living* (Columbus, O.: Merrill, 1977), and Marcus G. Raskin, *Being and Doing* (New York: Random House, 1971).

of a talent to settings designed or selected to encourage expression of that talent.

Fundamental to any consideration of setting characteristics is the element of choice. Choice is especially important in settings made available to children and youth in a diverse community. What decisions can children, youth, and the community make about settings with which they interact? At a more specific level what choices are available to children within a given setting? Can they choose among options for solving problems, for manipulating materials, for expressing artistic abilities, and for testing ideas?

The third perspective from which characteristics of settings can be viewed offers some new ways of thinking about settings for children. Since people cannot be considered as either/or in their talents, settings in which individuals interact must contain within them possibilities for more than one kind of experiencing. Individuals—those who initiate as well as respond, who bring something to a setting as well as change it, and who take something from it—need settings that have the potential to encourage multifaceted behaviors or interactions. The following proposals for potentials that such settings can hold for people interacting with them should guide the selection and designing of settings that highlight and encourage a broad range of talents.

Outreach-Inreach. What are the potentials for children moving out into the community? How might the community come into and become part of the setting? How can outreach and inreach efforts combine so each grows and uncovers new possibilities for movement beyond what is?

Simplicity-Complexity. Does a setting present children and youth with opportunities for solving complex problems and for dealing with questions that have more than one possible answer? On the other hand, are some aspects of settings characterized by simplicity in that few ideas, materials, or interactions are used? Do settings provide opportunities to ponder or work with a single idea or material, exploring it in depth?

Predictability-Surprise. What potential does the setting hold for predicting what might happen but at the same time being surprised by and taking pleasure in the unanticipated or that which conflicts with what was predicted?[4]

Knowledge: Personal-Public. What possibilities do children and youth have for dealing with personal knowledge as well as public knowledge? What potential is there in settings for children to test personal meanings in

---

[4] See Israeal Scheffler, In Praise of the Cognitive Emotions, *Teachers College Record*, 1977, (2), 171-186, for a discussion of the significance of surprise.

a variety of situations, changing and revising when appropriate? What are the potentials for hunching, imagining, and intuiting?

Involvement-Detachment. What opportunities do individuals have for totally immersing themselves in an interaction as well as for standing back, removing themselves to gain perspetive, or just resting? What opportunities do participants have for being spectators at times and participants at other times?

Leading-on Power-Closure. Do settings encourage children to deal with ideas and materials and interactions with others in such a way that one idea builds upon the other? Are settings changed to facilitate this branching and in-depth exploration? At the same time, do settings provide opportunities for bringing closure when participants deem it appropriate?

Individual-Community. What are the possibilities for working alone, with another, or with many others? Do children in settings have opportunities to change them to include others as needed to explore an area of interest? Do settings have inherent within them the potential for children to feel, express emotion, and learn about themselves and others?

Process-Product. How does a setting encourage children and youth to focus on the processes by which they learn, as well as on the outcome of their interactions? Are there opportunities for producing in a variety of ways by using different kinds of symbols? Are there opportunities for children to participate in designing settings and suggesting alternative uses for their surroundings?

Other potentials that settings might hold for persons interacting with them could be delineated. The potentials presented above are representative of the range that can be used to ensure a balance within settings. (The juxtaposition of what might be considered opposites is meant to discourage a linear view of potentials that settings can have for encouraging a variety of talents.) It is possible that there would be much movement back and forth within sets of potentials inherent in these settings.

In the next section the talent of compassion is defined and settings that would highlight and encourage the surfacing of compassion described. These settings may be examined in light of the potentials just discussed to determine which opportunities for acting on, changing, and taking from a setting are inherent in them.

Compassion: Settings and Identification Procedures

What follows is an explication of ideas presented up to this point as they apply to the talent of compassion. Suggestions made can be viewed as guidelines for defining a talent, identifying or designing settings that highlight or encourage the emergence of a talent, and describing aspects of the talent as they become evident in the settings. The suggestions made can also be viewed as jumping-off points for identifying new talents. The process should not stop with identifying talents. Rather, information generated in this process should be used in planning experiences that make it possible for children and youth to further develop the talent by testing and applying it in a variety of settings.

Defining the Talent

Webster's *New World Dictionary* defines *compassion* as sorrowing for the sufferings or trouble of another, or others, with the urge to help. In everyday usage compassion often means expressing a deep concern for others, showing an awareness of an individual's plight, and pouring forth feeling. Another way of viewing compassion, a moving beyond oneself, is found in Cobb's discussion of compassionate intelligence. Cobb proposes that individuals who possess compassionate intelligence can identify and participate in "otherness" while still retaining a sense of self.[5] Still another expression of a reaching out to others is found in the concept of peopling, "the process by which a person can enjoy, obtain comfort and give comfort to, and live fully with others."[6]

Although definitions of peopling, compassion, and compassionate intelligence may vary in shades of meaning, the concern for others evidenced by a moving beyond the interests and welfare of self pervades all three. The need to recognize and nurture the talent of compassion is underscored by the fragmentation of life we experience in the discontinuities between people and between persons and their environment. Wynne's documentation of research findings that young people are increasingly self-centered and less willing to participate by giving to society lends further support to the need to provide children and youth opportunities to develop the talent of compassion.[7] Cobb also alludes to this condition when she cautions that the extreme efforts to improve, realize, and gratify self can result in separation from the world and therefore one's fellow man.[8]

---

[5] Edith Cobb, *The Ecology of Imagination in Childhood* (New York: Columbia University Press, 1977), p. 22.

[6] Louise M. Berman and Jessie A. Roderick, *Curriculum: Teaching the What, How and Why of Learning* (Columbus, O.: Merrill, 1978), p. 88.

[7] Edward A. Wynne, Behind the Discipline Problem: Youth Suicide as a Measure of Alienation, *Phi Delta Kappa*, 1978, pp. 309-315, 312.

[8] Cobb, op. cit., pp. 109-110.

Settings Highlighting Compassion

Teachers, parents, and people in the community can collaborate to identify and design settings in which children might see opportunities to express compassion if that is a gift they possess. Such settings should make it possible for children and youth to show compassion beyond what might be considered a surface awareness of others. Various ways of defining such awareness are found in recent publications and intelligence assessments.[9]

The following settings have the potential for highlighting and encouraging the surfacing of the gift of compassion. The settings relate to situations that deal with the classroom, school, and local and world communities.

•*Setting A:*	Children with identified handicaps and children without handicaps interact with each other for the purpose of helping each other become competent in life skills.
•*Setting B:*	Children in a classroom or a school communicate to other children and adults appreciation for their having reached out to the children in order to help and encourage them or to introduce them to new people and experiences.
•*Setting C:*	Children have an opportunity to become friends with a person in a home for the elderly, a nursing home, a hospital, a foster home, or a place where a person who wants to change a life pattern such as drug abuse is receiving help in doing so.
•*Setting D:*	Children visit the site of a natural disaster, such as a flood or fire, or different areas of their community to talk with people in their homes. Children might ask the people what they are concerned about, what they wish they could do, learn, or share with others. The children might also ask what kinds of help these people would like to give and receive.

[9] *Aware: Activities for Social Development* by Phillis Elardo and Mark Cooper (New York: Addison-Wesley, 1977) is a practical guide on how to facilitate children's social development in classroom settings. A test measuring cultural awareness that includes social understanding and sensitivity among four areas of academic competence has been developed by Jonathan R. Warren at ETS in Berkeley.

•*Setting E:*   Children have the opportunity to plan a
multimedia presentation about the gaps
between so-called developed and developing
nations.

•*Setting F:*   Children have the opportunity to role play a
meeting of persons from countries who wish to
discuss the problem of hunger or the impact of
the nuclear arms race on the peoples of the
world.

Some of these settings involve direct participation with others in a
setting inside as well as outside the school building; some involve development of materials; and one involves the more indirect experience of role
playing. In any event, settings should be examined in terms of potentials
described earlier in this chapter. For instance, what potential does Setting
D, where children visit persons in the community, have for encouraging
Outreach-Inreach, Leading-on Power-Closure, and Individual-Community
pursuits? Perhaps a key considertion for examining settings that have the
potential to encourage compassion is Involvement-Detachment or Noninvolvement. As settings related to specific talents are examined, certain
potentials will appear more appropriate than others. Finding which potentials of settings seem to match the nature of certain talents will also help in
devising procedures for identifying these talents that emerge and are
expressed within the settings.

Identifying Talents—Compassion

Expressions of talents, in this instance compassion, can be identified
and recorded in a variety of ways. Many procedures for identifying talents
must be employed, because children vary in how and when they express
ideas and feelings related to their talents. A discussion of some of the
procedures and possible information they might generate about compassion
follows:

Observing. Children can be observed while they interact with others in
settings. Which persons does a child approach when given an opportunity to
seek out and help others? Does a child consistently initiate interactions with
others in a positive manner? Does a child reach out physically to support,
encourage, and express friendship to a person in a hospital or nursing home?
Is a child able to vary his approaches to others in terms of his assessment of
how an individual responds or how a person might feel? These and other
kinds of nonverbal behaviors that suggest a reaching out posture can be
recorded in a format such as the following:

Child ___12___

Setting ___Nursing Home___

Date	Initiates reaching out behavior.	Varies approaches to persons in terms of assessment of situation.	Comments
6/8/78	Takes book to X. Sets up reading stand.	Waits for person to request help before offering.	

Categories from the *Pupil Nonverbal Category System*[10] might be used to systematically record observations. Descriptions of observed behaviors may also be made in diary-fashion narratives.

How much time a child devotes to a project or interaction involving compassionate behavior may be recorded as an indication of expression of the talent of compassion. Returning again and again to a setting that holds opportunities for compassion and building on or enhancing experiences emanating from such a setting can also be indicators of a child's commitment to compassionate behavior.

Listening to Children. What questions and comments are heard before, during, and after a child's engagement in an activity? Are these questions about how children can help individuals become more independent, more able to gain control over their lives? Do children ask questions about how sorrow or suffering might be eased, even prevented? Do children comment on what they, their family, or friends might do to comfort a person or group of people? Do children encourage others to join in efforts to understand, support, and encourage? As in recording observations of nonverbal actions, verbal utterances related to compassion can be recorded in narrative form or in more formal ways such as the following:

Child	Setting	Questions and Comments Related to Compassion

Reflecting on Activities. Children can be given written or oral stimuli for reflecting on their experiences in settings that highlight compassion. A child may reflect on his visit to a nursing home by responding to questions such as these: What did you notice about the people you talked with today? Which person did you talk with most? What did you talk about? How do you think you let this person know you cared? How might you help this person the next time you visit? Do you look forward to visiting with this

---

[10] One form of the *Pupil Nonverbal Category System* is found in Berman and Roderick, *Curriculum*, pp. 176-177. This reference also contains other ideas for generating information about persons interacting with settings.

person again? Which people might be of help to you as you prepare for your next visit? Responding to questions such as these facilitates a child's carefully thinking through his own reaction to having interacted with people in a specific setting. Sharing these reflections with another person helps others get at how a child takes in and integrates experiences. In essence, this technique tells something about how the child perceives himself and his world.

Examining Products. Children's writing as found in stories, diaries, recordings of observations, paintings, and constructions can provide insight into the nature and degree of compassion children possess or experience. What do children record during and after interacting with settings highlighting compassion? Is language of feeling expressed? Is language that describes plans and that conveys hope used in compositions and recordings of experiences? What do children's autobiographies reveal about compassion as they see it in their lives and the lives of families and friends? Although reading the works of others is not a product or artifact, the kinds of books children read can be noted. Do interactions with settings that have the potential for highlighting compassion encourage children to read prose and poetry that deals with compassion? Do these settings encourage children to express compassion in their paintings, sculptures, and drama or in other ways they express themselves? For example, what do children reveal about their own feelings of compassion in their discussions of caring about and giving to others as presented in the book *Bridge to Tarabithia*?[11]

Perceptive teachers, parents, and children can use a multitude of techniques to identify talents that emerge in settings that highlight and encourage the surfacing of gifts. Variety and complexity of identification techniques are necessary to generate information about complex talents as they emerge in different ways in different settings.

New Talents

When all children are seen as possessing talents, the range of talents to be identified and encouraged automatically increases. Included among possible new talents, those not usually identified in the more traditional ways, are the following:

- Moral responsibility.
- Compassion.
- Humor.

[11] Katherine Paterson, *Bridge to Tarabithia* (New York: Thomas Y. Crowell Co., 1977).

- Statesmanship.

- Sensitivity.

- Independence.

- Courage.

- Manual dexterity.

- Talent for innovation and improvization.

- Zig-zag thinking—a combination of vertical and lateral thinking.

As children and youth are given opportunities to interact with a variety of settings, and as people who assume responsibility for the education of youth become better observers of children in these settings, more talents will be identified. In addition, procedures for identifying and nurturing talents will be refined and sharpened.

A Gifted/Talented Magnet: Montclair, New Jersey

When an educational program is based on diversity, as well as on a sense of community, the following assumptions can be made:

- All children have gifts, and these gifts vary from child to child.

- All children should have the right to develop these talents in diverse settings.

- Identification of talents and gifts should take place in a broad context that includes home, school, and community, presupposing that many persons, including parents and significant others, are involved in the process of identification and follow-up programming.

- The availability of program options to children possessing varying talents and gifts is critical.

- Children, teachers, and parents should be partners in the process of achieving a match between program options and children's talents and gifts.

The Gifted/Talented Magnet of the Montclair, New Jersey, Public Schools, a part of the school board's efforts to offer educational choices to its culturally diverse community, was based on the preceding assumptions about children and opportunities for their learning. Key questions raised by the staff when considering the schooling of the community's children were these: Who are the gifted? What are their needs? How can instruction be differentiated for them? What are viable alternatives for the children and youth in the community? Not surprisingly, when the Montclair community began considering these questions, people generally assumed that (1) the focus would be on the intellectually gifted child, (2) IQ tests would be used to identify the gifted children, and (3) the Montclair program would be an elitist one with few minority children in it. There was marked tension between those who vociferously supported the elitist notion and those who opposed it. The school administration offered another perspective. To the question, "Who are the gifted?" they responded: "All children have gifts and talents and it is the responsibility of educators, parents, and interested others to identify those talents and to differentiate instruction for them."

Initial Matching of Child with Program

Parents, children, and teachers decided in which educational experiences each child would take part. An early communication to teachers, parents, and children from designers of the program was entitled "Who Will Benefit from the Gifted and Talented Magnet? Some Questions to Help You Decide." That document, consisting of a list of indicators, also proposed that every child has talents, gifts, and/or special interests perhaps as yet unknown to others or even self. This statement had major implications for program development, for it indicated that talents had to be discovered and developed during a child's early years in school.

To help children achieve the benefits of their own talents and gifts, the Gifted/Talented Magnet was developed. This special school organizes learning experiences around the ABC's—Aesthetics, Basics, and Creative I. In the Basics component children receive instruction in heterogeneously grouped classes in reading, math, science, and social studies. In the Aesthetics component children and their parents, in cooperation with teachers, choose exploratory learning experiences from the following areas: art, creativity, dance, drama, foreign language, futuristic studies, language arts/social studies, leadership, math/science, music, philosophy and logic, physical arts, contemporary institutions, and film. In the Creative I the child has the opportunity to do something about a specific experience, to apply knowledge in a new way, to dream, or to pursue an idea in great depth and breadth. In this dimension of the program, a child can receive private music lessons, design and carry out a special community project, or receive small group instruction in a foreign language if special proficiency is shown. Students are scheduled individually into a personalized program.

In order to see if such a program would be appropriate for a particular child, developers of the program made available "Who Will Benefit from the Gifted and Talented Magnet?" as already discussed. The document asked parents, teachers, and students to answer questions about how they perceived the gifts and talents of the child being considered. There were no correct answers or passing score. These questions were not designed to exclude children or serve as an entry qualification. Rather, they represented an attempt to call attention to some of those incidents, behaviors, or interests that would help in choosing a place for each child. This questionnaire contained sixty-five questions referring to a broad range of behaviors and interests. These general questions were followed by questions that addressed specific areas of special talents. Thus the first step in identification began— matching the child to that alternative school where he/she might benefit.

This identification effort went beyond the school into the child's home and community. Others who participated in the matching effort included members of the child study teams, the home-school liaison worker, and the superintendent and his staff. Because the deficit model of what is wrong or lacking had been rejected in favor of a talents and gifts model, it was important that all classified children be reviewed with an eye to placement where they could best benefit. Thus it was that the child study teams considered their clients and made recommendations to parents about the preferred alternative program for a particular child.

Recognizing that potential may be identified through cultivating, channeling, rechanneling, or releasing creative energies, case studies were prepared for staff discussion of individual children. In such a fashion, members of the child study teams made their contributions to the initial matching of child and program option. Representative samples from two of the case studies follow. The case study reported:

> Gail is a third grader, an underachiever placed in the resource room. Gail is an affectionate, easily distracted child who is often approval-seeking and manipulative. She is very active and communicates more easily by touching, feeling, and moving. She tends to wander and does this both at home and in school. She is aggressive and angry and often uses negative physical behavior to release her anger and to command attention. Though unaware, she releases and communicates her feelings through performance.

> Should we not further consider and recommend this child so that she might have the opportunity to rechannel physical energy through the expression of movement, dance, and drama?" asked members of the child study team.

> John is a first grader functioning at grade level.

> John's use of responsive language is adequate; appropriate use of his own child-initiated expressive language is limited. His voice quality is weak, barely audible with little expression or emotion. His body movement is constricted; i.e., he sits rigidly, runs with his arms held close to the body. He does not spontaneously participate in physical activities. He seldom exhibits feelings.

Should we not find this child the opportunity to discover himself through body movement, dance, and drama?'' child study team members asked.

The superintendent and members of his staff as part of a larger public information effort also made contributions to the matching of students and programs. "Road Shows" were presented in all elementary schools. Using videotapes, slides, and teaching materials, the staff showed parents a visual explanation of what the alternative programs would be like. Teachers, central office staff, and the superintendent participated in these sessions.

Livingroom dialogues or small group sessions were held in private homes throughout the community. In these meetings six to twenty neighbors and friends gathered in the host family's livingroom to discuss with the superintendent and members of his staff assumptions about high-quality elementary education. Concerns and apprehensions were voiced and questions asked. Parents were listened to, received answers to their questions, and were reassured that choice making is not easy because it involves ambiguity and tension. However, parents were also assured that they would not be pushed into making a decision before an insightful choice was possible.

All of the person-to-person communication was backed up by a five-month-long public information campaign. News coverage, newsletters, personal contacts, and small and large group meetings were used to provide parents with needed information.

Continued Matching of Students and Program

How does identification work for children once they are in the school? If children differ one from the other in kinds and degrees of gifts and talents, how do school people design programs that address the differences not of children but of the individual child?

Experiences in the Gifted/Talented Magnet have been organized around what have been previously discussed as the ABC's. With this organizational scheme it is possible to observe students as they interact in various environments or contexts during the day. All children receive a minimum of twelve hours instruction per week in Basics. These include math, science, reading, language arts, and social studies. Content in these subjects is prescribed, and districtwide adopted texts are used. In this dimension of their schooling students learn that which culture dictates or determines important, the Basics.

Aesthetics, the exploratory/exposure portion of the program, represents the first level of the gifted/talented program and the second phase of student identification. It is in the Aesthetics portion of the curriculum that expanded offerings are made available, choices given to children and their parents, certified and noncertified teachers used, and artists and expert practitioners employed. The course offerings are highly motivational. Through interest alone students can gain access to anything they wish, studying what they want to know. Students choose from seventeen different areas of study, including some content areas customarily found in schools—science, math, social studies, language arts, and reading. Also included are music and less common areas, such as futuristics, contemporary living, dance, drama, art, horticulture, philosophy and logic, physical arts, foreign language, leadership, creativity, film and media, and mini-museum. Implicit in these options are assumptions about the future: that it will be different from the present or the past and that new ideas about schooling are therefore necessary; that the varieties of subject matter, competencies, and skills should be extended; that a variety of contexts should be supplied for the surfacing and nurturing of talents; and that nonacademic skills will be prized and rewarded as will academic skills.

In choosing among options in the Aesthetics students demonstrate their interest, their competencies, and their passions. Social competencies, mechanical skills, athletic, political, artistic, or adapting skills may surface; so, too, may alternative thinking strengths. In Aesthetics, interest is the key factor in determining grouping. Groups are small, and teachers share with children something that is uniquely satisfying and important to them, such as horticulture, reptile studies, futuristics, or dance. In some cases the learning takes place in a regular classroom. In other instances students may go to an art museum, or their activities may be based in a Mini-Museum, an environment that they change according to purposes they determine.

Thus a wealth of opportunities exists in which children, their parents, interested others, and educators may gain insights into special talents of each child. No attempt is made to educate all children in the same way, although there are commonalities in the schooling experiences of all children. There is a strong focus on academic skill development, but not to the exclusion of other potential talent areas, and time is provided in the school day for the student to demonstrate his/her talents to the class.

In this second phase of identification taking place within the school, students are involved in identifying their own talents. An instrument is used in which students classify their strength areas into three categories: Talents I Know I Have, Talents Others Know I Have, Talents No One Else Knows I Have.

Talented professionals and nonprofessionals also are involved in the process of talent identification and development. Included are professional dancers, musicians, poets, artists, actors, costume designers, film makers, photographers, writers, native-speaking foreign language teachers, persons wishing to share their cultural customs, as well as woodworkers. These and many others provide themselves as texture to a child's learning. They share their love and their knowing and help elicit the special competencies that all children love.

The Creative I is the C part of the ABC's, the final part of a program organization designed to address the diversity of children. From the Basics and Aesthetics portion of the curriculum children who demonstrate outstanding competencies are identified. They are then scheduled into special groups that meet two times a week for forty-five minutes each. In this Creative I portion of the program children take greater responsibility for what they learn. They can determine the depth and breadth of a project they wish to pursue. They may do accelerated study in math or science, for example, or they may receive special lessons in music, dance, art, or the physical arts. They may participate in the school orchestra or the Mime-Time Players, initiate a community project, or take a student sabbatical. Whatever is done, teachers pay attention to self-acceptance and to prizing the special talents of each child. In the Creative I students find an environment in which it is safe to boldly display their special competencies. Through experiencing they begin to recognize and develop a broad range of behaviors, and they develop competence in assessing the territory and determining what behavior they will choose.

Selecting children for the Creative I is the third phase in the identification process, beginning with 4-year-olds and continuing throughout a student's learning life. Teachers make nominations and serve as advocates for their nominees before a panel of persons, specialists as well as administrators, with administrators having final responsibility for placement. The nomination process is largely judgmental. Results from standardized tests are used only as a check where appropriate; teachers are asked about students not nominated for math, for example, who nonetheless had ranged high on standardized math measures.

Judgmental measures utilized by teachers include teacher observation and anecdotal reports, pupil product evaluation, nominations, and self-assessment. Teachers also use the indicators provided earlier for parents to help determine initial placement for their child. In creative arts areas the intensity of interest and involvement is noted along with evidence of advanced skills and imaginative insight. Professional artists, specialized teachers, and experts in the field are members of the placement panel.

It is the belief of the Montclair community that, if this model is to be fully successful, every child should ultimately be identified for a second-level Creative I. Because of knowledge, program thrust, and new research, Montclair is moving into an expanded concept of the gifts and talents of children. The next section proposes possible ways of dealing with this task.

Forward to New Identification Procedures

- Use a variety of instruments.
- Continue the identification process over time.
- Continue to ask, "Who are the gifted?" and continue to develop ways in which special gifts and talents can surface.
- Involve parents and children in the identification process.
- Listen and watch. Observe carefully.
- Sharpen your powers of observation. Heighten your perceptual sensitivity. "Observe the fishes. They will teach you how to fish."
- Develop the tools that will enhance the insights of others.
- Be open. Grant that a child will have special gifts and talents, and set about the business of identifying them.
- Know that knowledge, program thrust, and new research will move persons toward new notions about children's gifts and talents.
- Move to the hallways and play yards—to those places where children initiate their own activities—and watch carefully.
- Resolve to view children as craftspersons—people who can do many things well.

Do all of this with an eye to achieving that which Sri Aurobindo, Indian philosopher, meant when he said, "The chief aim of education should be to help the growing soul draw out that in itself which is best and make it perfect for a noble use."[12]

---

[12] Quoted by Seymour Fersh in *Asia: Teaching About/Learning From* (New York: Teachers College, Columbia University, 1978), p. 7.

9

YVONNE L. BLANCHARD, National Council for Teacher
Accreditation

Exponential Alliances— Home, School, and Community: A Referent for Triadic Relationships

Introduction

In surveying the growth and development of major educational initia-
tives to develop programs that accommodate the needs of the gifted child,
American education can be likened to underdeveloped countries—groping
for skilled and informed intervention.

Likewise, when one begins to examine the accepted definitions of
giftedness and the exclusionary application of such definitions in American
public schools, such American education can be labeled "elitist." Many of
the more recognized definitions have been limited to gifted ability identified
and defined through intelligence testing, a process generally predicated on
some hit-or-miss standardized assessment tool that seeks to measure knowledge that is often culturally or regionally restrictive, or that has not been
taught, or that has not been taught universally. Many states have instituted
laws or policies which establish IQ scores of 130 (often with a −5 variance
where it can be justified) as a defining variable for inclusion in gifted
programs. Intelligence tests, as currently constructed, tend to assess retentive
one-dimensional abilities based on predetermined correct answers and to
denounce the multidimensional, divergent, and often creative youngster
who is not satisfied with one-dimensional responses and processes but is

compelled to seek alternatives to problem solving and varies responses to any given question or circumstance.

Taylor and Holland make the following statement on this notion:

> Evidence is gradually accumulating that traditional intelligence tests, at best, reveal only minor variations in creative performance, they do not directly involve the ability to create new ideas or things.[1]

The hit-or-miss character of IQ tests, when used as a defining element for giftedness, renders the gifted identification process suspect and it also limits those who administer the process in their ability to define creativity. Those students not identified as gifted are labeled educational writeoffs, whereas those students defined as gifted as a result of the defining process form an elite group of intellectually conditioned and programmed students. The latter group are often subjected to academically prescribed, narrowly focused educational plans as they participate in school systems that define giftedness as a one-dimensional and often ambiguous entity—intelligence. In too many instances, past and present, the process for identification and selection of students for gifted programs has been a process that excludes, stigmatizes, and demeans those not in the top 3—5 per cent of their class. In defining creativity or giftedness, one must be careful not to restrict the process by dealing solely with criteria related to intelligence or IQ.

Creativity Defined

Throughout the literature, the nature of creativity in American culture is defined differently by each theorist who has pondered the multidimensional construct. Some define the creative process as the emergence in action of a novel relational product, growing out of the uniqueness of the individual on the one hand and the materials, events, people, or circumstances of his/her life on the other.[2] Marksberry and others describe the process as a kind of psychological creativity—which is not measured by the resulting product but rather by the way an individual approaches the problems and circumstances of life.[3]

Marksberry defines creativity as the result of activities born of circumstance and human conditions that serve to improve on psychological, intellectual, and aesthetic expression for the purpose of rendering functional the individual and his/her interaction processes. Creativity defines itself in

---

[1] Calvin Taylor and John Holland, Development and Application of Tests of Creativity, *Review of Educational Research*, 1962, *32 (1)*, 92.

[2] Carl Rogers, *Client-Centered Therapy* (Boston: Houghton Mifflin, 1951) p. 65.

[3] Mary Lee Marksberry, *Foundation for Creativity* (New York: Harper & Row, 1963), pp. 5-6.

degrees. It is conceivable that one may be creative in several disciplines with a predominance of creative product development in a specific area. Creativity defies the external expectations of monolithic people and institutions and is nurtured by multivariate, free-flow activities. Creativity is then the ability to execute any activity, not to please anyone but to satisfy a personal, internal, kinesthetic, spiritual urge to spontaneously create something not yet undertaken.

Push Outs

Often the gifted are students who are pushed out of school because of bureaucratic overkill, ambiguity in the curriculum, unimaginative classes or teachers, or poorly trained teachers and administrators. These students generally leave school because they can define or develop a more complex, stimulating, and efficient learning experience in the streets or in the community.

Current educational program demands and funding guidelines require a much broader, more inclusive definition of giftedness, one that accommodates a broader range of skills, abilities, and talents influenced by a broader range of student interests. Educational programs and school personnel must make alliances with parents and community—the two fundamental ingredients in defining the quality of the educational experiences; two requisites for mediating life's contradictions and monitoring the quality and level of participation of all children in exemplary educational programs.

As we anticipate the future and prepare young people to meet the challenge of space age encounters, we must carefully contemplate the factors that will make schooling more efficient for all students generally and for those students with gifted abilities and unexercised, often unidentified, talents specifically. The schooling process must be inclusionary without "set asides." All children, despite social class or ethnicity, have some kind of gift, special talent, and/or ability that, when appropriately nurtured, absorbs energy from surrounding environmental (community) resources and blooms into persona maxima.

Persona maxima is the highest recognizable form of personhood or individuality: the complete being—mind, body, and soul or spirit—endowed with reason, subsisting in itself and cooperating in the maximization of the personal execution of any task of activity. When environmental stimulus is deemphasized and deenergized, persona minima results. This is the less impressive presentation to the world of an individual in a state of underdevelopment and superficiality.

Perhaps the challenge of defining processes for gifted educational programs and the identification and nurturing of gifted and creatively endowed children can be made simpler and more meaningful by posing and responding to a series of subject-related questions such as these:

- What must parents, community, and educators do to create more amenable conditions for the maximization and development of gifted ability and excellence in multi-dimensional skill areas?

- What kinds of circumstantial and condition-related changes must be institutionalized to accommodate a redefinition of giftedness and creativity for the child who deviates from the average or the norm?

- Is creativity a construct born of psychological, intellectual, cultural, physical, or environmental processes? or a combination of all of these?

- Must creativity be observable and measurable? Why or why not? Is creativity limited to products and processes?

- Can parents and community share the responsibility for defining, developing, and managing giftedness and creativity? How? Under what circumstances does the defining of creativity and giftedness evolve?

- To what extent does a progressive community recognize and foster gifted/talented educational programs?

- To what extent and in what ways is a progressive community a direct consequence of individual and multifaceted creativity?

- Does creativity exist with variance and degree in all human beings despite the human condition? If so, how does it manifest itself?

- How can schools and gifted education programs be more responsive to the changing needs of children, parents, and communities?

- How can parental interface with gifted children be more child directed and efficient?

The answers to these questions will influence a more inclusive redefinition of what giftedness is as it relates to school programs, varying needs, interests and abilities of students, and the development of a parent-community knowledge transfer model for nurturing and managing creativity in the home and community. Such a model cannot be wholly conceptualized or developed without examining some interacting factors that influence the relationship of the learner to school. These factors are *parent, school, and community*. In *aggregate, they constitute an exponential alliance, a referent for triadic relationships that accommodates unknown variables in the gifted education defining process.*

The Alliance

These factors—parents, school, and community—constitute a very distinct and powerful relationship that must assume greater responsibility for defining school programs, giftedness, and curriculum planning. The cultivation of critical discernment in the areas of aesthetics, academic excellence, scientific and technological advancement, the training of consecutive and critical thinking, and the psychosocial precepts of leadership depends on the interaction of this triad.

This three-way exponential alliance must assume responsibility for redefining giftedness in terms of performance and for guiding each student to the enjoyment of what he/she produces or excels in, as opposed to the misguided triviality and ambiguity of experience and participation that characterizes the schooling experience of so many public school children. The alliance of parents, schools, and community can have a unifying influence on the quality of the school experience of many gifted children and can ensure the integrity of that experience.

It is only through such a three-way interaction of parents, community agents, and school personnel that each becomes more skilled in assessing the knowledge acquisition processes and the divergence of the knowledge base initiated by gifted students. Such interaction will allow more youngsters to be appropriately identified as gifted and fewer as troublesome and deviant. Failure to involve the parents and community invalidates the forthrightness and integrity of the schooling processes, and relegates millions of youths to misclassification, labeling, and tracking into poor educational circumstances.

If education for gifted students is to be successful in increasing individual creativity, productiveness, and participation, it must align itself with the whole community and motivate young people to maximize their giftedness, often in the absence of formal curriculum designed for the maximization of their gifts and talents. The alliance among parent, school, and community becomes an instrument for educational reform, as it marshals more creative educational enterprises to accommodate the multidimension needs of gifted students. As one considers the role of the parent, school, and community in monitoring, managing, and motivating giftedness, one must consider the critical nature of creativity and formulate some questions that will illuminate how parents, schools, and communities can form alliances to address student needs, extend gifted programs and activities, and encourage cooperative arrangements to maximize the use of resources.

Parents as Pioneers in School Involvement

Parent involvement in schools has been recognized as a critical factor in monitoring and assuring proper emotional, physical, intellectual, social, and creative development in school programs. Such involvement is necessary to ensure that children will be able to properly negotiate a healthy existence in a rapidly changing world. Parental failure to assume responsibility may result in serious problems later in adolescence, when deficits are cumulative and strategies for change are least effective.

Since the advent of federally supported education programs and the legislated requirement to establish parent advisory councils to advise and monitor educational programs, schools and school personnel have become more sensitive to parent committees and to the priority needs of children. Such legislated parent involvement has the effect of reinforcing positive school-community relations, enforcing instructional accountability, and keeping in check negative attitudes and behavioral expressions toward children, parents, and communities of ethnic or low-income status.

Parents are perhaps the most powerful lobby in education. However, too few parents are aware of the power they have to influence and demand changes in contentless curriculum, in the quality of educational programs, and in processes for delivering services and products.

Parent involvement is not always easily attained. Economic conditions often restrict the extent of school participation. As parents must devote time to occupational and life-sustaining activities, limited and less desirable time frames remain for other social and school-related activities.

Because of the demands imposed by their occupational condition, many parents are too fatigued to assume school-related responsibilities. Years later they may discover that their lack of involvement has had a profoundly negative effect on the social, emotional, intellectual, physical, or creative skill development of their youngsters—with a correspondingly negative effect on their future employability. Unfortunately, today it is only when youngsters become consumed by crises and trial that many parents begin to seek solutions to their children's problems. Failure to identify strategies or solutions often results in punitive handling or mishandling of children.

Effective parental involvement in school affairs may well be linked to parent education programs, both of which are central to high-quality educational experiences for youngsters. Parental involvement cannot be achieved without establishing rapport with school personnel, understanding school philosophy, and becoming familiar with school programs. It is well known that where you find an involved parent, you find better communication between home and schools, fewer discipline problems, greater student motivation and responsibility for learning, and greater academic achievement than that of the peer group whose parents are less involved in the defining and decision-making process of schooling.

For a long time parents in general, and low-income parents in particular, felt threatened by the school because the behavior of school personnel was often demeaning, assuming, and imposing. Because the education and schooling experiences of many parents have been limited, they tend to feel intimidated by the school, teachers, and administrators. They are often ashamed of their speech pattern, health, clothing, and a host of other factors that affect self-image.

As with the school, many parents are intimidated by their youngsters' knowledge base, formal or informal, and generally will not become involved with their youngsters on an academic level because they often do not have the tools or resources to help kids realize aspirations or do not want their children to see their deficiencies. They prefer to maintain a parent-child authority interaction to lessen feelings of inferiority and uneasiness and maintain the children's respect.

Traditional educational methods and lack of resources and creative curriculum planning may in theory and practice be responsible for low-level aspirations, lack of employable skill, or lack of ability to transfer skill to other forms of employment, therefore contributing to poor academic and financial circumstances in the home.

Schools, or professionals within schools, are often as uncomfortable in dealing with parents as parents are in dealing with them. Many school professionals, teachers and administrators alike, are so accustomed to relating and interacting with children that attempts at interaction with adults or other professionals outside their own professional area of expertise are unsuccessful.

Often the more assertive, less inhibited parents—or parents whose occupational status is flexibly designed—will offer assistance in the classroom to no avail because school professionals are intimidated by parental offers, feeling so threatened that they refuse the assistance and thereby the involvement of parents. Parents without formal training or advanced degrees are often intuitively more creative and knowledgeable about child development and behavior management than trained professionals who make the mistake of assuming parental ignorance.

Strategies in the Two-Way Alliance

Effective schooling strategies must be developed to facilitate the building of alliances. Some critical factors that must be considered in developing strategies are the following:

- *Parents* must be trained to know and understand the educational processes in their school system, school philosophy, course offerings, and school policies.

- *Schools* must not assume differences in the level of parental understanding of the schooling process but realize that even more learned parents are often not involved in the schooling process.

- *Parents* should be involved in designing, implementing, and evaluating school programs for their children.

- *Schools* too often assume or disseminate false notions of difficulty about curriculum design and program implementation and evaluation, making all such functions appear ambiguous or mysterious. What better assessment tool can any school system have than involved parents who have observed the effect of school programs on their children? Like school personnel, parents can identify the strengths and weaknesses of various components and understand the adaptation of the child to the program and the integration of children's learning skills with teaching methodology, curriculum learning styles, and community resources.

- *Parents and schools* should acknowledge other parents as resources who have varied skills and levels of expertise and respect the depth of their experience despite social, economic, and educational diversity within groups.

- *Schools* should assist parents in establishing parent task forces, steering committees, or parent councils with board of education monies, as opposed to discretionary federal monies attached to federally subsidized programs; using federal funds undermines the position of parent committees and to a large extent inhibits consecutive planning by these groups.

- *Parents* should be trained in the areas of program planning, organization and coordination, and implementation. They should participate in the selection of teachers for school programs. This will enable parents to monitor programs more effectively.

- *Schools* should develop parent internship. Through parent education or adult education courses parents would learn strategies for and methods of curriculum and educational program planning and classroom organization and management.

- *Parents* should understand that they can, and do, have a strong effect on the schools and that constructive involvement is a responsibility as well as a right.

Developing a Parent Education Program as an Outreach Model.
The most important ingredient in building alliances is establishing trust. Trust allows parties to rationally discuss and transcend differences. The

second most important ingredient is acknowledgment of each party as a legitimate entity equally responsible for defining a purpose and course of action. The third ingredient is defining the rights and conditions of the alliance and establishing an organizational structure to carry out the purposes of the alliance.

Subject to actualizing these three critical ingredients, the alliance of parent and school can go forward with the development of a plan for organizing a parent education outreach program, developing skills to monitor and manage giftedness and creativity at home and at school, and extending the educational opportunities for the gifted child. Although many types of parent education and parent training models exist, the alliance should consider first the needs of the parent population—particularly in light of the level of awareness regarding what constitutes a gifted and talented and creative student, how the gifted are identified, and how children can be taught to be creative.

Drs. Hanne and Havighurst have stated that

> Creativity is something that can be taught. It is also something that can be discouraged and allowed to atrophy. Since creativity can be taught, it is important for educators to put their minds to the task of developing it in every child, but in particular in the gifted child.[4]

Any parent education program to foster giftedness and creative development must include and be cognizant of the following factors and concerns:

- Information about the gifted/talented programs.

    a. Structure of local and statewide gifted programs.
    b. Identification and selection criteria for the inclusion and participation of the gifted children.
    c. Funding sources and eligibility criteria.
    d. Program needs, objectives, activities, and evaluation results.
    e. Personnel.
    f. Long- and short-range goals for programs.
    g. Facilities, supplies, equipment, and consulting services when necessary.

- Parent-community involvement in programs.

    a. Involvement in identification and selection process.
    b. Development of alternative course offerings and community-based programs external to the school.

[4] Robert F. Hanne and Robert J. Havighurst, *Educating Gifted Children* (Chicago: University of Chicago Press, 1961), p. 362.

   c. School policies and practices that affect the program.
   d. Social, economic, and cultural position of the community.
   e. Goal defining, planning implementation, coordination, monitoring, and evaluation of gifted/talented programs.
   f. Budgetary constraints in financing special school programs.

- Equal access to programs.

   a. Children with handicaps may also be gifted.
   b. Minority children are often not selected for gifted and talented programs because selection criteria are often skewed in favor of intelligence quotients. Alternative approaches and strategies for identification of the gifted/talented assure equal access.
   c. Minority children are often stereotyped into categories of giftedness: athletic-physical creativity in sports or dance and music, ignoring other profoundly distinct intellectual, social, and emotional-psychological skills.
   d. Expectations and cultural demands of school and the demands of the home should be examined for congruence.
   e. Selection criteria in many states are limited to mental giftedness (intelligence), with 130 IQ established as the level for defining giftedness.
   f. Gifted programs in many states come under the jurisdiction of Special Education departments, which makes many parents suspicious of the intent of programs.

This model of a parent education program provides the framework for the many pieces of information that must be explored to strengthen the alliance between parent and school. From this framework, needs of parent outreach can be made more explicit and resources can be more carefully assessed and creatively aligned.

Parent Outreach. Another more social strategy for bringing parents together is that of social gatherings. Activities may include but not be limited to

- Family day.
- Gifted/talented parent-pupil picnics.
- School carnivals.
- Community potluck suppers.
- Community-sponsored dialogues.

  a. Churches.
  b. Businesses.
  c. Industries.
  d. Social public welfare agencies.
  e. Social agencies.
  f. Cultural organizations.

- Coffee hours at parents' homes.

- Livingroom dialogues—small group discussions in parents' homes.

- Student performances.

Schools must assume the responsibility for creating a sense of inclusion, need, and belonging before parents will actively assume meaningful roles in actualizing and strengthening an alliance with the school.

Parent–Child Interface—Managing Creativity in the Home. Creativity develops in the minds of children free of trauma and social and psychological pathology. The forms of pathology most commonly observed in families are

- Low parental expectation and aspiration for the child.

- Constant abuse and neglect of children.

- Childhood loneliness due to working parents.

- Antisocial deviant peer groups.

- Results of negative and/or exclusive school politics and poorly implemented desegregation plans.

- Lack of social acceptance by peers.

The lives and minds of some youngsters are bombarded by so many survival-oriented stimuli and tasks that there is little privacy or time for creativity. For these children, that which is created is done under pressure and seldom under comfortable circumstances.

In many situations, the parent-child relationship today is analogous to that of a sick or diseased patient—feeble, maligned, uncomfortable, feverish, and painful. This is largely caused by a deferring of parent responsibility, changing conditions in the home, increases in the female work force, single-parent families, and a host of other factors. To reduce the fever, make the relationship more comfortable, and provide opportunities for more healthful conditions, it is necessary for parents to examine the needs of their children, understand the implied diversity in needs, and assert a new interest in what children do for six hours a day one hundred eighty days a year. This is fundamental because it yields understanding and intellectual curiosity, which in turn motivate other quests for knowledge.

Parents must have high expectations and aspirations for their children. Parents of gifted children must be principally concerned with the adaptation of the child to the gifted program and the integration of the child's skills, personality, and learning style into the selected program. The relationship of the parent to the gifted child is one of guidance. Parents should be concerned with understanding the cognitive explanation of the learning process—including the relationship of the child to the school, the relationship of parent to the school, and the relationship of parent to the child. They should be concerned with the stated definition of gifted and the identification and selection processes, as well as with the active integration of pupils with programs. Pupil alienation resulting from the distortion and misperception of the child's abilities destroys motivation.

Parents must begin to examine alternative education models to select an education for their child that is comprehensive. Open communication between a parent and child will enable parents to examine and understand the difference between the child's wish to please parents and the child's wish to develop aesthetic standards of creativity for him/herself. It is extremely important and necessary for parents to recognize that forced competition may not be valued by the gifted youngster and may limit his/her participation in the creative process. Working with children at home, parents must always remember to reward all children with recognition and esteem for what they produce and encourage personal and tailored choices in creative activities.

When gifted/talented programs are designed as magnet school components to facilitate voluntary desegregation, it is extremely important for parents to pay careful attention to the adaptation and integration of their child into the gifted programs. It is also important that parents discuss with children what the desegregation process will entail; what the curriculum changes will consist of; how the curriculum complements or fails to complement their heritage and socioeducational needs; and how they must compensate. Parents must examine standardized tests and instruments for identifying gifted students for cultural specificity in those instruments.

Facilitating the Desegregation Experience

In schools that are in the process of desegregating, children are often preoccupied with acceptance by peers, teachers, and community. Because of this preoccupation, the child who is in the minority and who comes from outside the community is not going to experience the same freedom to create as the child whose presence is legitimized by the fact that she/he belongs in that school or community. *This is where the parent-school-community alliance is best utilized to facilitate belonging and participation in all school programs.*

Minority children are the topic of discussion at many PTA or board of education meetings as groups of uninformed or misinformed parents discuss the low achievement and poor test scores of low-income or minority group children and fail to discuss low scores for other nonminority children. They discuss how low scores affect the academic standards in their schools but not how such low scores, often resulting from academic exclusion, may have a negative effect on the psyche and social, emotional development of low-income minority group children. These same minority children are bound by negative community expectations as evidenced in negative public discussions of their school performance. It is little wonder that the psyches of minority children are often too depressed to develop creative and gifted abilities.

Children who don't demonstrate high IQs are sometimes considered by teachers to be less desirable to work with than children who do test well. They tend to have a lower in-school status than the youngsters who realize their creative potential through well-disciplined apprenticeship, intensive training, and teacher encouragement.

What school personnel and parents must understand is that children of sparse means, with a paucity of material items in the home, tend to be preoccupied with the inventiveness of making much from nothing and making functional playthings from junk.

Parents must be aware of the fact that many childrren, because of the circumstances in which they interact, choose not to excel, exert, or acknowledge their giftedness for fear of ridicule, peer pressure, social ostracization, or administrative separation from the activities they value most—social and peer relations and other educational and cultural activities.

The School: The Mediating Ally

In the quest for a powerful alliance we have considered the role of the parent as one powerful exponent in the formation of a triadic relationship. The second component to consider is the mediating ally—the school. Looking at the role of the school as one of responding to the needs of gifted students, we see that role as one of making individuals more efficient managers of their environment. More to the point, this means they become truly efficient users of information, efficient resource developers, definers of their source experiences, change agents, peer counselors to the less talented and skilled, social organizers, and consumers of knowledge.

The role of the school, however, cannot be wholly or properly conceptualized without including the interacting factors—parents and the community—that constitute the whole as they influence the relationship of the child to school. School administrators must provide high-quality educational programs of a creative nature and make them available to all children and youth with a predisposition to giftedness, or to whose skill levels indicate proclivity for creative development.

School curricula are often dysfunctional, irrelevant, and ill-fitted to meet the ever-changing needs of gifted students. School administrators, who propose to develop educational programs to respond to the needs of gifted and talented and creatively endowed children, must undertake a critical review of their curriculum, instituting changes on a continuum. In so doing, children and their environmental experiences must be taken into account to ensure that the curriculum is multiethnic and multicultural, thereby accommodating a natural blending of the cultural experiences of a world community.

Curriculum must be organized to provide ample opportunity for participation in aesthetic development in the physical arts, sciences, mathematics, crafts, literature and linguistics, fine arts, music, and futuristic foundations of learning. School administrators would be wise to involve parents and community agencies in assessing the effectiveness of the school curriculum as measured by pupil growth, development, and interaction.

School personnel must be properly trained to be more efficient observers of strengths, weaknesses, and limitations in abilities, so as to design educational programs to maximize student potential. They must take care to develop curricular and extracurricular activities that do not require monetary input from students and parents, because poor financial means often inhibit participation, thus stifling creativity by disallowing the experience.

Another major responsibility of schools and school personnel is that of interacting with the community to enlighten the general public as to the educational offerings available in the schools and how community agencies and resources may enhance and improve them. Likewise, schools must expand these offerings to accommodate the multidimensional talents and abilities of the entire student body. This can be done by planning courses in consultation with local communities so as to develop a talent pool that corresponds to local community needs.

Community: Completing the Alliance

Community involvement holds a very important place in public education. Its role has been that of monitoring school programs and policy—insuring proper use of public finances for education. Increased community involvement has resulted because federal program regulations require community involvement, or because "points" are awarded that directly influence the level of funding.

Cooperation between schools and community is essential to a balanced approach to improved educational standards for all children. We must realize that the lives of today's youth are influenced by factors in the school as well as factors in the community. More community-related experiences are often called on to assign significance to experiences found in the school and the reverse. In the past schools have tried to exclude community agencies from the halls of learning primarily because community groups demand more stringent accountability measures, programmatic summing up, and comprehensive planning by school personnel. With community intervention one evidences more intensive observation and monitoring of the school, school programs, school processes, policies, and students. For many schools this is a very uncomfortable occurrence. Schools that have involved the community as curriculum consultants have experienced better results and produced more competent, informed, skilled, and creative children and youth.

Comprehensive Planning for Community Involvement. In developing comprehensive plans for involving the community, schools and parents must decide what groups, agencies, and organizations must be involved. This should not be determined solely on the basis of what groups have historically interacted in building better schools and educational programs, but should include groups and organizations represented by the parents of children in school programs.

The criteria for community involvement should include the following:

- Membership in local community groups, churches, organizations, agencies, or businesses.

- Interest in the public schools and their impact on the business community.

- Interest in the school budget and how tax dollars are spent.

- Interest in developing special linkages betwen the school and the business community for gifted and creatively endowed students with specialized interests and abilities.

A comprehensive plan for community involvement should include, but not be limited to, the following activities. The plan should be disseminated to parents, school personnel, and community groups for modification and expansion and be reviewed by a community task force for refinement. Activities should include the following:

- Developing a resource file of local community groups, agencies, organizations, churches, businesses, and professional associations.

- Drafting a "Dear Community" letter explaining the nature of the gifted/talented education programs and inviting representatives to visit the schools and participate in the programs.

- Involving representatives from community groups in developing a list of ways in which the community may be meaningfully involved with the schools.

- Organizing a community task force to serve as an advisory committee to monitor program effectiveness.

- Extending an invitation to the whole community to visit the gifted/talented programs in operation. Involve radio and public broadcasting, television stations, and so on.

- Appointing a community relations administrator to coordinate community—school activities.

- Encouraging community agencies that have been active in the schools to nominate other agencies, organizations, or community groups for inclusion on the task force. Do not limit participation to visible community groups or traditional groups that have *always* been approached.

- Encouraging community groups to participate in fund raising to finance special gifted/talented courses, parent training, and field trips.

- Providing effective dissemination of information about gifted and talented programs, policies, and program selection processes.

- Assisting the school in identifying equitable selection criteria for participation in gifted/talented programs.

- Evaluating the internal effectiveness of gifted/talented programs in the schools.

A more specialized role for the community in the exponential alliance is the sharing of the responsibility for effective delivery of educational services. Such activities should include, but not be limited to, the following:

- Sponsoring athletic activities.

- Organizing tutorial programs.

- Establishing career information centers.

- Organizing multicultural, multinational seminars.

- Conducting human relations training for parents, school personnel, and community agencies and representatives.

- Underwriting multicultural film projects.

- Sponsoring gifted/talented curriculum development seminars.

- Providing parent education seminars for guiding giftedness and creative development at home.

- Sponsoring intensive creative development laboratories in fine arts, physical arts, music, science, math, futuristics, leadership, literature, and linguistics.

The degree to which the activities outlined in the comprehensive plan can be implemented and realized, and the extensiveness of that implementation will depend on the social, ethnic, economic, and political nature of the community.

Conclusion

A holistic presentation of parents interacting with schools and community has been used to illustrate the importance and dynamics of the exponential alliance. In its aggregate state, it exerts a powerful influence on the proper and equitable development of educational standards and specialized school programs for gifted and creative children and youth. Care should be taken to ensure the quality and preserve the structural integrity of educational programs for the gifted.

Parents and community agencies must form alliances to prevent premature failure of chidren and to at least educate youngsters to understand that failure is temporary and momentary and very much a part of any learning process.

The alliance must make certain that each component—home, school, and community—undestands how the gifted defining process operates, how the pupil program evaluation process functions, and how the product development process is often different for minority and poor youngsters than for nonminority youngsters and ensure against inequitable differentiation between groups.

Parents of gifted children must realize that their children are a minority in any mix of ethnicity, sex, or socioeconomic status and must learn to embrace their children psychologically and motivate them to be flamingoes and not ostriches—teach them to be bold, proud, confident, self-assured, and colorful—not afraid, insecure, or ashamed—teach them to hold their heads high, not to bury them in the sand.

Parents of gifted children must understand that there is a consequence in being different that can be traumatic unless monitored very carefully. Such monitoring is a role best suited to parents to be shared with school and community—the exponential alliance.

10

ROBERT L. SINCLAIR, University of Massachusetts
WARD J. GHORY, Cincinnati Public Schools

Connecting Teacher Talents to Student Gifts

According to observers of childrearing practices in different cultures, parents and families in the United States devote extraordinary attention to the elusive task of determining each child's potential.[1] From infancy a child's characteristics, behaviors, and interests are scrutinized for clues that may reveal just what talents and strengths this child possesses. Indeed, one popular tradition describes the child's potentials as "gifts" (from heredity or the heavens), and woe be to the parents who dare rest before completing the task of precisely identifying the hidden talents (or, increasingly, the latent disabilities) of their child. In this context, children singing, dancing, leaping, stumbling, and so on are continually being assessed for their potential strengths and weaknesses so that some children can be hurried into special lessons while others are spared extensive training. Because we are optimistic people we believe that each person has some gift or talent, some strengths or special interest. Yet, as cost-conscious parents and educators, too often we lavish educational resources and special attention only on developing the potentials of the children with extreme and obvious talents or needs.

The responsibility is now shifting to the teacher and the school to identify and respond to the extremely gifted or talented, as well as to the notably handicapped. The rationale is clear: unless the special nature of these children is taken into account by teachers, these pupils will become

141

disconnected from productive and satisfying participation in the learning environments of the school and thus may never achieve their full potentials. In this chapter, we propose that one key to improving this important connection between learning environments and children is for teachers to recognize and respond to the gifts, talents, or potentials present in each child. The mounting educational concern for the gifted and talented, then, should seve as a catalyst for teachers to discover the special strengths or interests of all children; teachers can then begin to create school environments and learning opportunities that are responsive to individual characteristics. Discovering talents and creating matching learning environments is the nub of education for the "talented and gifted" as it should be for all teaching and learning. Simply administering more pretests and purchasing more reading series featuring paper-and-pencil exercises at varying degrees of difficulty will not accomplish this task. Instead, the search for the unique abilities of each child implies expanded instructional leadership roles for teachers so that such learning environments can be designed and implemented.

As one means to extend the concern for the gifted and talented to all children, this chapter will focus on the common and sometimes perplexing situation of a teacher in a classroom of multiability learners. Specifically, we will suggest the awareness a teacher can develop as preliminary and ongoing conditions for continual curriculum improvement. Next, the chapter will describe considerations a teacher should remember when diagnosing the multiple interests, attitudes, and skills of a learning group. Further, instructional leadership responsibilities of teachers for creating learning environments that draw on and foster the talents and inclinations of children will be suggested. Finally, environmental assessment techniques teachers could use to gauge students' perceptions of the success of their school and classroom environments will be discussed. In short, this chapter identifies selected issues any teacher should heed in his/her efforts to develop the unique talents that are potential in every young person.

Teacher Awareness

Three suggestions that teachers should consider when developing curricula that connect student talents and needs are as follows:

Become Aware of the Characteristics of Gifted and Talented Children

If "gifted" children were the only ones capable of possessing certain behavioral characteristics to an advanced degree, then the usual approach of segregating these pupils for specialized treatment or acceleration might make more sense. But if some of the advanced behavioral traits were indeed possible for other pupils when they were provided with different environmental conditons and training, the rationale for special gifted programs for a small number of pupils would be weakened. Classroom teachers have grown justifiably wary of judgments about young children that label them in negative ways or that serve as a basis for segregation and special treatment within the school. When presented with the lists of positive traits of gifted/talented children, the same skepticism would be reasonable, if similar labeling and segregation are the planned results.

Various research efforts[2] have identified intellectual, emotional, social, and physical traits that are likely (within levels of statistical significance) to be present among a gifted group and not likely to be present among other student groups. Given this research, our first recommendation is that teachers should become aware of the behaviors (and consequent problems and needs) considered indicative of gifted/talented children, so they can create and foster learning environments and characteristics for all children.

Table 10-1 presents one useful summary of the learning characteristics of gifted children, with some of the concomitant problems and needs such traits might create for a child in school environments. Perhaps the greatest value of such a list is that teachers can immediately recognize traits of some of their "problem" students. Examination of lists such as this one helps teachers recognize positive traits which may be implicit in problematic behavior. If the actual learning characteristics of each child were accurately identified, students could be provided sanctioned outlets for their preferred learning styles; a sort of multiple environment school would exist. This approach promises improved learning and reduced group management difficulties.

Become Aware of the Potentially Narrow Range of Behaviors Your Classroom Permits

To an important extent, the labels *gifted, average,* or *problem student* identify a certain set of environment-related tasks and expectations. The intellectual, social, and physical conditons in the setting serve as a threshold for encouraging or eliciting or, in some cases, hindering student behavior. As Torrance[3] notes, convergent evidence from the research of more than five

---

[2] See William K. Durr, Characteristics of Gifted Children: Ten Years of Research, in John C. Gowan and E. Paul Torrance (Eds.), *Educating the Ablest* (Itaska, Ill.: F. E. Peacock Publishing, 1971), pp. 23-32, and James J. Gallagher, Characteristics of Gifted Children: A Research Summary, in Walter R. Barbe and Joseph S. Renzulli (Eds.), *Psychology and Education of the Gifted,* 2nd ed., (New York: Irvington Publishers, 1975), pp. 127-150.

[3] E. Paul Torrance, *Gifted Children in the Classroom* (New York: Macmillan Publishing Co., Inc. 1965), p. 21.

TABLE 10-1. Learning Characteristics of Gifted Children[4] with Concomitant Problems and Needs

Learning Characteristics	Concomitant Problems and Needs
a. Keen sense of observation; willingness to examine the unusual	Possible gullibility; possible social rejection; need for interesting environments
b. Power of abstraction, conceptualization, and synthesis	Occasional resistance to direction; rejection or omission of detail; need for structured problem-solving opportunities
c. Ability to apply concepts; interest in cause-effect relationships; love of truth	Difficulty in accepting the illogical; concern for deception and injustice; need for opportunities to take reasoned stands
d. Attraction to system and consistency—as in value systems, number systems, and clocks or calendars	Nose for hypocrisy; need to invent own, sometimes conflicting systems
e. Verbal proficiency; breadth of information	Escape into verbalism or theoretical thinking; need for opportunities to develop and use specialized vocabulary
f. Retentiveness in long- and short-term memory	Dislike for routine and drill; need for early mastery of foundation skills
g. Questioning attitude; intrinsic motivation	Possible lack of sufficient stimulation by home or school environments; need for self-initiated problem-oriented projects

h. Power of critical thinking;
   skepticism and evaluative testing

Critical attitude toward others; excessive discouragement from selfcriticism; need for acceptance of self and others

i. Creativeness and inventiveness; versatility and virtuosity

Rejection of the known; need to create for oneself; need to develop basic competencies

j. Power of concentration; capability for persistent, goal-directed behavior

Resistance to interruption; stubbornness; need to set own pace

k. Sensitivity, intuitive empathy, and courage in relationships

Defensiveness about friends; potential problems in social leadership; needs for emotional support

---

[4] Adapted from a list provided by the Office of Gifted and Talented, Department of Health, Education, and Welfare, United States Government.

---

independent investigators supports the conclusion that whenever the way of teaching children is changed, different children become the star learners and thinkers. For example, children with high IQs who have excelled at receiving information from teachers and textbooks may temporarily flounder in classroom environments requiring critical thinking and distinctively individual physical or manual productions. In one study comparing environmental demands many high-achieving learners from a traditional setting became average, run-of-the-mill students in the "creative and productive" setting, where several formerly average learners now excelled.[5] Proof is that if any large and divergent group of learners is subjected to a relatively monolithic learning environment where only certain behaviors are recognized and rewarded, children will separate into clearly different groups along the relevant dimensions. Yet, these "differences" among children may be deceptive or even superficial, because they are so environmentally specific.

    Teachers need to become aware of the learning behaviors their classroom environments permit. Without this awareness they cannot begin to

[5] William L. Hutchinson, Creative and Productive Thinking in the Classroom (Ph.D. dissertation, University of Utah, 1961).

diagnose the strengths and potentials of all their students because in typical classroom settings many behaviors and strengths will not appear in ways that can be rewarded and approved. For example, school environments may be giving undue rewards to students (and teachers) for being courteous, prompt, obedient, popular, and acquiescent to authority, and they unduly punish the good guesser, the child who is courageous in her convictions, the emotionally sensitive person, the intuitive thinker, the visionary person, and the person who challenges ideas presented without sufficient evidence. Moreover, only two of ten characteristics that identified an ideal student in a national teacher's sample were included in the top ten characteristics of the ratings of a panel of experts judging the essential characteristics of a productive, creative person.[6]

Teachers should clearly question how much of their own and their students' time is spent in procedural routine (attendance taking, distribution of materials, announcements, and group management directions), how much in reproducing the thinking of others (as in dittoed drills or most tests of low-level cognitive behaviors), and how much in critical thinking and student production of unique ideas and creations. Furthermore, teachers should examine their own and their students' environments for opportunities to practice Guilford's[7] five intellectual operations (cognition, memory, divergent thinking, convergent thinking, and evaluative thinking), or the five nonintellectual learning processes suggested by Taylor[8] (intuitive, perceptual, emotional, social, and physical). Until we better understand the impact of school environments on student behavior, our judgments of who is gifted and how they are gifted will remain skewed.

Become Aware of Environmental Variables That Contribute to Student Involvement or Disconnection

In most schools and classrooms some students consistently perceive the educational environment as blocking or inhibiting them from learning. An important contribution of the gifted/talented researchers has been their finding that among these marginal learners will invariably be found gifted students. Yet educators still lack adequate data as to which environmental conditions and events force some pupils to the edges of their classrooms. This information is critical as the schools are called on to accept into their learning environments previously excluded or stigmatized groups—the new-

---

6 Torrance, op. cit., p. 14.

7 J. P. Guilford, Three Faces of Intellect, in Barbe and Renzulli, op. cit., pp. 75-91.

8 Calvin W. Taylor, Educational Changes Needed to Develop Creative Thinking, in Mary Jane Aschner and Charles E. Bish (Eds.), Productive Thinking in Education (Washington, D.C.: National Education Association, 1968), pp. 245-264.

comers to a recently desegregated school, or the educationally handicapped or gifted.

Based on the perceptions of 1,692 students in thirty-one alternative public high schools from six Eastern states, we have tentatively identified five evironmental variables that contributed significantly to the connection or disconnection between students and their alternative school learning environments. Alternative schools were specifically chosen because of their commitment to create flexible learning arrangements that better meet the needs of individuual learners. Nevertheless, we found that these alternative learning environments contributed in direct and statistically significant ways to marginal behavior in school settings.

First, the academic expectations, standards, and procedures were usually not so clear to marginal learners as they were to other learners. Second, marginal learners perceived greater discrimination against themselves in school environments than other students did. Third, marginal learners generally perceived that their teachers did not make as many special efforts to help them learn. Fourth, the communication processes used in sampled alternative schools were often not as effective at providing marginal learners with the information they needed to succeed. Fifth, learners identified as marginal generally perceived more responsibilities and difficulties from outside the school that interfered with the successful accomplishment of their work.[9] In sum, these environmental variables (entitled Clarity, Discrimination, Outreach, Communication, and Extraschool Priorities) represent but five of many dimensions of school environments that contribute to the difficulties of some learners and the success of others. When a surprising number of our most gifted youngsters do not complete high school, and many other gifted youngsters do not go on to college,[10] teachers must look carefully at their educational environments for the partial sources of the marginal behavior and low motivation of these students. For example, Torrance identifies six curriculum conditions that are widely responsible for low motivation: namely, no chance to use best abilities, no chance to learn in preferred ways, learning tasks that are too easy or too difficult, learning that is lacking in purposefulness, and interest in content rather than grades.[11] The implication here is that less time should be spent searching for the characteristics that signal the presence of a gifted child and more time spent

[9] Ward J. Ghory and Robert L. Sinclair, Views from the Margins: Student Perceptions of Educational Environments in Public Alternative High Schools, paper presented at the National Conference of the American Educational Research Association in Toronto, Canada, March 1978.

[10] Louis Fliegler, Curriculum Planning for the Gifted (Englewood Cliffs, N.J.: Prentice-Hall, 1961), p. 2.

[11] Torrance, op. cit., pp. 28-37.

examining and creating school environments that effectively connect with all learners.

Diagnosis of the Gifts and Talents of All Learners

To diagnose the gifts and talents of learners, both the individual and the environment must be taken into account. Based on this premise, teachers should shy away from an overreliance on testing or test scores for accurate and sensitive assessment of student characteristics. Rather, teachers themselves, as the persons closest to the learners, are in the best position to read environmental conditions and observe student conduct. The state of the diagnostic art is not far advanced. In particular, two concerns over the content and process of diagnosis should be raised.

Types of Diagnostic Information

Much of the confusion in the literature on the diagnosis of gifted children can be related to one common flaw: the purpose of the typical diagnostic procedure is to locate with maximum effectiveness and efficiency a group of gifted children. We suggest that a more practical approach would seek to define in usable terms the actual or potential gifts of each child. After all, even if a so-called gifted group were identified, more precise diagnosis of student abilities, talents, and learning styles would be necessary before effective curriculum could be developed. *But the flaw needs to be underscored for a more important reason: identification devices aimed at selecting one group of gifted children mask the strengths of other children and could ultimately limit their opportunities for education.*

For example, Taylor identified six types of talent based on world-of-work needs (academic talent, creative and productive talent, decision-making talent, planning talent, forecasting talent, and communication talent).[12] He argued that efforts to identify and cultivate only one talent group denied many other students the opportunity to be recognized or treated as above average (let alone gifted) for other talents. Supportive research estimates that to identify gifted children based on measures of intelligence alone would miss about 70 per cent of the creatively gifted children.[13] Further, types of giftedness other than creativeness and high IQ are likely to be overlooked in classroom situations, where the abilities to write, to engage in abstract thinking, or to cooperate with a group has led diagnosticians into a thicket of difficulties. One path out of these thorny

[12] Calvin W. Taylor, Be Talent Developers, *Today's Education*, December 1968.

[13] Torrance, op. cit., p. 25.

troubles is to collect information concerning the abilities, interests, and preferred learning strategies of *each* child. These data will serve as a more compelling basis for curriculum development.

Experience and observation in classroom settings suggest that a combination of subjective and objective diagnostic information should be collected.[14] Teachers might wish to seek subjective information of the following seven types when diagnosing individual gifts. First, superior performance of a task certainly reflects aptitude to some extent. Yet a child's gifts are occasionally blocked by emotional problems or lack of interest in the instructional approach. Second, the intellectual, emotional, social, and physical traits listed previously in Table 10-1 are a clue to the gifts and needs of young people. Third, the interests of children are an often discredited source of information for curriculum and environment development. Clearly, high motivation contributing to higher achievement and prolonged attention span results when learner interests are pursued (as when viewing favorite TV shows, eating preferred foods, or visiting special animal or human friends). In fact, it is reasonable to presume that interests are aroused when several of the child's abilities and previous experiences can be brought to bear on a learning task.

Fourth, the structured and unstructured activities of children should be consulted. The items they spontaneously collect, the hobbies and games they prefer, the organized groups (religious, scouting, teams) they join, or the musical instruments they play can be probed for what they reveal about a child's personality and motivation sources. Fifth, by noting imaginal themes (like the concern for invention, construction, and achievement prevalent during the latency period of early school age; or the passion for justice, revolution, reformation, or utopias characteristic of puberty and adolescence),[15] the teacher can identify topics that different learners respond to in group discussions or projects. Sixth, by identifying and calling on the varying cognitive skills of particular students (the one who can paraphrase, the one who uses metaphors, the one who makes generalizations, or the one who likes detail) the teacher develops and reinforces student strengths. Finally, a child's attitudes and values indicate to some extent the level of the child's social and emotional maturity, stressing needs that arise from accelerated or retarded development in these areas.

Four types of objective evaluation are also potentially useful to a

---

[14] See Marian Schiefele, *The Gifted Child in the Regular Classroom* (New York: Teachers College Press, 1953), Chapter 1, for a more extensive summary of subjective and objective evaluation information.

[15] See Richard M. Jones, *Fantasy and Feeling* in Education (New York: Harper & Row, 1968), pp. 130-131, for a table relating the developmental life stages, cognitive stages, imaginal themes, and emerging social orientations of children.

classroom teacher—if their limitations are understood. First, the teacher should consider the results of individual intelligence tests (such as the Stanford-Binet or the Wechsler Intelligence Scale for Children) but remain aware that the words and situations used in such tests place children from many cultural and social backgrounds at a disadvantage. Next, subject matter achievement tests, given in battery form at regular intervals in many school systems, attempt to compare individual test performance to group norms. Yet, research consensus opinion is that gifted children are apt to achieve far below their potential capacity, making them (in terms of possible achievement) among the most seriously retarded pupils in our schools today.[16] This finding also questions the extensive use of norm-referenced tests. Instead, individual diagnostic or criterion-referenced testing in one or more of the curriculum areas would reveal specific strengths and weaknesses with greater confidence.

Third, aptitude tests can also be consulted when identifying a child's potential for development in special areas. Yet, in general, the tests measure performance or achievement rather than talent, and do so by sampling only a few of the several abilities involved in a particular talent. Moreover, many researchers question the validity of measuring artistic abilities in a test situation that differs from most everyday experiences of a child. Nevertheless, aptitude tests of musical talent, art judgment, visual arts abilities, and measured aptitudes are available. Finally, personality inventories considering such positive factors as leadership ability, resourcefulness, responsibility, social participation, and initiative are occasionally administered to students. Again, these instruments claiming objective measurement of intangible qualities should be approached warily. They are usually based on comparison of an individual to a behavioral norm established by testing other individuals, and it is questionable whether a "normal personality" can be reliably defined.

Diagnostic Situations

The key to successful diagnosis is to create conditions that require or allow the desired behavior to occur. Testing conditions provide a familiar example of this axiom, because all the environmental conditions are geared to individual concentration on narrowly defined tasks. The extremity of a test environment raises questions over the reliable transfer of performance in this setting to performance in other settings. Thus a teacher truly interested in understanding children would collect diagnostic information of the types outlined previously from a number of observations in a variety of settings.

A diagnostic situation normally involves a task or stimulus (either

---

[16] Schiefele, op. cit., p. 19.

planned or emergent) and a method of recording behavior for further analysis. Within this general framework, the variations are limited only by the imagination and creativity of the teacher. For example, Taylor has proposed several exciting ways for teachers to create situations to identify creatively gifted children, such as (1) permit students to plan activities or make group decisions and observe which ones are the most dependent and which are the most self-determining; (2) pose complex issues and see which children take a hopeful attitude and which children have little hope that improvements can occur; (3) assign students a task they have done before but take away most of the facilities previously available, and then watch the resourceful people improvise.[17] One of the authors simply has his son collect some inchworms; then he releases them on a table piled with manipulative materials and gadgets and observes the students as they experiment and try to discover characteristics about the worms.

Ways of recording behavior are equally as diverse but not attempted so often. In fact, one of the tragedies of school organization is that the vast diagnostic information accumulated by a teacher on each child is rarely systematically recorded or shared. Yet the task is not unmanageable. As teachers of writing realize, students can reveal key information when they record their own behavior, as in autobiographies, diaries, or open-ended themes. Furthermore, many teachers keep anecdotal records in a file for each child in which classroom occurrences, parent contacts, or counseling interviews are briefly noted. As a running record develops over a period of several weeks or months, patterns in the learner's interests, concerns, problems, and strengths emerge. Other teachers make use of role-playing or discussion techniques requiring the student to put himself in the place of a character in a story, picture, or situation. The motives for acting in different ways can then be discussed by children and recorded by the teacher. More formally, observers of various types can be used to take notes describing a child's behavior at stated intervals. In sum, the measurement of human capabilities cannot be limited to an illusory test or easily administered instrument. Instead, the efforts to diagnose student gifts as a basis for curriculum development must be as emergent and developmental as the pupil's conduct itself.

Instructional Leadership Responsibilities of Teachers

To adequately diagnose student gifts and to create curricula and learning environments that connect with student talents is ultimately the

[17] Calvin W. Taylor, Developing Creative Characteristics, *The Instructor*, 1964, *73(9)*, 99-100.

responsibility of the teacher. Although often committed by supervisors to certain textbook series, limited by budgets to certain instructional options, hemmed in by schedules, and overwhelmed by group size, the teacher still can exercise considerable autonomy on the final, but critical, frontier of classroom learning environment. The perspective taken here suggests that teachers need to develop multiple environment classrooms where particular learning conditions are matched to the needs, gifts, and strengths of specific students and groups. In particular, three leadership responsibilities of teachers are advanced:

First, teachers are responsible for understanding their own dominant instructional style. Research on the effects of instruction suggests that each instructional style implies a model of learning and a particular instructional content that are most appropriate for this style.[18] For example, a lecturer is effective when presenting well-organized, somewhat technical information to large groups of students who can receive and record information rapidly. By contrast, a programmed instruction approach is appropriate when sequential or hierarchical information is presented by a highly structured book or learning machine to students who need extensive drill or repetition to develop and reinforce learning. Alternatively, an inquiry approach works best when source documents or exploratory resources are available to students fluent with problem-solving and interpretive approaches. Although many other instructional approaches could be described, the concern is that most classroom environments are set up to favor the instructor's preferred or dominant teaching style. Frankly, classrooms are often organized for teaching more than for learning.

By becoming aware of one's dominant instructional style, a teacher becomes aware of the learning tasks and learning styles that are favored, as well as inhibited, by a certain learning environment. It is easier in this context to identify the needs and gifts of learners who do not fit or connect well with the teacher's dominant instructional approach. Instead of punishing or ostracizing these students, the teacher can attempt to extend his/her repertoire of instructional approaches to allow for multiple learning environments within the classroom.

The second responsibility of a teacher who wants to match learning environments to student gifts is to investigate different criteria for grouping pupils. Normally, teachers are assigned pupils on the basis of administrative convenience (alphabetical listing or computerized numerical order), ability groups, or curriculum prerequisites. Within the classroom pupils are often grouped for convenience in instruction, i.e., according to the textbook level

---

[18] Bruce Joyce and Marsha Weil, *Models of Teaching* (Englewood Cliffs, N.J.: Prentice-Hall, 1972).

they are using or for easier group management. In a learning environment where extensive and ongoing diagnosis is taking place, many groups will form and dissolve or terminate on the basis of several additional criteria. First, students with particular skill needs can work together until the skill is mastered. Second, students with special gifts and talents could divide their time between individual projects allowing them to develop their abilities in depth, accelerated group work with other advanced students, and peer tutoring groups with pupils in need of assistance. Third, students with special interests (like dinosaurs) or special cognitive skills (as in problem solving) could team up with like-minded or divergent classmates for a unit of study. Fourth, heterogeneous large groups could collaborate on common projects like the staging of a play or the construction of a model. Fifth, all individuals could be assigned open-ended projects centered on a common theme such as the meaning of the good life that would allow different solutions and permit considerable sharing of ideas and common methodological instruction. In short, when learning needs, gifts, and skills replace instructional and administrative convenience as the starting point for instruction, flexible grouping and multiple instructional approaches become necessary.

The third leadership responsibility of a teacher is to identify and teach varying levels of complexity in curriculum content and process. Differentiated teaching strategies should be chosen on the twin bases of appropriateness for the learner and appropriateness for the curriculum content or skill. The closer these three variables (teaching strategies, learner characteristics, and curriculum content) mesh, the more affective the instruction will be. Various models of human development and intellectual or emotional functioning (Piaget, Erikson, Kohlberg, Bloom, and Guilford)[19] are recommended for study by teachers who wish to develop teaching strategies and curriculum content that provide appropriate challenges to pupils at various stages of cognitive, moral, and physical development. One useful synthesis for the classroom teacher of several of these models has been developed by Dr. Frank E. Williams. Williams's approach for teaching cognitive and effective behaviors in the classroom relates eighteen specific teaching strategies or modes of teaching to four types of intellectual process (fluent thinking, flexible thinking, original thinking, and elaborative thinking) and to four types of affective process (curiosity, risk-taking, complexity, and imagina-

---

[19] See Jean Piaget and Barbel Inhelder, *The Growth of Logical Thinking from Childhood to Adolescence* (New York: Basic Books, 1958); Erik Erikson, *Childhood and Society* (New York: Norton, 1950); Lawrence Kohlberg and Rochelle Mayer, Development as the Aim of Education, *Harvard Educational Review*, 1972, *42(4)*, 449-496; Benjamin S. Bloom (Ed.), *Taxonomy of Educational Objectives*, Vols. 1 and 2 (New York: David McKay, 1956); J. P. Guilford, *The Nature of Human Intelligence* (New York: McGraw-Hill, 1967).

tion) for each of the major academic subjects.[20] Similarly, in a book for elementary teachers, Michaelis, Grossman, and Scott[21] discuss how teachers can evaluate pupil progress and select matching instructional techniques by blending cognitive and affective processes for teaching the elementary subjects. The common message of these models is that professional teachers have the responsibility for using various teaching strategies that provide learning opportunities for students at all levels of cognitive and affective development.

As theoretical solutions to the complex role of a teacher these models are promising, but the daily burden of creating effective learning environments falls squarely on the teacher. For this reason we are suggesting that a teacher's leadership responsibilities can be assumed only in an institutional environment providing continual support and ample resources to teachers. Thus ongoing methods for assessing and improving the total school environment are necessary for creating classroom settings that successfully connect with learners.

Environmental Assessment Techniques

The perceptions of students toward school environment can be an important source of information about the ways environments influence student behavior. Specifically, student perceptions provide clues as to how different environmental dimensions of the school or classroom affect the conduct of various individuals. For example, some learners are intellectually, socially, and physically at home in a school. Other learners are uncomfortable strangers there. Yet both groups are acting based on the ways they perceive their school settings. It follows, then, that when existing environmental conditions are perceived in a different way by two groups of students, it is likely that the behaviors of these groups will also differ.

For this reason educators interested in matching students with appropriate curricula can better understand learner behavior by systematically consulting student perceptions of curriculum conditions. If student perceptions indicate that a learning environment is not serving them adequately, their perceptions of the specific environmental conditions that affect them provide a starting point for actions to correct the mismatch between the environment and the student. Further, student perceptions of school climate can identify environmental forces that may be hindering or assisting teachers in their leadership efforts for curriculum improvement.

[20] Frank E. Williams, Models for Encouraging Creativity in the Classroom, in Gowan and Torrance, op. cit., pp. 222-233.

[21] John Michaelis, Ruth Grossman, and Lloyd Scott, New Designs for the Elementary School Curriculum (New York: McGraw-Hill, 1967).

The Center for Curriculum Studies at the University of Massachusetts (Amherst) has been conducting research into the associations between students and learning environments for the past ten years. Three research approaches we have developed will be described in this final section as examples of environmental assessment techniques that contribute to curriculum improvement.

First, student perceptions of six environmental conditions that promote individualization of instruction and improved achievement could be gathered using the Elementary School Environment Survey (ESES). The ESES identifies similarities and differences in the educational environment as seen by students. In this perceptual process students rate the environment in terms of the Involvement it permits, the Autonomy it allows, the Humanism it reflects, the Morale it encourages, the Resources it provides, and the Equity it establishes. Information concerning the relative presence or absence of these factors can be used by professional staffs when identifying environmental changes that would support teacher efforts to improve the curriculum. The ESES process has been used across the nation, notably with a sample of more than six thousand children in Massachusetts.[22]

Second, student perceptions of three curriculum conditions that foster a multicultural classroom environment could be collected using the Multicultural Environment Survey (MES).[23] With this approach, students report whether they are learning the Skills, Attitudes, and Knowledge that are likely to lead to cooperation and understanding among cultural groups. Creating environments that foster multicultural harmony is the responsibility of all teachers, regardless of the cultural composition of their learning groups. It is a familiar finding that many of the gifts of poor and minority children are not identified partly because of the limitations of their school environments.[24] For this reason it is important to assess the multicultural press of classrooms if environments that provide equal educational opportunities relative to the gifts of all students are desired.

Third, the environmental variables that contribute to student involvement or disconnection in a learning environment have already been mentioned in the Awareness section of this chapter. The Alternative School Environment Survey (ASES) collects student perceptions of eleven curriculum conditions that are important in any secondary classroom or school where the movement toward individualization of instruction has begun.

[22] Robert L. Sinclair, Set the State for Response, *The Instructor*.

[23] John Browne, An Investigation of Multicultural Press in Elementary Classrooms (Unpublished Ed.D. dissertation, University of Massachusetts at Amherst, 1975).

[24] See E. Paul Torrance, Creative Positives of Disadvantaged Children and Youth, in Gowan and Torrance, op. cit., pp. 253-262.

Furthermore, use of this instrument makes it possible to compare the perceptions of pupils identified as disconnected from the learning environment to the perceptions of pupils who are involved and productive in these settings. The gaps or differences in the perceptions of these groups highlight environmental variables that contribute to the difficulties of disconnected pupils. With these data, teachers can alter their classroom environments to connect more effectively with marginal students.

Through the eyes of the learners, it is possible to identify the extent to which the educational environment is characterized by certain intellectual, social, and physical conditions. This perceptual approach provides important information about various factors that contribute to student behavior. It is the transactional relationship between the student and the environment that either fosters or hinders learning. An awareness of incongruity between educational environment and learner needs, and its consequences, encourages teachers to look critically at the conditions that influence the behavior of learners. Deciding and then acting on the reality of the school and classroom are necessary for individual and institutional improvement. Teachers can simply use student reports about the environment as data for identifying and eliminating conditions that hinder learning and for creating and maintaining conditions that provide productive connecting tissues between the student and the school.

Conclusion

Teachers, parents, and pupils who have attended more than one school quickly sense that each school has unique environmental characteristics, somewhat comparable to what we know as personality in individuals. Some schools, similar to personalities that lack capacity for renewal, are dominated by traits that resist improvement. In these schools that defend their particular set of learning conditions, the job of a teacher who wishes to create a classroom environment responsive to student gifts is doubly difficult. Other schools, similar to a creative and expanding personality, are receptive to new ideas and adapt smoothly to emergent needs and opportunities. In these schools that support ongoing improvement, a teacher concerned with the connection among the learning environments and the gifts, strengths, or potentials in each child can diagnose pupils and alter learning environments with the confidence that lasting improvements will result. To a certain extent then, the traits recognized as characteristic of gifted children and appropriate for their educational environments are too precious to be reserved for a special, elite group labeled as "gifted/talented." For, in an effective school program, the distinction between gifted learners and other learners should diminish, not because the gifted have been mainstreamed into the existing program or segregated for special treatment, but because all learners have been approached with the ongoing attention necessary for creating and improving educational environments best suited to their evolving academic and personal talents. The real gift is not in the person, but in the quality of the interaction between the educational environment and the learner.

11

CANDICE NATTLAND, Montclair Public Schools

Considering the Talents of Children or What You See Is What You Get

Diversification as an Educational Tool

All children are entitled to optimum development of their potential. Our most cherished beliefs speak of this, yet our educational systems are only now beginning to accept their responsibility in accomplishing this goal. If this is to be a primary aim of education, then the substance and ritual of the school must change. Fostering and directing this change are tasks for administrators and teachers. As a teacher in a school whose philosophy is to nurture the talents and gifts of children, I find myself confronting daily questions about this change. Why do I do what I do in my classroom? What are the students learning from the routines I establish and the activities I provide? Do these say what I want to say? Do they educate or confuse? Analyzing what you do with children is the beginning of an education that develops talents and gifts.

The difficulty with analysis lies in the nature of a teacher's close daily contact with children; there is seldom time for reflection, introspection, or asking why. I am working, teaching, and writing, balancing the heat of my interaction with children with the cool logic of the lesson plan book.

Changing basic assumptions about school changes what you do there each day. On a pedagogical level, implementing a philosophy that holds that all children possess talents and gifts is the issue for the teacher, and it raises many difficult questions.

Let us begin with a careful look at the developing child. I teach 7-, 8-, and 9-year-olds. Over the years they have taught me many things: for the most part they want to do things well; they need to feel competent to feel good about themselves; they become interested in something because of who is teaching them; they frequently learn best when shown something by a peer and then practice it; they can talk about things without understanding them; they can be enthusiastic and can concentrate great amounts of energy on learning what is interesting to them; they often like to talk about themselves; and they like to have best friends.

Children in the middle years enjoy and learn about ideas best by examining, poking about, handling, trying out, and manipulating concrete objects and situations. Art, dance, and drama for all children at this age are primary teaching materials. Because they are unable to think abstractly, young children can work conceptually through the arts. For example, a child can memorize a definition for the word *territory* and be unaware of what it means. A dramatic improvisation in which a group of children protects its corner of a room from a second group can concretely teach the meaning of *territory*.

Talented/gifted programs, when they broaden the ways in which children are taught, can provide many opportunities for involvement in numerous kinds of concrete learning. A school that teaches dance, drama, cooking, physical arts, graphic arts, and woodworking involves its students in experiences that can be used to develop high levels of conceptual thought. The experiences alone, however, will not teach this. Teachers need to know how to use concrete materials to make abstract concepts accessible to children; they do not understand ideas by being told about them. Talented/ gifted programs, in moving away from paper, pencil, and workbook teaching, can teach all children how to think about the complex phenomena of our physical and social world.

To a keen observer, what children say and do is a rich source of information that can be used to develop effective teaching activities and structures. Because each group is unique, there are different things to be seen and used all the time. This is one difficulty in following a rigid curriculum that tries to fit the children to its objectives. It frequently has nothing to do with the interests of the students. Teachers who believe that it is important to involve their children as personally as possible in what they are doing so that they can learn about themselves and the world will work alongisde their students, allowing them to shape what happens in school. The flexibility of a talented/gifted program, which works with children to tailor their schedule of activities to their unique needs or interests, encourages students to make a deep commitment to their learning.

Curriculum in a talented/gifted school must allow for a wide range of ability, encourage the diversity of children's interests, uncover latent talents, and teach each child how to work in a group. The nature of the curriculum should be integrative. Children's experiences in school should connect the things they are learning.

Traditional schooling does not concern itself with the fragmentation of learning that occurs when subjects are taught as if they had nothing to do with one another. The potential for fragmentation of curriculum in a school where there are a highly diversified kinds of learning is great. The danger of this fragmentation for middle-years children is that they are unable to connect what they learn; they resort to the ritual of doing (or not doing) what the teacher says simply because he/she says it, instead of working and learning because what they are doing makes sense to them and gives them a sense of their own competence. Adults know that solutions to problems require an ability to analyze particulars, balanced with an ability to think holistically. It is important to help children understand interrelationships of subjects taught in school and the relation between experiences they have in and out of school.

Another kind of fragmentation may occur for certain children in a school where they work daily with many different peer groups and teachers. My children work with me for two hours each day. They also spend time in classes chosen from an extensive array of offerings in language, mathematics, science, visual and performing arts, and physical education. There are advantages for a child who is involved in several groups during a day, but some children have difficulty in finding their place in each situation. Teachers need to be particularly sensitive to these youngsters. A child's involvement with the life of the group contributes to his emotional, moral, and cognitive growth. Teachers can help by encouraging strong group interaction and providing the support necessary for children to cooperate, recognize their interdependence, and value others for their uniqueness.

It is important that the teacher never lose his/her sense of being the leader of the group. Children frequently are interested in things that schools are not. Within a class there are many different interests. A teacher cannot arrange for every interest to be explored; school is a group experience as well as a place for individuals. The way in which the interests of the children are used determines whether a teacher is educating or entertaining his/her students.

A Model of Structured Spontaneity

With these ideas in mind, I began to develop a social studies and language arts curriculum. The content was an examination and comparison of three regional Indian cultures, two of which exist today. The children worked with the ideas of culture, community, environment, territory, natural resources, past and present, the relationship between a culture and its environment, and how the art of a culture reflects its environment. The children had an opportunity to develop basic skills in reading, research, writing, drama, art, crafts, mapmaking, listening, and discussion. These same objectives could be accomplished with many other content areas. I chose this study because this age group is fascinated with Indians, resources and materials are abundant, and I was interested in it myself.

The first culture examined was that of the Navajo Indians. The study began with an investigation of the desert region. Several children painted tempera paint scenes of the desert, others collected desert pictures for a display. Three children used the library to look up desert in the encyclopedia and dictionary. We discussed each activity in class meetings. I encouraged the more adventurous children in the tasks they chose themselves and made specific assignments to others. The group began to share their thoughts about what it would be like to live there. As always with 8- and 9-year-olds, they began to explore the new ideas from their own perspective. During this period I read aloud fiction and nonfiction stories about Navajo family life and provided books for the children to read themselves. It was better to be selective rather than overwhelm them with every book available on the subject. Each paragraph and story was chosen for a particular aesthetic or informational reason. Some books were read from cover to cover, others in part, and others were examined closely for what their pictures had to tell.

By this time several children had discovered that the Navajo are known for their extraordinary weaving skill. A teacher intern and a child who had taken the school's woodworking workshop built a Navajo loom. They warped it with several children who had taken the school's weaving class, and compared this type of weaving with other techniques. Soon everyone was involved in weaving a large hanging as well as purses, belts, and bags on simplified cardboard looms. The children insisted on authenticity and planned elaborate designs. We discussed the natural dye colors and how they are made from what is available in the desert. The children's paintings showed their heightened sensitivity to the desert landscape.

A delicate balance developed between the direction I had established and the activities in which the children became involved. As we became more deeply involved, they brought to the social studies unit what they had learned from the other classes in the school. Two students, Jemal and Errol, organized an elaborate ceremony for a Navajo feast the class prepared. They created songs, chants, music, and a dance. Another student, Rebecca, organized an improvisation based on a story I had read aloud. I invited the school's language teacher to teach us Navajo words, and Charles wrote a story using many of them. Maizie wrote a story about a Navajo girl who befriends a wild horse. When Maizie moved away, she dedicated the story to the school. As I worked with individual children, I tried to identify and encourage their strengths; it was sometimes difficult to maintain my focus as a teacher of a group of children. The school offers many opportunities for children to pursue their interests; but I could not be a private tutor for twenty-four talented individuals, nor did I want to be. An important function of school is to socialize children to work effectively as individuals within a group.

The class grew to form a productive group because there was a genuine basis for sharing. They made individual choices, but these grew out of a common theme. For example, Patricia wanted to know about Tim's water-color, and he about her natural weaving, because each project was a piece of the total study. Many children were intrigued with Ted's model of a mesa because they had written, drawn, and pretended about mesas in their own work. Working groups formed and reformed to write stories, put on plays, set up showcase exhibits, prepare frybread, and design jewelry. The structure allowed the children to investigate the varied activities as deeply as they chose and allowed me to assign work in needed skill areas.

As the children revealed more of themselves through their choices and their work, I kept notes on possible workshops to suggest for the next cycle of classes. At that time they would be able to schedule themselves into new workshops. For example, Jemal, the boy who invented the Navajo ceremony, became involved in the activities of the dance studio. Rebecca was chosen to be in the school play. The wide variety of workshops also increased the kinds of talents I came to value by allowing me to see new possibilities for children. I saw this school saying that every child can discover that he/she has something special and valuable to contribute to the group. It seemed that the more ability I saw in the children, the more it developed.

Along with the social studies unit, I taught formal reading skills with standard curriculum materials, for a portion of each day. The children did extensive reading and writing connected with their social studies projects. Listening, language, and spelling skills were taught from the materials the children wrote and performed. They bound many of their stories into books, creating a classroom literature about desert life and Navajo culture. They consulted these books many times throughout the year for information and sometimes, I felt, as a way of reminiscing about their successes. They loved to compare what they were doing with what they had done and laugh over funny episodes in the class that the stories evoked.

There were times when the study seemed to run dry because no one was excited about any project, or activities scattered from the many directions in which the children carried them. During these times I would organize a large group project, deliver new content, or teach a new skill.

This refocused the children on the material. During private or small group conferences I also helped them select several specific skills that I thought they should work on either to improve or expand their abilities. I observed the common weaknesses in the children, then designed activities to strengthen these areas. For example, in the bimonthly essay assignment I critiqued and helped the children refine their work in preparation for its final draft. Of course, there was a core of skills that were not optional; everyone was expected to read and write each day.

As I accepted their work seriously, the children grew to see it in that light. Class meetings became a time when children presented their projects to the group for discussion. It was then that I could tie the individual activities together so the children could understand the ideas the activities taught.

After working on the study for two months I wanted to see how much they had learned. I had been giving formal reading tests all along, but the social studies material demanded a different kind of evaluation, something more than a multiple choice test. It was then that I realized that I had been evaluating their progress each step of the way and used that evaluation to plan my next steps in the unit. I had the children organize and work on a large group cutpaper mural. Working in committees, they painted desert scenery and cut and pasted animals, shelter, people, and ways of transportation. I recorded the groups' discussions as they worked; it was clear where they were in their thinking by the kinds of animals they chose and the homes they made for them, by the type of natural phenomena they placed in the environment, by the way they constructed the homes, and by the way they dressed and positioned the people. They argued over where to put the hogans in relation to the mesas, where the sheep should graze, where the location of the trading post should be, and how many snakes could live on a certain size territory. The discussions revealed their careful thoughts, their consideration for each section of the mural, and their 8-year-old logic and social finesse. The mural seemed to them to be a celebration of how much they knew.

One of the most exciting projects that developed out of the study was a group improvisation directed by a drama specialist who was visiting the school. We provided several blankets, tables, and chairs for props, and she asked the children to become either a desert animal or a Navajo man, woman, or child. The scene was morning, and they were to wake up as the sun rose and go about their daily business. The children immersed themselves totally in the fantasy, and a fascinating drama began to develop: a bobcat barricaded himself in a corner with a sign that said "Beware," a tiny lamb huddled under the teacher's desk waiting to be found, old grandmothers started fires, mothers herded sheep, and fathers ordered everyone about in Navajo. Their play was punctuated with screams when blankets collapsed, but the children remained in character and repaired their hogans. After forty-five minutes the natural leaders had organized the group to build one elaborate hogan rather than many small shaky ones. The leaders, in this case all boys, instructed the women to stay home and prepare frybread while they went out to kill coyote and snakes. The hunting and killing were carried out with intense realism and exquisite control. Afterward the children discussed how they did not like being bossed around by the chief, how hard it was to get a big family to agree, how frightened the animals felt when the hunters attacked them, how the desert was a hard place to live, how hard it was to build a hogan, and how much they had accomplished while working in a group.

For many weeks after the experience the children asked for the blankets so they could continue the play. They replayed the themes each time, working over peer relationships, leadership positions, and feelings of competence within the Navajo context. The safety of "it's only a play" allowed them to deal wih issues much too emotionally powerful to be addressed directly. One of the boys spontaneously wrote dialogue, cast parts, and staged a play about a Navajo boy asking his father to get him a wildcat for a pet.

Several weeks after we had completed the Navajo study, an article appeared in the newspaper about a land dispute between the Navajo and Hopi Indian tribes. I read it to the children, planning to discuss what problems the Navajo would face if they had to leave their land. The children had so identified themselves with the Navajo that they became furious with the Hopi's demands. Errol jumped up and yelled, "Let's go get guns and help those Navajos out." Several children agreed, but Rebecca diplomatically suggested that Errol's idea wouldn't work because they do not sell guns to children. She suggested that we write letters to the President because, as most 8-years-olds believe, he can do anything. Everyone was enthusiastic, and many wrote letters. Ivan became interested only when we reminded him that he should write what he wanted to. The following excerpts reveal much of the depth of learning and feeling the study created, the confusion about difficult political issues typical of 8-year-olds, as well as the independence of some children.

> Dear Mr. president,
> please don't force the Navajo's off
> the land. Because they've been living
> on the desert for centuries and I
> don't know why the Hopi Indian's

are not proud of the land they
have. They've been living on their
land for centuries. And how would like it
if someone went up to your house
and said GET OUT OF OUR HOUSE!
And it really wasn't their house
and if we started a war it wouldn't
do much good and I think that
the Navajo's are doing the right
thing there defending there own
land are not going to move!

> Sincerely,
> Brett Abramson

I wish you'd give the Navajos a chance to
think up a solution for this tragedy . . . .
They need that extra land for crops and animals
and for food.

> Sincerely,
> Douglas Makin

Can the Navajos stay
on their land? they got all their hogans
and cactus

> Sincerely,
> Charles B.

Dear President,
I Don't care IF they
Take the land. I Want you to
take Force and BesiDes
I Don't like indians. But I like war
Movies with John Wayne. But You Write
to Me. O.K.
From,   Ivey Ageren Wright
P.S. Do You like Starwars?
If you Do I'll Draw You a Picture.

For the remainder of the year this class went on to study many of the broad concepts developed in the Navajo unit through units on the Netsilik Eskimos and the Algonquian Indians. This structure encouraged many comparisons, and by the end of the year children began initiating comparisons with their own lives. They grew more independent with each study, and the activities they suggested grew in sophistication as they participated in more workshops.

Conclusion

May and June are the months when teachers look back to September and reflect on the changes their students have made. Children work comfortably with their friends in the daily routines. This year the children unanimously feel that their school is the best place to be. They have already begun planning the workshops they want to take next year. Jemal has decided that he wants to be an actor, Tim an artist, Kim a singer. Of course, their feelings will probably change many times before they grow up. The school has opened up possibilities for them that had not existed before. It is not our intention to create precocious artists or dilettantes but to provide children with the opportunity to explore many alternatives in the arts and sciences. We want children to feel comfortable with the process of choosing; to receive the support to do what they want to do; to produce plays, dance and music recitals, science fairs, museum exhibits, poetry readings and art festivals; and to understand the discipline it takes to accomplish these things. A school that works with the talents of all its students is a place where every child can become involved. It can be a place that children love—a place to find friends, love, care, excitement, safety, challenge, and knowledge.

12

HARRY MORGAN, Syracuse University

Sensorimotor Development: Linking Cognitive and Affective Growth

An important goal of schooling in America is to enable all children to experience their own excellence. All learners have a need to fully comprehend basic concepts from cognitive perspective and to be able to demonstrate this understanding through figuring, writing, computing, reading, and other functional performances. There should also be opportunities to advance these basic skills beyond the minimal uses to which they can be put. Affective opportunities are necessary to enable learners to build on their knowledge in active, thoughtful, and creative ways. For example, we know that good individual performances in activities like ballet and gymnastics are subject to the laws of physics, and that music takes shape through the use of mathematical formulas. We also know that physics and mathematics serve only as a backdrop to these creative arts and a cognitive understanding, a feeling for the basic elements, is an essential ingredient for a fully satisfying experience.

Researchers in education have attempted to separate this feeling from function by using the terms *cognitive* and *affective*. These terms have evolved from earlier basic notions—they now imply identity, self-worth, and the attainment of competence that can come from one's *belief* that one can do well in formal (classroom) and informal (outside of school hours) learning environments. The environment in which formal learning takes place has

169

three fundamental elements: teacher-student interaction, student-student interactions, and planned activities. From the learner's perspective, the teacher, the classroom, and the materials are all a part of the environment.

There are different styles of learning and various methods of teaching that alter classroom interactions and activities.[1] An understanding of teaching styles and methods can be obtained by examining the relationship between the learner and the environment. The didactic or lecture method allows very little ongoing interaction between teacher and learner. Because the teacher is a part of the learner's environment, the lecture method provides an active role for the environment and a docile role for the learner. The opposite of the lecture method would require the teacher to become an observer, an omnipresent resource person as needed by the learner. The environment would be inactive whereas the learner, needing the motivation necessary to exploit materials, facilities, and adults to promote his own learning, would become active.

Teaching methods that encourage students to be active participants in their own learning are probably more effective than those methods that have fewer opportunities for student interaction with teachers and peers. I suggest a method that is between the aforementioned extremes—an active role for both the learner and the environment.

It is also important that educators and parents make a firm commitment to the belief that it is part of the essential nature of our civilization to fully recognize ethnic and cultural diversity. Therefore, it should be the right of all children to experience a learning environment that provides an understanding of the various cultures continuously fashioned by the human race. This commitment is as important in racially isolated schools as it is in the most fully integrated. It is essential that we place the concern for human betterment at the top of our priorities; if we are successful, a belief in human dignity will pervade the educational experience for children and teachers. The education establishment needs to be directed away from the insidious way in which schools can reinforce stereotypes in books, programs, and behaviors—where girls are herded into homemaking and black males into football for the wrong reasons. Many curriculum innovations, designed to further academic opportunities for children are, in fact, designed for political reasons unrelated to better education.[2]

How can we develop an educational environment for human behavior that includes a conceptual comprehension of basic skills and the capabilities

---

[1] Nathan Kogan, Cognitive Styles in Infancy and Early Childhood, *LEA*, 1976.

[2] Harry Morgan, Demands for Recognition—and Beyond Educational Leadership, *Journal of the Association for Supervision and Curriculum Development*, 1969, 27(3), 229-231.

to put these skills to work? Such an environment should provide a variety of activities and instructors. Occasionally, the instructors would need to perform their tasks in a discrete didactic manner, as in a lecture. For the most part, instructors would facilitate the student's participation in the learning/teaching process.

To encourage participation, students need an opportunity to select activities from a variety of attractive possibilities. A thoughtful approach to integrate the basic elements of these activities into the curriculum of the school is essential. For example, students who read well can probably get a more rewarding experience from theater or industrial arts because of their reading skills. Students in athletic activities can improve their performance if they are academically self-fulfilled; they could also work problems out logically and thoughtfully.

Some athletic directors, not aware of this, try to get star players excused from regular classes to enable them to practice longer in the gym or on the playing field. This special treatment too often creates an arrogant athlete and other dissident players annoyed by this unfair practice. Embedded in some athletic circles is the notion, promoted by early researchers, that suggested that children were able to excel only in physical activities or in academic activities—not both. A low level of academic achievement was assumed for the best players. The occasional excellent scholar who did well in athletics was seen as the exception. Many parents discouraged their children from athletic activities and sports for these same reasons. In fact, activities like basketball and football require high levels of cognitive and physical output simultaneously. The player must process a vast amount of information in an extremely short period of time, then transform this knowledge into behavior most suitable for the rapidly changing and unfolding action. This displays individual competence for cognitive (information processing) and motoric (physical output) outlay—with coordination and circular reinforcement from one domain to the other.

It now appears that black males excel in athletic activities far beyond their representation in the general population. Black athletes have transformed basketball into a fast, rocketing, active game to fit a style that for many years could be observed only in inner city playgrounds. Playground athletes in the black community contrasted sharply with white-dominated basketball fifteen years ago. The earlier style was conservative, formalized, and contained neither innovation nor unpredictable behavior. This apparently advanced sensorimotor development in black children displays itself not only in adult athletic activities but also at several intervals along the life span. We know from pediatricians who treat multiracial and multicultural families that black infants have more advanced motor skills than white infants. Black infants frequently reach certain sensorimotor milestones (crawling, sitting, standing, and walking) ahead of their white counterparts.[3]

Black children are energetic, spirited, and aggressive learners. They possess an almost voracious appetite in their desire to take in everything within their purview. This is a constant challenge to the teacher who must stick to a lesson plan, and unsettling for institutions that are unable to assimilate this form of creativity.

Rural black children, for the most part, assimilate into the methodological didactic process and rarely strike out against it. This is also true of black children who are in the extreme minority in white schools. We may never know how much of their learning potential is sacrificed in these settings.

Their urban counterparts are a different matter. They assert their energetic style of learning, make heavy demands on the institution, constantly test the system, and in the process lay bare its ambiguities, failures, and inconsistencies. These children tend to get into trouble in the process.

Nancy Bayley, in making a comparison of mental and motor test scores among black, white, and Puerto Rican babies, found no significant group differences in mental test scores. The black babies, however, scored higher than the Puerto Rican and white babies on the motor scale.[4] Superior motor development was observed in American black infants to exist through the age of twenty-four months. It was also reported that black and white infants compared equally in other areas of behavioral development.[5] Similar precocity was observed among black babies of Jamaican West Indian parents. Other investigators reported that these infants surpassed American white infants in reaching certain milestones—creeping, standing, and walking.[6] Williams and Scott, in comparing 104 black infants from moderate-income families with fifty infants from low-income families, found significant differences between the two groups in motor development. Infants from the

---

[3] M.D.S. Ainsworth, *Infancy in Uganda: Infant Care and the Growth of Love* (Baltimore: Johns Hopkins Press, 1967); M. Geber, Developpement Psychomoteur de l'Enfant Africain, *Courrier*, 1956, *6*, 17-29; M. Geber, L'Enfant Africain Occidentalise et de Niveau Social Superior en Uganda," *Courrier*, 1958, *8*, 517-523; M. Geber, Problemes Poses par le Developpement Du Jeune Enfant Africain en Fonetion de son Milieu Sc Social, *Le Travail Humain*, 1960, *23*, 97-111.

[4] Nancy Bayley, Comparison of Mental and Motor Test Scores for Ages 1—15 Months by Sex, Birth Order, Geographic Location and Education of Parents, *Child Development*, 1965, *36*, 374-411.

[5] B. A. Pasamanick, A Comparative Study of the Behavioral Development of Negro Infants, *Journal of Genetic Psychology*, 1946, *69*, 3-44.

[6] M. W. Curti, F. B. Marshall, and M. Steggerda, The Gesell Schedules Applied to 1, 2 and 3-year-old Negro Children of British West Indies, *Journal of Comparative Neurology*, 1935, *20*, 125.

low-income families showed a more advanced motor development than those from moderate-income families.[7]

Another important aspect of schooling affecting black children is a phenomenon that has become known as the "third grade syndrome." From some sophisticated group measures, it appears that most children—black and white, male and female—achieve at about the same academic rate until the third grade. After third grade, black children seem to do less well academically than white children. Why? There are several theories, and each, in part, may contribute to this phenomenon. The inequality hypothesis asserts that school systems do not distribute resources equitably That is, middle-class schools are favored in the assignment of staff, classes, materials, and other resources. The culture gap hypothesis assumes that the values and status of teachers tend to be incongruent with those of students and their families. Another theory, the self-fulfilling prophecy, suggests that learners tend to achieve at a level expected of them by their teachers; if the teacher holds a student in low esteem, the teacher will teach indifferently and convey negative attitudes. Students will sense this and reduce expectations of their own competence, thereby fulfilling the teacher's prophecy. Where these aforementioned circumstances exist, they can account for some academic disparity.

It is my view that because of the sensorimotor development of black infants, an active environment appears necessary for maximizing their learning potential, rather than what the child might perceive as a docile, sterile classroom. Three essential aspects of classroom learning—child—child, teacher—child interaction, and nurturing often found in the early grades—cease at the end of the third grade. It is here that black children, in group-measured terms, stop keeping up with white children academically. My observations also suggest that an unusually large number of black children who do not read well in junior high school have reading scores between 3.0 and 4.0. This further indicates that their successful encounter with schooling stopped at the third or fourth grade.

In a research project conducted in cooperation with the Syracuse Public Schools, several eighth grade classes were observed for one academic year. An English teacher was asked to establish a classroom environment where students would be allowed to interact freely with her, their peers, and selected materials in completing their classroom assignments. We suggested this teaching style because we wanted to observe styles of students in their

[7] J. R. Williams and R. B. Scott, Growth and Development of Negro Infants: Motor Development and Its Relationship to Child Rearing Practices in Two Groups of Negro Infants, *Child Development*, 1953, *24*, 103-121.

174 Curriculum—Leadership, Philosophy, Strategy

approach to school work. Our video tape recordings of these class periods revealed that black male children interacted with the teacher and other students many more times than other students. Black females were the next most active, white females the least.[8] In the absence of an active learning environment, some black children, I suspect, tend to get into trouble because of their learning style.

Initially, I am suggesting that the black child's energy is not intended to be chaotic or disruptive, but strategic to his style of learning. Schools need to expand the ways in which knowledge can be properly disseminated by the educator—and received and synthesized by the learner. Often, the interaction between the active child's motor energy and the school's common reaction to it inadvertently compels a miniature battleground.

The Children's Defense Fund, a project of the Washington Research Project, compiled statistics directly related to this subject. They reported that more than one million children were suspended from school one or more times during the 1972–1973 academic year. There did not seem to be any substantial differential based on geographic location or size of school district, city, or state. More than 63 per cent of the suspensions were for minor offenses such as cutting into the lunch line, talking back to the teacher, and truancy. Less than 3 per cent were for serious acts of destruction, criminal activity, or use of narcotics. In those districts from which the statistics were derived, one out of every twenty-four students was suspended. For black secondary school children, the suspension rate was *one out of every eight*.[9]

Many school environments and teaching styles require docile quietude; too often this results in a negative view of active encounters with learning activities. This can establish a punitive school policy toward student spiritedness and stifle creative use of facilities and materials. However, children could be provided opportunity to move about the classroom and school on their own for independent work in the library, gymnasium, auditorium, or resource areas. A comprehensive approach to planning would design school activities and learning environments that serve to expand children's learning opportunities. When such a comprehensive approach is contemplated, there are at least two important areas to study. One is teaching styles; the other is a planned set of activities that support sensorimotor needs.

Within the highly socialized environment of the early grades black children progress at a regular learning rate. The early childhood classroom is an efficient workroom where play is viewed as work, not merely movement without planned, purposeful involvement. The facilitating teacher would

[8] Elizabeth Einstein, Classroom Dynamos, *Human Behavior*, 1979, *8(4)*, 58-59.

[9] Washington Research Project, *Children Out of School in America* (Cambridge, Mass.: Children's Defense Fund, 1975).

introduce activities aimed at increasing the children's awareness of the world around them. Themes would be elaborated: first from the environment, such as communications, media, transportation, food supply, organizing chores, caring for pets and plants, building, cooking, music, and dance, and then from those aspects of the community in which the children see relationships, solve problems, and use skills. A well-organized classroom would provide teacher—child and child—child interaction as a basic aspect of the fundamental design. As children move up through the grades a typical school should encourage activities that provide for physical expression and integrate these activities into the regular school program—not merely offer an isolated sport here and there. Activities such as theater, dance, music, and gymnastics are included in the physical arts. Other activities, like trips, school and classwide projects, and student-directed activities, provide opportunities to positively direct and thereby diffuse the child's buildup of natural energy.

Sensorimotor differentiation as I have described it implies that school environments now in common practice are apparently designed to suit the learning needs of children from white families as opposed to the natural characteristics of certain black children,[10] and, if this is true, public schooling is making it increasingly difficult for black children to comply with the demands made upon them by the system. The fact that these children establish their own set of behavior norms, to which individuals and groups can conform, should not surprise us. Their behavior can be disruptive when a planned learning environment lacks elements that ought to complement sensorimotor energy.

As adults, we become frustrated when utility companies or department stores seem uninterested in a problem we might have with them, or unwilling to resolve it in our favor. We can become assertive and even hostile when they are not as impressed with our problem as we are. When learners interpret teaching behavior as not really interested in what they are feeling and needing, they, too, tend to become rude and boisterous. For them it is more than a simple phone call to the manager—it is going against a system that has the support of all levels of school administration, their neighborhood and often their family.[11]

The family should be kept aware of school programming and student achievement. If families are expected to support the work of the school, they need to be well informed. In very fundamental ways the family contrives to be the prime source of education for its members. Schooling has never constituted the whole of one's source of information. For this reason, as well

---

[10] C. J. Rich, The Difference at Birth (quote of T. Berry Brazelton), *Race Relations Reporter*, 1973, *4(17)*.

[11] Harry Morgan, op.cit.

as others, educators need to connect what they do to the learner's world of reality outside of school. Despite the fact that the entry point for schooling is age 5 or 6, and junior high school personnel do not see children until they are age 12 or 13, educators need to be in touch with children prior to their entry into their particular network.

Child-rearing practices in our country have varied somewhat over the years, having been influenced primarily by middle-class norms. Trends known to affect parental styles have been introduced by child-rearing professionals who are read and respected by members of this socioeconomic group. Lower socioeconomic families striving for higher status readily adopt attributes that they identify as appropriate to the group(s) above them. Lower socioeconomic people are willing to acquire many such attributes to remove the barriers between themselves and the middle class.

Black parents in general, and black low-income people in particular, are afraid that if their children do not modify their spiritedness they will not be able to assimilate into the American middle class. It is often true that as black parents they have not been able to assimilate into the cultural mainstream of America themselves. Too often, because of this fear, they will equate their child's motoric activity with aggression and devalue their child's naturalness by defining their activeness as "being bad."

We now know that cognitive capabilities and a readiness to learn have been identified at birth, or a few hours thereafter among black and white infants. Parents need to know that they can begin to support the work of the school early in their child's life. They need access to the most learned information in this regard. Good, up-to-date information, materials, and advice should be available to all families whether their children attend school or not.

Black mothers ought to be encouraged to play with their babies and share in the enjoyment of active, frequent eye contact and exciting periods of child rearing. They need to be encouraged to interact with their infants' motor excitement and support their natural capabilities. The mother's reciprocity is vital to a sustained growth environment for her baby because of cultural expectations. The infant's rapid buildup early in life can be expected to diminish if, through adaptational stress, black parents are forced to bring their family personalities into compliance with the dominant white culture.[12]

Conclusion

I have attempted in this chapter to promote an educational environment that enables all learners to become as competent as their natural talents will

[12] C. J. Rich, op.cit.

allow. I believe that the goals for educating all children should be the same. To focus solely on cognitive skills, learning deficits, or affective development would perpetuate a dangerous one-sidedness by depriving children of the attributes that all children need to develop active, thoughtful, and creative ways of coping with their environment.

PART THREE Curriculum— Specific Educational Models

This section deals with specific educational programs for the gifted/talented student from the preschool years through high school.

The Strickland chapter describes desirable components of an educational program designed for the pre-elementary and primary grades. Emphasis in this chapter is placed on knowing the child and providing a responsive emotional and physical environment. The author stresses the need for balancing cognitive and affective concerns and points out the possible detrimental effects on gifted/talented children when human qualities are neglected because of an overemphasis on cognitive skills.

Based on the premise that school programs cannot and must not be the same for all students, the Marks chapter describes in detail three alternative choices for the gifted/talented adolescent, all within the public school system. Explained in detail for each school within a school are organizational composition—such as the composition of staff and students—guidance, sites, grouping, content focus, decision making, evaluating students, and building schedules.

The Stave chapter deals with gifted/talented students as they move through the upper grades of a public school system. Planning and implementation of alternative programs within the high school are detailed by Mr. Stave. He shares with the reader past experiences and future expectations.

13

DOROTHY S. STRICKLAND, Kean College of New Jersey

Nurturing the Gifts and Talents of Young Learners

The significance of the early years of schooling cannot be overestimated. Universal acceptance of the importance of the prekindergarten, kindergarten, and primary grades has never been greater. What does or does not happen during this critical period will most assuredly affect the child's general posture toward school and toward learning in general. The total range of the child's development is thus influenced.

The pre-elementary and primary grades are generally considered to be the place to build the foundation for the basics. What the basics are and how they are to be developed are questions that curriculum decision makers struggle with constantly.

Most would agree that any sound program for young children will seek to foster health and physical development, provide intellectual stimulation, promote social awareness and a positive self-concept, and promote curiosity and creativity. The means toward these ends will vary from school to school and from district to district. They will depend on the values of the decision makers and their conviction about what is or is not important in an educational program. Their convictions will be based on a combination of factors: their philosophy of education, their beliefs about how children learn, and their perception of contemporary societal values.

The school can and must provide an educational program at this early childhood level (ages 4 to 9) that will offer opportunities for every child to discover his/her gifts and talents and simultaneously provide alternatives for those children who demonstrate unusual ability. The decisions that determine how this is accomplished should be based on current knowledge in the field relevant to knowing the learner and providing a responsive environment.

These should be considered with the ultimate goal in mind of helping children internalize what they learn, so that they may apply their knowledge, strengthen it, and put it to use for personal self-expression.

Knowing the Learner

Knowing the learner involves a knowledge of and respect for each child's individuality.

> Whenever a teacher, parent, therapist, or other person with a facilitating function feels basically that the individual is of worth in his own right and in his own unfolding, no matter what his present condition or behavior, he is fostering creativity.[1]

Probably the single most important principle for educators to keep in mind as they plan for children is that each is an individual worthy of dignity and respect for his/her uniqueness. This requires parents and teachers to have faith in children and in their potential. Such faith should not be based on past performance or products but on the child's present state, no matter what it may be. It says to the child, "Take risks. Try something new. You are allowed not to succeed. Not succeeding is not the same as failing. It is an important and necessary part of the learning process."

A respect for individuality suggests that the early childhood programs must be flexible enough to accommodate a variety of cognitive styles and learning rates. Materials and activities must broaden the range of options rather than reduce them to a lock step, narrowly defined curriculum.

Respect for individuality should in no way imply that early childhood programs must provide classroom instruction that is primarily one-to-one. Such an organizational pattern would be inefficient and inappropriate, because children need the stimulation and benefit of interaction with their peers in small and large group situations.

What is implied is an organizational pattern that provides for a planned balance among whole group, small group, and one-to-one instruction. Even in whole and small group situations, however, teachers should be adept at getting varied response and follow-up to a single stimulus.

For example, the responses to a literature selection read aloud to a

[1] Carl R. Rogers, Toward a Theory of Creativity, in Sidney J. Paines and Harold F. Harding. (Eds.), *A Source Book for Creative Thinking* (New York: Scribners, 1962), p. 70.

group of children may be planned so that individual expression is fostered and a wide range of opportunities for success are offered. Following are just a few of the possibilities that might be offered for children to extend their enjoyment of a story read aloud:

- Browse through the book individually.
- Draw a picture or construct something related to the story.
- Draw a picture related to the story and dictate a caption.
- Draw a picture related to the story and write a caption on your own.
- Help dramatize a part of the story.
- Retell the story, possibly using a tape recorder.

Knowledge of the learner's individuality becomes important as the teacher plans options and helps children select them. By providing options that reflect both variety in mode of expression and variety in levels of ability, children are allowed to reveal their talents and abilities. The observant teacher learns more about the children in the group and is better able to challenge their strengths.

Programs that are narrow in scope and primarily require all children to do the same task in the same manner have little or no opportunities for options and reveal only what children know or do not know about the given tasks. In such programs special talents and abilities may go unnoticed and fail to be nurtured because they are not discovered. It is not uncommon to find children in such programs whose ability to read or excel in some other area goes unnoticed by a prekindergarten or kindergarten teacher. Most important, the possibilities for such talents to develop naturally are lessened.

Knowing the learner involves providing opportunities for children to learn through a variety of firsthand interactions with people, materials, and natural resources in their environment. Young children learn best when they have an opportunity to explore through their senses. They need to touch, taste, feel, and see for themselves in order to learn. Direct experiences with natural phenomena and with people who have interesting things to share should be encouraged. These direct experiences can act as catalysts for activities, such as the options described earlier as possible responses to literature.

Field trips, experimentation with materials in the classroom, and utilization of community resource people are critical ingredients in the learning process. Opportunities of this sort with appropriate follow-up offer exposure to new ideas and opportunities to explore them and try them out.

Opportunities in the classroom for cooking foods, growing things, and caring for live animals are just a few of the many possibilities for direct experiences. Any of these can be extended through experience charts that detail recipes, or directions for planting, or caring for an animal. Books containing additional information may be read to or by children and then discussed. Media presentations, such as films and filmstrips, may be used. Visits to a local bakery, nursery, a neighborhood garden, or a pet shop may serve to extend understanding. Visits to the classroom by appropriate people should also be arranged.

As teachers engage groups in such activities, they should always be observant of the child who demonstrates a special penchant and ability in certain areas. These abilities need nurturing. For example, the youngster who asks good questions of the neighborhood gardener might be asked to interview the local florist or nursery owner. A list of two or three questions may be generated and either dictated to the teacher or written by the child. Parental help should be enlisted to provide transportation to and from the interview. This could be a special assignment for the child: interviewing a community person and reporting the results to the class.

The prekindergarten youngster who shows a special talent in math or reading might be the one to set the timer for baking or help explain the various abbreviations on the stove controls. Older children or academically advanced young children who are capable of reading can be encouraged to read through simple recipe books designed for children. Again, parental help both in and out of the classroom can be invaluable here. Most parents are eager to help, especially when their children are excited about learning and trying things out on their own.

Visits to the classroom by knowledgeable or talented local people can add immeasurably to children's understanding. Local artisans and others involved in the creative arts help children to realize that people help to create the beauty around them, thus children become aware of the range of possibilities for their own creative urges. One caution, however! When visitors are invited to the school to share informally with children (as opposed to performing), keep the groups as small as possible. One or two classes listening to a local potter tell about and show his/her work are far different from the same presentation given from a stage in an auditorium filled with all the kindergarten and primary classes. The latter is not truly a firsthand experience in the sense that it is meant here.

Firsthand experiences are important for all children at every age. The observant teacher will make use of such experiences to identify particular talents. This information should be used to plan special firsthand projects in the areas of interest to the individuals identified. Most important, they act as a catalyst for additional firsthand and vicarious learning activities that are generally restricted only by the imagination and energy of the adults in the classroom.

Knowing the learner involves offering numerous opportunities for children to experiment with and test-out both materials and ideas.

The importance of firsthand experiences has already been emphasized; some would call it the key to learning among young children. Actually, when we provide that key we are opening the child to the opportunity to experiment and to test. This is where the real learning takes place.

Opportunities to use manipulative materials and to discuss their ideas (conceptions and misconceptions) about things are vitally important to children's learning. As children manipulate objects, they grow in understanding—not because of any properties inherent in the objects alone or by what we as adults tell them about the objects. They learn because of what they do with those objects.

For example, at a very early age children can learn to recite the names of numbers or letters of the alphabet. This is largely because of their marvelous ability to imitate. It tells us very little about their knowledge of number concepts or about their ability to read.

When young children experiment with water, sand, blocks, and other materials, they are learning about such concepts as quantity, distance, size, number, and space. They may match or count to determine how many more blocks are needed to complete a structure, or who has "too many" or "too few" of the cookies that are being distributed.

When children discover similar words and letters on a chart story that has been dictated and discussed, they are beginning to learn something about the speech-to-print process, and how our alphabet operates as a code. Children become involved in the process, ask questions, and begin to experiment on their own. The encouragement of this experimentation and interest often becomes the means whereby the gifted child is challenged and moves ahead. For all children, however, it is the means whereby the concepts become their own.

Creative teaching in which opportunities are presented to solve problems is an excellent way to challenge children to experiment and test. The problem should be related to something of interest, such as a topic currently under study. Small groups of four to six children seem to work best for this purpose. The children are presented with the problem. Materials for solving the problem are available, but not identified as such. The children are then left to brainstorm possible solutions, select those that appear most worthwhile, and test them out. Children who show extraordinary ability in such activities should not only work with small groups but also be given additional more challenging problems to solve.

Knowing the learner involves encouraging children to communicate in a wide variety of ways. Children learn to communicate by listening, talking, making gestures, moving, exhibiting facial expressions, and by reading and writing. A program for young learners should be broad enough to provide experiences with all of these. Truly nurturing gifts and talents means going beyond the academic gifts to foster an atmosphere of respect for the talents children demonstrate.

This requires a program with planned opportunities for graphic arts, woodworking, modeling, music and movement, and physical activities—as well as the usual academic components. Unless children are given opportunities to express themselves in a variety of ways, neither they nor the school will be able to discover unusual gifts and talents.

Again, the most fundamental need at this point is for the classroom teacher to plan special projects and provide special opportunities for the development of the interests and abilities uncovered. Beyond this, some schools may wish to provide pull-out classes or groups where children may explore their special interests. These may take the form of after-school clubs or special programs for talented/gifted children.

Knowing the learner involves allowing children to share in decisions related to what and how they learn. Children learn best when they are active participants in the instructional process. Even very young children can be a part of decisions concerning what will be studied and how to go about it. This by no means suggests an abrogation of authority on the part of the teacher. It merely suggests that teachers be alert to the natural interests of children and seek ways to use those natural interests to develop the basic skills and key concepts in each subject area included in the curriculum.

For example, concepts of space, time, change adaptation, variety, interrelationship, equilibrium, and balance are all basic or key concepts of science. An understanding of these concepts may be explored in a variety of ways. It becomes the responsibility of all those who determine the curriculum to decide which aspects of these concepts will be explored at any given stage, and whether it be taught at the introductory, mastery, or review level. The actual content for exploration of the concept becomes less important than the children's ability to use these understandings to organize their experiences and process new information about their world.

For example, a trip to the zoo might precipitate a discussion of how various animals adapt to the winter season. Caring for animals within the classroom can do the same thing, however. Whenever possible, children's suggestions about how to proceed in their investigation should be sought and acknowledged as an important part of the learning process. Suggestions about projects, books to share on a subject, and ways to display or demonstrate what has been learned are all possibilities for children to share in decision making.

Knowing the learner involves providing opportunities for children to express both what they know and how they feel.

Children need opportunities to communicate their feelings and to share in what others are feeling. The curriculum should be designed to simultaneously foster affective and cognitive development in young children. For example, children who are surrounded by books and who are introduced to good stories and poetry learn in a most enjoyable way about written communication as both an affective and a cognitive experience. They learn to respond to plot and characterization and to be sensitive to poetic expression. They learn that their own ideas and feelings can be transmitted through the written word.

Opportunities to express and share feelings through writing, art, dance, and music will be important to all children. Children who demonstrate particular talent in these areas need outlets, both to discover their own gifts and to share them with others.

Knowing the learner involves encouraging unique, child-initiated approaches to a given task. At first glance, this principle may seem to be identical to the one just previously discussed. The two are quite different, however. Encouraging unique, child-initiated approaches to a given task goes beyond soliciting children's advice in the decision-making process. It allows children at least some opportunities to proceed in ways that may appear inappropriate to the teacher.

Respect and faith in the child who appears to see things in a different way do not come easily to many teachers and parents. It is easier and safer to be supportive of efforts that typify a more standard or commonplace way of doing things. Indeed, at first it is not always easy to distinguish between true creativity or ingenuity and nonconformity for its own sake. Nevertheless, an open flexible atmosphere is important. When the child's desire to create new ideas or things is consistently stifled, he/she may either become a discipline problem or retreat into a pattern of conformity in order to gain approval.

Creating a balance between the needs of the individual and the constraints of working in a group setting is not an easy task. The more capable the teacher is at creating a good balance, the better the gifts and talents of the learner will be nurtured.

Knowing the learner involves recognizing the need for pleasurable learning experiences. Among early childhood educators, phrases like "Play is the child's work" and "Thinking is child's play" are often used. Such phrases point out the importance of play in the life of the child and its relationship to learning.

In the early years almost everything the child does is perceived as play to him/her. Teachers often refer to learning activities as games. But whether what children do in school is referred to as work or as play is unimportant. What is important is that children find learning a pleasurable activity. When children derive pleasure from learning as its own reward, they are better motivated to improve their skills.

If schools develop their curricula by what is known about how children learn, they will attempt to provide as many pleasurable experiences as possible for children. Children are naturally curious, happy, and eager to learn. These are attitudes on which to build and expand into lifetime postures.

Knowing the learner involves providing a flexible structure—balancing planned and incidental learning.

When principals are asked what they look for when selecting teachers of programs for talented/gifted children, invariably the word *flexibility* will be included in the description. Flexibility suggests teaching that makes maximum use of both direct and incidental methods. It suggests a program that has specific objectives but is not so locked-in that the experiences leading to mastery of those objectives are fully prescribed in advance. It also indicates a program in which some purposes and objectives actually grow out of the experiences themselves.

King contrasts direct and incidental teaching of the development of prereading skills in the following manner:

Direct Teaching	Incidental Teaching
Objectives projected into experiences.	Purposes arise out of experiences.
Emphasis on intellectual development.	Emphasis on psychological and social climate.
Analysis of knowledge and skills necessary.	Assessment of potential of children and environment.
Sequence of specific learning experiences.	Integrated learning experiences based on needs and interests.
Formal scheduling with definite time allocation.	Informal scheduling through large blocks of time.
Objective evaluation.	Skills embedded in interdisciplinary studies.
	Subjective evaluation.[2]

Balancing direct and indirect teaching has numerous instructional

----

[2] Ethel King, Prereading Programs: Direct Versus Incidental Teaching, *Reading Teacher*, 1978, *31*, 504-510.

implications; it implies a lack of dependency on published materials. Certainly, the use of a single reading, math, or science program should be avoided. While preplanned, direct teaching should be an important part of the day's activities; it should not be done in a regimented restrictive manner. A high priority should be given to pupil-initiated activities and to instruction that requires pupils to make their own association and generalization.

Providing a Responsive Environment

The Emotional Climate

In the previous section on "Knowing the Learner" much was said relevant to providing a positive emotional environment in the classroom. Teachers need to respond to children's feelings as well as their academic accomplishments. Talents and gifts related to areas beyond cognitive or measurable accomplishments must be valued.

A sense of security will prevail in a classroom where children are allowed to help make decisions about goals and activities and where their ideas are encouraged and respected. Such a program expects challenging ideas from children, not passive compliance. Teachers will ask questions designed to provoke thinking and elicit active participation.

A responsive environment requires that every child be given opportunities for success. In every sense it will be the school's responsibility to nurture the gifts and talents of every youngster regardless of the form they take. This means providing alternatives and options within the classroom and offering special opportunities that might take the form of a pull-out program.

The Physical Environment

The physical environment can add to or detract from the emotional climate in the classroom. It can serve to establish boundaries and promote natural control. It should be both comfortable and efficient.

The physical arrangement of an early childhood classroom will contain numerous interest areas and displays of concrete materials. Displays of children's work will adorn the walls and counters. These materials will not merely serve as background for an attractive classrom; they also will be used as part of the instruction.

The physical arrangement will facilitate active rather than passive learning. Furniture will be arranged so as to accommodate whole group, small group, and one-to-one instruction. A variety of media for self-expression will be available. Pupils will be taught to use the materials independently as well as under teacher direction and to care for materials, books, and equipment in a responsible manner.

The importance of encouraging pupil independence in classroom management cannot be overestimated. Among the gifts and talents to be nurtured in young children are leadership and responsibility. Unless children are given leadership roles and share responsibilities in the classroom, they will not discover their own strengths in these areas, nor will these strengths be discovered and nurtured by others.

Equally important, when children assist in the planning and maintainance of the physical aspects of the room, they tend to use the facilities with greater ease and effectiveness, thus freeing the adults from some of the routine matters related to instruction and allowing more time for quality interaction with individuals and small groups.

Although an attractive, varied atmosphere within the school is essential for getting the most from children, it should only be considered as one part of the total learning environment. The "classroom" is wherever teacher and pupils are learning. This may be in any part of the school building or the community at large.

Balancing Cognitive and Affective Concerns

The trend toward earlier identification of gifted/talented children and the creation of special programs for them have produced positive and negative criticisms. On the one hand, such programs have the potential to ensure a richer and more stimulating environment for all of the children in a given school or school district. This happens when teachers recognize that a more stimulating and interesting learning environment is conducive to better learning for all children—no matter what their intellectual capacities or special talents may be.

Special programs for talented/gifted children can have a detrimental effect, however, when there is an overemphasis on the development of cognitive skills. Such overemphasis often results in the neglect of important human qualities needed to produce successful, well-rounded individuals. Indeed, qualities such as curiosity, self-expression, and creativity—all characteristic of gifted/talented children—may actually be thwarted rather than nurtured in such an environment.

The move toward providing extensive intellectual content in the pre-elementary curriculum has had important implications for the teaching of reading, in particular. In some schools it has produced a radical change from the complete absence of any hint of formal reading instruction to the inclusion of highly structured reading/language programs in which large groups of children are taught in a routine, systematic way. School administrators may boast that their gifted pupils are not allowed to merely "play" in school. Gifted readers may sometimes be placed in upper grades to receive advanced instruction, with little thought given to their emotional and social developmental needs. Whether or not special programs exist for them, young gifted children need opportunities for reading and writing instruction within their own peer group setting. This is consistent with the need to provide a wide range of materials and opportunities for learning at many ability levels within every classroom.

Providing a proper balance between affective and cognitive goals and objectives can be a serious problem for those seeking to enrich their programs for gifted/talented young children. In many schools a false dichotomy has been created between affective and cognitive learning, when in fact an effective program should stress the use of one to foster the other. Specifically, the language program should keep opportunities for learning to read and write in proper perspective, providing them as a part of a total language arts program and offering a wide range of experiences for self-expression. These experiences should develop naturally from those things children care about. In this way young children will begin the task of learning to read through exposure to reading about themselves and their world.

Conclusion

As educators of young children we are constantly making decisions that affect their lives. Indeed, making decisions is perhaps one way to describe what teaching is all about.

Decisions must be made about what to teach, when to begin teaching it, in what order (if any) it should be presented, what materials are best to use, what instructional practices to employ, and so on. The challenges seem endless. But, in one way or another, they are met.

Our values are implicit in the kinds of decisions we make, and thus they are ultimately reflected in the nature of the program we provide. Our convictions about what is or is not important in an educational program for young children stem from a combination of factors: our philosophy of education, our beliefs about how children learn, and our perception of contemporary societal values. Ultimately, our goal is to nurture the development of each child to his/her fullest potential. Lowenfeld stated it well:

> You can teach subjects and subject-matter forever, you can "adjust" a child to his environment forever; and, if you are lucky, you may find a way to teach a

child subject matter and "adjust" him at the same time; but—and this is the big but—if your child cannot apply creatively his knowledge, he cannot make the kinds of contributions to society which "break through barriers."[3]

---

[3] Victor Lowenfeld, Creativity: Education's Stepchild, in *A Source Book for Creative Thinking* by Sidney J. Paines and Harold F. Harding (Eds.) (New York: Scribners, 1962), pp. 10-11.

Education for the Gifted/Talented Adolescent

The major and most important areas affecting children in a school system are its curriculum and instructional program. Curriculum in a general sense encompasses all that happens as a result of school activity. This includes both planned and unplanned, structured and unstructured activity. Curriculum is the "stuff" that schools are about. Instruction involves technique, method, style, and/or delivery of the school activity, or stuff. The total school program then is the umbrella under which curriculum and instruction operate.

Schools develop personalities as a result of their programs. Facilitators of this personality development are curriculum and instruction—which can be characterized by rigidity, by flexibility, by creativity, by sharing, by serving a rule, by a student orientation, by a faculty orientation, and so on.

The school program for the gifted/talented should be a smorgasbord of experiences prepared by students and staff for the gifted/talented. The keys to good curriculum are flexibility and creativeness, held together with the desire to create in an atmosphere charged with the idea that our task is not always to prove, but to improve. The curriculum cannot and must not be the same for all individuals.

The modes of instruction must be seasoned with the condiments of variety, shared planning, and experimentation. The point is that a public school system that maximizes consumer choice legitimizes new as well as old educational approaches to common objectives. The new educational approach will be made operational by public consent. Moreover, educators will also be able to choose from among these educational alternatives, possibly enhancing their sense of professional satisfaction.

The aspect of experimentation allows for failure to be perceived in a different manner. Rather than fearing it, teachers and administrators realize that it is part of the process and use it to their benefit—in terms of adapting future programs or using it to jump off to further experimentation. The very nature of experimentation removes failure as a threat and makes people more willing to try new and more varied ideas. For those teachers uncomfortable in an atmosphere of continued change and innovation, careful attention must be given to providing administrative support.

Teachers should be placed in this program who will be stimulated by its challenges and demands. The vehicle of different organizations under one roof offers the benefit of allowing educators to work in close collaboration with their colleagues. Those who see team teaching as a preferable method of teaching are afforded that opportunity. On the other hand, teachers who feel more effective in an autonomous situation can work in that manner.

This choice model, therefore, tends to minimize conflict among interest groups because each individual is making direct decisions in educational affairs. Furthermore, as a supply and demand model the choice system has a self-revitalizing capability. As the options prove successful, they will increase in popularity—thereby increasing the flow of successful programs into the public schools and generating a renewal process for public education. School systems are currently structured to present only one model or pattern of education to students and parents. It should be possible to develop within one school or cluster of schools within a neighborhood, district, or system several different models that would offer real choices to all those involved in the educative process.

In this belief the planning of a differentiated program can be accomplished in the following manner:

First, a basic outline of three distinct educational models is formulated.

Second, a series of large and small group meetings should be planned with all staff involved with the program to present these ideas to students and their families.

Third, a number of advocate teams should be established to brainstorm these new components. These teams—consisting of teachers of various levels and disciplines, administrators of various levels, central office staff, guidance teachers, plant management personnel, and parents—should be organized in such a way as to provide great diversity among the participants. The advocate teams are then given the basic outline of the structure of each component and asked to fill in the specifics of each part of the program (student composition, staff composition, guidance, parent's role, site considerations, grouping concepts, content focus, process of decision making, evaluation, scheduling considerations, and resources). The emphasis here is on dreaming toward the best possible organization. Although considerations such as cost, feasibility and so on should not be entirely ruled out, they ought not be of primary importance in this process. The teams, wary at first of this freedom, will soon begin to dream, discuss, advocate, and debate the specifics of these new programs. A report with specific recommendations will result from the efforts of the advocate teams.

Fourth, a convergent team should be organized for each concept model. These teams, composed of individuals who have served on the advocate teams, are charged with taking the reports of the advocate teams and putting together a practical and feasible plan—one that will embrace the dreams but also deal with realities such as the characteristics of student population, the backgrounds of personnel, and the existing physical facilities.

Fifth, once the various components are approved by the board of education, teaching staff can be chosen. Teachers can then begin to address many of the details of their specific programs such as ordering supplies and materials, developing parent/student handbooks, reorganizing classroom space, developing schedules, assessing student needs, and meeting with the administration.

There are those in education who suggest that the essence of learning lies in having choices about the conditions of learning; the prospects for improved learning appear bright as more options are introduced. Suggested here is an internal system under which the student and his family are offered a variety of types of schooling, all within the public school system. Educators for years have talked about individualized instruction and methods by which teachers can individualize without providing a school organization that is consistent with the theory of individualization. The method proposed here lays the foundation for classroom individualization by providing an organization that reinforces the concept throughout the school.

Gifted/talented adolescents not only need curriculum and instructional programs that are different, they also need an organization within a school to meet the needs of adolescents. This curriculum recognizes the variety of these needs and provides for the adolescent intellectually, while taking into account his/her emotional, physical, and social needs. The schools within a school are labeled Concept I, Concept II, and Concept III. The specific curriculum and instructional processes used in Chapter 7 ("Reaching Out to All Children") are used for each concept described in this chapter.

Concept I

Concept I organizes learning into a seven- or eight-period day with each period running in length from forty to fifty minutes. Learning is accomplished through discrete subject matter offerings in each of the eight periods during the day. The curriculum is subject matter centered and is offered to students through classes organized on grade levels. Materials are selected by the teachers and dictate to a large degree the curriculum of this program. The program is teacher directed and is organized and taught in the fashion most comfortable to the teacher.

Concept I involves seventy-five to a hundred students grouped according to discrete grades, beginning at (5) 6, 7, and 8. Each of these houses is assigned four subject-centered teachers in the areas of reading/language arts, math/science, and social studies. Related arts and other activities are scheduled during the eight-period day. Learning and media centers are utilized to supplement instruction within the Concept I program.

Organizational Composition

Student Composition. Grades (5) 6, 7, and 8, racially and sexually balanced across total school population, are heterogeneously grouped with a class size of approximately twenty-five students. Concept I is selected by parents who desire this type of education for their youngster.

Staff Composition. There should be a minimum of four teachers to a house of seventy-five to a hundred students. Teachers should be committed to the philosophy and goals of Concept I; that is, they should be highly trained in subject matter areas and believe strongly that youngsters are happier and develop to a fuller extent when subject matter is mastered. Teachers should have a choice in determining if they should teach in Concept I, but the final placement of staff in Concept I should rest in the hands of the principal.

There should be some paraprofessional or aide time available for teachers in Concept I.

Guidance. The guidance counsellor is an essential component in Concept I. The counsellor is basically involved in dealing with the emotional growth of students as it relates to accomplishment of the subject-centered curriculum of the program.

Site Considerations. The Concept I houses should be grouped as closely together as possible and should be separated from Concept II and Concept III in the building if possible. Four regular classrooms would be needed for the program.

Grouping Concepts. Students will be heterogeneously placed in each of the homerooms within Concept I and will move accordingly throughout the school day into the various periods scheduled for their academics. During the periods when related arts, media center, and learning center are

TYPICAL STUDENT SCHEDULE
CONCEPT I

PERIOD	MONDAY–TUESDAY	WEDNESDAY–FRIDAY
HOMEROOM		
1	TYPING*	JOURNALISM*
2	PASSPORT TO ADVENTURE*	VOCAL TECHNIQUES*
3	LANGUAGE ARTS -	
4	SCIENCE -	
	LUNCH	
5	SOCIAL STUDIES -	
6	MATH -	
7	PHYSICAL ARTS -	
8	THE MACHINES OF MATH*	ARCHEOLOGY*

*Aesthetic classes—part of Gifted and Talented Program. These courses change after 18 weeks. The rest of the schedule does not change.

HOMEROOM — for attendance, information, etc.—10 minutes.
PERIODS   — 40 minutes.
LUNCH   — 30 minutes.
THURSDAYS — periods shortened to 30 minutes to provide for parent conferences.

FIGURE 14-1

scheduled, students will be regrouped based on selection of different courses. The grouping will be done by grade level, with the exception of the related arts, which will be multiaged.

Content Focus. The content for the basic instructional program in Concept I is focused through textbooks and board of education adopted materials. It is based on adopted curricula for each of the grades within Concept I, and teachers are asked to follow this material. There should be a textbook for every youngster in every subject area in Concept I.

In an eight-period day approximately four periods will be utilized for basic instructional activities, with four periods remaining for students to take courses within the gifted/talented part of the program. These would be aesthetic and Creative I offerings, which are explained in detail in another chapter of this book. In all aesthetic and Creative I offerings students are grouped in multiage fashion.

Process of Decision Making. Concept I is a teacher/administrator-directed program, and students have little responsibility relative to decisions affecting organization, teacher style, content, and so on. Parents are involved in the decision-making process through parent—teacher conferences, which are held weekly for those parents desiring input into the program. The principal of the school determines the schedule and what subject matter is offered at what time.

Evaluating Students. Students are evaluated by report card, and grades are determined by the teacher who utilizes accomplishment of subject matter as the key to rewarding students through letter grades.

Scheduling Considerations

Adequate Planning Time. In each of the houses of approximately a hundred students the four teachers should be given a minimum of one planning period per day, and this planning time should be a common planning time with the four teachers in each house. Because teachers do not teach in teams in Concept I, it is absolutely imperative that they have this planning time so that they can share concerns relative to students within their concept. This also provides additional time for the teacher to meet with students in a guidance capacity. A typical schedule for a student in Concept I is shown in Figure 14-1 on page 197.

Concept II

Concept II organizes the components of learning—pace, interest level, skill development, and maturation of students ages 10—14—in a new perspective. It considers time as a flexible factor in learning and addresses self-development through the use of a thematic approach to curriculum. Teachers skilled in content areas select appropriate materials and activities for each student. This selection comes after consultation with students for the purpose of setting goals, motivating interests, and involving the student in the decision-making process. Through this participation cooperation is greatly increased, making it easier for students to identify with teachers and the school. Teacher emphasis will be on positive reinforcement.

The curriculum is characterized by the following:

- Integration of subject matter within the thematic approach.

- Teachers, in the role of facilitators, participating in the learning process with the ultimate goal of enabling students to become self-directed.

- Student/facilitator counseling.

- Parent involvement.

- Heterogeneous grouping on a multiage, cross-graded basis.

- Math as a multilevel approach, organized to meet individual needs and growth patterns of students.

- Small group excursions to enhance learning experiences beyond the limitations of the classroom.

- Utilization of various external resources, e.g., professionals with expertise in various fields, community resources and agencies, environmental study areas, and so on.

- A learning environment in which a total effort is made to reveal the gifts and talents inherent in all children.

- A realization that the learning process involves emotional sensitivity to the needs of others and a trusting relationship among the partners in the learning experience: parents, students, teachers, and administrators.

- A complete and thorough evaluative process evolved through the cooperation of parents, students, teachers, and administrators.

Concept II involves seventy-five to a hundred students from grades (5) 6, 7, and 8 in a multiage open classroom model. An integral part of this program is the incorporation of related arts in the academic experience through the thematic approach. There will be flexibility in structure and activities that offer choices to encourage creativity, exploration, more active participation, and socialization.

Material resource service centers (possibly equipped with creative materials, interesting experimental equipment, books, study carrels, listening centers, and other audiovisual material) form a real and accessible component of the school.

Organizational Composition

Student Composition. Grades (5) 6, 7, and 8, racially and sexually balanced according to school population, are heterogeneously grouped with no more than thirty and no less than fifteen students from each grade level.

In keeping with the goals of Concept II the house will be a multiracial, multiage group with different ability levels—including students in special programs—heterogeneously and coeducationally grouped.

Staff Composition. There should be a minimum of four teachers to a house of seventy-five to a hundred students. Teachers must be committed to the philosophy and goals of this alternative. Teachers should have a choice in determining whom they work with in Concept II. Teacher selection should not be based solely on academic certification. Teachers should have input for any replacement staff.

Although in each house there is a team leader for whom remuneration is provided, this role takes on added significance in this concept. In this situation the team leader schedules and organizes team planning sessions, coordinates the work of professional and nonprofessional staff members, acts as an intermediary between the team and the administration, formulates proper evaluation procedures, follows student progress in the gifted/talented program, communicates with teachers in other houses and programs, and is responsible for guidance and discipline in certain situations.

Because of the nature of this component, team members work more closely together in this concept. Team teaching is common, with certain teachers taking specified responsibilities (such as large group instruction), acting as a resource for a particular task, or specializing in developing diagnostic/prescriptive programs for students.

There should be one aide per house. The house teachers should choose their own aide on approval of the building principal. Adequate training should be provided for all aides in Concept II.

There should be at least three student teachers. Selection of student teachers should be based on their ability and background in order to fit the needs of the team. Student teachers will share in the responsibility of team planning and execution of programs. Student teachers will share current materials and ideas from their colleges. Preference should be given to student teachers who are interested in the middle grades and the open concept.

One administrator should be assigned to Concept II. The administrator should provide instructional insights and help in house planning.

Guidance. The guidance counsellor is an essential member of the Concept II house. One counsellor should be assigned to the house on a shared basis with other houses. His/her schedule should provide for involvement with students as well as teachers in the concept. Counsellor input should provide valuable information concerning the emotional growth of the students and the development of positive attitudes toward self and school. A counsellor should be called on to instruct in areas of emotional maturity, value training, and decision making.

Parents. A parent advisory committee should be set up to communicate with teachers on such matters as social functions, field trips, ongoing projects, and classroom help.

Site Considerations

Concept II should be grouped together—at least on the same floor. Minimum space available should be equivalent to five rooms. Students should have a place to go to relax and socialize. Students should help design the environment. Whenever the need arises in the program, a school-without-walls concept should be utilized.

The surroundings of the physical plant should be utilized as much as possible for the following:

- Units or themes that require nature studies.

- Large group instruction where indoor facilities are inadequate.

- Individual projects that need minimal supervision.

The maintenance engineer, in conjunction with students and facilitators, should conduct a feasibility study to determine those areas where remodeling, landscaping, and construction are desirable for a more positive learning atmosphere.

Any space or locations outside should be considered a classroom. Offices, plants, homes, the neighborhood, museums, parks, camps, or any other meeting place should be made available to the group to be used as a learning environment. In order to provide a variety of offerings, space is essential to avoid overcrowding. Any open setting requires more planning because of the multiage grouping technique. Therefore, so as not to shortchange any child, it is desirable to have more space to accomplish the goals. Space should be provided for daily and/or weekly counseling.

Grouping Concepts

Grouping is a flexible technique designed to facilitate positive learning experiences. Planned as well as natural or informal groupings may have various dimensions. It is expected that the grouping process will cross age and ability levels. In keeping with the decision-making process, grouping will be planned by students and facilitators.

Groupings and regroupings within Concept II will be based on the following considerations: interest, ability, instructional levels, performance levels, social preference and development, physical maturation, sensitivity to ethnic and sexual considerations, and levels of sophistication.

Some general guidelines for grouping follow:

- Groups should be flexible.

- Continual regrouping based on achievement and interests is inherent to the whole philosophy of Concept II.

- In terms of Concept II, a group may consist of one to a hundred students.

- In the traditional academic subject areas, such as mathematics, grouping should be based on the student's needs. For example, a student who has not mastered fractions can be grouped with other students who need help in this basic skill.

- The criteria we suggest for grouping in order of importance are (1) teacher and student input and (2) achievement tests.

- In areas where a choice is available, such as team or individual sports in physical education, the group is based on what activity the student elects to take.

Grouping should allow and provide for the vast differences that exist among any aggregation of individuals. The great variety of interests and purposes and the wide range of talents and skills necessitate fluidity of grouping and should provide for increased interaction with a variety of individuals.

Content Focus

Content focus should stem from interest and needs as perceived by students—with sensitive counseling. Units of study should be based on cross-disciplinary themes. Given a variety of options, students will also choose programs for sequential skill development and critical educational needs. As a result of thematic and sequential skills experiences, students will develop individual interests and assume increased responsibility for their own learning.

Cross-disciplinary experiences will be related by common themes, such as "man and environment," "technology," "fact and fantasy," "exploration," and "conflict." From these, student and facilitator will set up a variety of options that will allow them the opportunity to explore the theme fully. Assuring the sequential development of skills and critical educational needs will involve contracting. Students will pursue individual or group projects of their choice based on contractual arrangements with the teachers in the program. The interest of the students will determine the nature and length of these projects. Students will be free to choose and form their own individual interest activities, eliciting the aid of the facilitator as they see the need. Themes and options from which students choose will be determined by the team of teachers.

Process of Decision Making

The decision-making process should be an integral part of Concept II program. The middle school pupil should move from a dependent learner to an independent one. Therefore, assuming responsibility becomes an important part of the learning process.

Decision making is a shared process between students and teachers. It has as one goal the identification of those students who need more direction than others. Teachers and students come to decisions regarding schedule and schedule content. One method of evaluating options for decision making is to use the following criteria:

- Is the choice something a child could reasonably choose to do?
- Is the choice related to what a student can't do, but wants to do?
- Is the choice related in some way to what a child might want to do?

Considerations affecting decision making are these:

- Availability of funds.
- Scheduling—how often to change, what to include.
- House management, discipline, and activities.
- Logistical feasibility.

Parents, students, teachers, aides, and student teachers should contribute to the decision-making process.

Some ways to involve these groups in the decision-making process include the following:

- Town meetings to air problems and resolve problems.
- Student learning contracts to help students decide on projects and interests.
- Schedules with time blocked out for sharing student/teacher concerns.

An ongoing self-evaluation is one of the keys to the ultimate success of the Concept II program. The major purpose of evaluation is to improve the educational program so that the needs of the students can be met effectively. The evaluation process should not be used solely to judge; for if it is used in this fashion both the program and the evaluation will fail. Facilitators, administrators, students, and parents should serve as evaluators through cooperative efforts. This practice will encourage and bring about self-directed improvement. Self-evaluation is a powerful and essential ingredient in changing individual and group behavior. Meaningful feedback from students, staff, and parents is an integral part of this ongoing evaluative process.

Evaluation is a function of the decision-making process. It involves information about students, making use of resources, knowing the community served, and designing a multifaceted curriculum geared to meet the needs of all students served.

The group of teachers should meet daily to plan the activities for the next day. Overall long-range plans would be set, but daily planning is necessary. A student advisory group should be included in the planning sessions. This group can be rotated for decision making. The group of teachers may rotate the leadership of the group among themselves.

Evaluating Students

It is recommended that the house develop a reporting system, possibly anecdotal, in concert with the principal. A summary, continuously recording student progress throughout the years, is essential as well.

Scheduling Considerations

Adequate Planning Time. Adequate planning time should be considered as a most important principle, because it is only through mutual planning, preparation, and sharing of strategies by the teacher team that the demands can be met for an effective program. The teachers should be allowed to come together as needed, as well as to use this time for advisory situations with individual students.

Flexibility in Structure. The student also serves as coplanner of his individual schedule. It should be necessary for the teacher and student to change the individual schedule on a systematic basis as needed—for example, every two to four weeks.

An activities schedule should be posted, including in-school and out-of-school activities. Required activities will be scheduled so that a student has more than one opportunity to participate (i.e., a required film or presentation will have more than one showing). Whole-day experiences will be scheduled for an individual student or a small group that will take them into the community.

Activities that may be rigidly scheduled—orchestra, YM-YWCA, community activities—should come at the end of the day so that flexibility of the remainder of the schedule is not threatened. This will also allow students additional time in areas in which they might want to extend their involvement.

Resources Available Outside System

Community resources and resource persons should be closely linked to the learning experience of students. The most meaningful learning experiences are often those that are gained firsthand. Firsthand knowledge can be gained by the field trip or through resource persons who have been invited in to the learning area by the students and facilitators. In addition to enriching and supplementing learning experiences, field trips and resource

TYPICAL STUDENT SCHEDULE
CONCEPT II

THEME: CONFLICTS

PERIOD	MONDAY	TUESDAY	WEDNESDAY	THURSDAY	FRIDAY
HOMEROOM					
1	WRITE ON* – – – – – – – – – –		LOOKING AT LEADERS* – – – – – – – – – – –		
2	PHYSICAL ARTS –				
3	MATH	IND. READING	MATH	IND. READING	MATH
4	SCIENCE EXPLOR.	INTER-ACTION	SCIENCE EXPLORATIONS	INTER-ACTION	SCIENCE EXPLOR.
5	CONFLICTS AND SOLUTIONS		CONFLICTS AND SOLUTIONS		CONFLICTS AND SOLUTIONS
	LUNCH				
6	PHOTO ESSAY * – – – – – – – – –		FINE ARTS* – – – – – – – – – – – – – – – – – – –		
7	CIVIL WAR	MATH	CIVIL WAR	MATH	CIVIL WAR
8	POPULAR MECHANICS* – – – – – – – –		PHILOSOPHY AND LOGIC* – – – – – – – – – –		

*Aesthetic classes—part of Gifted and Talented Program—40 minutes. These courses change after 18 weeks.

HOMEROOM — for attendance, information, etc.—10 minutes.
LUNCH — 30 minutes.
THURSDAYS — periods shortened to 30 minutes to provide for parent conferences.

All other classes—theme classes.
Theme times are flexible, e.g., Interaction—80 minutes.
Theme times subject to change based on need.
Themes change every 6-8 weeks.
Theme classes are dropped on rotating basis in order to provide time for counseling, goal setting,
    town meetings, journal writing, silent sustained reading, etc.
Interaction—heterogeneous group-centered experiences in reading, writing, listening, and speaking.

FIGURE 14-2

persons within the community help the facilitators learn more about the
environmental background of the students. Knowledge of this background
should bring about a closer relationship between students and teachers.

The making of a guide for community resources and resource persons
might be compiled by a Concept II house to provide a means for administrators and teachers to evaluate the available resources. Possible outside

resources might include parents, aides, student teachers, speakers from various fields, libraries, museums, theater groups, governmental agencies, art centers, police stations, stores/businesses, fire stations, parks, poultry and flea markets, zoos, health officers, local newspapers, travel agencies, parks and recreational facilities, processing plants, and corporations.

Concept III/Fundamental

Concept III is a skill-oriented program that allows for guided freedom in the academic pursuits of students. This program recognizes the development of talents as being important, but it recognizes that specific skills are a necessity in this development. Concept III is a structured program that emphasizes through homework, character education, and highly structured activities the goals of the program—which are to impart 4-R education to the students in the program.

Teachers skilled in content areas are chosen to participate in Concept III. These teachers volunteer for the program and are selected from the list of volunteers. The program is teacher directed with little interference from either parents or administrators. Parents are asked to show their support for the program through an agreement signed with the teacher and the school that they will cooperate with the teacher in checking homework, assuring attendance of students, and participating.

Concept III is organized in grades 5 and 6 with two teachers and fifty students, whereas in grades 7 and 8 it is organized at grade level with a hundred students and four teachers at each grade level. There is no multiage grouping within this model. Related arts, media, and learning center activities are scheduled based on selection of these programs by the students. All material used in the teaching process is selected by the individual teachers within the Concept III program.

Organizational Composition

Student Composition. Concept III incorporates grades (5) 6, 7, and 8 in racially and sexually balanced programs. All students are grouped heterogeneously and by grade level. Concept III is selected by parents who desire this type of education for their youngster.

Staff Composition. The pupil/teacher ratio within the Concept III program should be in the neighborhood of 25:1. Therefore, each house would have two teachers for each fifty students and four teachers for each hundred students. Teachers will be committed to the philosophy and goals of this program. Teachers should have a choice in determining whom they will work with in Concept III. Teacher selection should be based solely on academic certification and proven ability in skill teaching. Teachers should have input for any replacement staff.

There should be a paid aide per classroom. The teacher should choose the aide, based on approval of the building principal. Adequate training must be provided for all aides within the program, and all training should be done by the classroom teacher working with the aide he/she has chosen.

It is crucial that the administrator have a feeling for a Concept III/Fundamental-type alternative and be supportive of this type of program.

Guidance. The guidance counsellor is an essential part of Concept III/Fundamental and can help with the 4th R, which is character education. In this component students deal with topics of self-concept, brotherhood, attitudes, and values. The guidance counsellor is an integral component of the teaching of character education within a Concept III program.

Parents. It is important that parents select this concept based on their own personal philosophy of what schools should do. Their responsibility then is to support the program through checking homework that has been assigned by the teacher four nights a week, by signing a contract supporting the program, and by attending activities of the school.

Site Considerations

The program should be grouped together and should be isolated as much as possible within the larger school. Regular classroom space is all that is needed for this program.

Grouping Concepts

Students initially should be grouped in a heterogeneous way but should be regrouped throughout the day based on achievement levels of students. In addition, teachers within a Concept III/Fundamental program may group, based on interest as well as achievement.

Content Focus

The curriculum areas and instructional methodology are determined by the classroom teacher. Teachers are charged with the responsibility of utilizing materials that in their judgment best impart to the student skills in mathematics and reading.

There is no districtwide text to be used, and there is no set curriculum or course of study to follow. It is imperative, however, that before such a program is started, the teachers agree on what the curriculum should be and what skills should be taught at each grade level. Social studies and science are taught through the reading program as well as the math program. The crucial curriculum for adolescents in this program is to expand their horizons in the area of language arts/reading and to expand their horizons in the area of mathematics and science. This is not a program that is heavily oriented toward the arts, but the program does provide for a youngster to take aesthetics and Creative I offerings as discussed in an early chapter.

Process of Decision Making

Teachers have much autonomy in this program. Simply put, the decision-making process is such that each teacher determines what would be most effective. They may want parent-teacher conferences at their discretion. They may want telephone conversations with parents whenever necessary. They have nearly equal responsibility with the building level administrator in making decisions that affect their classrooms.

Evaluating Students

Students are evaluated on an A, B, C, D, F report card. Grades are given based on the accomplishment of subject matter on grade level. Awarding of grades is based on teacher judgment relative to student achievement.

Scheduling Considerations

Adequate Planning Time. Teachers should be provided with a minimum of one period per day of common planning time with other teachers in the house.

Flexibility and Structure. The structure of the student day is totally in the hands of the teachers working within Concept III/Fundamental. On any given day they may spend large amounts of time in reading/language arts; on another day they may spend large blocks of time in a math/science or laboratory situation. It is not necessary that students meet in every subject area every day. In summary, the structure should be determined by the teachers within the program.

Inherent in housing various alternatives are a variety of concerns. Although similar in nature to the problems faced by all schools, the nature of housing different models in one school presents new variations and challenges that must be resolved.

An old problem of all middle schools has been exacerbated somewhat by the varied organization, that of providing a smooth transition for a student from the middle school to the high school. Since the implementation of these components, both the middle school and the high school have recognized the need to accommodate their organization to the other. The middle school must provide the student with the preparation necessary for

TYPICAL STUDENT SCHEDULE
CONCEPT III

PERIOD	MONDAY	TUESDAY	WEDNESDAY	THURSDAY	FRIDAY
HOMEROOM					
1	PHYSICAL ARTS/HEALTH				
2	SOCIAL STUDIES				
3	LANGUAGE ARTS				
4	SCIENCE				
5	MATH				
	L U N C H				
6	RELATED ARTS				
7	READING				
8	CITY PLANNING*	PHILOSOPHY AND LOGIC*			

*Aesthetic classes—part of Gifted and Talented Program—40 minutes. These courses change after 18 weeks.

HOMEROOM — for attendance, information, etc—10 minutes.
PERIODS   — 40 minutes.
LUNCH   — 30 minutes.
THURSDAY — periods shortened to 30 minutes to provide for parent conferences.

Basic subjects are taught by an interdisciplinary approach.
Basic schedule changes to meet needs of students. Changes may occur after 9 or 18 weeks.
Examples:
    Reading may be silent, developmental or remedial.
    Learning Center experiences are provided in Math and Reading.
    Supplemental Instruction/Resource Room may supplant a basic subject.
Recess—provides time for counseling and social interaction.
Related arts—courses in music, art, home economics, and industrial arts.

FIGURE 14-3

the high school. Equally important is the need for the high school to adjust its organization for the students who come to them from these varied programs.

Thus a program of coordination between the two schools has been established whereby teachers meet to articulate curriculum, share philosophies, and receive inservice education. Also, teachers swap teaching assignments for a few days and make visitations to the different schools in order to get a better perspective on the total student experience.

Now that parents are presented with an array of different organizations, how do they make a proper selection of program? Although seen as a drawback by some, this can be utilized as a benefit. Under this plan the parents cannot simply drop a child at the doorstep and let the school pick him up from there. This plan actively engages them in the process of their child's education. Of course, the school must provide parents with the necessary support to aid them in the decision-making process.

Teacher recommendations, evening orientation meetings, classroom visitations, and literature outlining both program and student expectations have been established to enable parents to decide on the appropriateness of a concept for their child. Parents are assured that no decision is irrevocable and that the ultimate goal is to place their child in a program that capitalizes on his/her learning style.

Doesn't the creation of such a program with differing philosophies deteriorate staff unanimity? Of course, all faculties have interpersonal problems to some degree. However, under such a varied organizational stucture it is preeminent that the administration treat all programs and faculty equally. Different treatment or wider flexibility is to be determined by the nature of the program, not because of the administrator's predisposition toward one program or another. His concern must be the total school, and he must hold the view that all programs, although significantly different, are in no way better in their effectiveness. He must seek to avoid rivalry among concepts and to provide the teams with the resources, equipment, and support they need to do the best possible job. He must also establish clear lines of communication among all groups in order to share ideas, problems, concerns, successes, and failures, so that their efforts can be understood and appreciated by all members of the school. Only through a formalized airing out can differences of opinion, grievances, and mutual suspicion be properly resolved.

In this chapter I have outlined the organizational components of schools within schools for adolescents. Overlaid on top of these concepts then would be the gifted/talented curriculum explained elsewhere in this book. Students in all three concepts would participate in the aesthetics and Creative I offerings of the gifted/talented program. A matrix summarizing some of the differences as well as some of the similarities of the three concepts appears on pages 212-13.

Conclusion

In summary, it is important to remember that parents are responsible for choosing either Concept I, II, or III/Fundamental based on what they know of the programs and the type of education they want for their youngster. The concepts outlined are not all inclusive, but they do speak to openness. They value diversity. They are nonexclusive. They embrace human growth and development and are unswerving in their recognition of individual worth. Within these bounds is an infinite spectrum of alternative possibilities in creating new and additional learning forms.

We have sought to establish a middle school with its own identity. Each component of our program seeks to fulfill the functions of the middle school as formulated by William Alexander in his book *The Emergent Middle School*.[1] That is, to help the pupil understand himself as a unique human individual with personal needs and shared social responsibilities, to assure every pupil a degree of success in understanding the underlying principles and the ways of knowledge in the areas of organized learning, to promote individual growth in the basic learning skills, to foster independent learning on the part of every pupil, and to permit wide exploration of personal interests.

[1] William M. Alexander et al., *The Emergent Middle School* New York: Holt, Rinehart and Winston, 1968), pp. 84-86.

TABLE 14-1. Summary of Concepts

	Concept I	Concept II	Concept III/Fundamental	Gifted/Talented Aesthetics and Creative I
Personnel	House of 100 students Teacher/student ratio 1:25 Student teachers—teacher choice	House of 100 students Teacher/student ratio 1:25 Student teachers encouraged Community resource persons	2 teachers/50 students Teacher/student ratio 1:25 1 teacher aide Student teachers encouraged Community resource persons	Open access electives Teacher/student ratio 1:20 Aesthetics; 1–10 Creative I Team/interdisciplinary teaching Community resource persons Adjunct teachers utilized
Scheduling	Day divided into periods Constant class schedule	Flexible time Periodic revision of individual schedules	Flexible time Periodic revision of individual schedules	May consume up to 40 per cent of student's day 18-week cycles minimum Individualized schedules Aesthetics: parent/child determined Creative I recommended by teacher

Curriculum	Grade level approach to academic disciplines	Thematic approach to curriculum Integrated interest	Heavy emphasis in computation and language Teacher directed Frequent homework Parent involvement Frequent reporting and character education emphasized Peer tutoring	Belief: All students have gifts and talents (6 areas of giftedness) Aesthetics in academic and related arts (17 areas) Interdisciplinary approach Mentorships in Creative I Work in many environments Work with people of all ages
Grade composition	Grade 6: Semidepartmentalized Grades 7–8: Completely departmentalized	Multiage grouping (6–8)	Grade level grouping grade 6 Multiage grouping grades 7–8	Multiage grouping (6–8) generally Some grade level groupings
Decision making	Teacher determination	Student, parent, teacher determination	Teacher determination	Student, parent, teacher determination

Perspectives for the Gifted/Talented in a High School

I once came across a statement (in an old high school course description catalogue) to the effect that a young person really could not be considered fully educated unless he had completed at least two years of Latin and two years of Greek, and had additional mastery of modern languages. This gave me some concern because I had long before concluded that, no matter how well educated we are, each of us is a "sweat hog" someplace or other. It might be the mathematics student on the gym floor or the football player in the physics lab. Very few of us excel outside our own area of expertise. In the process of going from high school to graduate school we become more and more specialized; very few of us become concerned that "the renaissance man" is no longer a priority. It would seem reasonable that a youngster's talents be developed all through his/her educational career rather than wait until the third year of college, or even graduate school, to develop a specialty. The next logical step would be to develop alternatives on the one hand and some specialties on the other.

Elsewhere in this book, Mario D. Fantini outlines the development of educational alternatives, suggesting that earlier modes generally were outside the public school system—in some cases they were even alternatives to education, such as work training programs.

The professional literature is filled with discussions about alternatives or options. Almost all would agree that there are few generalizations in education that are universally agreed upon, but one of them is that people learn at different rates. It seems strange, therefore, that educational systems, supposedly dedicated to providing the best education for all students, are so structured that they block these differences.[1]

However, up through the 1960s the alternatives and options were most apt to be in the nature of restructuring the traditional school by such means as the school within the school. Textbooks for administrators showed how the needs of students could be met by these organizational changes, while fully admitting that the structure was based on "a truly randomly selected cross section of the entire student body."[2]

As the 1960s faded, it became more and more evident that, no matter what the educators were saying, the students were dropping out, dropping in, and, in general, fighting the system. Apparently their needs were not being met often enough, and real changes were being proposed from the outside as well as the inside. Strong materials began to appear, such as Ellen Lurie's book *How to Change the Schools: A Parent's Action Handbook on How to Fight the System*,[3] a remarkably conservative book considering the times.

More and more publications began to examine options and alternatives. The entire September 1973 National Association of Secondary School Principals bulletin was devoted to alternatives, and principals began to look into the future.[4]

Authors such as David Tyack clearly outline the philosophy behind the educational system. Tyack indicates the effects of what he calls "one best system" and concludes that it is necessary to inculcate and demonstrate certain values and skills to a large heterogeneous population. The system is designed by and under the control of an economic and social elite, and the values of that group are imposed on the educational system.[5]

It should not be concluded that this is necessarily bad for large numbers of youngsters—the problem is that in many cases it simply does not work. Some writers openly fault the system for its values and its misconduct:

[1] Baird W. Whitlock, *Don't Hold Them Back* (New York: College Entrance Examination Board, 1978), p. 4.

[2] Robert D. Ramsey, Owen M. Heresai, Harold L. Hula, *The Schools-Within-the-School Program: A Modern Approach to Secondary Instruction and Guidance* (New York: Parker Publishing Co., 1967), p. V.

[3] Ellen Lurie, *How to Change the Schools: A Parent's Action Handbook on How to Fight the System* (New York: Random House, 1970).

[4] The National Association of Secondary School Principals, *The 80's: Where Will the Schools Be? (A Response of 14 Principals)* (Reston, Va.: NASSP, 1974).

[5] David Tyack, *The One Best System* (Cambridge, Mass.: Harvard University Press, 1974), pp. 126, 127.

it is in the schools . . . that the mass . . . learn that life is inevitably routine, depersonalized, venally graded, that it is best to toe the mark and shut up; that there is no place for spontaneity, open sexuality and free spirit. Trained in the schools, they go. to the same quality of jobs, culture and politics. This is education—mis-education, socializing to the national norms and regimenting to the national "needs."[6]

The alternatives described in this chapter were created at one urban high school and came about not through any great philosophical discussions but as a result of school administrators' seeing that they had to meet the particular needs of each youngster. Most of them agreed that there is no best way in which to frame an educational program that would suit everyone. As Yvonne Blanchard says elsewhere in this book (Chapter 9), gifted children are found everywhere and come from every social class and ethnic background. The problems come when students are not properly identified and programs provided that best meet the needs of their gifts and abilities.

In the course of seven years, alternative programs were created that reflected this initial conclusion. The first alternative—the Storefront Academy—was viable for eight years. Other alternatives known as Interim I and Interim II, the Team School, and the School of Performing Arts were created over a period of seven years and are still operating.

The Storefront Academy

The first alternative program was created in 1968, as a result of a series of violent incidents in the high school with the sit-ins and demonstrations that seemed to be part of the school culture of the late 1960s. The same students seemed on occasion after occasion to become involved in acts of aggression against their fellow students—they refused to attend classes on a regular basis and created an educational atmosphere that made for an unhealthy learning environment. As school officials saw it, they had two options: go to the board of education and ask for expulsion of these youngsters or create an educational program separate from the main body of student activities.

With assistance from the director of pupil services and the guidance director, a storefront was acquired approximately a half mile away from the main building. A teacher and support persons were assigned to help. The philosophy of the storefront academy was to put education second and understanding of self first. The social worker, the school psychologist, the individual consultants who came on a regular basis—all helped to reconstruct the individual and to help the youngster feel proud about who he was so that

[6] Paul Goodman, *Compulsory Mis-Education* (New York: Vintage Books, 1964), p. 29.

the learning process could be reestablished. It was a difficult task because the skills of the youngsters were in almost every way below grade level, but the potential appeared to be there. Progress appeared likely. Over the years progress, indeed, was made. Youngsters graduated, youngsters went on to college. Some eight years later the Storefront Academy was closed, and two new programs—Interim I and Interim II—were created within the high school complex.

Interim I and II

School officials felt that separateness was unnecessary because violence-prone students were no longer a problem. However, there were a number of students whose learning potential was not matched by achievement. As a result they absented themselves from class and fell through the educational cracks. Interim I and Interim II were created to serve as a hub of educational and sports activities for periods of time that vary from student to student depending on needs. Some classes are taken with a core teacher(s), other classes with regular subject matter teachers. Some students remain in the program for the majority of the high school years—others spend as little as a month in the program.

The Alternative School

Another alternative developed when school officials identified a group of students who realized that they did not have to drop out of school to quit going to school—they could come and go, pick and choose, sit and do little, and, in a number of other very imaginative ways, keep from attending classes on a regular basis. School officials became very alarmed about this because the students identified as having this syndrome had some talent—in many cases, a good deal of talent—that obviously was not being used. One particular group of fewer than two dozen students had a high potential equaled only by their low achievement rate. In fact, many of the students could be called brilliant in many areas—musically very talented, highly articulate, verbally skilled. After a good deal of discussion with professional guidance persons and school psychologists, it was agreed that not all youngsters can succeed and mature at the same speed even though all standardized tests suggest that they should do well in school.

In looking for explanations and patterns, it was found that as a child grows one parent, usually the mother, becomes the person whom the child looks to for guidance, help, and support. When that child goes to school, we slowly wean away the allegiance from the one person at home to a dual allegiance—the second portion going to the kindergarten or prekindergarten teacher. As the child progresses through the school system, we begin to add more individuals into the child's life—a separate art teacher, very often a separate physical education instructor. By the time the youngster reaches middle or junior high school, he/she has allegiances and obligations to probably six or so adults. As the youngster goes up through the grades, he/she becomes more independent and the number of individuals continues to expand so that one class is almost wholly independent of another. For some youngsters this separation and compartmentalization cause an academic breakdown and they cannot cope with the total situation that confronts them.

An alternative program, the alternative school, was planned so that allegiance would be to only one person—the teacher—in a self-contained classroom. After some discussion with the guidance department, an alternative school was created that met for only four hours each afternoon apart from the mainstream of the high school program. The ground rules were rather simple—students could study such subjects as they and the teacher agreed could be studied successfully in this very separate environment. The philosophy was explained and accepted, and the program was started.

On the high school level, this certainly makes no educational sense whatsoever, but school officials were less concerned about educational value than they were about the psychological adjustment and security building, which they felt would have to precede any meaningful learning experience. As a result they were looking for a very unique teacher, a person who could relate to youngsters who were a little "different." He builds up each person from, as the cliché says, where the person is to where he wants him/her to be.

In this program a student may study history, botany, literature, philosophy, or drama, with the teacher guiding the student closely into and through each study area. When mutual consent arrangements are made at the appropriate time for a youngster to take a single course—perhaps a lab course like chemistry—he/she may be permitted to do so in a high school program while remaining in the alternate school for the balance of the program. If that venture out is successful, then other courses may be taken outside the alternate school. The aim is, of course, to slowly feed the youngster back until all courses are outside the alternate school and only the home base backup system remains—and eventually even that is phased out. Through the years some students have been in this alternate program for almost all of their high school career; others have had just a short stay to regain their educational composure and then successfully transfer back into the main program and on to education beyond high school.

Loyalty of most parents and students to the program is fierce—instead of being quiet about it or concerned about being "different," they hold their banners high, they are proud of it. When some discussion came up during a budget hearing that the program might be abolished, their careful, deliberate, and very clear analysis made school officials proud to have them as part of the educational programs.

The chief difficulty in a program like this one is in staff selection. A unique individual took a framework that was thought to be sound and put flesh on the skeleton and created a living organism. School administrators have serious doubts that the program would survive if this vital staff member left. It certainly would be difficult to conceive of it as being as successful as it has been. A well-designed, well-constructed program written by administrators may help, but unless the leeway and flexibility and basic choices are left to the people who run the program on a day-to-day basis it will be doomed to failure.

The Team School

A third alternative program called the Team School came about as a result of the educational experiences some high school teachers had as far back as the 1950s, when a humanities program was created by an art teacher and an English teacher. The concept was that the artist, the writer, and the musician reflected, accepted, or rejected the period that produced them. The standard English course and the standard history course should approach the subject by looking at it from the point of view of the arts. The difficulty with the program was that it took a block of time out of the educational structure, which caused scheduling conflicts. Field trips that were an integral part of the program caused difficulties outside the subject areas studied. The math teacher complained that the field trips apparently always came on test days, and the science teacher felt that the constant absences due to the humanities scheduling made life too difficult for all. As a result, teachers who had worked in the program sat down and worked out the skeleton of a humanities program, setting up its major areas—which included English, foreign languages, mathematics, science, art, and history. School officials wrote a short prospectus, advertised it to the staff, students, and parents, and the following fall opened the Team School for six teachers and 125 students.

The Team School tried to reflect the philosophy of the humanities program and offered this program to a cross section of the high school student population, with an emphasis on personalized instruction, flexible schedules, independent and small group study programs, and student decision-making a very important ingredient. It produced almost unlimited opportunities for students who were able to organize their time and share in the opportunity of developing a learning environment with the teachers and fellow students. They set up three-hour chemistry labs two days a week. They spent whole mornings each week on field trips, and although they studied the traditional subjects of math, Spanish, U.S. history, and the like, the interrelationships of all these subject areas was at the core. School administrators soon discovered that this program had an enormous appeal to youngsters because it provided an opportunity for students who were self-starters to move ahead at a more appropriate speed rather than remaining in structured 45-minute classes several times a day each day Monday through Friday, September through June.

But as with all alternative programs, there were some built-in problems. The teachers became very much interdependent, their lives became closely interwoven with those of the students, and when the classroom went outside the school building, such as in the week-long bike hike-canoe trip, where the history of the area was studied and written up as part of the English class, many teachers felt that the fishbowl effect was hard to endure. It requires a unique, extremely capable, always confident teacher to survive the constant attention. Free periods became student conference time, teacher planning time was given to planning with fellow teachers, and evenings became sessions with parents. It was wonderful, it was exhilarating, but it was draining! As staff turnovers due to moving, pregnancies, transfers, and so on occurred, school officials found that the nature of the programs changed as the personality of the staff changed. They soon found there were some teachers who definitely did not want to teach in such an environment. At the same time, there were some students who felt that all of their needs were not met in the Team School. Obviously its teachers could not teach all of the courses taught in the main program, and soon students were beginning to attend some classes in the main program. That began to fracture the solidarity, because while one student might be in a German class in the main building and another in a mechanical drawing class, the rest of the Team School was in a town meeting deciding some future program commitments.

Over the years, then, teacher burn-out, student impact, and the educational times in which the town found itself caused the nature of the program and the commitment of the students to change radically. As the years progressed, the Team School became more and more traditional and less and less a genuine alternative program. This is something that can be observed whenever one looks at the history of alternative programs.

The School of Performing Arts

The next alternative to be created was the School of Performing Arts. For those persons who grew up in cities like New York, where there are several different high schools created for separate purposes, such as the Brooklyn Technical High School for engineers, the Bronx High School of Science for math and science, and the High School of Music and Arts for the performing arts, there seems no reason why at least a performing arts component should not be constructed within a traditional high school, if the high school is large enough.

After long meetings with staff, students, and parents, a program was designed where the morning would be devoted entirely to academic subjects—such as math, science, foreign languages—and the entire afternoon to programs in the arts. It might be dance, a chamber music group, a videotaping class, or a course in theater history. At the very outset of the planning it was obvious that existing staff personnel could not deliver the expertise needed in the various areas. As a result, four staff people in the area of physical education/dance, English/theater, and music were set up as core staff to coordinate a core of adjunct staff whose expertise would qualify them to teach on a part-time basis. A professional musician taught strings several hours a week in the late afternoon to a chamber music class; set design was taught four hours a week in the middle of the afternoon three days a week, and so on.

Conclusion

All the alternative programs have to a large extent served their purpose and continue to do so. All are alive and functioning well, although with a good deal of alteration over the years. Some changes have come about internally to a particular alternative program, whereas others reflect changes in society that render an alternative less applicable than it once was. The needs of youngsters change, and, to meet the talents that walk in the door, some changes have to be made inside the door. The main programs continue to draw 85 to 90 per cent of all the students in the school, which is what one might expect. Alternatives therefore try to capitalize on the talents of some youngsters, providing an educational environment that best suits them without sacrificing the academic core, so that the student who goes on to higher education does not find himself in a situation where his background is inadequate.

School officials know that over the years different kinds of alternatives will be constructed but under very different circumstances. Declining enrollments in many school systems will force a rethinking of the structure of the alternatives currently available to students. Limits on spending will cause a closer fiscal examination, and, finally, many of the old solutions will no longer meet the needs of future youngsters. Programs will change to meet the needs of a new age.

PART FOUR Curriculum in Content Areas

Chapters in this section examine curriculum development from the perspective of various content areas. The Weiss and Clerico chapter discusses the development of communication skills through the use of a thematic approach. A typical student's day is described and suggestions are given to ensure the participation of all students.

Jerome D. Kaplan discusses the problems in implementing the mathematics curriculum and stresses the need to allow each child to advance at his/her own rate. He suggests the desirability of remodeling early childhood mathematics, developing classroom management systems for skill development and problem-centered teaching.

Science is a stimulating area for many gifted children. Warren M. Singer discusses the curriculum in this area for gifted children. He stresses the need for a wide range of exploratory and enrichment experiences and the importance of encouraging students to develop initiative in dealing with complexity.

Alice Miel describes the purpose of social studies as helping students to understand themselves and others and to develop the knowledge, skills, and attitudes required for participation in society. To this end, she provides a number of suggestions regarding ways in which social studies can help students become more skilled at understanding, caring, and acting.

The arts have traditionally enjoyed relatively low status in the school curriculum. Elliot W. Eisner discusses this condition and asserts that it reflects a limited concept of intelligence. He calls for greater curricular attention to the range of symbols that individuals use to express themselves and notes that "The use of

223

intelligence to encode and decode visual form is no less demanding than its use in history, or in music, or in mathematics." Moreover, there is "rich interaction between symbol systems . . . and inability to use any one of the symbol systems available in the culture can be a liability for the use of others." Thus expanding the concept of giftedness and talent to place more emphasis on the arts can provide opportunities for many children to further their intellectual development.

16

M. JERRY WEISS, Jersey City State College

LOUIS CLERICO, Montclair Public Schools

A More Global Look at Language Arts

These few pages include sincere attempts to describe the need for a real involvement with life, with a love of learning, and with resources and strategies that can develop communications skills. This presentation is an escape from the real worlds of drill and skill sheets and workbooks with pages unrelated to specific substance and content. We are leaving behind the right-wrong, unfeeling, unemotional, statistical, overstructured, and strictured curricula that are the antithesis to a love of reading and writing.

Real questions need to be answered if changes are to take place:

- Isn't school more than the mastery of skills?

- Aren't there interests and attitudes to be developed?

- Shouldn't we reexamine values and help students find personal values for themselves through a genuine search for truth and knowledge?

- What books will best meet the interests, needs, and abilities of a particular school's students?

- Is there any relationship between technology and humanity?

- What are the most practical ways for stimulating creative and critical thinking?

- Where is there room for individualism?

- What experiences will best allow students and teachers to express their feelings on major issues and events?

A very important ingredient of any language arts program is the teacher. In a special program for the gifted/talented the teacher is without a doubt the single most important ingredient. All the sophisticated, modern materials on the market are only as effective as the person implementing the program. This chapter will discuss ways a teacher can implement an exciting program by ensuring that all skills are presented in a slightly different manner.

Any successful teacher has a structure in which he/she functions. Within that structure there should be a unified, coordinated plan incorporating such basic points as the four listed here:

- *Philosophy:* A definition of what language arts embodies and a reflection on the enthusiasm of the teacher in encouraging the following:

    a. *Skill needs.* These skills must be recognized and integrated into the curriculum—not dealt with in isolation.

    b. *An active and creative environment.* There needs to be an environment that will provide students with a variety of outlets through which the individual can demonstrate the impact of learning. Some of the outlets are drama, puppetry, art, dance, music, role playing, creative writing, and so on.

    c. *Critical thinking.* This is essential in any language arts curriculum. Students have to draw conclusions, make decisions, document findings, tell fact from opinion, and be aware of propaganda techniques.

    d. *Sensitivity.* Developing sensitivity to the nature and value of language involves helping students see the many different ways authors and illustrators use to tell their stories. There are a wide range of trade books on the market that may be more appealing than most materials used in the regular classroom.

    e. *Independence.* Students are encouraged to select books and to express their ideas based on their own needs, experiences, and personal values.

- *Diagnostic tools:* A broad view that recognizes experiential background, physical development, intellectual abilities, social development, attitudes, and mastery of skills directly related to success on prescribed assignments. (Examples: interest inventories and grouping sheets—specific skill needs, counseling and building the ego of the child, health records.)

- *Teaching strategies:* The thematic approach reflecting experiential background and interest of students in a particular class. In the primary grades the units may be three or four weeks, in the middle grades as long as eight weeks. Some of the topics that have been extremely popular with children are animals, fantasy, monsters, humor, space, adventure, and suspense.

- *Ongoing evaluation:* An evaluation of the extent to which the student mastered the skills and concepts being taught.

  a. How has the student grown in his/her own ability to express ideas—through writing, speaking, or the arts?
  b. How has the student developed independence in being able to find materials to meet his/her needs?
  c. How has the student grown socially in being able to work cooperatively with others in group projects and reports, and how well does the student respond to the suggestions and ideas of others?
  d. How has the student demonstrated initiative in being able to stimulate ideas of others and in presenting group findings in an original and interesting manner?

Following is an example of how one teacher might approach the teaching of a Thematic Unit. You will note the employment of the previously mentioned strategies to totally involve all students. Rachel Brown, teacher, sent each of her 125 students this invitation:

Friday, the thirteenth, has been declared a "howlyday." For you, all classes are suspended. You will report to the auditorium at 8:48 to participate in the Scare-Fest, an event designed to make you tingle by letting you sample some haunting delights. This is not for the squeamish. Parental approval, as well as your doctor's, should be presented in written form before entering the inner sanctum. Anything WILL happen! Accept this invitation at your own risk.

Now is the time to double your insurance value. I shall provide a crypt; but only you can provide a body. Once you enter, you will never be the same again. But, then, do you really want to be????

The die was cast with the principal's permission to carry out a one day in-school field trip. All of the 125 students would be together the entire day to participate in this unusual event. Ms. Brown was determined to help her students justify their claims of how macabre school could really be.

Time: 8:45. The auditorium doors had a *CLOSED* sign prominently displayed. What student is really going to believe that? Even the *DO NOT TOUCH* sign just above the door handles did not stop one brazen girl from grabbing a handle. She screamed as the Vaseline-greased handle challenged her touch. "That woman's sick!" commented a soothing companion. Others laughed. "What the hell's coming off?" others inquired. No response. The locked doors offered no clues.

Time: 8:47. The students stood outside buzzing, discussing, laughing, curiously involved, reacting, and responding to an invitation that explained nothing. The only promise: Anything WILL happen.

Time: 8:48. A click. A door is unlocked. Another student, brave Joe, unhappily touches the greased handles and opens the door to find a dark curtain just waiting to be pushed. Utter darkness. Joe leads the pushing crowd into the once-familiar auditorium. Now, without benefit of light, students bump into misplaced chairs, wastepaper baskets, and other carefully placed obstacles that inform the stumbling students they are on alien territory.

Time: 8:50. A voice over the auditorium's public address system: "Freeze! Stand where you are! There will be light. Sit quickly and quietly. Do not disturb the environment. You are a guest here. Everything is carefully designed to welcome you to *SUSPENSE*, a very special place."

Dim houselights illuminate the room with just enough light to cast shadows on the rows of seats that have not been corded off. The seats, selected according to a maze of sorts, beckon the students to sit and to wait. Giggles, titters, whispers fill the room.

"Sit down! Shhhhhhhhhhhhhhh!"

A candle appears. The houselights go down. One single light. Then incense provides the aroma that separates the outer sanctum from the inner sanctum. A screen is lowered on stage. Lights out.

The movie *And Then There Were None*, starring Barry Fitzgerald, begins. The class is intrigued by Agatha Christie's clever plot, which centers around invitations sent to ten who will encounter death according to the little poem "Ten Little Indians." Before the last reel is shown, the houselights go up. Ms. Brown steps forth and says, "You have all witnessed the strange behavior in this mansion. Now you must think. Each of you will be given an index card. On it, sign your name. And write who you think is the murderer and explain how you reached that conclusion. Be very careful to think through your solutions."

During the next fifteen or twenty minutes Ms. Brown lets the students talk among themselves and write the concluding scenes for the movie. She then collects the cards and calls upon students to express their opinions. She eagerly watches the interaction among the students as they agree and disagree. She offers no comments.

After this short period of discussion Ms. Brown identifies four students as "star witnesses" to the crimes. She tells them to organize the sequence of events as they remember them and to recall as many details as possible. The rest of the class is to do this on an individual basis. Any one of them may be called for additional testimony. At this point she introduces Detective John Proust of the local police department. Detective Proust has been called in to gather as much information as possible about the murders.

The next half hour reveals an interesting series of interviews with the star witnesses. Detective Proust explains his methods of gathering data and how a modern detective bureau goes about solving crimes. Detective Proust is quite efficient and frank in interrogating the witnesses. He listens and sometimes challenges statements, checking for facts versus opinions.

It is now lunch time. The students are asked to keep their observations to themselves. They will report back in forty minutes for further adventures in *SUSPENSE*.

When the students return, they note that a Detective/Police Bureau has been established. As the students file back into the auditorium, they see several chairs behind a large table. On each chair hangs a sign that represents a popular television policeman/detective. *Columbo, Barnaby Jones, Police Woman, Kojak, Starsky and Hutch,* and *Quincy* are some of the labels on the chairs. Each student goes to the chair of the detective he/she wants to assist in solving the crime. Groups are then formed, and students are assigned seats in the auditorium based on their detective choices. For the next half hour each group drafts a plan of how their detective would go about solving the crime. A recorder summarizes the findings and proceedings and turns the report in to Ms. Brown.

This report is the background for developing short stories or plays or television scripts that will feature the further adventures of the chosen detectives. Ms. Brown then leads a discussion about the techniques used in the film to create the suspense. She points out the artistry demonstrated by the actors and actresses, the director, the cameramen, the film editors, the composers of the musical score, the costume and set designers, the makeup specialists, the special effects artists, and so on.

This then leads to a good discussion of how successful mysteries are developed in books. Ms. Brown introduces a series of writers who are well known for their abilities in startling readers. Among the authors listed are Edgar Allan Poe, Arthur Conan Doyle, G. K. Chesterton, Ellery Queen, Ian Fleming, Dorothy Sayers, Agatha Christie, Shirley Jackson, Bram Stoker, Joan Aiken, John Buchan, Raymond Chandler, Wilkie Collins, Graham

Greene, Dashiell Hammett, Harry Kemelman, John LeCarre, Ross Mac-
Donald, Ngaio Marsh, Rex Stout, Daphne DuMaurier, Victoria Holt, Robert
Ludlum, Helen MacInnes, Alistair MacLean, Jay Bennett, Patricia Windsor,
Mary Shelley, Louisa May Alcott, Josephine Tey, Ray Bradbury, Rod
Serling, Alfred Hitchcock, Erle Stanley Gardner, and Mary R. Rinehart.

Ms. Brown points out that tales of mystery and suspense are very
definitely popular forms of literature. Basically, a mystery story deals with a
crime and its solution. An author has a wide range of approaches that may
be followed from crime to solution. The techniques and ingredients used
may vary from super labs and high-powered detectives to careful dropping
of clues along the way to challenge each reader to decide "whodunit." Some
authors may even invoke the supernatural to create an atmosphere of
mystery. Others, in the name of science, calculate their inventions to create
monsters out of control. The setting may be anywhere and everywhere.

Finally, Ms. Brown concludes her introductory remarks by showing the
final reel of *And Then There Were None*. Students discuss the conclusion
and voice their reactions to this classic "whodunit."

Class dismissed.

The goals of this unit are (1) to acquaint students with some of the
outstanding authors of mystery and suspense; (2) to show students the
different forms of this genre: gothic tale, detective story, science fiction, case
history of a psychopathic criminal, tales of the bizarre and occult; (3) to
show students that stories of this type have a long and popular history; (4) to
acquaint students with specific techniques that authors use for the development of characters, plots, settings, moods, atmosphere, suspense, and
emotions; (5) to help students see the difference between "media" mysteries
and those created by outstanding writers; and (6) to provide a range of
suggested activities for involving the students' creativity in expressing their
ideas and talents related to this theme.

In discussing differences between media mysteries and those mysteries
meant to be read, students will realize that in a film all the elements of
suspense and terror must be developed visually. For example, Dracula's old,
decaying castle in Transylvania should, through visual effects, draw the
viewer into the vampire's domicile and power. Also, music, lighting, acting,
special camera angles, and effects are important ingredients in creating
television and movie mysteries. In a book the author uses written words to
develop an interest in his characters and events.

Students should read intensively and extensively. All assignments will
emphasize mastery of reading and writing skills as related to the purposes
and materials used for this unit. Students will be expected to participate in
class discussions and to participate in panel or dramatic presentations.
Presenting scenes from such plays as *Sleuth* or *Arsenic and Old Lace* or *The*

Mousetrap will offer opportunities for explaining character interpretations. Seeing the film version of *Dracula* with Bela Lugosi and seeing the current Broadway presentation can spark interesting comments in the form of oral or written reviews.

Alfred Hitchcock in *Life* magazine (July 13, 1959) described suspense as follows:

> Let us suppose that three men are sitting in a room in which a bomb has been planted. It is going to go off in ten minutes. The audience does not know it is there, and the men do not know it is there either, so they go on talking inanely about the weather or yesterday's baseball game. After ten minutes of desultory conversation, the bomb goes off. What's the result? The unsuspecting audience gets a surprise. That's all. Suppose the story were told differently. This time, while the men still do not know the bomb is there, the audience does know. The men still talk inanities, but now the most banal thing they say is charged with excitement. When one finally says, "Let's leave," the entire audience is praying for them to do so. But another man says, "No, wait a minute. I want to finish my coffee." The audience groans inwardly and yearns for them to leave. That is suspense.

Students can be encouraged to create several suspense scenes based on the explanation given by Hitchcock. Some can develop ideas for television shows or short films, whereas others can present their ideas in short stories and novellas. Several written selections might form the basis for a new mystery magazine published by the class.

Students interested in art might illustrate the original stories written by other students. Art students might turn the classroom into a ghostly, ghastly environment. Pictures and posters and artifacts can be hung to lure readers into the realm of suspense.

Listening experiences will be developed through recordings of Lucille Fletcher's "Sorry, Wrong Number," or Edgar Allan Poe's "The Tell-Tale Heart." There are now readily available reissues of Basil Rathbone in dramatic episodes of the *Adventures of Sherlock Holmes*. Recordings of such famous radio programs as *Inner Sanctum, Lights Out, The Green Hornet*, among others, are available in record stores. Who can ever forget the shocking impact of *War of the Worlds*?

In this lesson, developed thematically, all students would be guided into reading with which they could succeed. Skills would be taught that would enable the students to meet the reading, writing, speaking, listening, and visual literacy assignments related to this unit of study. Most students would be motivated by such a topic and could draw on their experiences to develop individual and small group projects that would reflect their learnings. All of the related arts—music, theater, art, puppetry, dance, mime, and journalism—as well as reading and writing would be at the disposal of the students as means to interpret and/or explain the impact the unit was having on each and every one. This topic is a natural for developing critical thinking. Students would have to be able to predict outcomes, be alert to facts and opinions, be able to make inferences, and be sensitive to the nature and values of language as developed by print and nonprint "creators."

Conclusion

Independence is a major objective of any communications program. The media center would be the source for many books, magazines, reference materials, and all kinds of nonprint materials necessary for the fulfillment of this unit. Students would choose on their own those resources that would help them fulfill their objectives for the course.

A most important factor in this type of program is that it does provide for individual needs and abilities. All students can and do participate. All students are contributors. Each student has talents that he/she can bring into play as the unit progresses over six or eight weeks.

17

JEROME D. KAPLAN, Seton Hall University

A Different View of Content: Implementing the Mathematics Curriculum

Mathematics offers every student the opportunity to be successful within the context of the school experience. This potential is clearly not fulfilled. On the contrary, numerous surveys and attitude indices have shown that mathematics is often ranked as the school subject liked the least. The study of mathematics produces anxiety in learners that sometimes leads to high achievement but often is a debilitating factor, causing students to quake in Pavlovian fashion at the mere mention of the word. Even mature, successful adults when faced with a bit of real mathematics become paralyzed at the sight of an equation or mathematical statement.

The anxiety is deep and real. It starts early and continues building over many school years. Ask adults to trace the roots of their mathematics phobia and discover that a series of early school experiences is at the heart of their problems. Because mathematics anxiety is widespread at the early stages of schooling, many students experience frustration and fall behind. School districts spend many dollars and teachers spend many hours trying to help students who are having trouble. High anxiety means low efficiency. If some of the anxiety were reduced, students would become more confident and competent, and teachers would be more effective.

Why Is Mathematics Difficult?

Mathematics is perceived by many students as being difficult. There is justification for this belief for these reasons:

- Mathematics is often expressed symbolically.

- Mathematics lacks redundancy.

- Mathematics learning is cumulative.

Its symbolism gives mathematics the appearance of another language. Whether at the first grade or graduate school level, mathematical ideas are rarely expressed in standard English expressions. During their first years of school children learn symbols for numbers, operations, and relations. Many students are eliminated early on if they cannot master the ideas, logic, and language of mathematics.

Not only do symbols represent a language, but also when used together they provide mathematical presentation with little or no redundancy. Redundancy characterizes most texts on most subjects; in fact, most explanations are redundant. But mathematical statements appear carrying the bare bones of the message. Their compactness of thought and expression minimizes the amount of available "review."

One of the biggest problems confronting teachers is the sequential aspect of mathematics. Each year is built on the learnings of the previous year. Multiplication requires addition; division requires multiplication and subtraction. Most skills of the school mathematics curriculum lean heavily on previous learning, creating a network of dependencies that reaches back to primitive number concepts. If the chain is broken at any stage or skill, then the student will have difficulty with new concepts and skills.

These characteristics—the presence of symbols, the lack of redundancy, and sequencing—define not only higher level mathematics but also first grade mathematics as it is frequently taught today. Other subjects do not possess all three characteristics.

Because mathematics turns out to be difficult for so many students, it gains a reputation for being difficult, creating anxiety that gets passed on from one class to another, from one generation to the next. Often, the same teachers who are in a position to reduce anxiety are themselves anxious about teaching mathematics.

A Curriculum Proposal

The cycle of difficulty and anxiety continues. To disrupt the cycle a major revision of mathematics instruction would be needed. One possibility would have only mathematics specialists teaching mathematics to children.

They would not only specialize in mathematics but also be enthusiastic teachers. Excitement about teaching is certainly an important ingredient for any school subject. However, the idea of specialists is too impractical for today's schools; more practical is curriculum change.

Curriculum changes do not alter the basic attitude of teachers toward the teaching of mathematics, but they can create situations that enable teachers to be more relaxed while teaching it. This chapter suggests three curriculum directions that, when taken together, have the potential of changing the school atmosphere for teaching. The chief goal would be to allow *all* students to advance according to their potential. The three components are as follows:

- A remodeling of early childhood mathematics. In the mathematics program from kindergarten to second grade, emphasis would be placed on the tactile, not the symbolic. Few schools truly practice a Piagetian curriculum—early nonsymbolic contexts for developing basic concepts.

- Classroom management systems (CMS) for the teaching and maintenance of skills at all grade levels from second to twelfth grade. The CMS proposed here is diagnostic/prescriptive and functions to bring together key information for the teacher about instruction— mathematics objectives, student diagnosis, available prescriptive materials, evaluation, record keeping, and management techniques.

- Transference of skills to solve problems. From the second grade onward the curriculum would be extended beyond skill development and skill maintenance to include problems of differing value— mathematical, personal, environmental, vocational, and economic. Problems would include games and puzzles, dice and cards, newspapers and books—in short, any situation or material that enhances thinking by giving students an opportunity to use their skills.

None of these proposals is new. Each has been installed in different schools in many ways, requiring little in additional resources. Perhaps what is new is the proposed implementation of all three components simultaneously throughout one school unit. The combined curriculum framework is unusual not because of the specifics of the design but because of the requirement that it be articulated across the grades. Ultimately, good leadership and open communication are at the heart of the proposal. The leadership required must be prepared to take some risks. In this time of back-to-basics and grade-by-grade accountability, the climate is not suited for risk taking. A description of each of the three components will confirm that the proposal is modest indeed. Figure 17-1 shows the placement of the components into the school context.

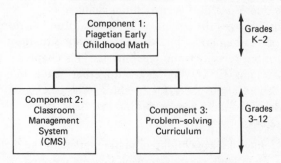

FIGURE 17-1. Grade placement of components.

Nonsymbolic Early Childhood Mathematics

Jean Piaget has written much about children's intellectual development—in particular, number concepts, logic, and space.[1] He has not had too much to say about curriculum and practice. But numerous interpretations of Piaget's work have pointed to the role of concrete experiences for children in the preoperational stage. During this period (approximately 2–7 years old), children often confuse a substance's measurement with the physical appearance of an object or material. For example, preoperational thinking concludes that there is more liquid in a tall thin tube than in a short wide beaker even after the two quantities have been compared and found equivalent. A child who draws this conclusion is not able to conserve liquid.

In the case of number, the child may exhibit preoperational thinking through another of Piaget's tasks on conservation. In this task, the child is shown two equivalent parallel rows of objects (e.g., black and red checkers):

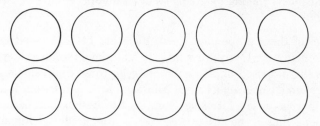

FIGURE 17-2. First step in number conservation task.

[1] J. Piaget, *The Child's Conception of Number* (London: Routledge and Kegan Paul, 1952).

In the first phase of the task, the child is asked which row has more objects (the red one or the black one?). Most school-age children state that the two rows have the same number of objects. One of the two rows is then rearranged, usually by elongating it:

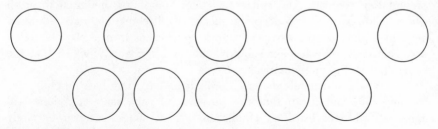

FIGURE 17-3. Second step in number conservation task.

The child is asked the same question as before. At this point many children age 7 and younger state that the longer row has more. The child's understanding of one-to-one correspondence, or conservation of number, is not permanent.

Piaget used tasks such as the liquid and number conservation tasks to determine the stage of the child's intellectual development. For Piaget, conservation is the basis of rational thinking. His results and those of many others who have experimented with his tasks show that most children become operational thinkers around the age of 7. This is not an exact age: there are children who are preoperational before 7 and children who are operational after 7. The difference of thought between these two stages is significant—the operational child thinks logically with respect to substance and quantity; the preoperational child shows an attachment to the physical dimension of a task, often demonstrating ambivalence about a phenomenon.

The preoperational, nonconserving child does not seem to be able to integrate two dimensions simultaneously, e.g., the amount of liquid and the shape of the beaker. The ability to classify objects according to separate dimensions may be an important key concept missing in preoperational thinking. If so, then the role of classification and sorting activities would seem to be important in the early childhood program.

The nature of Piaget's theory and the specific characteristics of the tasks have caused many observers to infer that the preoccupational period requires a learning environment that accents variety and activity. Variety means that concepts are presented in several contexts over a period of time.[2] Activity means that concrete materials become the media for modeling concepts. It also means that symbolic modes are delayed for most children. The latter

[2] Z. P. Dienes, *Building up Mathematics* (London: Hutchinson Educational Ltd., 1960).

point is often not present even when good modeling is present. Children need to explore each concept continuously through different models.

A single model may be instinctive to some children but not to all. The probability of reaching all children is raised by increasing the number of presentation contexts. And conceptual understanding is heightened for all when children "see" a concept by means of different materials. Children need to explore on their own and draw conclusions from their interaction with materials. The teacher should guide children's activities so that the system fosters key mathematical concepts.

To state that concrete materials provide an important base for children's learning does not mean that the presence of such materials alone will enhance children's learning. Haphazard use of materials never or rarely directed to conceptual enhancement misses the point. Teachers must be able to extract from each set of materials the relevant concept at the appropriate time. This attribute requires an undertaking of concepts, materials, and management. Because the goal of concrete activity is conceptual development, it is an axiom of the early childhood period that children must play, explore, and discover.

To illustrate the two elements of variety and concrete activity, the concept of addition of whole numbers, usually introduced and practiced during kindergarten and first grade, must be examined. The basic idea behind whole number addition is the union of two disjoint sets. The sum is the number of the union, the addends are the numbers of the two sets. Consider two sets of objects as an illustration of how the definition translates into a specific model (Figure 17-4) where the x's and o's represent concrete objects such as chips, shells, stones, or buttons.

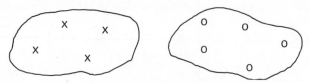

FIGURE 17-4. Two sets of objects, disjoint from each other.

The number of the combined set (Figure 17-5) is 9, which is the sum of the numbers (4 and 5) of the two sets. This model, the standard used for introducing addition, should be presented using many different kinds of materials. Furthermore, each set should be composed of materials of different sizes, shapes, and colors. Often a set presented to a child or constructed by a child is made up of the same objects (red chips, yellow cubes, or green blocks). Varying the objects that make up each set is often overlooked, but this idea represents a step up the hierarchy of number. Some children who conserve number when the objects are all alike cannot conserve when the objects are different.

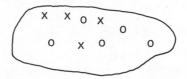

FIGURE 17-5. The union of the two sets of figure 17-4.

Classroom Management System (CMS) for Maintenance of Skills

A management system for the classroom is the means by which critical information is brought together and placed at the disposal of the users—teachers, supervisors, students—so that the best curriculum decisions can be made. One aspect of information retrieval for decision making is often neglected: namely, the instantaneous availability of information. Much information gathered about student performance often does not get back to teachers until after a week, a month, or a school year goes by. CMS provides information regularly and immediately; in fact, as frequently as required by its users.

The main purpose of creating CMS is to provide teachers with a diagnostic/prescriptive system that offers information about the status of the basic skills of students. CMS is the second component of an overall program designed to give students a full opportunity to realize their potential. CMS does not become operational until the second grade and continues, in some form, through the grades to be used as necessary by each teacher. It exists specifically to teach, reinforce, and maintain skills in computation, geometry, and measurement.

When CMS is fully operational within each classroom it enables teachers to differentiate instruction by providing these broad areas of information:

- The entry status of each student on a hierarchy of skills.

- The available instructional methods and materials that teach the identified skills.

- The specific objectives that each student has mastered and the individual rate of mastery.

- The degree to which each instructional resource can teach each of the skills.

The main components of the CMS will now be described:

1. Curriculum Objectives (CO's)

The starting point of CMS is a series of curriculum objectives arranged in hierarchical fashion according to the design of Gagne.[3] These objectives consist of those skills chosen by teachers and supervisors as being important for students to learn and master. Although the objectives that result may be those necessary to satisfy a testing program, in the end it is hoped that objectives would be more student centered. What are students' interests and students' goals? How can the curriculum be filled with concepts and skills that make the learning of mathematics personal, intellectual, and practical? Is there an overwhelming pressure to produce increased test scores at the expense of student interest? These and other questions must be aired before a good set of objectives is chosen. Finally, for CMS it is clearly not necessary for the objectives to be graded. CMS is a mastery curriculum that promotes children through the system when they demonstrate successful performance.

2. Curriculum Based Tests (CBT's)

The CBT's serve as tests of mastery for the CO's. Among the CO's there are those that are critical to the curriculum. A critical CO is one that culminates a unit or a sequence. The objectives in the sequence preceding a critical CO are the prerequisites for that CO. A CBT is available for each CO; a critical CO consists of ten items, whereas a prerequisite CO consists of five items.

3. Enabling CO's

For the critical CO's the prerequisite of enabling CO's allows teachers to diagnose a student's difficulty further by backing up to an earlier CO that the student has not mastered.

4. Prescriptions

Two kinds of prescriptions are available:

- Correlations to the major textbooks used in school.

- Correlations to all supplementary materials available to teachers.

[3] Robert M. Gagne, *The Conditions of Learning* (New York: Holt, Rinehart and Winston, 1970).

5. Recordkeeping System

- Classroom Profile—kept by the teacher to record each child's curriculum and progress, CO's, assigned and mastered.

- Student Progress Form—each student maintains a record of CO's mastered and those requiring additional instruction.

6. Answer Keys

Answer keys are available for easy checking of CBT's by teachers and students. In addition to answer keys for all tests, answer keys to all instructional materials must also be available.

7. Management Techniques

CMS is an arrangement of the instructional environment to provide diagnostic/prepscriptive teaching in the basic skills. The key aspect that ties together all other components is not visible itself. It is a process that includes such diverse activities as modifying materials, moving furniture, rewarding behavior, and other maneuvers that prepare the classroom so that students can have easy access to instructional materials, answers, records, and tests; so that recordkeeping is simple; and so that individual diagnosis and prescription can be achieved with a minimum of interruption and waiting time. One main goal behind CMS is to increase the independence of the students, to give each student an expanding role in managing his/her environment.

Good management is the medium by which appropriate and accurate information gets to the people who need it. To ensure that students have a role in managing the environment, it is useful to teach students the procedures and logic of the system early in the year. Such seemingly minor issues as acquiring of tests or materials, or reading an assigned prescription, or returning materials, or recording progress (these, and many more) are the guts of the system proposed. In fact, overall classroom management depends on the students' management of their own curricula.

If the choreography and logic of classroom management are understood and put into practice daily, teachers can be free to perform more central teaching functions. The end product of CMS is to release teachers from clerical functions and put teachers back into teaching. This CMS section is incomplete without the final component on problem solving that parallels it. Both run concurrently—one with fewer children, the other with more children. It will sometimes be difficult when the full two components are operational to tell where one leaves off and the other begins. But suffice to say that CMS is not designed to be teacherproof, not at all! In fact, it is not planned for an entire class. It is for some students some of the time.

Any move to CMS must be done slowly. The following implementation plan envisages four phases. Although the structure of these phases should not be thought of as absolute, they should be seen as goals that can be achieved by many teachers by the indicated time periods or earlier. These graduated phases are based on experience in setting up management systems in many classrooms and on the realities of today's classroom. The different phases will take on different time frames depending on many factors: the age of the students, the experience of teachers in setting up management systems, the motivation of teachers, the support of administrators, and the attention span of students. One of the main ingredients on which CMS is postulated is the management technique employed by teachers. With good management, teachers can start the diagnostic/prescriptive process relatively early in the school year. There should be particular emphasis in "start up" procedures during Phase I when the classroom and materials are organized and students prepared for differentiated learning.

An outline of the four phases follows:

- *Phase I—Startup procedure*. Setting up classroom. Modifying materials. Preparing students. Start Project Math. Creating forms. Initial diagnoses.

- *Phase II—Continued modification of materials*. Prescriptions. Instruction with small groups. Student independence. Variety of materials. Continue Project Math.

- *Phase III—More students diagnosed and prescribed*. More students diagnosed and prescribed. Increased independence of students. All forms and records up to date. Flow automatic. Mechanics solved.

- *Phase IV—Full class diagnosed and prescribed*. Variety of teaching modes: lecture, small group, individual students. Traffic flow. Student independence. Students managing environment. Schoolwide projects.

Problem-Centered Teaching

The third component has been designed for one main reason: to enable as many students as possible to use their skills to solve problems—in short, to think. Too frequently students become skillful, pass tests, and are declared proficient, but their efforts are almost rotelike and mindless. Even if the endless drill and practice of some classrooms do not bore students, it is unconscionable to exclude the part of the curriculum that appeals to the mind. In the problem-solving component there are no restrictions on the type of activity that can take place as long as it is intended to be stimulating or relevant or both. Teachers here may use games and puzzles, cards and dice, newspapers and magazines, telephone books and almanacs, coins and calculators, and so on. The standard and not-so-standard manipulative materials (Cuisenaire rods, chip trading, fraction bars, and geoboards) are included here. So are activities related to measurement and geometry. In fact, an entire curriculum can be based on measurement problems using computational skills to find solutions.

In this problem-solving component the curriculum reaches out beyond the border of mathematics and attaches itself to other school curricula such as geography, social studies, reading, science, art, and music. Central themes such as symmetry and symbols can be studies starting at the upper elementary school years. Within these themes separate curricula mix together into an integrated whole. In addition to these aspects of problem solving, there are exercises of experimentation and data gathering. One major motivation in mathematics is the search for pattern. It is almost everywhere—in the number systems, the figures of geometry, and in measurement activities. Collecting data and recording the results via tables and graphs should start early in the child's mathematical life because the world is full of statistics and data collection. The child must realize that arithmetic is a tool to be used in both practical and intellectual purposes.

This problem-centered teaching component of the overall curriculum design has several interesting by-products. The plan calls for CMS (the second component) and this one to coexist from the second grade on. The proportion of CMS to problem solving depends, of course, on the skill development of the students. Both components are to be taught in parallel, not in linear, fashion. They are intended to assist each other in the sense that problems apply basic skills and thus motivate the learning of skills. If a problem (or a puzzle or game) has interest for a student, then presumably the skills required will have to be learned by the student.

The plan envisions part of a class working in CMS while the rest of the class is in the problem mode. For the teacher, the problem-centered activity should provide the opportunity to be creative and stimulating. This component offers considerable latitude to each teacher to assemble materials and ideas. The accent should be to involve as many students as possible in thinking about problems in a low-anxiety atmosphere. Many teachers thrive on the opportunity to be freed from following a rigid curriculum, to pursue a strategy of their own making. The freedom must be accompanied by knowledge that students live in the real world of school. Therefore, while teachers foster problem solving, they must communicate their curriculum to other teachers. Graphing techniques developed only in the third grade would leave students vastly underdeveloped in this area.

Conclusion

All teachers within a building should be a party to the curriculum moves proposed here. An articulated list of skills properly communicated does not stifle growth; it raises teachers and students to expected levels carefully defined. Strands of curriculum thinking should run across the grades with the commitment to exchanging ideas with colleagues.

The entire proposal, modest in its separateness but bold in the combination of all three elements, demands leadership and communication. It is the belief here that all parts already exist, that it is now a question of assembling the parts—getting it all together.

18

WARREN M. SINGER, Montclair Public Schools

The Gifted Child in Science

Introduction

Concern for the education of the gifted is not new. History reveals that Plato over two thousand years ago advocated the institution of specialized instruction for gifted children in a variety of academic areas. Under the leadership of Suleiman the Magnificent of the Ottoman Empire concerted efforts were made to accommodate the gifted with special training in the sciences. The concern generated for educating the gifted seems to be a manifestation of the social and political beliefs of the society and the time.[1]

As Gallagher points out, American society is faced with "a new sense of urgency" for addressing the needs of gifted children in the educational system.[2] With this in mind, the writer proposes to suggest a curriculum of concern for the gifted student in the study of science.

Thorndike characterizes the gifted as the "best thinkers," and their education should be an "education for initiative and originality."[3] There is

---

[1] Samuel Kirk, *Educating Exceptional Children* (Boston: Houghton Mifflin, 1962), pp. 35-37.

[2] Ibid., p. 37, citing James Gallagher, *Analysis of Research on the Education of Gifted Children* (Springfield, Ill.: Office of the Superintendent of Public Instruction, 1960), pp. 1-2.

[3] Paul Witty, *The American Association for the Gifted Child* (Boston: Heath, 1951), p. 60.

need to provide a curriculum for rapid learners different in degree, but not essentially in kind, from the traditional curriculum for all children.[4]

Gifted children learn rapidly and easily. These children often read above grade level and retain what they have read or heard without appearing to need much drill practice.[5] They often possess large vocabularies. Further, gifted children frequently are capable of recognizing implied relationships and comprehending diverse meanings. They often ask penetrating, searching questions, probably an outgrowth of their natural curiosity and investigative manner. These children appear to possess a long attention span and are flexible and resourceful in problem-solving techniques. That is, gifted children are individuals who are characteristically independent, individualistic, and self-sufficient.[6]

Terman regarded the gifted as "the most retarded group in education when mental age and chronological age are related to their actual school experience."[7]

Children gifted in science are often curious and want to know. They readily toy with an idea. They are willing to question, explore, and follow an inclination to determine what might happen. These children are keenly inquisitive and observant by nature. They are curious about people, objects, and situations; they question everything and everyone. They often explore mechanical things, constantly searching for *why*. Gifted children are more apt to question why things are not done differently than the usual way.

These children have strong imaginations; they can visualize and dream about things that have never happened to them. They are challenged by complexity. They seem to thrive on complicated situations. They become intrigued with problematic situations, frequently delving into complicated tasks. They most often want to figure things out for themselves, without help, while seeking more difficult answers rather than accepting an easy one.

Programming for Gifted in Science

Any discussion of programming must start with an assessment of each child and then continue to placement within the appropriate school environment and school experiences. Plowman contends that the desirable environment and experiences should be planned to promote behavioral characteris-

---

[4] Ibid., p. 60.

[5] Ruth A. Martinson, *A Guide Toward Better Teaching for the Gifted* (Ventura, Calif.: Office of the Superintendent of Schools, 1976).

[6] Ibid.

[7] Ruth A. Martinson, *Educational Programs for Gifted Pupils* (Sacramento, Calif.: California State Department of Education, 1961).

tics of the gifted student and to provide an atmosphere in which it will be possible to draw out and develop the child's uniqueness.[8]

Programming is an ongoing process and, as such, must be founded on the continual evaluation of development of specific intellectual skills, interests, knowledge, traits of creativity, attitudes, values, and aspirations. The teacher then must be continually aware of the level of each pupil with respect to skills, knowledge, and concepts. The teacher becomes an educational diagnostician and a prescription specialist, attempting to "articulate learning sequence in such ways that there appears to be a natural flow of ideas and development from one position to the consideration of a whole galaxy of ideas."[9]

Science Curriculum Planning

I have determined in my investigation of the gifted that educators appear concerned with engineering an educational environment for gifted children that encourages diversity and excellence. Science teaching must be defined in terms of opportunities for both independent and interdependent learning.

The curriculum designed for gifted students in science must place emphasis on advanced concepts. Hawkins formulated a three-phase approach to arrive at advanced conceptualization:[10]

- *Phase I. Exploration:* Children are provided with time devoted to free and unguided exploratory work. They are given equipment and are permitted to construct, test, and experiment without any instruction.

- *Phase II. Elaboration:* "On hand" material must be provided with written or illustrated guidance. It is designed for the greatest diversity of study topics.

- *Phase III. Synthesis:* This encompasses experiences that will provide children with opportunities to go from the "concrete perceptual to the abstract perceptual."

"Gifted students, particularly, will profit as they learn to understand the larger theoretical positions and generalizations that follow from the specific phenomena that they originally observed."[11]

[8] P. D. Plowman, *Programming for the Gifted Child, Exceptional Children*, March 1969, pp. 547-549.

[9] Ibid., pp. 547-549.

[10] James J. Gallagher, *Teaching the Gifted Child* (Boston: Allyn and Bacon, 1975), p. 126.

[11] Ibid., p. 127.

Gallagher points out that it is not solely in the process of science that students need to be taught, but in the conceptual realm that signifies new ways of looking at the world around us.[12]

The best way to teach the skills involved is not to focus on them directly but rather to utilize the processes in an attempt to construct general scientific principles.

Gallagher has further postulated that the process or method should not be studied as an entity in itself; it is more important to study how to make use of the method or tool in a specific problem area. "Science is not a body of knowledge but a method of obtaining new knowledge,"[13] he states.

As Fliegler points out, children who are gifted in science frequently possess an intense curiosity about natural phenomena; they want to know how things function and why.[14] Fliegler has suggested that the science teacher design (in advance) a series of problems that each child can attempt to solve by his/her own methods. The child's real pleasure comes from designing his/her own experiment and solving it.[15] The answer may be of secondary importance. This excitement is often generated when children pursue problems that hold special interest for them. Stress is too often placed on scientific products. It is of the utmost significance that gifted children learn that the true nature of science is a vehicle for searching out the truth. Emphasis must be on active student participation in science combined with the highest level of complexity each child can master.[16]

Identification of the Gifted

Any program for gifted students must necessarily begin with some form of identification procedure. All too often, many students who might be potential candidates for such programs are denied access because they exhibit asocial behavior or an interest in a nonacademic subject. The school has the major responsibility for identifying a child's uniqueness.

In schools where children can be observed in a wide variety of learning activities, teachers have a much better chance to detect indicators of giftedness. The Montclair, New Jersey, program for the gifted/talented is one example; it offers children a wide range of exploratory learning experiences. Teachers can observe children in a broad spectrum of electives,

[12] Ibid., p. 139

[13] Ibid., p. 139.

[14] Louis A. Fliegler, *Curriculum Planning for the Gifted* (Englewood Cliffs, N.J.: Prentice-Hall, 1961), p. 142.

[15] Ibid., p. 143.

[16] Gallagher, op. cit., p. 144.

thereby providing opportunity for gifts and talents to surface. The child whose talents are masked by disruptive behavior may eventually be identified through participation in such enriched educational programs. Enrichment of this kind often generates the motivation necessary to arouse the child's interests. Giftedness, which might otherwise go undetected, may then be discovered and nurtured.

Identifying the Gifted in Science

An early attempt to identify children gifted in science was conducted by Jean Piaget. He devised an experiment to determine the development of conceptual ordering in children. A liquid was poured from a wide container into a narrower cylindrical one. The children were then asked if there was more liquid in the second container than in the first. They generally determined that there was more liquid in the narrow container even though they saw the experimenter pour the same amount of liquid from the wider to the narrower one. Piaget concluded that they had not, at that level in their development, understood the concept of "constancy of volume." Gifted children were able to come to the conclusion that the amount of liquid remains constant earlier than the other children with fewer "manipulations of the operation."[17]

A broad criterion of giftedness was presented by Dr. P. A. Witty that focused its attention on potential leaders in science. It was developed so that teachers and parents can work collaboratively in supplementary efforts to identify these children. Witty's criterion includes the following:

1. Early and accurate use of a large vocabulary and unusual proficiency in other aspects of language development.

2. Keen observation and retention of facts.

3. Early interest in calendars and telling time.

4. Attraction to picture books at a very young age.

5. Unusual ability to give and sustain attention.

6. Discovery, when the child is young, of cause and effect relationships.

7. Demonstration of competency in drawing, painting, singing, and other creative abilities.

8. Rapidity and originality of verbal responses.

[17] Teaching Gifted Children Science, Department of Public Instruction (California State Department of Education, 1973), pp. 8-9.

9. Early interest and proficiency in reading and a great liking for books—including encyclopedias, atlases and dictionaries.[18]

In 1961 Dr. Louis Fliegler developed a comprehensive checklist for identifying children who are gifted in the science area:

1. Interest in science during the preschool years.

2. Curiosity as to what makes things work.

3. Ability to understand abstract ideas at an early age.

4. Strong imagination in things scientific.

5. A love of collecting.

6. Abundance of drive—willingness to work on a science project for long periods of time in face of difficult obstacles.

7. Better-than-average ability in reading and mathematics.

8. Unusual ability to verbalize ideas about science.

9. High intelligence. IQ of 120 or more.

10. Tendency to think quantitatively—to use numbers to help express ideas.

11. Willingness to master the names of scientific objects.

12. Tendency to write stories about science, including the writing of science fiction.

13. Creativity in science projects and delight in studying science for science's sake.

14. Evident discontent with reasons which other children readily accept for things scientific.

15. Exceptional memory for details.

16. Willingness to spend long periods of time working alone.

17. Ability to generalize from seemingly unrelated details.

18. Ability to perceive relationships among various elements in a situation.[19]

[18] Pearl W. Schwartz, Compendium of Methods for the Teaching of Science to Gifted Children, *Science Education*, 1968, 53, 131, citing Witty (1964).

[19] Ibid., p. 131, citing Fliegler (1961).

Development of Logical and Scientific Thinking

Dr. J. Richard Suchman emphasized that human knowledge is acquired through perception, analysis, inference, theorizing, and verification. Suchman's Inquiry Program has had exceptional adaptability for use with gifted children in science education. The program's goals are to develop leadership characteristics, critical thinking processes, and a systematic approach for discovering facts and concepts. According to Suchman, one of the most outstanding strategies of the inquiry process is "the identification of properties of objects and systems." Once the properties have been verified, through further inquiry and experimentation the student is better able to predict behavior. The chief role of the teachers is "to stimulate and support the creative and analytical thinking of his students."[20]

Some practical techniques for use in science programs for gifted students have been proposed that involve learning the structures and processes of thinking. These thinking techniques are critical, convergent, divergent, inductive, deductive, and comparative.

Critical thinking can be manifested in open-ended questions. Through analysis, comparison, and evaluation the child is able to make a judgment. Such a question might be stated, "What do you think would have occurred in this experiment if . . . ?"

In convergent thinking the individual starts with some given facts and then proceeds logically and systematically to construct the one correct solution to a given problem.

G. P. Guilford acknowledges a distinction between the operations of convergent thinking, which are represented by the kind of abilities that standard IQ tests measure, and divergent thinking, which includes fluency, foresight, and flexibility.[21]

Divergent thinking is not often measured in most aptitude tests used in schools.[22] An example of an assignment designed to promote divergent thinking might be to suggest possible uses for paper that decomposes one year after having been exposed to the air.

Inductive thinking teaches children to reason from specific observations to a general conclusion: "How are these situations related: Placing a jar under hot water so it can be opened; sagging telephone wires; and movable joints on a bridge."[23]

---

[20] Ibid., p. 133, citing Suchman's "Inquiry Program."

[21] Gallagher, op. cit., p. 53.

[22] Ibid., p. 53.

[23] Schwartz, op. cit., p. 134, citing Berenson (1966).

Deductive thinking involves reasoning from the general to the specific: "If air contracts as it cools and some liquids expand as they freeze, what would happen to each of the following at thirty-two degrees Fahrenheit: a bottle of soda, a bicycle tire, an inflated balloon?"[24]

Comparative thinking involves comparison for differences and similarities. The teacher might ask the student to test the consistently rising or falling temperatures of a bicycle pump as it is being vigorously pumped.[25]

Children should be given opportunities to generate their own ideas relative to systems as a whole. If not, they are overwhelmed with specific information that is often difficult to integrate into generalizations and new understandings. Curricular efforts should lead to generalizations: "There are one hundred and two known elements. How were we able to learn about the structure of atoms and molecules we never have been able to see?"[26]

Children derive considerable satisfaction from investigating and discovering what makes things happen as they do. The gifted child in particular appears to be challenged by a variety of new and different materials and, as a consequence, enjoys being involved in the task of solving problems. One can readily perceive that gifted children are scientists by disposition. It is this intense natural curiosity toward which a science curriculum for gifted children should direct its program thrust.

Although many of the commercial science programs have considerable educational merit and viability, they fall short in balancing the dimensions of content and process. In order to be effective, each dimension should become the vehicle for the development of the other. The process dimension seems to be overly stressed. The students should learn skills as a means to increase their knowledge of subject material. Although it is not the function of the elementary school to produce scientists, the school must be held accountable for what the child has or has not learned. It is not realistic to expect children to have suddenly acquired all the skills necessary to learn content. The children should be developing knowledge, facts, and concepts along with the processes.

Units and activities should be designed so that gifted children are placed in situations that give rise to complex problems for them to solve in their own special way. In short, the program should be one that encourages the children to use their highest intellectual resources.

Experienced educators have discovered that one of the most successful techniques of getting a student to perform more industriously is to build on some established interest. Drawing from the children's experiences and

---

[24] Ibid., p. 134.

[25] Ibid., p. 134.

[26] Gallagher, op. cit., p. 143.

creating a problem approach stimulates both curiosity and "the desire for masters."[27]

It is not the function of the elementary school to begin producing technicians and science specialists. It is education's task to provide experiences for children that demonstrate the interrelationship of all knowledge.[28] Content should then be designed so that students have a wide range of opportunities to manipulate science materials, thus enabling them to attempt scientific approaches to the solution of problems.[29]

Suggested activities will provide examples of how many important concepts gifted children can investigate and learn. It must be kept in mind that the performance of these science activities and the mastering of the concepts by the children are not ends in themselves. It is essential that the students take an active role as they investigate specific phenomena. Similarly, they must be guided into productive and meaningful avenues of exploration.

The curriculum, in sum, should provide for maximum student participation in things scientific and should be representative of activities that involve high levels of complexity.

Students should be given many opportunities to generate their own ideas relative to systems as a whole. Critical thinking activities can be manifested in open-ended questions. Creative writing and discussion sessions can be built around any of the following open-ended questions:

- What would happen if all the electricity were turned off in your town?

- How would Montclair, New Jersey, be different if moved to Alaska?

- Suggest possible uses for paper that decomposes one year after having been exposed to the air.

Special programming for gifted elementary school children should concentrate on instructing them in critical thinking skills and problem-solving techniques that will enable them to become independent learners.

The science content should be designed in such a manner that students have the chance to express ideas of their own in their own way. Creating a problem approach to learning stimulates curiosity and enhances the children's desire to participate in many learning experiences.

The "Time Machine" and "Proximity" are lessons developed by Marvin

[27] Norma E. Cutts and Nicholas Moseley, *Teaching the Bright and Gifted* (Englewood Cliffs, N.J.: Prentice-Hall, 1957), p. 142.

[28] Benjamin Fine, *Stretching Their Minds* (New York: E. P. Dutton), p. 110.

[29] Ibid., p. 119.

J. Gold, past-president of the Association for the Gifted.[30] These lessons attempt to stimulate the creative and critical thinking processes. They provide the children with a large number of possible associations and problem solutions.

The Time Machine

Objectives:

1. Students will gain an appreciation of the effect of various individuals on history.

2. Students will gain insight into the intricacies of, and possible solutions to, problems that confront contemporary society.

Process Skills:

Drawing inferences, evaluation, synthesis.

Procedures:

A historical personality is transported to contemporary times for the purpose of solving a critical problem. The individual's work and background should be such that he/she is qualified to solve the designated problem. The student should study and analyze the individual's life experiences related to the problem and be prepared to draw inferences as to how this individual of the past might deal effectively with a modern-day problem.

Activity Options:

1. Individuals research figures of the past and some topics of concern; a report is written.

2. Small groups of students participate in panel discussions or dramatizations.

3. Committee work is done by the whole class to investigate the appropriateness of one of many historical personalities who could possibly deal with the problem.

Illustration:

Benjamin Banneker is charged with solving a contemporary city planning problem.

Theodore Roosevelt is charged with solving modern ecological problems.

Variations:

1. Have a leading figure of the present transported back in time.

---

[30] Marvin J. Gold, Introducing the Gifted, *Exceptional Children*, 1971, *38*, 593-596.

2. Have this same character sent into the future.[31]

Proximity

Objectives:
Convergent thinking, divergent thinking, and evaluation.
Procedures:
This is an exercise that shows the relationship of one thing and/or fact to another. The activity is initiated with one "cue" science term; each pupil adds a related term. The students work against a time limit while adding on additional terms. The activity is terminated when time is exhausted.
Activity Options:
1. An individual child constructs his/her own sequence or chain of terms. The child records the sequence to compete with himself within a period of time.
2. Children competing in small groups or teams have approximately six minutes to prepare their lists of terms. The team with the longest list (without errors) wins the match.
3. The activity can be done by the entire class. Children are called on randomly to add items to the list.
Example:
Electricity (cue), circuit, switch, relay, current, wave, tide, moon, satellite, TV, communications, etc.
Variations:
1. Proceed in the least possible number of steps from the cue to an unrelated terminus word.
2. Work from the cue term back to itself without repeating any item.[32]

I have found that the following activities suggest ways to broaden the child's understanding of the skills he/she has acquired during a unit on electricity:
1. Make an electric game or toy of your own design.
2. Design an experiment to demonstrate how an electromagnet functions.
3. Invent a burglar alarm system that sounds when a window or door is opened.

[31] Ibid., p. 596.
[32] Ibid., p. 594.

4. Prepare a written report that discusses the similarities of the scientific contributions of Thomas Edison and Lewis Lattimer, or Benjamin Banneker and Benjamin Franklin.

5. Design an automatic switch that sounds a buzzer when a tub fills with water.

Conclusion

Gifted students are often held to activities that have been designed for the average student. This often proves to be regressive, as the bright student becomes restless and regards school work as routine. Consequently, the bright child may either withdraw into his own world of fantasies or seek "kicks" from aggressive behavior.[33]

The enrichment program should be so designed as to encourage the bright child to develop initiative. This can be attained through rich opportunities for the student to select activities in which he/she wishes to become engaged.[34]

Although the enrichment program is a horizontal extension of the student's regular program, overlapping between enrichment and acceleration will inevitably occur. This program must assist in increasing the child's level of skills beyond those in the regular subjects. This will help the child to foster a deeper understanding of what he/she is studying and will broaden his/her base of knowledge.

As Paul Brandwein concludes, "Finally, in adopting any program, any testing device, any proposal, it is worth remembering that there is no one way of doing what is worth doing. Teaching is a personal invention."[35]

[33] Cutts and Moseley, op. cit., p. 39.

[34] Ibid., p. 44.

[35] Paul F. Brandwein, *The Gifted Student as Future Scientist* (New York: Harcourt Brace, 1955), p. xii.

19

ALICE MIEL, Teachers College, Columbia University

Social Studies for Understanding, Caring, Acting

Every class, community, and nation contains a few persons known for their unusual leadership ability, their political skill, their charisma. Of all types of giftedness in the human family, talent in the sociopolitical realm is totally group linked. It cannot be developed or demonstrated except in a social context. This places on social studies (organized studies of the social) a special responsibility—to help students understand themselves and other human beings as social creatures with the intelligence to shape and benefit from group life and to help them develop the knowledge, attitudes, and skills needed for optimum participation in their society.

As with other curriculum areas, social studies programs must be designed with a whole range of people in mind, from those who seem to have intuitive social and political leadership potential to the other extreme. Five reasons follow:

- Sociopolitical natural talent left in the raw can be dangerous. Such talent needs to be informed and directed to social rather than antisocial ends if it is not to be misused.

- Some young persons may discover a strong interest in becoming researchers if their social studies experiences give them a proper introduction to those fields of investigation.

- Those persons in society who are more highly gifted and talented along other lines (intellectual, artistic, athletic) often share with the socially gifted the role of opinion leader and social model. If they are not to be as socially ignorant and inept as they are brilliant in their own proficient fields, they will need a suitable social education.

- Democracy demands that every citizen participate intelligently and carefully in the process of selfrule. Although not all can be Gandhis, Churchills, or Martin Luther Kings, they can be among the many educated leaders democracy requires in the private as well as the public sector—in families, social institutions, organizations of all kinds, and government from the local to national level. The demand will continue; developing persons talented in social relations is the only intelligent course.

- Conditions in the modern world call for cosmopolitans, persons who can transcend national loyalties and provide leadership for the common good of all humankind. New kinds of social education are required to develop specialists in world affairs. Furthermore, those specialists cannot be effective without the informed support of the average citizen. Therefore, social studies must have an international dimension as well. A worthy goal is the development of a global perspective in an increasing number of persons throughout the world. American schools must do no less than their share.

Socialization in a Postindustrial Democracy

Social Studies for Understanding

If social studies is to contribute both to an increase of political giftedness and to socialization of the broad population (with its gifts and talents varying in kind and degree), the program must have certain characteristics. It must be designed to develop a cognitive base for understanding the conditions and demands peculiar to a postindustrial democracy on an increasingly interdependent planet. This may be called social studies for understanding. Understanding includes awareness of conditions as they are, and as they might be. Understanding that human beings are capable of both good and evil, that there are strife, conflict, and exploitation in the world, but realizing the many examples of heroism and altruism as well is essential. Furthermore, there are many tested mechanisms for action to correct or ameliorate conditions.

Social Studies for Caring

Social studies must educate feelings so that people have positive attitudes of self-respect, trust, and esteem and concern for fellow human beings. At the same time they must be taught to dislike cruelty and injustice and to distrust the motives and actions of oneself and others when evidence dictates. Otherwise, naive trust, when broken, may turn into generalized distrust of humanity. Achieving a proper balance between trust and distrust necessitates recognition of varied experiences and values within one's own culture as well as in other cultures. Also necessary is a willingness to reexamine one's own values, while maintaining basic beliefs about how human beings should treat one another. Included should be development of positive feelings toward all that is living and nonliving on this earth, a feeling of linkage with the past, and a sense of responsibility for the future. All this falls within the concept of social studies for caring—what some might call moral development.

Social Studies for Action

Social studies must help people to develop the inclination and skills to carry thought into deed and to engage in joint ventures requiring decisions— social studies for action.

Social studies alone cannot socialize America's young, but it can help. The remainder of this chapter is devoted to suggested content for social studies for understanding, caring, and acting. Content as used here includes ideas (sometimes referred to as subject matter), feeling content, and skill content. Content so broadly defined necessarily draws some of its subject matter from disciplines such as sociology, political science, social psychology, and anthropology, as well as the familiar geography and history that composed social studies in the past. To be effective and feasible the approach must be interdisciplinary (across disciplines) and interdimensional (across cognitive and affective dimensions). Only representative suggestions are given here. Some of the suggestions are more appropriate for middle and upper school students. Others may be adapted for younger children. They are grouped under three headings: (1) developing social meanings, (2) extending lifespace and (3) learning to take socially useful action.

Developing Social Meanings

Miss Barron wanted her first grade children to know what they were saying when, following a rule of the school, they pledged allegiance to the flag each morning. She spent several weeks building concrete meanings for each word in the pledge, starting with *I*. She used every explanatory and clarifying device she could think of until she was satisfied that the children were not just mouthing nonsense when they repeated the pledge. She then introduced the United Nations flag, explained that organization with the same care, and helped the children compose a pledge of allegiance to the world organization.

Young people need such patience and care in developing meanings for words like *democracy, freedom,* and *justice.* These concepts are not learned at one time but continue to take on fuller meaning as a person grows older. They also are concepts that must be enlarged and changed as the world changes around the individual. For example, what happens to one's freedom to play a stereo loudly at a late hour when one moves into an apartment building? What happens to one's right to smoke when taking a seat in a theater or on an airplane? What is one's obligation to the next generation when consuming nonrenewable resources?

An exercise for building meanings for certain crucial social terms is to delve into word origins. When students discover that democracy means rule by the people and autocracy means rule by oneself, they can begin to unlock other terms: *cracy* is the part of the word that means *rule, demo* is the part that means *people.* If *aristo* means *best,* then aristocracy is rule by the best. But who are the best? Political philosophers have argued long over that question—are those of noble birth the best? those with the most wealth? those with the most intelligence? those with the greatest physical strength? What are the dangers in "rule by the best?" What did our founding fathers have to say on the subject? What of the modern concept *meritocracy?*

The students might also discover the theories supporting the three major beliefs about government—totalitarianism, anarchy, and democracy. In the first, the relationship between the individual and the group is relatively simple—the state is supreme, and the individual is subordinate to the group. Under anarchy, the individual is supreme, and absence of government is considered ideal. Democracy has a more complex relationship between the individual and society, one of several delicate balances with which members of a democracy must learn to cope. In a democracy individuals are encouraged to maintain their integrity and cherish their uniqueness in a group context. At the same time as the group supports and nourishes the individual, each individual supports and enriches the group. Neither the individual nor the group is supreme.

The relationship between freedom and restraint in a democracy also requires that seemingly opposite concepts be balanced in both thought and action. Democratic order is achieved when individuals claim their rights and exercise the freedom guaranteed them, and concurrently exhibit responsible behavior through a combination of self-control and obedience to rules and laws. That is, persons demonstrate loyalty in a democracy through a balance of protesting/conforming behavior. It shows loyalty to the principles of a democratic society to express disagreements and reservations and to protest unfair authority relations, yet cooperate with authority on the basis of intelligent appraisal. Neither protest nor conformity must get the upper hand.

A concept of justice is important for young people today. Justice is legally achieved through yet another delicate balance, that between rule of law and compassionate respect for the person. Social justice on a world scale makes new demands on persons everywhere because basic nutrition and health, let alone the "good life," are distributed unevenly and unfairly in many cases, both within and between nations. Young people can learn to face such realities as the world's oil supply—its location, distribution, and use. Facts about creeping deserts and starvation of huge segments of the planet's population present opportunities to consider the moral questions involved in global consumption patterns and to ponder how justice might be done.

It is often said that a democracy is based on majority rule, and so it is in a way; it certainly is not based on minority rule. Yet, more sophisticated techniques of governing exist than simply accepting a mathematical majority. People have learned that it pays to listen to the opposition and build a position that utilizes the most constructive parts of all views. When this process is used well, a consensus (wide agreement) is reached, for the minority can feel satisfied that their ideas have been heard; they have indeed had a chance to convert the majority and, if they wish, they can reopen the issue later, after living with the decision for a time. Students better understand consensus as differing from a mere voting procedure if they realize that it comes from Latin words meaning "feeling together" (the word has no connection with taking a census, which is Latin for counting people off by hundreds).

Young people can come to understand such concepts through wrestling with numerous illustrations of present, past, and possible future human dilemmas. Events in the classroom, school, neighborhood, newspapers, basic documents of our society, literature, and film are sources of material for lively discussions which can sharpen meanings. Young children just entering school have unique opportunities to take on new meanings for freedom and authority as they discover that other groups do things differently from their own family's ways. However, in concept development students should not be left with facile verbalizations; they should rather feel something "in their bones." Some minds find it easy to make a fast leap from the concrete to the abstract. This creates a danger of dehumanization. The remedy is to help them return often from the abstract to the concrete to test their ideas and add meaning to their concepts: "We have talked of justice. Was justice done in situation A, B, C? Now, have we reached a satisfactory conception of justice or should we revise our view of this term?"

Members of a society who have a grasp of order, loyalty, justice, and consensus appropriate for a democracy are equipped with concepts basic to such a society. They can understand that democracy rests on certain fundamental beliefs—belief in the worth and dignity of the individual, in shared decisions and cooperative problem solving, in reason and persuasion instead of force and violence, in the ability of human beings to govern themselves if they have the necessary information, and belief that cultural gains (the fruits of technology and research) should be widely diffused among the masses.[1] This very list could be the subject of research and discussion by students. Concerning the last item, it would be useful to explore the concept *culture*.

Extending One's Life-Space

Young people have a continuing problem of orienting themselves in their world and extending their life-space; the world about them does not stand still. A life-space has been defined as "a person's current world (a) as viewed through his own eyes, (b) in terms of the people, places, and times that he can identify or identify with, and (c) as shaped by his knowledge, human relationship skills, and values."[2] The world will be a better place as more of its inhabitants have fuller life-spaces. Following are several suggestions for helping young people extend their life-spaces.

Persons in My Life-Space

A teacher might begin by asking students to list the names and locations of all the persons they feel they know rather well—family, friends, and acquaintances (this also might be an interesting exercise for a family to undertake). All could be asked to form groupings within their own lists as a next step. After these groupings had been shared and discussed, students might agree on categories all would use for further work on their lists. As lists were refined, students might provide thumbnail sketches of persons' names. Following that, tabulations might be made showing what portions of individual lists (kept confidential) were composed of family members, close neighbors, persons in other cities or states, persons in other countries, persons whose mother tongue is not English, persons of different race or religion, and so on. At some point the concept of life-space might be developed with the students; they might speculate on how persons happen to include others

---

[1] Adapted from a list presented in a lecture by Professor Hal Lewis, University of Florida, May 3, 1978.

[2] Alice Miel and Peggy Brogan, *More Than Social Studies* (Englewood Cliffs, N.J.: Prentice-Hall, 1957), p. 30.

in their life-space. Lack of representation of some groups in certain individual lists might possibly lead to a study of prejudice and mechanisms of stereotyping.

As a follow-up to listing, locating, and describing persons in their life-space, students might be helped to see the desirability of extending their own life-space. Various means of doing so are observing people, talking with them, corresponding with them, exchanging pictures and information about each other's lives, doing something to help someone in need, and learning about others through television, films, books, and art. Learning how persons in other parts of the world perceive those in the United States might be intriguing to students. Pen pals, "sister" classes, schools or towns in another part of the world, travel, and making contact with visitors from other countries are possible avenues for extending one's life-space. The purpose is to help students broaden the boundaries of their lives, develop new appreciation for differences in people as well as their common humanity, and open doors to new knowledge and feelings.

Names of People and Places

The life-space activity might develop into a study of names. Such a study could include the concept of family and given names rather than first and last names, because in many countries family names come first (Mao Tse Tung would be Tse Tung Mao were he a North American). In Spanish-speaking countries the last name of a male is his mother's maiden name, the middle name is his father's: Tomas Ramirez Aguadillo is Senor Ramirez, not Senor Aguadillo. On the other hand, in those same countries women often keep their maiden names and add their husband's with the *de* in front of it: Senorita Maria Ramirez might become Senora Maria Ramirez de Cortez and be called, at least professionally, Senora Ramirez.

In old Denmark Soren Jensen would have been the son of Jens, perhaps Jens Hansen (son of Hans), who in turn was the son of Hans Rasmussen (son of Rasmus), and so on. This explains the number of Scandinavian family names that end in *sen* (Danish and Norwegian), and *son* (Swedish), although the custom of taking the father's given name as one's family name (son of) is no longer followed. In fact, a Danish girl could now be named Jen*sen*.

Students might find out why so many Russian family names end in *vitch* and Polish in *ski*. They might learn the significance of *von* in German family names, *van* in Dutch, *de* in French. They might discover that in Islamic countries it is an honor for a boy to bear one of the names of the prophet; thus common given names are Abdul, Ahmed, and Mohammad. Places to which Islam spread from the seventh century (Asia, northern Africa, Spain, and part of the Philippines) can be traced through such given names.

Another helpful clue in given names is that *a* is a common ending for a girl's name in the Western world, whereas some boys' names end in *o*. In Japan the reverse is true. In Africa many children who were educated in mission schools under colonialism adopted Christian names. Today however, they are more likely to use their African given names, especially within their own country.

Just as given names in English often have a meaning—rose, violet, pearl, grace—and family names have meanings like smith, barber, carpenter, miller, and baker, so do names in other countries. The strangeness of names in other parts of the world would be dispelled if these equivalencies were learned, but students should not expect that all names will have such meanings.

Within the United States the telephone book can raise many interesting questions regarding the preponderance of certain family names in a community. For example, why do Kims outnumber Smiths in one city?

Students may make treasure hunts of place names by using maps, atlases, and out-of-country addresses. Here it will be helpful to know words in the language for north, east, south, and west, for street, avenue, and so on, with their common abbreviations. Such knowledge will make the addresses seem less like nonsense syllables.

Even the names of places and streets within the United States will yield clues to some of the history of the area—the Spanish influence in the southwest, the French influence in Louisiana and Maine, American Indian names all over, and names starting with *New* showing British origins. The Danish word for village, *by*, can be found at the end of many place names in England and the United States. Why? What other endings are common and have special meanings?

An interesting way for students to begin to learn the meaning or origin of personal and place names would be from their personal correspondence with others. Work with addresses might include honorific titles and abbreviations used in different countries—*monsieur, madame, mademoiselle* for French-speaking countries, *bey* and *hanim* for Turkey, and so on.

The purpose of a focus on names of persons and places is to develop more of a feeling of closeness to others far away, as well as to assist students in orienting themselves in the world. Also it is important to recognize that name and home place are precious to the person concerned.

Making Depth Studies

Spending time digging into certain topics in small groups, or as individuals, is another way of extending one's life-space. Suggestions include the following:

• Exploring one's own roots and pooling the findings for a class survey.

In many classes it would be likely that only a few parts of the world were represented in the students' origins. Reasons for this situation could be explored.

- Investigating successive users of the same land area (block, neighborhood, or town) to discover who the people were, where they had come from, how they used the land, what became of them as a new group moved in, and so on.

- Making an intensive language-culture study of some other part of the world. If the choice were a nonwestern nation, the class would be more likely to study relatively unfamiliar areas.

- Making comparative studies of nations in all the hemispheres, noting differences in postindustrial, industrial, and developing nations of the third and fourth worlds. Basic problems faced by different peoples, types of exchange and interchange among them, and responsibilities toward one another could be discussed. Students could attempt to get a perspective on certain problems over a period of time or across cultures or both.

- Making a study of lifestyles in different periods: the Renaissance in Europe; slavery, immigration, depression, and post-World War II society in the United States.

- Making a study of a society's attitudes toward success and failure. What are the criteria of success in our society? What provisions are made for failure (judicial system, prison reform, forms of insurance, or welfare system)? In what way does our society create losers? How do losers feel? How could we reduce the number of losers? How would these questions be answered in another type of society— totalitarian or one with an extended family pattern?

- Collecting examples of ways people in different parts of the world work together for the common good. Responsibility for depth studies of a number of them could be divided among the class. Examples of cooperative efforts that might be studied are the international postal union (materials available from the U.S. Committee for UNICEF), overseas phone service, international weather service, international health organization, food and agriculture organizations, and Interpol, as well as UNICEF, UNESCO, and the United Nations itself. Nongovernmental organizations of educators, artists, scientists, and other professionals could be studied also.

Some of the most intriguing depth studies occur spontaneously when teacher and students pursue new avenues opened during a study, instead of stopping when initial plans have been carried out. This point is illustrated by what happened to a science-related study of water, as reported by a teacher in Montclair, New Jersey. The students became interested in the sinking of the *Titanic* and, among other activities, examined the statistics of women and children who were lost in comparison with the number of men passengers and crew members. This led to questions relating to women's liberation. For a teacher interested in helping young people to extend their life-space, such elaborations of a study would be most welcome. In fact, it is useful in curriculum planning to provide opportunities for consideration of social implications of developments in science.

Learning to Take Socially Useful Action

If classes have engaged in activities like those suggested, they will have been learning techniques of cooperative search, organization, discussion, and communication of results to others. They have been acting socially but have stopped short of the experience they need for being full-fledged participants in a democracy. As stated earlier, one basic belief on which a democracy rests is confidence in cooperative problem solving. In schools it is very important that young people be helped to understand and become concerned about community problems. But even that is not enough. Students need to learn how to take cooperative action to carry out solutions agreed on in group discussion. Learning how to go this final mile involves all the elements of problem solving—discovering, clarifying, and analyzing the problem, weighing alternative proposals for solution, deciding on a course of action, and evaluating the results in terms of what is indicated for the next such experience. All of this calls for an array of social skills (skills of thinking-feeling-acting in relation to others).

One set of such skills has to do with processing information—skill in gathering information through listening, observing, searching documents, and studying artifacts, accompanied by skills of organizing information into appropriate categories and evaluating its validity and worth. Evaluation skills include ability to decide among conflicting experts and authorities. What are their qualifications, their backgrounds, their special interests? How good are they at projecting into the future? Evaluation also involves ways of attaining reasonable objectivity.

For example, knowledge of propaganda techniques could give protection against partial, slanted, or erroneous information in political pieces and commercial advertising. It would be helpful for students to compare editorial policies of different newspapers and magazines and to make use of consumer reports.

Information skills include making decisions and solving problems after weighing facts and anticipating consequences of alternative solutions. The techniques of systems-planning, in which lateral as well as longitudinal effects of decisions and actions are considered, would also be useful. In addition, there are skills for sharing information and decisions with others in various forms (prose, poetry, art, graphics, sound, music, and the like) and through different media (from print to television).

A second set of skills needed by all participants in cooperative problem solving is group discussion techniques. These can and must be taught to those likely to be leaders of discussion and to group members as well, for in a democracy leadership is shared as different members initiate suggestions, raise objections, furnish needed information, redirect discussions, or assume other leadership roles.

Most of the social skills just presented can be practiced through various classroom enterprises in which teachers and students plan, act, and evaluate cooperatively. However, the critical test of acquisition of skills occurs when definite action on a real school or community problem is planned and executed. In such situations, students can learn how to cope with the present and to determine proper courses of action. Students need the lessons and the satisfactions that come with real experiences if they are to continue as active citizens in their communities, nation, and world.

In selecting problems to work on, it is important that teachers not try to "put old heads on young shoulders" and exploit children by having them attempt to solve problems their elders cannot solve. If the youngsters are involved in selecting and analyzing the problems they will work on, this danger can be avoided. In fact, they may surprise their elders with what they can accomplish.

Opportunities for problem solving by young persons are to be found in the school itself and also in the community: traffic conditions near the school, problems merchants, officials, and others may be having with young children or teenagers, conditions under which the elderly live, recreational needs of the community, need for community beautification, and need for support for education. Young people may deal with some issues by themselves with teacher guidance. Others must be worked on cooperatively with community adults. A balance of the two experiences seems ideal.

Conclusion

When social studies programs feature many rounded, in-depth experiences with multiple learnings cutting across familiar disciplines, students will need opportunities to see how the information they are gaining relates to existing bodies of knowledge. Teachers should help young people to organize their learnings and fill in gaps so that they are constantly building a more systematic view of the world. It also is important that students be helped to generalize on findings, evaluate their learnings, and apply them in new situations so that there will be the greatest possible reward from given experiences. Such work will benefit all young people as they continue to be lifelong social learners.

If students also are helped to observe, analyze, and evaluate the processes they are using in their learning, they will have more control over use of such processes throughout their lifetime. There could be no better equipment for political leaders and all participants in our democracy than knowing ways of gaining understanding, ways of extending feelings of caring, and ways of acting on convictions. Content for social studies should be chosen with this in mind.

20

ELLIOT W. EISNER, Stanford University

Artistic Thinking, Human Intelligence, and the Mission of the School

Philosophical Roots of School Structure

The schools of America participate in a cultural tradition extending back to classical Greece. This tradition, articulated most forcibly by Plato, distinguishes between levels of intelligence and the degree to which knowledge can be regarded as true. It is a tradition that has shaped Western philosophy and has influenced the character of its educational institutions. It is a tradition that in many respects is inhospitable to certain forms of consciousness and intelligence, of which the arts, as forms of experience and activity, are paradigm cases.

The tradition I speak of makes a sharp distinction between the abstract and the concrete, between thought and emotion, between the work of the head and the hand, and between the ideational and the material world. In the hierarchy of mind and knowledge that Plato formulated the arts were regarded as inferior forms of knowledge, artifacts created by people who did not have a clear view of what was true, good, or beautiful. Truth, for Plato, was achieved through a process of abstraction. It was the result of a form of thinking that did not rely on the material world, much less on the world of

269

material objects that artists created. To base one's knowledge on material objects or art forms was to base it on what is ephemeral and in a state of decay. Plato emphasized freedom from the material world so that the mind could clearly comprehend what is eternal and nonmaterial: pure form. For such a process to occur those modes of thought that did not depend on mere empiricism were crucial; one could not know what was true by using processes that depended on the changing and decaying furniture of the world. Mathematics and logic were the quintessential subject matters, dialectics the method. Emotionality and materiality had no place in the journey upward, except as stepping-stones to a truer, more beautiful, and better world.

School Curricula as Emphasized Today

For some readers the foregoing might seem like ancient history. It is. But it is more as well. Plato's ideas, the tenets he formulated about the nature of mind and the status of knowledge, have influenced educational practice in our educational past and do so in the present because they have influenced the culture in which American schools function.

Consider, for example, the status hierarchy that exists among subjects students study in school. At least two characteristics are prominent. First, it is clear that not all subject matters are given equal time in school programs. Second, it is clear that not all subjects are regarded as equally "intellectual." With respect to the first, the way in which time is allocated to various subjects in a school curriculum says something about their importance in the curricular hierarchy. The arts at the elementary school level consume about 3–4 per cent of school time each week. Half of all secondary schools in the United States offer no work in the visual arts, and, of those schools that do, only 15 per cent of the students enroll in the visual arts courses in the four years they are in school.[1] Music fares a bit better, but not much.

Although the allocation of time to particular subjects in a curriculum is an operational definition of the value with which they are regarded, time is only one indication reflective of Plato's conception of mind and knowledge. A second indication of the status hierarchy among subjects is what is regarded in school as being intellectually demanding and, consequently, who is regarded as "smart." Using this criterion it is also obvious that some fields of study are thought of as "tough" or "solid," requiring high degrees of intelligence: mathematics, physics, chemistry, geometry, and sciences in general are the most vivid examples. These are the fields that count in evaluating the intellectual power of students. These fields are regarded as

[1] Music and Art in the Public Schools, *National Education Association* (Research Monograph, 1963-M-3, 1963).

abstract, having little to do with emotion and practically nothing to do with "being good at your hands." The arts, by contrast, are considered less intellectual, more emotional; ability in the arts is thought of as the result of talent rather than intelligence. The school curriculum can be seen as an expression of what the culture or the community believes important; fields of study either are placed at the center of the circle or occupy peripheral positions.

The marginality of the arts is expressed not only in the small amount of time allocated to them in the school week, but also in the location of the week during which they are taught. In the elementary school the arts are taught in the afternoon rather than in the morning, quite often in the latter rather than in the earlier part of the week. This, too, serves as a type of corroboration of the marginal, nonintellectual view of the arts. Additional corroboration is provided by the fact that in our own professional culture, the culture of professional education and social science, we have come to distinguish between cognition on the one hand and affect on the other. Cognition refers to thinking and affect to feeling, again a distinction rooted in the Greek distinctions between the noetic and the poetic. Therefore, subjects regarded as cognitive, such as reading, arithmetic, writing, spelling—the 3 R's—are taught in the morning when the children are fresh and can think. Subjects regarded as affective—the arts—are taught in the afternoon when the need to think, or the need to think clearly, is not as important.

The school is reflective of the culture, and the culture is reflective of its traditions. The structure of curriculum priorities teaches as surely as didactic instruction in the multiplication tables or spelling lists, but more softly and infinitely more covertly. What children learn in school is not only what is taught; they also learn what counts, what it takes to get ahead, what receives high praise, who is regarded as smart, who is not so smart, who is dull, who is talented, and who is not. (This is commonly referred to as the implicit curriculum.) Insofar as school is a subculture, as it surely is, it teaches through the values that pervade it. Those values are not simply those that are given public testimony through words (words might be among the most feckless expressions of what we value), but through the way choices are made and resources are allocated. One of our most precious resources, time, is minimally allocated to the arts. Children quite correctly infer that it is not a high priority in school. This conclusion is reached not as the result of systematic empirical investigation. That's not the way it occurs. Children come to establish in their mind's eye an image of schooling as a result of their experience. School comes to mean a place in which time is arrayed in certain ways, characterized by certain forms of activity, and guided by certain rules. What school comes to mean for children is determined largely by the way in which the school itself functions. These images, born of experience, serve later as criteria that many adults use to determine what is educationally appropriate for their own children's education. The tradition is sustained.

The Use and Abuse of Intelligence Tests

Thus far I have focused my attention on the way in which decisions about the allocation of time to various fields of study express a set of values to children who attend school. A status hierarchy among fields of study also exists that reinforces conceptions of intelligence because different fields are not considered intellectually equal. It is this last point that warrants additional attention here, not by rooting it in Greek distinctions between thinking and feeling, but by relating it to more recent developments in the history of education: the development and uses of the intelligence test.

Intelligence tests, like other tests, are validated in large measure by their ability to predict the status of an individual or a group of individuals within a larger population within some context. The score secured on an intelligence test thus becomes an expectation for an individual's future performance. How an individual does in school becomes an index of his or her intelligence. If modifications on intelligence tests are made so their ability to predict school success is regarded as an index of the validity of the tests, we have a mutually validating process occurring. The validity of the test as a measure of intelligence is determined by its ability to predict success in school, and success in school becomes explained on the basis of an individual's intelligence. Yet even if one viewed intelligence test scores as nothing more than a prediction of school performance, the use of such test scores would still pose difficulties because of their conservative influence on the content and aims of school programs.

However, intelligence tests offer more troublesome problems. Intelligence tests are believed to measure intelligence in *general,* independent of context. Such a view violates the Darwinian theory upon which intelligence testing is based. Darwin's theoretical views of the survival of the fittest referred to the fittest *in a particular context.* However, in the process of translation it becomes overgeneralized. Richard Shaw, speaking of this overgeneralization, writes:

> This idea [survival of the fittest] is hardly revolutionary; it has been with us since Darwin. But it was distorted along the way by Victorian Englishmen and their American cousins, who construed "survival of the fittest" to mean "fittest for *all* likely situations." The modern western white man was God's supreme achievement and all other forms of humanity could be rank ordered according to degree of match with him. Central to this achievement was man's intellectual ability, so a measure of this characteristic should be the prime basis for such

ranking. This misconstrual of Darwin's nonetheless fit with older folkways. The captains of all civilizations, ancient or modern, rose from the ranks through mental, not just physical, prowess.

Binet sought originally to develop a series of tasks that would predict success in conventional schooling. He was commissioned to identify those students in the public schools who were not likely to succeed under conventional treatments and who thus needed some kind of special treatment. In effect, one could say, he was commissioned to study the Aptitude Treatment Interaction (ATI). But the growth of the mental testing movement centered on the prediction problem. Many of the specialized tests, as well as the general tests, used today are spinoffs from tests first tried by Binet. Mental tests diversified further as the personnel selection and training problems diversified across the two world wars. But the core of mental testing remained concerned with prediction of achievement in conventional educational institutions. Thus, "Aptitude" became synonymous with "scholastic aptitude," which in turn came to be thought ae the essence of "general intelligence."[2]

The significance of such tests becomes even more important when one realizes that not only do standardized tests have little to do with artistic modes of thinking, but also that tests such as the Scholastic Aptitude Test and the Graduate Record Examination are used by institutions to appraise students' intellectual ability and to determine acceptance to those institutions. If either the school's curriculum or the test itself is modified to increase the levels of prediction from one to the other, a circle or self-fulfilling prophecy is drawn. Institutions select students on the basis of test scores that are designed to predict performance in a curriculum that itself was developed to reflect the tasks and to teach the skills measured by what the tests are designed to predict.

The low status of the arts in relation to a conception of human intelligence becomes even clearer when one considers that many colleges and universities do not take into account secondary school students' grades in art, music, theater, or dance in calculating the students' grade point average—a bit of information that can determine the students' acceptability to college. (The University of California, to name one major example, does not consider art or music grades in calculating secondary school students' grade point average.) Not only are the arts given a marginal place in the curriculum, they also are given a marginal place in our conception of mind.

These factors alone appear sufficient to illustrate the ways in which school programs and testing procedures affect our conception of human intelligence. But even these examples do not exhaust the ways in which the arts are given short shrift in American schools. In some states such as

[2] Richard Snow, Toward a Theory of Aptitude, Invited Address to Division C, American Educational Research Association, Toronto, March 1978.

California, schools that identify students whose measured IQ is 130 or over receive additional funds from the state. These students are referred to as MGMs—mentally gifted minors. But what is giftedness? In this view it is unambiguous. It is a score of 130 on a group intelligence test. What about artistic giftedness? Is it not a form of mental giftedness? What about social or athletic giftedness? Are these forms of human aptitude nonmental in character? How does one justify funds for one type of mental giftedness and deny funds to others gifted in ways that are not now tested?

The structure of secondary school programs should also be considered. Comprehensive secondary school curricula exist for the college bound and vocational programs for those who are to enter the work force when they leave school. These programs formally not only differentiate the vocationally and nonvocationally bound adolescent, they also distinguish between the intellectually inclined and those inclined toward nonintellectual matters.

Students are usually labeled quite early in their school career and placed or counseled into these two streams. One finds a remarkably high probability that children of the upper socioeconomic classes will occupy places in the college preparatory stream while those in the lower socioeconomic classes will occupy places in the vocational program. Those who can work well with their head have access to further education in the university, whereas those who work well with their hands leave school in order to join the work force. Thus the structure of school programs, the use of testing procedures, and the differences in the amount of time schools allocate in various fields of study set conditions that are inhospitable to the arts and to children whose interests or aptitudes reside in their pursuit. The structure of school programs differentiates subjects and students in terms of intellectual ability, the testing process rewards those whose aptitudes are consonant with a limited conception of intelligence, and the time devoted to the arts in the curriculum tacitly, if not formally, assigns them a marginal place in the status hierarchy among subjects taught. All of these factors help define the bright and the dull, the intellectual and the mechanical, the theoretically inclined and the practical, those good at thinking with their head and those adept with their hands. Plato's view of mind and knowledge emerges in the culture of schooling that we have created. The "really bright" go into mathematics.

Toward a Wider View of Cognition

What kind of argument can be mustered to counter such a venerable tradition? In what way can intelligence be more adequately conceptualized? What are the potential benefits of a wider view of cognition? And what are the practical consequences of a wider view for schools and for the children and adolescents who are compelled by law to attend them? It is to these questions that I now turn.

Reflect for a moment on the ways in which humans come to know the world. *Cognition*, a term ubiquitous in discussions of schooling, refers to the process of knowing, the means through which the organism becomes aware of the environment. (The *Dictionary of Psychology* defines ·*cognitive* as a generic term used to designate all processes involved in learning.) That process requires an active organism, an organism that must select from a multitude of qualities that constitute the environment. This process of selection and organization requires mentation. Perception of the world is the product of a mental activity in which humans construe form, select what is salient or significant, and confer meaning on it. The sensory systems that humans possess provide options for such contact. For example, we can choose to regard the world visually, auditorily, or through smell, taste, or touch. We can linger over the qualities of our experience either refining and experiencing our sensations or using the qualities of our experience for purposes of classification linguistically, quantitatively, or, even more specifically, historically, chemically, or psychologically. Our experience of the environment depends in part on how we choose to attend to that environment. The essence of perception is that it is selective. What we choose to select depends on what we seek, what our purposes are. In short, in our transaction with the environment both the environment's qualities and our own intentions determine what aspects of the environment shall be experienced.

Initially our experience is qualitative in character. That is, although we may later classify qualities with verbal surrogates—words—our immediate experience is with the qualities themselves: the experience of greenness, or largeness, or warmth. We taste the sweetness of sugar, feel the wetness of water, or recognize a familiar face. What is empirical is initially experienced as a quality, and later—at times in microseconds—we transform what has been experienced into a member of a class and label it as such. Thus a tree of a certain stature, texture, and color is labeled as sycamore, but only after the qualities of the tree are experienced. Even the numerals 2 or 4, 5, and 9 must be experienced qualitatively before the numerals become numbers. Our sensory systems are the channels that provide options for such contact, and what those channels provide can remain as experienced, or they can be transformed into a symbolic form.

The perception of the qualities of the environment is inself an act of intelligence. The world does not organize itself for the organism; the organism must do this itself. Reality is, in this sense, a personal construct. Individual differences among humans in aptitudes, interests, intention, and needs cause each to select different qualities from the environment and organize them differently. Each of us constructs our own universe and, because we occupy a common culture, there is sufficient overlap in the worlds we create to make it possible to share a common but not an identical world.

The process of construing the world requires the use of intelligent abstraction. Because we cannot ingest the world whole, we select from it, we organize our selections, and we form such selections into concepts—concepts that might be visual, numerical, verbal, tactile, or olfactory. Our sensory apparatus provides the channels for contact, and our intelligence selects and organizes, a process requiring abstraction from the many possibilites open to us. Thus *perception* (a word that has an unfortunate passive connotation) is a cognitive event. The recollections of our perceptions are formed as concepts related to the sensory modes in which the world was experienced or transformed to serve the purposes we might have.

The import of these remarks is to correct those who believe that concepts can only be linguistic: concepts can be formed in any of the sensory modalities and symbol systems humans can use. Thus a concept of man himself can be visual, or it can be as a *Homo sapiens*. It can be tactile, or it can be as an example of the mammalian species. Thinking is not limited to mental operations confined to one symbolic form. It is wider than internal speech. Humans have options with respect to the modes of thought they can choose to use.

Symbol Systems in Externalizing Perception

My discussion thus far has focused on the idea that thinking is not limited to words or numbers, that the organism must be active in order to make sense of the world, and that the way in which the world is perceived or experienced is a result of a process of intelligence dependent on the ability to abstract certain features from the world. But what I have said so far focuses on an internal process. To share our awareness or understanding of the world, it must be made public with this process; our use of symbol systems becomes crucial. Symbols are manmade forms that present aspects of reality to his consciousness and to others. Symbol systems are organizations of symbols used to elaborate that reality. From the conceptual forms that an individual has constructed for himself on an internal level, he must be able to create some public vehicle that conveys to others the qualities of his experience. One symbol system that is prevalent in all human cultures is spoken language. Speech inefficiently expresses what we actually think. In our culture speech varies in precision, in vocabulary, and in syntax. To become acculturated means developing some proficiency in the use of discourse. Similarly, acculturation also occurs in the acquisition of literacy. Speech becomes the basis for the skills of decoding written words. We learn to read and to write in order to comprehend and to express certain features of what we know, or what we can come to know.

But not everything that we are able to conceptualize can be expressed adequately in words as words are commonly used. Although words go a long way from a functional point of view to inform, they fall short of describing or conveying certain aspects of our mental life. Words in their ordinary use fail to capture our experience with certain particulars: the quality of an April morning in New York's Central Park, the character of *that* rose, *this* dog, *that* love affair. This view of the function and limits of language is perhaps nowhere more articulately expressed than in the writing of Susanne Langer. Speaking of the relationship of nondiscursive to discursive knowledge she writes:

> Such knowledge [nondiscursive knowledge] is not expressible in ordinary discourse. The reason for this ineffability is not that the ideas to be expressed are too high, too spiritual, or too anything else, but that the forms of feeling and forms of discursive expression are logically incommensurate, so ttat any exact concepts of feeling and emotion cannot be projected into the logical form of literal language. Verbal statement, which is our normal and most reliable means of communication, is almost useless for conveying knowledge about the precise character of the affective life. Crude designations like "joy," "sorrow," "fear," tell us little about viral experience as general words like "thing," "being," or "place," tell us about the world of our perceptions. Any more precise reference to feeling is usually made by mentioning the circumstance that suggests it—"a mood of autumn evening," "a holiday feeling."[3]

As Langer says, our knowledge is wider than our discourse. The ability to express the ineffable through propositional language does not leave man "speechless." Fortunately humans have created a variety of symbol systems other than propositional language to express ideas that will not take the impress of discourse. These symbol systems are exemplified in dance, in the visual arts, in music, in mathematics, and in the nondiscursive use of language itself: poetry and literature. Each of these symbol systems is available in the culture and serves as a vehicle for expressing ideas, images, or feelings. Each contains its own parameters; the potential and limitations of dance are not those of mathematics, and vice versa. Hence what one can know and express in dance is not the same as what one can know or express through other symbol systems. But to deal with dance as a symbol system one must be able to exercise intelligence with respect to it. This means that in order for symbolic forms to communicate intelligence must be used in both the encoding and decoding process. Inability at either end diminishes the power to communicate.

What I have said about the need to exercise intelligence in the symbol system called "dance" applies a fortiori to the array of other symbol systems

[3] Susanne Langer, Imitation and Transformation in the Arts, *Problems of Art* (New York: Scribners, 1957).

available in the culture. The use of intelligence to encode and decode visual form is no less demanding than its use in history, or in music, or in mathematics. Becoming literate in its wide meaning refers to an ability to construe meaning from the forms represented in a variety of symbolic systems. Because the characteristics of these systems vary, because they emphasize the use of different sensory modalities, because they employ different forms of syntax, because they are regulated and appraised by different criteria, the kinds of meaning one can secure from them also varies. What one knows is determined by one's ability to encode or decode within a symbol system. As Olsen puts it, intelligence is being skilled in a medium.[4]

There are several other features about the relationship of symbol systems to intelligence that are worth mentioning. One of these is that the relationship between the modes in which conceptualization occurs and the symbol system used for expression is not isomorphic. That is, one cannot conceptualize in one mode and transfer exact meaning to another. An alteration in the content of such conceptualized material inevitably occurs from at least two sources. First, if there is a shift from a visual mode conception to a verbal mode of expression—a linguistic symbol system—the content of what has been visualized undergoes an obvious transformation. Pictures and words are not the same. Although what is said has some relationship to what has been visually conceptualized, it is not a replica of it.

Second, the task of transforming images, whether auditory or visual, into a public form requires the use of some media (paint, sound) and the skills necessary to treat those media so that they convey what has been conceptualized. In this process the medium itself makes a contribution to the expressed quality, and the skills with which an individual can work influence the extent to which intentions are realized. Therefore, communication is hampered because ideal transference of meaning between media is impossible, and the level of skill with which an individual is able to work is different.

Another aspect of the relationship between symbol systems and intelligence deals with the contribution of the *act* of expression. Until now I have spoken of this act largely as though it were unidirectional: from conceptualization, to transformation, to expression. The process is not so straightforward. In engaging the set of materials in a context, ideas are born. Indeed, some philosophers such as R. G. Collingwood have argued that it is in the process of expression that ideas are formed, or, more succinctly, "How do I know what I think until I say it?"

This view of the relationship of the cognitive process emphasizes the

[4] David Olson, From Utterance to Text: The Bias of Language in Speech and Writing, *Harvard Educational Review*, 1977, 47(7).

constructive aspect of concept formation and the idea that opportunities for action are themselves generative in two ways. First, opportunities for action on a material motivate thought. Countless professional papers are written because of the need to present a paper at a professional conference or convention. The occasion motivates the creation.

Second, the act, once engaged in, is never wholly conceived in the cortex. What might be conceived is a theme or image of a general nature. The process of working with actual material is a process that clarifies, confers detail, and provides the material on which revision and correction can be made. In this sense the opportunity to use a symbol system within a particular medium is an opportunity to form ideas, not simply to express those already formed.

The final point I wish to make regarding the relationship of symbol systems to intelligence is with the ways in which symbol systems interact. Consider, for example, the creation of literature and its consequences on our experience. To write, an author must be able to see. By this, I mean that a novelist, say someone like Saul Bellow who writes of Mr. Sammler and of Jerusalem, must be able to perceive the qualities of the characters or situations that he writes about. The author must construe the reality that serves as a subject matter for his literature. Without the ability to see what is subtle or significant, the content of the literary work is limited, or at worst empty. But once having seen what is subtle or significant the writer must transform these forms of consciousness into a literary structure that gives them expression. The author's ability to perceive the world with sensitive intelligence provides the content that is eventually transformed into that symbol system we call literature and thus becomes a public, sharable form.

Once such literature becomes a public document, a vehicle is created that educates our own vision. Although the literary work is created within literary symbol systems, it generates a visual reality for the reader.

What we have in this example is the completion of a conceptual circle. Intelligence in the visual perception of the world provides much of the content for literary expression, and the literary expression confers vision on our eyes. In this sense the visual arts contribute to the literary arts, and the literary arts contribute to the visual arts.

But the transactions among symbol systems and forms of internal representation do not terminate with the visual and the literary. Verbalization is instrumental in mathematics, and mathematical forms of thougtt contribute to the treatment of problems that are not themselves mathematical. Although the precise ways in which modes of cognitive interaction occur are not well understood, there is little question that such interaction occurs. Thus inability to utilize certain modes of thought provides a cognitive handicap not only in those symbol systems where those modes of thought are used directly but also in other symbol systems where such forms of thought may be useful.

To sum up: schools in the United States reflect the conceptions of a culture that regards human intelligence in limited ways; the roots of these conceptions find their origin in Greek philosophy and have been reinforced by testing programs that limit their attention to a narrow range of human aptitude and then overgeneralize the meaning of the test scores.

Furthermore, school programs also reflect a limited view of intelligence and reward individuals differentially with respect to the aptitudes considered important. Thus artistic ability is regarded as a product of talent rather than the expression of a form of intelligence. Even when such intelligence is manifested by students, it is regarded of less value than intelligence expressed in some other areas.

A view of the organism as a creator of meaning has been described together with the argument that one's conception of the world is a personal construct that profits from the symbol system available in the culture, that the kind of knowledge humans can create is determined by the kinds of symbol systems they are able to use, and that these symbol systems provide humans with different kinds of knowledge—what can be known in numbers cannot be known in pictures and vice versa. In addition, the process of interacting with a medium influences the forms that ideas, images, and feelings eventually take. And, finally, there is rich interaction between symbol systems and modes of conceptualization; and inability to use any one of the symbol systems available in the culture can be a liability for the use of others.

Conclusion

Although it might be apparent that what I have said about condition and school structure bears directly on our conception of giftedness in the arts and elsewhere, it seems prudent to make the argument explicit.

I have attempted to illustrate some of the ways in which thinking occurs. As we have seen, thinking is manifested in a variety of sense modalities and can be represented through a variety of symbol systems. One's ability to think in these systems is the function of the interaction between genetically endowed characteristics of the individual and the opportunities the individual has to learn. The school is an institution that provides a program that helps the young become proficient in the use of these symbol systems. We call this program the school curriculum. But, as we examine this curriculum, we find that the opportunities provided to children to learn how to use these symbol systems varies enormously. Some systems receive thirty-five times as much attention during a typical school week as do others. The difference in the opportunities afforded children to learn to use particular symbol systems has two extremely important consequences for them. First, these children whose aptitudes are consistent with the symbol systems that dominate the school curriculum also have the best opportunity to do well in school and to secure a positive sense of self-esteem from it. Those children whose aptitudes are less related to what school programs now emphasize are handicapped in the competition for grades and positive reinforcement from the school.

Second, the absence of adequate attention to some symbol systems within the school curriculum makes it difficult for students to experience the kind of meaning and to secure the type of knowledge that these systems make possible. In this regard the arts are a prime example of neglect. Because works of art are often subtle and complex, tuition is necessary to deal with them adequately. When this tuition is absent from school programs, children do not become literated in the system. What the arts provide that children do not learn to experience becomes unrealized potential, particularly for those with strong artistic aptitudes. Neglect of the arts in the school curriculum becomes an unrealized form of experience for all students. In this respect our limited conception of talent or giftedness or intelligence supports, in practice, a form of cognitive deprivation. Because we have drawn our circle too small, we have deprived a great many children of the opportunity to cultivate their intellectual potential. In the long run the limited conception of intelligence that has dominated our thinking exacts a price not only from the students the school is designed to serve but also from the society as well because it reduces the likelihood that children will be able to draw on their most significant aptitudes to contribute to the society in which they live. In the final analysis, our conception of human ability, particularly our conception of intelligence and giftedness, needs to be broadened not only because it is more consistent with the facts as they exist, but because a society that aspires to the ideal of equal educational opportunity must also recognize the different ways in which talent, giftedness, and intelligence can be cultivated and manifested.

PART FIVE Evaluation, Finance, and Facilities

The final section discusses support services necessary to sustain programs for gifted/talented students. One common concern to all program areas is evaluation. Daniel L. Stufflebeam discusses the evaluation of educational programs from philosophical, conceptual, and practical perspectives. He presents guidelines for organizing evaluation activities and illustrates several evaluation techniques that are useful in school settings.

James A. Adams discusses strategies and sources for financing gifted/talented programs. He points out that a substantial part of the cost can likely be assumed in the regular budget. Beyond that, he speaks to the possibility of acquiring additional funds from both public and private sources.

In the concluding chapter, Stanton Leggett discusses the design and adaptation of space and facilities for gifted/talented programs. He presents a number of examples of facility adaptation to respond to programs oriented to particular talents. At the same time, he emphasizes the desirability of designing, innovating, and equipping spaces in ways that enhance flexible utilization.

Philosophical, Conceptual, and Practical Guides for Evaluating Education

Introduction

This chapter describes and illustrates certain philosophical, conceptual, and practical aspects of educational evaluation. The first part of the chapter discusses criteria for judging both educational programs and evaluations. The second part proposes a conceptualization of evaluation and, in particular, explains a given definition of evaluation. The concluding part presents procedural guidelines to use the proposed approach, illustrates the use of six novel evaluation techniques, and presents recommendations for organizing school district evaluation offices. Overall, this chapter is a general guide that groups involved in education can use to organize their thinking and activities concerning how to evaluate school programs.

Philosophical Considerations

Two basic questions that confront those who evaluate education are these: What constitutes good education? What constitutes good evaluation? This section posits certain principles for assessing education and evaluation.

Principles of Good Education

The principles proposed for deriving criteria to evaluate educational programs follow:

1. *Schools should uphold the ideals of a free society by promoting the common good and protecting the rights of individuals.* According to this principle evaluators should examine educational programs to ensure that they promote, or at least do not thwart, freedom of thought, speech, press, and religion; that they extend learning opportunities to all; that they discriminate against no group; and, in general, that they uphold the Constitution. In addition, evaluators should play an activist role in society: they should promote free choice by helping people and institutions to open up and assess alternative programs of teaching and learning; they should assess the extent that school curriculums respond to the needs of a mobile society and to the needs of students who must move from school to school; and they should aid educational institutions to prepare students for the challenges they will face in the future.

According to this principle, evaluations must not be value free, and the specification of criteria of merit should not be entirely negotiable. Whatever the interests of the client, an evaluator should always assess whether a given educational program is consistent with and contributes to the welfare of a free society and its individual citizens.

If the practicality of this point seems remote, consider that desegregation suits, Title IX, Public Law 94-142 (guaranteeing high-quality education to the handicapped) and the so-called sunshine laws have all underscored the relevance of democratic ideals to the evaluation of school programs. Also consider that the schools have an important role to play in equipping people to face such predictable challenges as space travel, overpopulation, food shortages, inflation, unemployment, environmental preservation, energy conservation, conflict resolution among nations, the breakdown of the family unit, and guaranteed human rights throughout the world. Evaluations that ignore the relevance of these and related concerns to education will be much less significant and helpful than they could and should be toward making education a powerful instrument for maintaining a free society.

2. *Educational programs should respond to students' individual and collective needs.* Given that the primary purpose of schooling is to foster human growth and development, schools must meet a wide range of student needs; and evaluators should assess the extent that programs respond to these needs.

The following seven areas of need are proposed for use in determining the criteria to be used in assessing the merit of school programs and the development of individual students:

- *Intellectual development:* Development of the power or faculty of the mind by which one knows or understands, as distinguished from that by which one feels and that by which one wills; the faculty of thinking and acquiring knowledge.

- *Emotional development:* Development of the capacity to deal effectively with feelings of joy, sorrow, fear, hate, or the like and development of a realistic and positive self-concept.

- *Physical and recreational development:* Development of motor coordination, body fitness, hygiene, and athletic abilities, interests, and habits.

- *Moral development:* Development of principles and habits with respect to right or wrong conduct and acquiring the ability to conform to these principles, rather than to custom or even to law when these are at variance with one's moral convictions.

- *Aesthetic and cultural development:* Development of a sense of, appreciation for, and ability to create beauty, especially as manifested in the areas of music, art, drama, and dance.

- *Vocational development:* Development of a conception of the world of work and of one's career interests and aptitudes, and preparation to engage in gainful and fulfilling employment.

- *Social development:* Development of the capacity and habit of living in friendly companionship with others in family and community settings and development and implementation of a sense of responsibility for promoting and sustaining civilization.

In assessing programs evaluators should pay great attention to the wide range of potential student needs and to the individuality of students. Plans and programs should be assessed for their response to all developmental areas, not just intellectual growth as too frequently is the case; both intended and unintended effects should be checked. Moreover, evaluators should encourage and give credit for creativity and diversity in educators' attempts to meet students' needs.

This principle is consistent with the expanded definition of gifted children proposed in this book. This principle recognizes that each child has unique talents and needs. It proposes a broad base of variables for assessing students' needs and the extent they are being met, and it asserts that educational offerings should contain whatever diversity is required to meet students' many and varied developmental needs.

3. *Educators should constantly strive for excellence in their educational offerings.* They should assess whether educational programs have the attributes deemed necessary to promote human growth and development to the fullest. Programs should be assessed for their theoretical soundness, economic efficiency, and operational adequacy. Variables used in assessing the excellence of program offerings are enthusiastic and effective teaching, efficient management, use of evaluation for program improvement, sound policy, innovative arrangements, adequate facilities, up-to-date materials, qualified staff, appropriate class size, staff morale, effective staff communication, good public relations, sufficient energy to heat and operate school buildings, safe transport to and from schools, safety in the school buildings, and sufficient finances. Strengths in these areas will aid schools to serve students well.

4. *Educators should plan and conduct programs that are feasible and appropriate to local conditions.* Concerns for quality and reality must go hand in hand. Educators must be frugal and design their programs so that they can be carried out with the available human, material, and financial resources. The programs should also prepare students to meet local as well as external challenges. Evaluators should consider the relative merits of competing programs in regard to practical criteria: cost, compatibility with existing programs, reflections of community needs and values, and exploitation of locally available educational opportunities.

The principles described are a necessary but not sufficient base for determining the criteria to judge educational programs. Specific, localized concerns must be considered in every evaluation; these can be derived only through close study of the particular evaluation situation. Hence the approach to evaluation to be described later in this chapter requires that evaluators employ criteria that reflect the four principles discussed and proposes a process by which they and their clients can determine additional criteria that pertain to the situation at hand.

Principles of Good Evaluation

In addition to determining and addressing the criteria of good education, educational evaluators must determine and implement principles of good evaluation. This section proposes that a good evaluation should have four main attributes. These are technical adequacy, utility, probity, and practicality.

1. The need for *technical adequacy* is based on the truism that evaluations should provide good information. That is, the information must provide dependable answers to the questions under study and must accurately assess all features of the object under investigation that determine its merit. In particular, the information should pass tests of reliability, validity, and objectivity. Overall, it should evidence truth.

2. *Useful* evaluations serve some purpose beyond providing accurate information or satisfying the evaluator's own curiosity or prestige needs. The fundamental purpose of an evaluation should be to help some audience to judge one or more things or to help them to do something better than they have done it in the past. To pass the test of utility, an evaluation must be oriented to the information needs of the audience and must provide all of its members with the information they need, when they need it, and in a form they can understand.

3. The *probity* requirements are important because evaluations can, and often do, have harmful effects on people. These effects may be brought about through the unlawful, unethical, or clumsy actions of evaluators. To meet the probity requirements evaluators must keep themselves informed about, and adhere to, laws concerning privacy, freedom of information, and due process. They must also manifest due respect for the people who are involved in, and influenced by, their evaluations and must strive to meet the ethical principles of the evaluation profession. In sum, a proper evaluation is one that is conducted legally, ethically, and with due regard for those involved in the evaluation.

4. The need for *practical* evaluations reflects the fact that they are usually conducted in a natural setting and that they consume valuable resources. To be practical, an evaluation plan must not assume skills and knowledges that are beyond the capabilities of the people who must carry it out. The plan must also be workable in the place where it is to be implemented and must not assume conditions that do not or cannot be made to exist. Finally, the evaluation must not consume more time, materials, and money than necessary to achieve its purpose. Practical evaluations are ones that are feasibly planned and efficiently executed.

To ensure that their evaluations are technically sound, useful, proper and practical, evaluators must carry out appropriate procedures. A list of concrete actions they can take toward this end is presented under the heading "Practical Considerations" later in this chapter.

Conceptual Considerations

Given the preceding discussion of criteria of good education and good evaluation, we turn next to an overall view of the evaluation enterprise. This conceptualization is described in relation to a proposed definition of evaluation.

Proposed Definition

In general, evaluation means the systematic determination of the worth of some object.

A proposed operational definition of this concept is *Evaluation is the process of delineating, obtaining, and applying descriptive and judgmental information—concerning the worth of some object's goals, plans, processes and products—in order to serve decision making and accountability.*

Steps in the Evaluation Process

According to this definition, evaluators must carry out three steps during any study. These steps are to *delineate* the information requirements, to *obtain* the needed information, and to *apply* the obtained information to certain decision problems and accountability requirements. Theee three steps portray evaluation as an interactive process. According to this approach, an evaluator should define his audience and involve them in clarifying the questions to be addressed and the type of study that is needed. Once some of the needed information is obtained, the evaluator and the audience should assess its merit, use it judiciously to guide decisions and serve accountability, and consider what further evaluative information is needed. Then they should repeat the cycle. According to this analysis, evaluation is a looping, iterative, cycling process; those who conduct it must be skilled in both the communication and technical aspects of evaluation and must be continuously sensitive and responsive to audience needs.

General Information Requirements

The proposed definition also notes that evaluators should collect "descriptive and judgmental information." Evaluators should collect and assess pertinent previously available information about the object, as well as up-to-date information. This information should be both objective and subjective.

Information that depicts the object as accurately as possible, without being distorted by one or more person's biases, is needed. But so is judgmental information. In fact, one of the best ways to get in-depth insights about an object is to tap the reflections and judgments of persons who have experienced and thought about it. Another advantage of purposely seeking judgmental information is that it helps the evaluators and their audiences to see the object from a number of different vantage points and value perspectives. Collecting historical and current information that is both descriptive and judgmental is necessary if evaluators and their audiences are to acquire rich, thoughtful analyses and avoid arriving at simplistic reports.

Specific Information Requirements

Beyond requiring that evaluators obtain descriptive and judgmental information, the proposed definition also identifies four classes of pertinent information. These classes include the information needed to judge a program's goals, plans, processes, and products.

1. The information needed to choose and judge goals—hereafter called *context information*—includes descriptions of the relevant environment (the local community); assessment of students' intellectual, aesthetic, physical, emotional, vocational, moral, and social needs; projection of enrollment trends; assessment of institutional needs (qualified staff, smaller-sized classes, parental support, or appropriate facilities); assessment of unused opportunities (such as federal grant programs or talented people in the community who are willing to volunteer their services to the schools); analysis of particular problems (e.g., a desegregation suit); descriptions and judgments of existing and/or proposed goals and priorities; and recommendations for needed changes.

The administrators of a school district are advised annually to convey context information to their district's board of education, staff, and community in a "state of the school district report." These audiences, together with the school district's administrators, are advised to use this report along with other information to assess existing goals and priorities and to help decide what changes are needed in school district policy and operation. In addition to this annual report, specific studies should be conducted to provide background information and direction for writing program and project proposals. Context information is as applicable to school, classroom, and student levels as it is to the district level; its main purpose is to assist in forming sound goals and priorities.

2. The information needed to judge program plans is called *input information*. It includes a characterization of the approach presently being used in the classroom, school, or school district (if the approach already is in operation), descriptions of alternative approaches that might be chosen, an analysis of all the identified approaches (in terms of potential responses to the district's goals and priorities, students' needs, costs, compatibility with the existing program, legality, propriety, and potential implementation problems), and ratings of the alternative approaches by those associated with the program as well as outside experts. The audience for input information might be a teacher, school principal, superintendent, school board, curriculum committee, or any other individual or group that has some measure of authority and responsibility for program planning. These audiences should use input information to identify available approaches (e.g., alternative desegregation plans or alternative textbooks), to decide which ones would work best in the given situation and to defend their choice.

3. The information needed to judge a program's implementation is called *process information*. It describes progress in implementing a plan, identifies instances in which the intended approach has not been executed, denotes deviations from the plan, analyzes implementation problems not addressed by the program plan, and documents any other special operational

problems (staff orientation, communication and morale, cost overruns, or equipment breakdowns). Those responsible for conducting a program or project need process information, both to help guide their efforts and keep them on track and to maintain an accurate record of the process of implementation so that program or project success can be appropriately interpreted at some later time.

4. The information needed to judge attainments at various points in a program is called *product information*. It includes descriptive and judgmental assessments of students' progress in all of the needed areas addressed by the program or project (assessments of intellectual, aesthetic, moral, physical, social, vocational, and emotional development). It assesses both intended and unintended outcomes and compares these to the costs and objectives of the program or project. Anyone who is responsible for operating a program or project should use product information as a basis for recycling or terminating the effort.

The Use of Evaluation for Decision Making and Accountability

Descriptive and judgmental information concerning a program's context, input, process, and product is potentially useful for both decision making and accountability.

To influence decision making, the information has to be pertinent to the decision makers' questions and be available before their decisions are made. In general, context information assists in goal formulation; input information aids in program planning; process information guides the implementation of a plan; and product information helps decide whether a project should be continued, expanded, or terminated.

In addition to guiding decision making, context, input, process, and product information can help people to be accountable for what they have done. By maintaining a record of the obtained information and the actions subsequently taken, the persons who operate the schools can be accountable for their work.

Context information provides a record of what goals were chosen and what information was available to inform this choice. Input information records the decisions made in determining how to achieve a given set of goals, identifies the alternative approaches that were considered, and presents the data and judgments that were available to compare these competing alternatives. Process information provides a record of the process as it actually occurred, assesses the extent that the intended process was actually carried out, and provides a basis for interpreting outcomes. Product information records identified outcomes and decisions to continue, modify, or terminate a program or project.

Overall, context, input, process, and product information are useful for focusing, structuring, implementing, and recycling programs designed to improve education; they also offer accountability to one's various publics.

Practical Considerations

The preceding explanation of the proposed definition of evaluation provides a general framework for use in planning and conducting evaluation studies. However, it provides little operational guidance. This concluding section contains guidelines for planning evaluation studies, sample techniques, and suggestions for organizing school district offices of evaluation.

The Procedural Guidelines

Table 21-1 (pp. 295–302) reflects a set of problems commonly encountered in evaluation. The table lists guidelines evaluators can follow to avoid or overcome the underlying problems and to meet the criteria of a good evaluation that were described earlier in this chapter. This list is presented as a tool for evaluators to use in planning and monitoring evaluation studies. The sixty-eight guidelines are divided into seven classes. These are conceptual, sociopolitical, contractual/legal, technical, utility, administrative, and moral/ethical.

1. The *conceptual guidelines* concern how evaluators conceive evaluation. These guidelines recognize that evaluations typically are team activities. If the team members are to communicate and collaborate effectively, they must share a common and well defined conception of evaluation and how they will apply it. To develop this common view of evaluation, the guidelines in Table 21-1 propose that the members of an evaluation team should answer the following general questions: What is evaluation? What audience will be served? What questions will be addressed? What information will be needed? Who will do the evaluation? What strategy will they follow? How will flexibility be maintained in the evaluation? What standards will be used to judge the evaluation?

2. The *sociopolitical guidelines* reflect the fact that evaluations are carried out in social settings and are subject to a variety of political influences. Unless the evaluators deal effectively with the people who will be involved in and affected by the evaluation, these people may subvert or even terminate the evaluation. The actions that the guidelines in Table 21-1 advise evaluators to take in order to deal with sociopolitical problems are to involve those who will be affected by the evaluation in planning and conducting it. They also serve to convince those whose work will be evaluated that the evaluation will be done fairly, convince external audiences that the evaluation will be done impartially and reported honestly, secure

advance agreements to participate from those who are expected to cooperate in the evaluation, maintain communication throughout the evaluation with the staff and audiences, and conduct a sound program of public relations for the evaluation study.

3. *The contractual/legal guidelines* denote that evaluations need to be covered by working agreements among a number of parties, both to ensure efficient collaboration and to protect the rights of each party. The underlying assumption is that successful evaluation requires that evaluators, sponsors, and program personnel collaborate. If this collaboration is to be effective, it needs to be guided by working agreements. If these are to hold, they often must be formally constructed, as in a contract or formal agreement. Such formal agreements should reflect possible disputes that might emerge during the evaluation and should give assurances to each party concerning how these disputes will be handled. The guidelines in Table 21-1 advise evaluators to reach agreements with their clients on the evaluation's purposes, products, schedule of activities and reports, budget, office space and equipment, personnel, protocol, procedures for keeping information secure from unauthorized use, use of human subjects, arrangements for collecting data, editorial authority, rules for releasing information, plans for dealing with value conflicts, rules for modifying the evaluation plan and budget, authority to use the evaluation for research, development, and training purposes, and rules for terminating the evaluation.

4. The *technical guidelines* reflect the fact that evaluators must solve many technical problems that have to do with collecting and reporting information. These problems pertain to the general investigatory framework, the sources of evaluative information, the instruments and procedures for gathering data, the ways and means of organizing and analyzing the obtained information, and the media and methods to be used in reporting the results. Table 21-1 presents seventeen specific guidelines for dealing with these problems.

5. The *utility guidelines* are intended to ensure that evaluations will be planned and conducted in order to meet the information needs of the evaluation's audiences. These guidelines advise evaluators to ascertain their audiences' information needs; formulate evaluation objectives that respond to those needs; report directly, clearly, and conclusively to each audience; use reporting media and methods that best serve each audience; and help each audience apply the evaluation findings.

6. The *administrative guidelines* reflect the fact that evaluations are often complex undertakings that require much careful planning and coordination. To help evaluators administer their projects, the guidelines in Table

21-1 remind evaluators that they should staff their evaluations appropriately, orient and train their staff, plan their activities thoroughly, manage the implementation of the evaluation plan, and be careful to conserve the resources used to conduct the evaluation. Moreover, evaluators should implement these administrative guidelines in such a way as to enhance the ability of the client agency to improve its long-range capabilities to manage evaluation studies.

7. The *moral/ethical guidelines* emphasize that evaluations are not merely technical activities but are also performed to serve some socially valuable purpose. Determining the purposes to be served inevitably raises questions about what values should be reflected in the evaluation. Deciding on value bases also can pose ethical conflicts for the evaluator. The final set of guidelines in Table 21-1 directs evaluators to treat all people involved in the evaluation with respect and dignity, present their evaluation of an object in proper perspective, conduct their evaluations so as to advance the cause of a free society, report judgments that reflect the pluralism in society, not allow their evaluations to be used improperly to justify past decisions, and evaluate objects in terms of how well they meet human needs.

TABLE 21-1. Guidelines for Conducting Evaluation Studies

____ 1. Definition	• Achieve mutual understanding among the participants in the evaluation study of the definition of evaluation that will guide the study.
____ 2. Audiences	• Specify the full range of audiences that are to be served by the study.
____ 3. Object	• Clarify what object is to be evaluated (e.g., a teacher, a textbook, a certain federal project, a given technique, a specified drug or an institution).
____ 4. Purposes	• Clarify the purposes of the study (e.g., a selection of persons or groups to participate in a program, allocation of funds, modification of a program, interpretation of program outcomes, or public relations).

_____ 5. Questions
• Clarify the audience's questions (e.g., which practitioners or institutions are in most need of assistance? What areas of an institution or program are most deficient? Should a particular innovative practice be adopted?).

_____ 6. Information
• Determine what information (e.g., employer judgments, patient records, students' test scores, and correspondence files) will best answer the audience's questions.

_____ 7. Agent
• Identify all those persons whose cooperation will be needed in order to conduct the study.

_____ 8. Strategy
• Characterize the evaluation approach that will be used (e.g., a case study, an experiment, a survey, a judicial hearing, or an expert panel).

_____ 9. Flexibility
• Ensure that the evaluation strategy will allow for the discovery and investigation of new questions as the evaluation develops.

_____ 10. Standards
• Define the standards that will be used to judge the study.

Sociopolitical Guidelines

_____ 11. Involvement
• Involve the audiences in planning and implementing the evaluation.

_____ 12. Internal credibility
• Convince those whose work will be evaluated that the evaluation will be conducted and reported in an objective, fair, and workmanlike manner.

_____ 13. External credibility
• Convince key external audiences that the evaluation will be conducted impartially and reported completely and honestly.

_____ 14. Subject cooperation

- Secure cooperation from all persons whose participation will be required to successfully complete the evaluation.

_____ 15. Communication

- Communicate throughout the evaluation with the staff and all the audiences.

_____ 16. Public relations

- At appropriate times, inform the press and public about the intent, methods, and results of the evaluation.

Contractual/Legal Guidelines

_____ 17. Commitment

- Ensure that the evaluation findings will be used honorably before agreeing to do the study.

_____ 18. Products

- Specify the products and services that the evaluators are to produce.

_____ 19. Schedule

- Reach agreement on a realistic schedule for the evaluation activities and reports.

_____ 20. Finances

- Reach agreement about a realistic budget and financial constraints.

_____ 21. Facilities

- Reach agreement on the office space and equipment that are needed to conduct the study.

_____ 22. Personnel

- Reach agreement about who will perform what evaluation functions.

_____ 23. Protocol

- Agree on what communication channels will be used and what policies and rules are to be followed in conducting the evaluation.

_____ 24. Security

- Agree on procedures for keeping the evaluation's basic information secure from unauthorized use.

___ 25. Informed consent

- Secure permission from those who are expected to supply personal data to the evaluation.

___ 26. Arrangements

- Reach agreement on any special conditions of data collection that will be necessary in order to meet the evaluation's sampling and treatment assumptions.

___ 27. Editing

- Reach agreement on who will have final editorial authority.

___ 28. Release of reports

- Reach agreement on who may release the evaluation reports and who will receive them.

___ 29. Value conflicts

- Reach a clear understanding about how conflicts over the criteria to be used in developing conclusions will be dealt with.

___ 30. Renegotiation

- Define procedures for revising and renegotiating the formal agreement (e.g., if there are cost overruns in certain budget categories or if unforeseen factors make it desirable to modify the evaluation design).

___ 31. Spinoff

- Reach agreement about how the evaluation can be used to train evaluators, do research on evaluation, and aid the audience to develop their own evaluation capabilities.

___ 32. Termination

- Agree on conditions for terminating the contract.

Technical Guidelines

___ 33. Investigatory framework

- Adopt a methodological strategy that is suited to the study purposes.

_____ 34. Independence

- Establish procedures for maintaining an independent perspective.

_____ 35. Sampling

- Define the population of interest and employ an appropriate sampling plan.

_____ 36. Attrition

- Provide for replacing persons who drop out of the study sample in a systematic and representative manner, or at least for keeping a record of the dropouts.

_____ 37. Description

- Fully describe the object of the evaluation as it exists and/or evolves during the study.

_____ 38. Instrument validation

- Ensure that the data-gathering instruments that are used in the study are valid for the purposes of the study.

_____ 39. Data standardization

- **Ensure that those data that are to be aggregated are gathered under standard conditions.**

_____ 40. Data cleaning

- **Remove as many scoring and coding errors as possible from the data before analyzing them.**

_____ 41. Data management

- Code, score, and retrieve obtained data according to a systematic plan.

_____ 42. Aggregation

- Combine data at those levels (e.g., school, district, or state) that are of interest to the audience.

_____ 43. Computer program

- Ensure that the computer programs used are appropriate and are not in some way flawed in the output they provide.

_____ 44. Analysis plan

- Have a competent statistician verify that the data analysis plan is appropriate and sufficient.

_____ 45. Interpretation

- Ensure that the norms and standards that are used for interpreting the results of the evaluation are appropriate for the evaluation's purposes.

_____ 46. Report editing

- Edit the evaluation reports before finalizing and publishing them.

_____ 47. Complexity

- Do not reduce the problem under study to a false simplicity.

_____ 48. Reanalysis

- Make the obtained data available for independent reanalysis.

_____ 49. Audit

- Obtain an independent appraisal of the evaluation report.

Utility Guidelines

_____ 50. Audience

- Identify the audiences of the evaluation, stay in touch with them, and periodically update your appraisal of their information needs.

_____ 51. Objectives

- Ensure that the objectives of the evaluation match the information needs of the audiences.

_____ 52. Targeted reporting

- Address each audience's information needs directly.

_____ 53. Precision

- Communicate the findings of the evaluation in clear and precise language.

_____ 54. Conclusiveness

- Provide conclusions and recommendations in the evaluation report.

_____ 55. Media

- Use that combination of media and methods that will best help each audience understand the evaluation findings.

_____ 56. Applications

• Help the audiences see how they can apply the evaluation findings to their practical situations.

Administrative Guidelines

_____ 57. Staff

• Staff the evaluation with qualified personnel.

_____ 58. Orientation and training

• Acquaint the persons who are to participate in the evaluation with their responsibilities and train them in the procedures required to carry out these responsibilities.

_____ 59. Planning

• Plan the evaluation systematically and collaboratively.

_____ 60. Scheduling

• Maintain up-to-date projections of what evaluation activities involving what persons will occur at what times.

_____ 61. Control

• Monitor and control the evaluation activities so that the evaluation plan gets implemented.

_____ 62. Economy

• Monitor and control the use of time and resources so that they are used as wisely and efficiently as possible.

Moral/Ethical Guidelines

_____ 63. Self-esteem

• Treat the people whose work is being evaluated with dignity and respect.

_____ 64. Comparisons

• Place the evaluation of an object in proper perspective by contrasting its strengths and weaknesses with those of other objects that are in competition with it for funds.

_____ 65. Common good

• Issue reports that reflect the best interests of a free society, but not the self interests of any group.

_____ 66. Value base

• Report judgments that represent broad, balanced, and informed perspectives.

_____ 67. Pretext

• Be careful not to allow clients to claim falsely that evaluation results are the basis for prior decisions.

_____ 68. Social value

• Report evaluation results in the context of how well the object of the evaluation meets human needs.

It is clear that evaluation is a complex process and that no concise set of data collection and analysis paradigms would be sufficient to deal with the wide array of applicable problems. Instead the methodology of evaluation must reflect principles and procedures from such diverse fields as moral and political analysis, legal analysis, historiography, cost analysis, communication, psychometics, and anthropology.

Selected Techniques

To upgrade their techniques, evaluators should constantly strive to invent new methods and to adapt existing ones that provide general responses to common evaluation problems. Six such past developments are the School Profile Technique,[1, 2] the Advocacy Teams Technique,[3] Goal Free Evaluation,[4] Experience-Based Test Development,[5] the Adversary-Advocacy Technique,[6] and adaptation of the Judicial Model.[7] These techniques will be illustrated in relation to a hypothetical situation.

[1] Daniel L. Stufflebeam, Walter J. Foley, William J. Gephart, Egon G. Guba, Robert L. Hammond, Howard O. Merriman, and Malcolm Provus, *Educational Evaluation and Decision Making* (Itasca, Ill.: F. E. Peacock Publishers, 1971).

[2] Howard O. Merriman, *The Columbus School Profile* (Columbus, O.: The Columbus Public Schools, May 1969).

[3] Diane L. Reinhard, Methodology Development for Input Evaluations Using Advocate and Design Teams, Ph.D. dissertation, The Ohio State University, 1972.

[4] Michael L. Scriven, Evaluation Perspectives and Procedures, in James Popham (Ed.), *Evaluation in Education: Current Applications* (Berkekey, Calif.: McCutchan Publishing Corporation, 1974).

[5] Henry M. Brickell, Needed: Instruments as Good as Our Eyes, The Evaluation Center Occasional Paper Series, Paper No. 7, Western Michigan University, July 1976.

[6] Robert Stake and Craig Gjerde, An Evaluation of TCITY: The Twin City Institute for Talented Youth, The Evaluation Center Evaluation Report Series, Western Michigan University, 1975.

[7] Robert L. Wolf, The Application of Select Legal Concepts in Educational Evaluation, unpublished doctoral dissertation, College of Education, University of Illinois, 1974.

Suppose that a parent-teacher association, with the support of their school board and superintendent, decided to evaluate the six elementary schools in their district. They wanted to identify the areas most needing improvement in the district as a whole and in each school.

With the help of the district's evaluation office, the PTA group chose ten variables to be assessed in each school: four were in the intellectual domain, and one each in the moral, aesthetic, social, vocational, emotional, and physical domains. Data were gathered such that at least one variable was assessed at each of the six grade levels. The committee rated each variable as equally important, and they agreed on a district wide standard for each variable to aid in interpreting the results for each school and the district as a whole.

The results of this hypothetical analysis are presented in Figure 21-1. The ten variables on which data were gathered are listed down the side and the district ideal plus the names of the six elementary schools are listed across the bottom. The maximum range of each variable, to the limit of the districtwide standard, is represented by the distance shown on the district ideal bar, and the results for each school are presented in the form of a cumulative bar graph.

The results show the following:

- No school's overall performance matches the district standard.

- Children from low-income families are distributed quite unevenly throughout the district.

- At least one school surpasses or comes close to matching the districtwide standard for all variables except number 5 (composition of the student body).

- Smith School is noteworthy for its consistently strong showing in spite of the fact that half its students come from underprivileged homes.

- Henry School's overall performance appears low, especially since only 4 per cent of its student body come from underprivileged homes.

- Every school has a strong showing on at least one variable.

The study group met with the PTA of each school to explain the results in Figure 21-1 and to consider their implications for program improvement. In each case the findings and discussion of them raised more questions than they answered. For example, the group at Jones School wanted to know whether their school's low showing on the physical fitness test reflected a

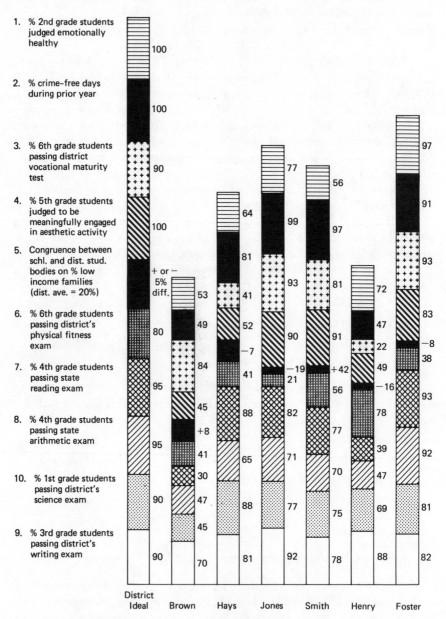

FIGURE 21-1. Indicators of educational development in the elementary schools of the Black River School District

lack of attention to this area; the groups at Brown School and Henry School wondered whether their school spent as much time on reading as did the other schools; and the group at Hays raised questions about their teachers' qualifications to teach art, music, drama, and dance.

With the help of the central PTA study team and the district evaluation office, a study team was formed at each school. Each team investigated those questions of most interest to the teachers, parents, and principal in the local school. The intent was to diagnose problems whose resolution would lead to improved performance in the local school.

A similar investigation was launched at the district level. The superintendent, concerned about the uneven distribution of underprivileged children and the uneven performance of the six schools in the district, directed his evaluation office to identify any instances of unequal educational opportunities in the district.

In responding to this charge the evaluators collected the information appearing in Figure 21-2. They also conducted hearings in each of the six schools, interviewed representatives of each school study team, and analyzed samples of teachers' lesson plans and of students' cumulative records from each school. The results appeared in a written report that was presented to the superintendent and distributed to the teachers, parents, and administrators who had been involved in the study. An oral version of the report was also presented at a meeting of the superintendent's cabinet.

Based on the results, the superintendent concluded that both educational achievement and opportunitty were too unequal among the six schools. He decided, with the board's concurrence, to launch a program of educational reform in the elementary schools and to seek an outside grant to support the program. In accordance with this decision, he charged the district's director of elementary education and evaluators to prepare an appropriate plan.

The new program was to achieve the following:

- Upgrade the overall performance of Brown School and Henry School.

- Preserve and strengthen the good performance in the other four schools.

- Ensure that educational services are equally available in all the schools.

- Obtain a more even mix of children from varying socioeconomic levels.

- Involve persons from all the schools in planning the program.

		Brown	Hays	Jones	Smith	Henry	Foster
1.	Hours per week of psychological services available to the school	4	12	12	12	5	12
2.	Hours per week per grade devoted to the district's character education program	0	2	2	4	1	1½
3.	Hours per week devoted to vocational education (6th grade)	1	2	2	1½	1	2
4.	Total hours per week of aesthetics education instruction (5th grade)	6	4	12	10	5	10
5.	% of teachers observed to be enthusiastic in their teaching	30	68	82	95	15	76
6.	Hours per week devoted to physical fitness (6th grade)	1½	1½	1	2½	6	1½
7.	Hours per week devoted to reading (4th grade)	2½	5	5	4	5	6
8.	Hours per week devoted to arithmetic (4th grade)	1½	3	4	2	5	4
9.	Hours per week devoted to writing (3rd grade)	1	3	3	2	3	3
10.	Hours per week devoted to science (1st grade)	1	2	2½	1½	2	2½
11.	Average years experience of teachers	2	5½	8	3½	4	7
12.	Average number semester hours earned by teachers	127	139	147	135	123	148

FIGURE 21-2. Indicators of educational opportunity in the elementary schools of the Black River School District

In launching the planning effort the evaluators and director of elementary education decided to use the advocacy team technique. Through this technique, competing teams devise alternative plans for improving a situation; the evaluators assess these plans against previously established criteria; a convergence team composed of representatives of the different advocacy teams reaches consensus on a compromise strategy; and the evaluators report the alternative strategies and their assessment of them to the group that must select a course of action.

As a first step in identifying advocacy positions and selecting team members, the district evaluators and director of elementary education met with each school's PTA study team. Each team reported its own findings and recommendations regarding problems in its school. In the discussions that followed these reports, certain advocacy positions emerged. The people from Brown School urged that a busing program be instituted. Members of the Henry School group strongly recommended that the principal be replaced. The Smith School team members argued that they had worked hard to reach their present level of achievement and didn't want their children from disadvantaged homes bused away or their staff broken up; in effect, they argued in favor of the neighborhood school concept. The groups from Hays, Jones, and Foster asked for increased resources but otherwise thought that things should stay pretty much the same.

Based on these discussions, the context information and the superintendent's directive, two advocacy teams were formed—one for curriculum improvement through desegregation and the other for curriculum improvement through neighborhood schools.

The teams were released from their other duties for one week and charged to develop and write up their plans. They were told to show how the implementation of their plans would respond to the superintendent's directive and the problems identified by the previous districtwide and individual school context studies. They were also told that their plans would be judged by the district evaluators for their potential effectiveness, compatibility with the existing curriculum, costs and general feasibility, innovativeness, legality, and political viability.

When the two reports were submitted, it was clear that there was no winner. The district evaluator and director of elementary education met with the two teams and the superintendent to discuss the results and to form the convergence team.

It was composed of members of the two teams, an outside expert on integration, and one on elementary education. This team met for one week to prepare its plan. The resulting plan incorporated the two prior plans but added a magnet school dimension.

Brown School was proposed to become a magnet school exemplifying the philosophy that all children had gifts and talents and providing a wide array of experiences in the creative and performing arts, plus a sound basic education curriculum. Henry School was to become a magnet school, emphasizing the philosophy of basic education; the principal in this school,

	Plan 1 Busing of Students and Redistribution of Teachers and Services	Plan 2 Upgrading Education in the Existing Neighborhood Schools
1. Potential to upgrade the overall performance of Brown and Henry Schools	Strong	Weak
2. Potential to preserve and strengthen performance in the other schools	Weak	Strong
3. Potential to improve equality of educational opportunities	Strong	Weak
4. Potential to integrate children of all socioeconomic levels	Strong	Weak
5. Provision for involving district personnel in the improvement program	Acceptable	Acceptable
6. Overall potential effectiveness	Weak	Doubtful
7. Fit with existing program	Weak	Strong
8. Costs and general feasibility	Weak	Strong
9. Innovativeness	Weak	Weak
10. Legality	Strong	Weak
11. Political viability	Weak	Weak
12. Fundability	Doubtful	Weak

FIGURE 21-3. Assessment of alternative advocacy team plans for upgrading elementary education in the Black River School District

who had by this time resigned, was to be replaced by the one from Smith School. The vice-principal of that school was to be promoted to principal. The Hays, Smith, and Foster Schools were to be retained as neighborhood schools and given individual grants to strengthen their programs. The hardest recommendation was that Jones School should be closed—to ensure integration and to reduce administrative costs.

To the extent possible, students were to be given their choice of the school they would attend, provided that this would result in each school having no more than 30 per cent and no fewer than 10 per cent of students from underpriviledged homes. Buses were to be provided to those students choosing a magnet school not within walking distance of their home.

The evaluators prepared their final report, which reflected Figure 21-4, and submitted it to the superintendent. After discussing it with numerous school groups, he submitted the report to the board of education along with his recommendation that a modified version of the convergence team's strategy be adopted. His modification was that Jones School would remain open during the first year of the program and subsequently be closed only if the plan's districtwide integration standard was not met during the first year. The board approved the recommendation and charged the superintendent to seek outside funding to implement the plan.

A three-year grant was obtained, and the program was put into operation. Evaluation of the program was coordinated by the district's evaluation office. During the first year the evaluation team concentrated on gathering and reporting process information. Every two weeks they met with a group at each school to apprise them of discrepancies observed between plan and performance and to help answer questions about particular operational problems. Evey six weeks they compiled their findings into an overall progress report on implementation of the plan and presented this report at a meeting of the superintendent's cabinet. At the end of the first year, they submitted a comprehensive progress report for delivery to the funding agency.

Among other things this report noted the following:

- Integration was within the prescribed levels, with all students and 95 per cent of the teachers getting their first choice of school.

- Excitement about the program—sometimes labeled "the Hawthorne effect"—was evident, especially in the two magnet schools.

- The costs associated with the added busing were 20 per cent higher than anticipated.

- Parent involvement, especially in the Brown School for Creative and Talented, was noticeably increased over what it had been in past years.

- The previously observed discrepancies in amounts of time devoted to the different parts of the curriculum were not so pronounced but were present.

	Plan 1 Busing of Students and Redistribution of Teachers and Services	Plan 2 Upgrading Education in the Existing Neighborhood Schools	Plan 3 Combination of Magnet and Neighborhood Schools
1. Potential to upgrade the overall performance of Brown and Henry Schools	Strong	Weak	Strong
2. Potential to preserve and strengthen performance in the other schools	Weak	Strong	Strong
3. Potential to improve equality of educational opportunities	Strong	Weak	Strong
4. Potential to integrate children of all socioeconomic levels	Strong	Weak	Strong
5. Provision for involving district personnel in the improvement program	Acceptable	Acceptable	Acceptable
6. Overall potential effectiveness	Weak	Doubtful	Strong
7. Fit with existing program	Weak	Strong	Strong
8. Costs and general feasibility	Weak	Strong	Acceptable
9. Innovativeness	Weak	Weak	Strong
10. Legality	Strong	Weak	Strong
11. Political viability	Weak	Weak	Doubtful
12. Fundability	Doubtful	Weak	Strong

FIGURE 21-4. Assessment of alternative advocacy team and convergence team plans for upgrading elementary education in the Black River School District

- Much developmental work remained to be done before the aesthetics part of the curriculum could be implemented districtwide.
- There were frequent complaints from the teachers that communication among the six schools was not as good as it should be, with some suggesting that the schools were competing instead of cooperating.

- Grant expenditures were distributed unevenly, with the Brown Gifted/Talented Magnet School getting a much larger share than originally planned.

- The schools had worked hard to implement the program as planned.

The superintendent sent a second-year plan—amended to respond to the problems revealed by the process evaluation—to the funding agency. The plan—which included an expanded budget to cover the costs of busing—was approved.

During the second year the evaluators pursued three parallel activities. They continued to monitor and report on the program as they had during the previous year. They developed "experience-based tests"—in the intellectual, vocational, physical, and aesthetic domains—for use during the third year in evaluating the program's outcomes. And they engaged an evaluation consultant to perform a "goal-free evaluation" of the program.

Experienced-based tests are devised to confirm the existence of observed unique effects, irrespective of what outcomes are intended. In the example under consideration, graduate interns in the school district were assigned intermittently to observe second, fourth, and sixth grade classes in each magnet school and one neighborhood school. They were to look for achievements that appeared to exist in one but not the other two schools and to write test items to reflect the idiosyncratic achievement. The intent was to identify and confirm the unique contributions of each type of school to students' growth and development. Periodically, as pools of items were generated, they were combined into short tests; and each one was administered on two occasions to two different samples drawn from each magnet school and one of the others. Item analyses to show performance differences among schools were performed, and those items having point biserial coefficients greater than 0.30 on both occasions were retained for inclusion in the tests to be used during the third program year.

While this test development continued, the outside consultant was performing a goal-free evaluation. He had purposely remained ignorant of the program's goals and planned procedures in order not to bias his data collection. He observed classes; interviewed students, teachers, and parents; analyzed lesson plans and student records; and performed time and cost analyses in each school. At the end of the year he prepared and delivered a case study report of the overall program and what he had found in each school.

Some of his main findings were as follows:

- A "bread and circuses atmosphere" prevails at Brown School, with some teachers concentrating almost exclusively on art education and others struggling to keep the kids up to speed in the basics. The students appear to be the rope in a tug of war; they are becoming disenchanted. Be prepared for many requests for transfer to other schools by both teachers and parents.

- Hays School appears to be a typical American elementary school. The principal pays attention to organization and runs a tight ship. Concentration is on reading, writing, and arithmetic. There aren't many frills here—not much excitement either.

- Smith School is really something. The parents could almost be described as a part of the staff. They tutor, monitor after-school study sessions, relieve the teacher for work with individual students, help make instructional materials, and work with their children in the home. Morale and pride are startlingly present wherever one looks in this school. The principal—an energetic, talented leader—is constantly careful not to elevate himself above the rest of his large team. The students in this school are avid readers and seem engrossed in their school work; many are obviously self-directed learners and pursue their studies far beyond their assignments. Everybody works hard here, but nobody complains.

- Quite remarkably, the comments about Smith School apply to Henry School. It seems that the real catalyst for the success observed at both schools is the principal, who presently is at Henry and previously was at Smith. Perhaps he could help the principal at Brown.

The outside consultant's report was somewhat of a shock to the superintendent. He had expected a comparative analysis of the neighborhood schools versus the magnet schools and an assessment of the integration effort. Instead his attention became riveted on the important role of the principal in the program. He decided that during the coming summer he would have to do something to improve the leadership situation at Brown but also realized that the solution would not be easy.

During the third project year the evaluators carried on four activities. They administered their experience-based tests to samples of students in all six schools and conducted a Multiple Range Test[8] of the results to detect differences among the schools.

They obtained data for comparison with those obtained by the district PTA group four years earlier.

[8] B. J. Winer, *Statistical Principles in Experimental Design* (2nd ed.) (New York: McGraw-Hill, 1971).

They assigned one graduate intern to review all the pertinent data and to write up the strongest possible defense of the program. Another intern was given the opposite charge: to review the data and write up the strongest possible indictment of the program. This phase of the evaluation was consistent with Robert Stake's "Adversary-Advocacy Reports Technique."[9]

The evaluators also organized and conducted a Judicial Trial of the program. Local attorneys were brought in to prosecute and defend the program, all previous evaluation reports were introduced as evidence. Evaluators, teachers, parents, students, administrators, and outside experts were called as witnesses. The public was invited to attend, and ultimately a jury decided that the program was "worthy of continuation and further development."

Finally, the evaluators prepared final reports on the program. They included an executive summary, comprehensive technical report, and a video tape based on the jury trial. The funding agency and persons in the local community were well pleased with the results.

Although this illustrative evaluation can be faulted on a number of counts—including technical adequacy and feasibility—it illustrates that evaluation can provide useful guidance for developing and operating programs. One of the vital elements in this example was the assistance provided by evaluation specialists. We turn next to the question of how school districts can obtain such assistance on a systematic basis.

Organization of School District Evaluation Services

Proper implementation of evaluation requires school districts in some way to organize and administer an evaluation program. The districts may contract with evaluation companies, hire consultants, participate in a consortium with other districts (as in a county or intermediate school district), or direct each teacher, specialist, and administrator to evaluate his/her own activities. They may also appoint one teacher in each building to serve as building coordinator of evaluation and pay that teacher a stipend for the extra work. These are useful approaches to evaluation; however, their quality and usefulness can be greatly enhanced if the district operates its own office of evaluation.

Such an office can serve many functions. It can conduct high-priority studies, provide inservice training and technical support to persons throughout a school district who need to evaluate their own programs, help the district to negotiate sound contracts for externally conducted evaluations, maintain a file of accurate information for the district to use in making

---

[9] Robert Stake and Craig Gjerde, op. cit.

accountability reports to the public, and, overall, help the district to write and implement policies to guide its evaluative operations.

A number of school districts have established evaluation offices to carry out the evaluation approach proposed in this chapter. These include, among others Dallas, Texas; Montclair, New Jersey; Saginaw, Michigan; Columbus, Ohio; Jefferson County, Colorado; Cincinnati, Ohio; Lansing, Michigan; and Austin, Texas.

In consideration of their experiences, the following recommendations are offered:

- To ensure its credibility, objectivity, and potential impact on school district policy and administration, the office of evaluation should report to the superintendent of schools, and the director of evaluation should be in close contact with the superintendent and board of education.

- To ensure that all vital evaluation functions are served, the office of evaluation should be organized internally to see that context, input, process, and product reports are obtained; that inservice training and technical support in evaluation are available to persons inside the office and to outsiders who need to conduct their own evaluations; that an up-to-date file of information for the preparation of accountability reports is maintained; and that evaluation reports are prepared and presented so that the audience will understand and use them.

- To carry out its functions, the office of evaluation must have an adequate budget. Based on a recent study of evaluation departments in urban districts,[10] it is proposed that 0.5 per cent of total school district expenditures is a reasonable level at which to fund a district's evaluation office.

Conclusion

This chapter has discussed the philosophical, conceptual, and practical aspects of evaluating education. It proposed that educational objects should consistently be assessed for their contributions to a free society, their response to students' needs, their professional excellence, and their appropri-

---

[10] William J. Webster and Daniel L. Stufflebeam, The State of Theory and Practice in Educational Evaluation in Large Urban School Districts, Invited Address presented at the Annual Meeting of the American Educational Research Association, Toronto, Canada, March 24–29, 1978.

ateness to local conditions. It argued that evaluations themselves should be assessed for their technical adequacy, utility, probity, and practicality. It defined evaluation as *the process of delineating, obtaining, and applying descriptive and judgmental information—concerning the worth of some object's goals, plans, processes, and products—in order to serve decision making and accountability;* and it explained an approach to evaluation that is based on this definition. The chapter listed conceptual, sociopolitical, contractual/legal, technical, administrative, utility, and moral/ethical guidelines to be followed in planning a study. It illustrated the use of the *School Profile Technique*, the *Advocacy Teams Technique*, the *Experience-Based Test Development Technique*, the *Goal-Free Evaluation Technique*, the *Advocacy-Adversary Reports Technique*, and the *Judicial Hearings Technique*. The chapter also proposed that school districts should invest about 0.5 per cent of their budgets in a school district office of evaluation.

It is hoped that districts that do not have such an office of evaluation will seriously consider the need to establish one. The systematic evaluation that can be obtained from such an office can help all educators to do their jobs better, to be accountable for their work, and to ensure that their programs respond effectively to the intellectual, aesthetic, physical, moral, social, vocational, and emotional needs of their students.

Funding a Program for the Gifted and Talented

From Challenge to Commitment

The first and most important step in funding a program for gifted/talented students costs nothing at all. It is the voluntary commitment of administrators, teachers, and citizens to the goal that each child in the community shall receive whatever help he/she must have to reach his/her full educational potential. Without this commitment limited educational funds may easily be wasted. With a common dedication to principle, a way can usually be found to achieve the goal despite the never ending array of demands placed on the public dollar.

When the commitment to inaugurate a program has been made, those responsible for its development must analyze their own educational system, assess local resources, make reasoned choices in program structure, set priorities, and seek whatever supplementary support will be needed. There are few external controls on gifted/talented (G/T) programs at this point. A system is relatively free to adopt whatever proven practices it may choose, to adapt them in any way it sees fit, or to design its own innovative approach. The program it selects will determine the financial support needed and may even suggest ways of securing it.

317

Analysis of the Local System

The educational structure already in existence must be reexamined as it relates to the proposed G/T program. At least in the developmental stages, it may be wise to avoid abrupt changes. Positive psychological values may well accrue when the new program seems to extend the best features of past activities. Several areas merit special attention:

Student Population

The number of students in the system will be an early determinant. A small system with five thousand students may not be able to identify enough students with similar needs at the same level to make grouping for gifted/ talented students practical. Another system with fifty thousand students would need only to verify the number of such students and locate them. A much larger system with half a million students could proceed with almost any plan with fair certainty that enough students could then be identified to justify its implementation subject to organizational and financial limitations.

Most systems have achievement and IQ test scores, grades, interest profiles, teacher evaluations, and other data on which to base an accurate estimate of the number of students in need of service without waiting for formal identification and placement.

School Size

Large schools with many children at the same grade level may find it easier to use ability grouping as a part of the plan, particularly if it is to include some components that involve integrating G/T students with the total student population, as in physical education, elective subjects, student government, extracurricular activities, and so on. On the other hand, availability of a fairly small school facility may encourage a system to operate a magnet school for children gifted in specific areas.

Community Factors

Often the cultural traditions of a community will influence the program chosen. Plans eagerly promoted in one locality may be totally unacceptable in another. Some value the arts, others emphasize mathematics and science or communicaton skills or career education. Some seek a balanced program, others want specialization. In some communities all college-bound students are considered to be gifted; in others, creative and divergent thinkers are seen as most in need of help.

Other community factors to be considered include the socioeconomic status of the families, their educational background, other educational institutions in the vicinity, and political positions related to schooling.

Staff Enthusiasm

Perhaps the single most important factor in determining the choice of program will be the attitude evidenced by the professional staff, both administrative and instructional. Their perception of the existent needs, their basic educational goals and philosophy, their willingness to contribute time and energy to program development, and their attitudes toward innovation and change will affect the kind of plan that will be attempted and will determine its success or failure.

Effective program developers have usually set up planning committees representative of staff and community groups so that all those to be affected by the program will have input and a feeling of ownership from its inception. Again it should be noted that this particular phase in any district is essentially cost free.

Inventory of Needs and Resources

Having determined that the system and community will support a program for G/T students, the next step is to determine the true amount of the need and to what extent it can be met without increasing the overall budget of the system. This entails careful estimation of total program costs in a number of categories, then subtracting the cost of providing a conventional program for the same students. *It is only the remainder, or excess over the regular cost, that can properly be charged to the new program; this is the amount of new funding that will be needed.*

Four categories of excess costs should receive special attention. Others may arise, depending on the type of program and the way it is institutionalized.

Identification of Students

Numerous definitions, criteria, tests, and so on are available for use in determining who should be in a gifted/talented program. Where routine procedures have been developed for other purposes, such as the child-find census for handicapped persons to be served under Public Law 94-142, there may well be trained counselors, data analysts, psychologists, and others who can simply build identification techniques for the gifted/talented into their existing procedures. It is important that identification be a constant process and that the program never be closed to qualified students. Even when some restriction such as class size may seem to leave no room for more, a waiting list should be maintained pending openings caused by family mobility or student withdrawals, and interim measures should be taken to provide whatever assistance is possible to the gifted/talented student just entering the system or not previously identified for whatever reason.

Closely related to the selection process is the evaluation of student progress in the program. This often implies retesting and comparison of data with those used in admitting students to the program. Altogether, provision for selection and the evaluation may require materials and personnel resulting in some excess cost beyond that of the regular school program.

Instructional Materials and Equipment

Whatever type of program adopted—enrichment, grouping, or acceleration—provision must be made for some specialized materials and equipment. Classroom techniques emphasizing discovery, exploration, creativity, and pursuit of individual goals need supporting materials that are broader in scope and different in vocabulary and difficulty from those most useful to average students. If acceleration is part of the program either in grade level or in content, whole courses complete with textbooks, supplies, and equipment will need to be added at the end of the sequence. Here the cost may be substantial—equipping a laboratory for advanced placement physics may cost more than one for regular high school physics, and the college-level texts may be expensive. Again it is important to emphasize that only excess cost should be charged to the new program: a student not registered in AP Physics must be provided some other class, text, and support, even though the course may offer little to his educational development. It can be argued that the ultimate cost to society is far greater when gifted/talented students are short-changed by their own schools.

At every level a gifted/talented program will place greater demands on the school's media center. Emphasis on independent study and research will necessitate more varied and sophisticated reference materials and audio visuals oriented to concepts and insights. Far greater demands will be made on the librarian/media coordinator than would be true for a conventional program.

A related problem is curriculum and materials development when commercial products cannot be found. This may call for substantial sums for substitute teachers, outside consultants, workshop supplies, and printing costs. But such developmental work is a reasonable undertaking once the program gets under way.

Administrative and Instructional Personnel

The classroom teacher ultimately determines the success or failure of the gifted/talented program. Thus no administrative duty is more crucial than the selection and training of teachers. Such a teacher must possess all those attributes associated with excellence of instruction in general. He/she must also be secure working with students whose potential abilities are far greater than his/her own. Intellectual honesty and enthusiasm for the job are essential.

In addition to the task of locating such teachers, the administrator must plan for their staff development, inservice training, and certification needs. Many state departments of education provide guidelines and assistance, but for a program of any size there will also be consultants' fees, workshop support, and perhaps tuition fees to teacher training institutions that offer special courses for teachers of the gifted/talented student.

With some approaches the number of teachers employed will actually increase because of limitations on class size. Whenever the number of students served is large, whatever the type of program, it may be necesssary to increase the supervisory staff and to add one or more administrators or directors to coordinate the program. That in turn would create a new secretarial position, with office expenses, travel allowances, and fringe benefits for all. Don't forget, though, that only those costs above the level provided for the general school program should be counted as gifted/talented costs; assigning new duties does not necessaarily mean that a new position has been added.

Another budget item may be the cost of bringing into the system skilled and talented professionals for short periods of time and for special purposes. Some funds for this purpose will likely be needed in almost any system, however large.

A study of personnel needs would be incomplete without considering the part school volunteers can and should play in the gifted/talented program. Large sums of money spent on imported professionals may not be as effective as the sharing of talents by local citizens. One reason is that it is obvious to the student, gifted or not, that when the imported professional leaves the district there will be little follow-up or caring about the outcome. But when the volunteer comes, freely giving of himself, he will remain in the community to see the results of the encounter and is himself a continuing testimony to the value of students' education.

Mentorship programs, too, are an example of community enrichment efforts that are extremely modest in cost. These match a student with a professional adult in a field of mutual interest. The program captures a little of the old apprenticeship system, but should not be confused with the part-time on-the-job training included in some career education programs that create an employer—employee relationship with pay.

A survey of the local community may produce a long list of organizations with programs for young people with special interests and abilities. These groups may provide some funds to the school for a special purpose, or they may provide enrichment experiences and services. Their presence is an invaluable asset to administrator and teacher.

Physical Facilities and Services

Generally speaking, provision of school facilities and services for a gifted/talented program should not require an increase in funds needed, but careful planning may disclose a few excess items.

If class size is to be limited as in some grouping and enrichment plans, the number of classrooms needed may increase (in many systems, declining enrollments have eliminated this problem; in growing communities it may be a serious cost item). Consideration must also be given to the location of available space. If students from several schools or a whole district are to attend, a central location may be needed and other classes may have to be displaced or district boundaries adjusted. Relocating materials and equipment costs money. So does transportation of students, especially when they come from a fairly large geographic area or when traffic patterns are inconvenient.

Even when space is available and well located, remodeling and decorating costs may be anticipated as buildings are adapted to their new use.

A Program with Priorities

In almost every case the careful preparation just outlined will produce an excitingly long list of resources already available in the system and in the community, and also a reasonable estimate of the costs associated with a program suitable to the system. Now it is time to determine the full structure of the program, to set short-term and long-term priorities, and to secure the necessary financial support. A comprehensive program can often be undertaken in phases, beginning with low cost procedures while financial support is sought for later, more costly steps. An NEA publication warns, though:

> Any attempt to provide for the needs of the gifted without making at least a minimum adjustment in the school's financial picture will necessarily mean that expectations for the program will be seriously limited.[1]

A 1970 study by Rossmiller, Hale, and Frohreich[2] showed that special programs for the gifted cost less than a hundred dollars per pupil above the average expense (needs adjusted for inflation!). Other estimates have ranged from "no extra cost" to 1.5 per cent of the total school budget. Most agree that the cost per gifted/talented student will be less than to educate any other exceptional student, but probably more than for an average child.

[1] *Administration: For the Gifted and Talented* (Washington, D.C.: NEA/NASSP, 1960), p. 132.

[2] R. Rossmiller, J. Hale, and L. Frohreich, *Educational Programs for Exceptional Children: Resource Configurations and Cost* (Washington, D.C.: National Education Finance Project, 1970) p. 127.

A final consideration in the planning process will be to separate annual costs from those anticipated to be one-time or infrequent expenses.

At this point the administrators should know what each component of the program will be and why it was chosen, what resources are at hand and what others will be needed, and what sequence of steps will have to be established to meet short-term and long-range goals.

The writer has taken the liberty to project the Winston-Salem (North Carolina) experience to illustrate the sequential nature of local program development and state commitment to G/T programs:

- Phase 1 — Commitment and planning for a comprehensive program including the identification and grouping of students, enrichment, acceleration, and financial structuring.
  - One sixth grade class identified, placed at an elementary school.
- Phase 2 — Program design complete, ESEA Title III Proposal submitted to the State Department of Public Instruction.
  - One third grade class, one fifth grade class identified, placed at Brunson Elementary School.
  - One seventh grade class placed at Wiley Junior High School.
  - Staff Development program begun.
- Phase 3 — ESEA Title IV funding for research and development. Summer enrichment program begun for Gifted/Talented students.
- Phase 4 — Honors program added for secondary students, now reaching grades 3—12 with ability grouping and summer enrichment.
  - Identification process operating in primary grades; no formal program in grades K—2.
  - Governor and State Department, on basis of evaluation results, secure legislation to support Gifted/Talented Programs statewide.
- Phase 5 — AP Program begun for grades 11—12, effectively extending the curriculum range to grades K—12.
- Phase 6 — The Governor of North Carolina and the State Department of Public Instruction established a summer enrichment program for 400 (boarding) students from across the state.
  - Local program expanded to two classes at each grade level 3—8.
- Phase 7 — State established the North Carolina School of the Arts, a

professional school in the performing arts, grades 7—12 and college, a part of the state university system.

— Arts in Basic Curriculum established at six elementary schools.

• Phase 8 — Local G/T Program is expanded to place classes in four other elementary schools, bringing number of children to be served at all grade levels nearer 10 per cent of the student population of the system.

— Governor's School is expanded to a second locaton.

— ABC program is implemented in twelve elementary schools.

• Phase 9 — On the horizon, with strong support from the current Governor, is a new state-supported school for the gifted in science and mathematics.

— ABC program expansion.

Ownership, Partnerships, and Linkages

A school system must retain *ownership* of its educational program. No outside party should be allowed to "buy into" the schooling process if local identity is diminished. A veto power must always be retained by the system along with control of policy, goals, and curriculum, all within the framework of federal, state, and local law. The system that pays its own program costs will never have to defend its ownership rights. However, there are often needs that cannot be met without outside help.

There are always *partnerships* that may be formed with other agencies and programs. These allow each party to augment the work of the other to their mutual advantage. Such arrangements often provide "risk money," funds that will allow the school system to try an unproven technique or develop new materials, for example. Once the initial plan is complete, it is expected that the burden of support, perhaps at a much lower level, will be assumed by the local system. The external partner frequently contributes organizational procedures, evaluation processes, and consultation services. These may be available on an almost permanent basis.

Finally, there are *linkages* that may be formed with civic groups, business and industry, professional groups, and so on. These usually result when a specific need of the system may mesh with a special interest of the group. Most often such groups offer leadership training, enrichment experiences, and person-to-person involvement. Sometimes though such organizations underwrite entire programs, as the Women's City Club did the Cleveland Major Works Program beginning in the early twenties.

The experiences of systems like Cleveland, Dallas, Evanston, Chicago,

Denver, and San Francisco show that a great variety of ways can be found to serve gifted/talented students, that wide variances in case and style can be found, and that funding can be had if vigorously and patiently sought.

There are a few certain sources available to finance special programs for the gifted/talented. Let us look briefly at several possibilities:

Local Budgeting Procedure

In many cases the local system can shoulder the moderate additional cost of a gifted/talented program, particularly where the school board has taxing authority. The problem becomes one of public relations, to show the program to the public so there will be no voter backlash. Where a tax referendum or bond issue is involved, the program must be shown to offer potential benefits sufficient to ensure passage. Special efforts must be made to avoid any elitist image and to show concern for many talents and all population groups. Objective identification procedures, parent-involved placement, and individual goal setting will help to convince the public that project goals are fair and desirable.

If funding is not complete after the local system budget is adopted, the next most likely source is still within the community—the organizations and groups that include parents of school-age students and others with past or present concerns for the school system. These groups have the highest stake in the local educational product—their own children, friends, and future employees are involved. If they cannot themselves provide the funds, they will likely join in the search.

State Aid

The state may provide direct support for the gifted/talented program. In North Carolina, for example, H.B. 824—Educational Opportunities for All Children Requiring Special Education (The Creech Bill)—includes the gifted/talented as a specific category. The initial funding of $15,000,000 is expected to increase as needs are better assessed.

A study in 1972 by Gallagher[3] explored the scope and depth of state actions for the gifted. Twenty-one states had legislation providing special resources or incentives to encourage local systems to increase their efforts, ten had study commissions contemplating such legislation, and ten had leadership personnel employed in the state department of education. Funds allotted were very limited. The states involved were scattered across the country.

These findings indicate that a local system has a good chance of

[3] James J. Gallagher, *Teaching the Gifted Child* (Boston: Allyn and Bacon, 1975).

securing some state aid, either in cash or in leadership assistance, and especially in teacher training programs.

Federal Programs[4]

There are no formula grants specifically targeting the gifted/talented student under ESEA or other federal education legislation. Gifted/talented students are included under P.L. 94-142, the Education of Handicapped Children Act of 1975, only as the gifted/talented handicapped. This program mandates a free, appropriate public education for children ages 5–20 (ages 2, 3, 4 by 1980). Funds may only be expended for excess cost beyond state and local spending levels for all children. Formula grants are based on the number of identified children in need of service. Appropriations of $2 billion a year are expected to increase as more special needs are met. There is serious effort being made, led by the Gifted/Talented division of the Office of Education, to add the gifted/talented child to the categorical listing.

There are several federal programs that offer project grants. These are highly competitive and usually limited to one year, possibly renewable once or twice.

One federal program directed to gifted/talented students is P.L. 93-380, The Special Projects Act, part of the Education Amendments of 1974. Administered in the Office of Education of the Department of Health, Education, and Welfare, the gifted/talented children program makes competitive grants directly to local systems in amounts from $6,000 to $100,000 (average $50,000) out of an annual appropriation of about $2.5 million per year. Projects must be directly related to education of the gifted/talented. They may include planning, differentiated instructional services, counseling, inservice training, graduate training, stipends, internships, and model projects for preschool, elementary, and secondary school students. Such a project grant may enable a system to get a gifted/talented program into operation but will not then sustain it.

Another part of P.L. 93-380, the Elementary and Secondary Arts Education Program (ESAE), was intended to assist state and local education agencies in making arts an integral part of elementary and secondary school programs. The John F. Kennedy Center for the Performing Arts serves as a national focal point for strengthening the arts in education. Funds of about $750,000 a year are used to establish and conduct programs in which arts are integrated into the school program and to identify and replicate outstanding programs of this nature. Included are the following:

- Inservice training.

[4] *1978 Federal Funding Guide* (Washington, D.C.: Education Funding Research Council, 1978).

- Use of art resource personnel.

- Use of visiting artists.

- Utilization of community art resources.

- Employment of an administrator.

- Curriculum development.

- Development assistance.

Project grants are competitive, range from $2,000 to $10,000, and average $8,000.

ESEA Title I, Part A, Aid to Educationally Deprived Children, has appropriated funds of $1.725 billion per year, dispersed through formula grants based on identified children in listed categories for the following:

- Instructional and service activities are provided, including cultural development, prevocational training and counseling, and teacher training.

- Services must supplement, not supplant, those normally provided by the state and the LEA.

- Services (local and state) must be at least comparable with those in non-Title I schools. (Title I money is extra, above funds provided on average to all children.)

ESEA Title I Part B, Educationally Deprived Children—Special Incentive Grants, with appropriated funds of about $25 million per year, makes formula grants to systems (through state departments) for "overcoming the effects of poverty."

While Title I funds are not directed toward the gifted/talented program, they may benefit it indirectly by raising the academic performance level of some children with specific talents.

The same thing is true of two other programs. ESAA Title VII is aimed at overcoming the educational disadvantages of minority isolation through support of special projects in arts, mathematics, student concerns, and so on; $21.5 million is available for such project grants. P.L. 90-222, Economic Opportunity Act, funds the Head Start and Follow Through programs. Again, these are not aimed at gifted/talented children but may assure that no such children are lost before ever having a chance simply because of neglect during crucial formative years. It is possible to design Title I programs for educationally deprived gifted/talented children if enough can be identified for a separate program.

Another similar source of funds is P.L. 94-482, ESEA Title IV, Parts B and C. Title IV-B—Library and Learning Resources—has appropriated funds of about $185 million per year. Formula grants are made to the states based on pupil population to be used for the following:

- Library resources, textbooks, and instructional materials.

- Instructional equipment plus minor remodeling for same.

- Testing, counseling, guidance, career information, encouragement to finish school, and postsecondary education.

Although none of these specifies target groups of children, all may include needs of the gifted/talented.

ESEA Title IV-C, Educational Innovation and Support, has appropriated funds of about $1.5 million that goes to the states as formula grants based on pupil population for use for the following:

- Supplementary education centers and services to stimulate and assist local systems.

- Demonstration projects.

- Increased state and local leadership resources.

- Dropout prevention.

- Nutrition and health services.

- Innovative research and development.

Research and development projects are competitive at the state level. They provide funding for a great variety of innovative programs, including those targeting the gifted/talented. Programs may be funded on an annual renewal basis for a limit of three years. Successful programs that pass state or national validation proceedings may be maintained for an additional period for demonstration purposes (usually with reduced funding). Results of successful programs are disseminated through a national diffusion network.

A final source of federal funding to support programs for gifted/talented children is P.L. 89-209, National Foundation for the Arts and Humanities. Three separate types of funding are set up:

- Special Innovative Projects in Arts Education grants to states and other agencies for pilot projects, curriculum development in the arts, and placement of artists or craftsmen in schools through two basic programs: (1) artists (craftsmen) in schools and (2) Alternative Education Forms Funding from the $5 million annual appropriation if on a $1–$1 matching of federal funds.

- Promotion of Arts—Federal—State Partnership provides formula grants and project grants through state arts agencies on a $1—$1 matching basis. Funding is about $15 million per year.

- Project Grants in the Humanities provide grants directly from the National Endowment, with 10 per cent matching funds expected. About $2.5 million per year is available.

Foundations and Other Organizations

The administrator seeking grants outside the educational funding sequence of local, state, and federal offices of education would again be well advised to start in his own community, where all institutions have a special interest in the development of the gifted/talented students who will benefit directly. Personal contacts may already have paved the way. But with local groups as with all others, a sound proposal carefully presenting objectivities, selected activities, evaluation procedures, and specific needs is an absolute essential.[5] When seeking financial support, the administrator must be careful to preserve the integrity of his program by seeking only partnerships that will further the system's goals. He must be prepared to defend every item in his own plan or to acknowledge that it is not essential. And he must be prepared for the possibility of rejection and be ready to seek alternate sources.

Although there are no large foundations with the specific purpose of promoting education for the gifted/talented, there are a number that have made substantial contributions in that direction. Carnegie Corporation has done most in terms of dollars, but the Ford Foundation, the Charles F. Kettering Foundation, the John D. Rockefeller 3rd Fund, the Joe Berg Foundation, and many others have been active in the development of our nation's cultural and human resources, often working with public schools by providing research and development funds, leadership training, and so on. Successful grantsmanship often depends on the selection of a target with goals very clearly and closely related to those of the proposed program. It should be kept in mind, too, that even though a partnership may not be formed, there is still the possibility of a linkage for some specific purpose or event. All such relationships should be maintained, because they may blossom forth at a later date. Educators are increasingly aware of the value of the arts to the perception of heritage and intercultural, interracial, and interethnic relationships. They now may bring together a number of agencies in a single program. An example is Urban Gateways in Chicago, funded by Model Cities/Chicago Committee on Urban Opportunity (CSA), Title VII (ESEA), Comprehensive Employment and Training Act (CETA), the Na-

[5] *Coming to Our Senses*, a panel report by the American Council for the Arts in Education, David Rockefeller, Jr. Chm. (New York: McGraw-Hill, 1977).

tional Endowment for the Arts, and The Illinois Arts Council. The program takes school students to cultural events, makes the arts a part of the curriculum in inner-city schools and those of all six counties in the Metropolitan area, encourages adults and families to share experiences, and established a teacher-training program and artist-in-residence projects.

Fund sources are sometimes not obvious; for example, a major supporter of the Dallas gifted/talented program is the local Board of Realtors. Always, the value to the funder must balance the cost.

Public funding always carries with it the inhibiting influence of accountability for tax dollars; private funding often fosters greater divergence of approach. Public funding means careful regulation; private funding comes with certain stipulations. Public funding usually is meant to build a program; the private sector may choose to finance a dream.

Conclusion

Education opportunities for gifted/talented students have improved in many school systems since Sputnik spotlighted their frequent neglect. Administrators have a persistent concern for gifted/talented programs, and teachers seek diligently for instructional techniques and classroom materials that will meet the special needs of these students. Community support has improved, although there are still many who feel that gifted/talented students should be able to "make it on their own." And they can. But "making it" alone may result in incalculable waste of human lives and social benefits. With the right help these students may be our richest national resource and our best hope for cultural extension. They are in our schools now, dependent on us. Our response to this challenge will determine their future and ours.

Space and Things for Educational Programs for Gifted/Talented Students

Some Limits

Space and its things, particularly in education, are curiously inert without the excitement of the activity of the occupants. Perhaps the great cathedrals have a life outside of the eyes of the beholder, but in education space is prosaic and seems to wait to come to life when it serves people. Walk through an empty school in the summer.

Where a school is assigned the task of cultivating the talents of its occupants, the facilities of that school are enlivened to an extraordinary degree, perhaps in direct proportion to the breadth of the definition of talent. Historically, research in this area started with a focus on genius; moved from genius to giftedness, exemplified by high intellectual achievements; broadened significantly in what must be considered a breakthrough to include creativity; and with the dam broken finally swelled out to include talents. Getzels and Dillon illustrate the scope of a definition of talent by the following generalizations:

For each . . . human activity there exists a corresponding talent.

If a thought, behavior or activity is possible to humans, some human somewhere has experienced it.

331

If a thought, behavior or activity can be experienced, someone somewhere can experience it superiorly.[1]

To this list one is tempted to add a fourth generalization, based on Taylor's work:

If young people were to be tested appropriately over a wide range of thought, behavior and activities virtually all persons tested would be well above average in at least one area.[2]

Stated another way—the greater the number of talents under consideration, the greater the chances that all young people will be shown to possess talent.

Society obviously selects those activities it chooses to approve, and the approval changes with time and fashion. Schools as an instrument of society are even more selective as education carries out the role of transmitting the culture. There is an uneasy balance between the conservation of society's traditions and knowledge, on the one hand, and the explosive quality of real cultivation of talents and gifts of each student in school, on the other.

A partial list of gifts and talents follows, listed in no particular order:

Art	Originality	Moral responsibility
Dance	Perceiving	Compassion
Music	Increasing skills in	Social vision
Movement	relationships	Humor
Drama	Valuing	Statesmanship
Improvisation	Assessing situations	Sensitivity
Expression	Becoming rooted	New kinds of gifts
	Oratorical skills	

Getzels and Dillon[3] point out that many talents focus on the problem-solving capabilities of students, neglecting the more creative act of finding and stating problems. Further, the same authors emphasize the following list of humanistic qualities, which they add to the predominantly marketable talents found in most lists:

a passion for life	to empathize	to survive
to love	to be of service	to get through
to understand	to care	

and, finally and delightfully:

---

[1] J. W. Getzels and J. T. Dillon, The Nature of Giftedness and the Education of the Gifted, *Second Handbook of Research on Teaching*. (Chicago: American Education Research Assn., Rand McNally, 1973), p. 704.

[2] Calvin Taylor, Multiple Talent Teaching, *Today's Education*, March-April, 1974, p. 71.

[3] Getzels and Dillon, op. cit., p. 705.

>to get along with grace
>and authenticity

Three classifications of talents and gifts are included in Getzels and Dillon's[4] report of the research in the field. Categorization is at the heart of the scientific method. Curiously the lists have a surprising measure of correspondence:

De Haan and Havighurst	Taylor	Rice
Intellectual ability	Academic	Academic
Creative thinking	Creative	Creative
Scientific ability	Communication	Kinesthetic
Social leadership	Planning	Manipulative
Mechanical skills	Forecasting	Mechanical talents
Fine arts	Decision making	Performing arts
		Psychosocial talents

An abbreviated look for limits in talents and gifts discloses no easy answers. When a school commits itself to the encouragement of these qualities, the school automatically is accepting the responsibility of pursuing the individual concerns and interests of each student as far as is possible, within the limitation that these activities be worthwhile or acceptable to society; obviously no school would encourage a talent for destruction of other students' work.

Predicting Activities

Space is provided and things are procured in order to support student activities. The usual school curriculum is a reasonably predictable set of activities. This curriculum is based on a selection from among all the worthwhile activities deemed appropriate for all students. A modest list of optional activities from among which students may select is offered. The process of instruction is also reasonably predictable; for example, homemaking courses are readily recognizable, and the activities involved in the courses are fairly well known in advance.

When a school expects to nurture the talents and gifts of its student body, a truly different problem is posed. Whereas some activities may well be expected of all students, the cultivation of gifts and talents becomes much harder to define, and the impact on the spaces and things of education becomes less predictable. For example, if creativity is a talent to be encouraged, by definition the school really does not know where that talent

[4] Ibid., p. 705.

will lead the student. Also, every new group of students probably will have a sharply differing mix of talents to encourage. This is further complicated because many students possess competence in a variety of fields. In addition, the talents to be encouraged do not necessarily have any relationship to the disciplines on which schools are so firmly anchored. Finally, the allotment of time appropriate to the development of a particular talent in a particular student is not known.

Although there are some common elements and activities, the encouragement of talents and gifts involves a degree of individualization of learning that sharply reduces the predictability of activities in a school situation.

How Can Spaces and Things Respond to Uncertainty?

Few new office buildings are designed and built with the knowledge of who the tenants will be. In fact, a surprisingly wide array of activities is accommodated by the structures. Dental laboratories, photographic studios, restaurants, banks, computer companies, and doctors' offices with their self-contained laboratories and display showrooms are among the tenants housed as readily as business offices with their bewildering requirements for electrical services and computer terminals.

School buildings can as readily accommodate a wide variety of activities and can change and respond to changing needs. What may be started as a series of classrooms can change to science laboratories and music studios. The technology exists to change space and things—probably to a greater degree than is required by educational programs that, to a considerable extent, are resistant to change.

There are limits to physical space changes. One such limit is changing low ceiling space suitable for typing to high ceiling space required by an automotive shop. The Indiana Vocational Technical College system solves this problem, an acute one in vocational area technical programs because of changing market conditions, by constructing large high ceiling buildings and dropping lower ceilings where needed. For the most part, school spaces such as gymnasiums, cafeterias, and theaters requiring high ceilings can be less readily changed.

Mechanical systems, stairs, and toilets are required spaces that are not themselves readily changed. Consequently, recent architecture has placed these functions at the perimeter of space that is otherwise flexible, or clustered this relatively immovable space as an island within flexible space.

Aside from these limits, most space in new school buildings can be delivered to the educational institution as empty space. The school can then partition, subdivide, leave open, furnish, and use the space at will. Proper storage for a bewildering supply of materials is essential. When change takes place, portions or all of the partitions, subdivisions, furniture, and equipment can be returned to storage, leaving the space empty and ready to be outfitted for different activities.

Not many educational programs take place in new buildings, however. The same process, moving from empty to furnished to empty again, can be utilized in existing buildings. The constraints will relate to the relative ease of adding or subtracting walls and the relative ease of providing water, waste lines, and electricity and other utilities, as needed, to locations within the existing structure. Three keys to using existing nonflexible buildings in a flexible way are the exercise of ingenuity, the use of more space rather than less, and the use of technology that contributes to the expansion of flexibility in the building. Whatever is done must be done with the full knowledge of the change that will inevitably occur.

A new school facility or a remodeled facility must be designed with the idea that the layout of space and things agreed on will change even before the school is occupied and will continue to change throughout the useful life of the building. The cycle of empty, filled, empty, refilled space is an ongoing expectation of all space.

A by-product of a facility that can be made to respond to changing needs lies in the ways in which space can be used in the instructional process. If it is assumed that one of the student talents to be encouraged is managerial quality, the realistic allotment of space and other limited resources to aspects of the instructional program is a critical aspect of the exercise of managerial skills. If students are involved in deciding on which strategy will be more effective and help assign space and resources to the activities depending on the value assigned to each activity, they will be deeply involved in planning, forecasting, and assessment of results—all aspects of an overall managerial talent. Decision making as to the uses of space and things of education is in itself a fertile area for the development of talents. The ability to deal intelligently with uncertainty is a considerable talent that can well be developed as an aspect of management of educational change and, therefore, management of educational space and things.

The Technology of Change

Walls and Enclosures

One of the significant developments of building technology in the last few years has been the use of interior systems in which walls, doors, power panels, and the like can be arranged and rearranged within a large space. Ceilings provide channels into which walls can be inserted at regular intervals. Demountable walls are furnished in standard width panels, secured to each other, and placed firmly on the floor, over carpet in many cases. The interrelated ceiling system allows heat, light, and air conditioning to be supplied to each module of space independently, so that what may be originally installed as a classroom can be subdivided into two conference rooms, and in turn a conference room can be subdivided into offices. Doors and walls are put in place; lights, cooling, and heating are rearranged as needed. Change continues.

Wall variations are many. Office landscaping uses self-supporting screens that provide demarcation within a larger space for territory. There can be centers of interest, workplaces for staff, or areas for a wide variety of other uses. Folding walls exist that when extended create sound-resistant enclosures. However, these walls can be moved in location only with considerable difficulty. The use of such folding walls is a tradeoff between instant change in room size and the inflexibility of changing the location of a folding wall. The latter inflexibility usually represents too high a price to pay for the privilege of opening up a wall instantly.

Within open space, tranquil islands can be arranged by movable enclosures that are rooms within a room. Designed to provide real sound-proofing, these movable enclosures can be used as music practice or rehearsal rooms, or general workrooms where even a power saw could be used in the middle of a library. Technology allows seemingly incongruous activity in the midst of a quiet learning center to take place.

Utilities

A major requirement for change is the ability to introduce utilities where needed. A whole series of quick connections for water, waste lines, hoods or ventilating systems, gas lines, and, of course, electricity exist. There are a variety of ways to provide ready access to all these utilities, varying chiefly as a tradeoff between cost and availability.

If utilities are to be available everywhere, it is more costly to do so. The variations include space between ceiling and floor or under floor where new utilities could run to new locations. This constitutes almost a separate floor for utilities. Its use is characteristic of heavy utility requirements of research laboratory buildings. A set of utility connections can be extended to one or more of the modules that make up the ceiling and partitioning system. When not in use, the utility connections in the floor are covered with a plate and do not interfere with any of the functions of the room. Sectional utility-rich areas that concentrate services in a building are another variation, as opposed to diffused utilities throughout a structure.

Finally, it is generally possible to make custom installations of utilities where needed—running a line under the floor or in some ingenious way making sure that water is provided where needed.

Things

The tools of education—furniture, books, charts, audiovisual equipment, writing surfaces, kits, paper, pencils, typewriters, microscopes, violins, saws, exhibit cases, file cabinets, cooking utensils, test tubes, pH meters, computers, brooms, pails, snake cages, graph paper, ovens, wrestling mats—are much more important than rooms.

It should be possible to outfit any space to fit the needs of those using it and to reoutfit the room when the needs change. For example, there are wall hanging systems available that allow the amount of chalkboard to be changed or moved to a better location, or to have bulletin board substituted for chalkboard. Shelves can be affixed to the same hanging system as can writing surface, cabinets, and exhibit cases. Alternatively, all equipment for a room should be movable. If more bookcases are needed, these can be brought in. If cabinets are needed, these can be supplied. Tables and chairs and pianos and power drills are all movable. The outfitting of a school can contribute enormously to the dimensions of the activities that take place.

Again, the process of providing empty space, outfitting the space from storage as needed, and emptying the room again ready to be outfitted for a new function provides an essential element of the ability of the space and things to respond to uncertainty. Most teaching spaces are outfitted permanently with standard equipment. Someone decides that 20 linear feet of chalkboard is needed, and this is sealed into the room without recourse. The wastefulness of the shotgun strategy is avoided when everything is stored but available when needed. A lesser number of a wider variety of things is possible for the same cost. A substantially increased variety of things is a prerequisite to support an educational program for gifted/talented students.

Probably the most underrated kind of equipment in a school that is trying to cultivate gifts and talents of students is a mobile cart. Mobility may be enhanced, for example, by the use in the school of an electric-powered forklift truck. When one or two students diverge from the direction other students are taking, a well-supplied cart can carry those things needed by a large per cent of student activities. Students can plan the activity and the materials needed and be provided with a cart in which a fairly complete inventory of things necessary for the projects' success are accessible. The cart can be returned to the storeroom for safekeeping in between uses and can be reequipped for new needs.

Technology as a Tinkertoy Set

Technology has placed within the hands of the educational profession an amazingly versatile environment. Well done, this environment costs little or no more than a rigid, thoughtless environment. The things of the environment must be accumulated, organized, made available, and used for the educational program.

In a setting for gifted/talented students, the environment can be manipulated with a real do-it-yourself approach. The gathering of resources from storage is one such task. Each school needs an operating manual so that students and faculty know the potential that exists for the space. There is a need for a catalogue of things available, presented in some fashion better than a card catalogue, that leads the searcher to snakes, video cassettes, computer printout paper, and the like. A computer search of materials available may be required. Advertisements at the storage area may show new things available. Catalogues are needed to order things not available. A school can provide the spaces and things that students and faculty can use to deal with uncertainty.

Some Generalizations

How much space is needed for a program for gifted/talented students as compared with a traditional school?

Little is known with any reliability about space needs for education for gifted/talented students. It can be argued that since there is a wider range of activities than in the traditional school, more space will be required. Another view is that with the necessity of providing some adult supervision, the area required for such a program may not vary much from the usual allotment. It is likely that increased space is needed as the variety of activities increases. One element of flexibility to meet uncertainty is an allotment of unassigned space to be used as and if needed.

What kind of atmosphere should be most evident in the school for gifted/talented?

If a school is really tapping the potential of its students, a building would be characterized by research—a workshop-laboratory kind of atmosphere where, in widely different settings, students are working intensively and with obvious delight.

What different kinds of communication problems exist in a school for gifted/talented?

In a school where the space and things are tools to be put together by students and faculty to serve gifts and talents, there is a major need to communicate to all how the space can be used, what things are available, and how the things can be used. Common understanding of and ability to use the environment makes the environment responsive. Students will use things creatively, in unforeseen ways, if there are ways to understand what is available.

The work of the students constitutes a resource that should be communicated to other students. A research job on clouds, for example, may result in a video tape that becomes an element of things available.

Communicating well is a talent. The school will have a highly developed communications network.

Display and performance capabilities of effective, usable quality are essential. The school is a museum in that the individual efforts of gifted/talented students are best made available to all students to enrich their experience and to open new doors for inquiry.

The school consciously uses the interchange of interesting ideas, forms, and symbols to increase the level of awareness of the student body.

How can all the wide variety of the world be reproduced in the school in order to nurture the gifts and talents of the students?

It can't be. That is why, at appropriate times, the students use the resources of the community around them and those of the larger world in which they live. The school learns to inventory those resources of people or organizations, to communicate this inventory of information to students, and to establish contacts between student and community.

How does such a school assess the work of its students?

Some research has suggested that where the student has been given responsibility for assessment of his/her work, the assessment process has the capability of adding to the utilization of the talents. At Alverno College in Milwaukee, Wisconsin, students helped plan their own assessment in which community members knowledgeable in their fields of study sat on an examining panel. The development of a presentation, subject to peer review and including evaluation from outside the school, may contribute to the effectiveness of the work. It becomes clear that assessment in the case of gifted/talented students becomes far more than a paper-and-pencil test. It is the demonstration of the talent. The space must provide ample forums for the demonstration of talent through its communications networks, platforms, museums, galleries, planning activities, and through the way students show their talents in the skills of living with others and living in the world.[5]

Some Applications

The following notions, conceived in abstract settings, are intended only to stimulate thought about an environment for the education of talented students. These are essentially illustrations of a set of categories of talents. Obviously not all gifts and talents will be touched on. For example, schools generally have well-organized programs to capitalize on the unique talents of students in athletics. Space and things are already in place to assist in this endeavor, and further treatment is not necessary other than to refer to well-done facilities.

[5] Ibid., p. 719.

Academic Talents

The academic talents representing experiences generally found in the traditional school curriculum are probably best accommodated where opportunity is presented for intensive individualistic or small group work in the usual disciplines (scientific talents are separately treated). The tools used are verbal and mathematical, focusing on inquiry. The areas tend to be interdisciplinary fields such as environmental studies, which are a mixture of science and social sciences with a heavy emphasis on economics and political science. A major growth area will probably be in the quantification of data in the social sciences. A project workroom, perhaps in some area of improving the quality of urban life, as an example, might be set aside for a team of students. The workroom would require tables and chairs, bookshelves, chalkboard and a large amount of bulletin board, a microcomputer or terminal, file cabinets, typing desks, and chairs.

Another location for a small group project could be in a library, which, for these purposes, could well have a much larger number of conference rooms, some of which could be assigned student projects. An example might be to use a library conference room for a three-hour meeting every other day for an advanced group of three elementary school students working independently in mathematics. Such a room would have a collection of books and a large chalkboard.

This room may also be used for regular meetings of three students who are in an advanced conversational group in Spanish. Perhaps one student is a native-tongue Spanish speaker who leads the group. Tape recorder, earphones, record player, books, magazines, newspapers, and similar things would be needed as a basis for improving spoken Spanish. The relationship between conference rooms and library allows for moderate supervision and assures that materials are at hand.

The library and its extension through a network of public and university libraries constitute a valuable resource for the academically talented. Because much of the work is reading and writing, the assignment of carrels to students who are consistently working in the library will allow for the accumulation of books, reprints, audio cassettes, notes, and the like bearing on the individual project. More complicated work may require an enclosed carrel or study space in order to keep materials together.

Scientific Talents

The student (or small team of students), at any level of the school system, who is scientifically talented represents a real problem in the use of space because such a student is involved in longer-term, more complicated projects, often requiring more support space and the setup of apparatus over long periods of time. When readings are made on an experiment several times a day for a period of a month, the experimental work cannot be carried on unless the equipment remains undisturbed throughout the experiment.

Most advanced work in science, however, places a greater strain on the use of journals in the field and on formulation and mathematical testing of conclusions than upon the laboratory aspects of science. A science area for encouragement of talent in this field would have resources available in terms of journals and books, perhaps in an area of the library, and a number of small conference or workrooms with computer availability and the capacity for providing laboratory space that can remain undisturbed while at the same time under adult supervision. The safety problems in science are obvious, and the school may not avoid responsibility for preventing accidents. Although small laboratory rooms off of large rooms are often seen as settings for the work of talented young scientists, much of the long-term work may involve systematic observations in the community, or of a swamp on the school site, or the use of a portion of a growth chamber, or cultivation of a mold in a saucer, and the like. A variety of storage conditions would extend the laboratory use tremendously.

Creative Talents

The Gestalt psychologists suggest that insight is a reorganization of perceptual patterns. This kind of creativity is represented all across the board of educational activities. The space and things response to creativity is outlined in the other descriptions of settings for the encouragement of talents. It is further nurtured by space and things that in themselves can be changed to respond to new needs.

Communication Talents

The major areas for the expression of communication talents lie in clear, persuasive, and interesting writing and speaking with equal clarity. As such, these talents are encouraged throughout the school and require no special space other than a quiet area for writing and the ability and time to engage in good conversation.

The trappings of the communication arts field involve the ways that written words or voices are carried to larger groups. A school should be able to reproduce the written words of its talented writers—using newspapers, yearbooks, literary journals, scientific papers of students, student-written cookbooks, technological manuals (how to keep a carburetor in working order, for example), and the like. The more students write, the better they will write. Their work must be seen by others. The school encouraging communications talent needs a printing plant.

Communications media have far outstripped the written and spoken word. Television, radio, and moving pictures are the newer media that less frequently are fully utilized in schools. The use of these media to encourage talents requires attention. With videotape recorders, instant-developing motion picture film, and sound recording and playback instruments, there are enormous resources for simple do-it-yourself procedures to cultivate the skill of conveying ideas.

Schools can also use some older devices. The Chinese wall posters are vivid reminders of the power of communication. Probably every school needs some provision, ranging from simple to complex, for reproducing the written word and for making possible radio, TV, or film production designed to convey ideas. The school itself is a wall for messages, and tte TV bulletin board is a teaching tool.

Manipulative-Mechanical Talents

There are four interesting prototypes in developing talent in the manipulative and mechanical areas. One is the development of trainers, in which individual students can learn skills at their own speed following instructions in picture and sound as well as in writing. The opportunity exists to take individual students far beyond the work of a class as students follow their talents.

Lewis Yoho developed a fascinating simulation of industry in "orchestrated systems approach" developed at Indiana State University. A summary can be found in Leggett et al., *Planning Flexible Learning Places.*[6]

The use of design as a unifying element in crafts shop, home economics, and the like creates an interdisciplinary effort in these fields—a problem-solving approach evolving beyond merely linking these areas as codisciplines. When students state a problem and tackle solutions expressed in words, mathematics, and drawings or in a three dimensional object, the manipulative-mechanical talents are being encouraged at a high level. Illustrating going beyond skill training to using one's mind and skills to fashion solutions, *Design Education in Schools*, edited by Bernard Aylward,[7] contains a most interesting detailed description of the evolution of the shop, arts, and homemaking areas to a new level of significance.

Different paths through the same set of tools provide a final creative prototype for developing and advancing the unique talents of the individual

---

[6] S. Leggett, C. W. Brubaker, A. Cohodes, and A. S. Shapiro, *Planning Flexible Learning Places* (New York: McGraw-Hill, 1977), pp. 151-152.

[7] Bernard Aylward (Ed.), *Design Education in Schools* (Russell Square, London: Evans Brothers Limited, Montague House, W.C.1, 1973), p. 175.

as postulated by Woodruff and developed in the Minuteman Vocational High School in Concord, Massachusetts.

Planning, Forecasting, Management, and Decision-Making Talents

Space needs for planning, forecasting, management, and decision-making talents are essentially related to the exercise of verbal and mathematical skills. The kinds of provision made in the academic talent area may well be appropriate.

Fine Arts and Performing Arts Talents

Encouragement of talents in the fine and performing arts requires, in terms of space and things, more of everything. For the serious exercise of these talents there is need for more studio space so that more time can be given to work. As work intensifies, small individual studio space, which may be used for long stretches of the day, should be provided for the talented students to work privately and keep supplies in this individual space.

In music, the talented will make good use of additional practice rooms and ensemble rooms and make more intensive use of large group rehearsal rooms. Portable, soundproof rooms will allow variations in the provisions for practice space.

Theater and dance require rehearsal spaces plus rich backstage spaces. There should be opportunities for a number of productions to rehearse as well as an auditorium with a major stage for actual performances. A school needs an effective theater, usable for dance as well as drama, in which music and theater can be combined, flexible enough to provide for solo musical performances as well as concerts. Talent is not only demonstrated on stage; the backstage technical and production crews also offer many opportunities for students.

The visual arts need a showplace for talent just as drama, dance, and music programs need an audience before whom to perform. The gallery, so arranged that it has reasonable security, is a significant part of any school. Neither should the impact and needs of the newer media—photography, radio, TV, and film—be overlooked.

Psychosocial or Interpersonal Talents

The considerable talents in interpersonal relationships are encouraged throughout a school. Its lunchrooms, student activities areas, corridors, classrooms, and shops are all areas in which the abilities to cope, to get along with others, to influence people, and to respond can be cultivated. Inefficiency of design is often related to the existence of a variety of pleasant places for informal student associations.

Special Places

The Changed Library

The educational process, as it relates to the education of groups of students, is resistant to change. Dealing with one student becomes difficult when educational economics sets limits on staffing and teachers are assigned for every twenty-five or thirty students. Ideally, the teacher of twenty-five students should treat each student individually and arrange a special and unique program for each student. This has generally not been the case.

The introduction of programs for gifted/talented students exacerbates the problem of individuality within a group. One answer is to cluster students of like interests or talents together. With five hundred students and twenty-five teachers, some twenty talents can be encouraged—with a range of interest and accomplishment in each talent in each class. One thinks of space in which the twenty students can gather, with the ability to separate the larger group into smaller groups or individuals based on the level and direction in which students explore a talent. This is essentially homogeneous grouping or tracking of talents. The key to its practical application lies in the talents of teachers that would ideally coincide with that of the students. It would be incongruous to offer a program of encouragement of the talent of students in which they were constrained to take courses based upon the talents of the faculty.

Conceivably, clusters of students will work together in some areas—indeed, in an area like theater, a group is essential. However, a fair percentage of students in any group will exhibit talents that are not readily absorbed into group work. What can be done without dulling the student or stifling the talent?

The current model of the school library, based as it is on a scaled-down university research library, needs to be made a more effective component of an elementary or secondary school. Exactly how the library will evolve is not known. However, there are a series of components, some of which have been stated earlier, that must be considered. These points are skewed to the problems of a school attempting to encourage talents of young people:[8]

---

[8] The notions expressed here about the emerging role of the library lean heavily on the work of and conversations with Robert Taylor, Dean, School of Information Science, Syracuse University. Among other works, reference is made to Robert S. Taylor, *The Making of a Library, The Academic Library in Transition* (New York: John Wiley, 1972). Mr. Taylor obviously is not to blame for the author's conclusions.

- *Substitute network for warehouse.* If a school is encouraging talents, it is obviously impossible to provide the collection neceesary to encourage all the talents because of the unpredictable nature of requests. The school's collection becomes a modest one, as long as there is access elsewhere to a substantial warehouse-type collection. The school's collection becomes almost bibliographic.

- *Information comes in new forms.* To print collections and audiovisual collections, add the electronics connections. The role of the computer as a part of the network, as a search instrument seeking information, and as a tool to deal with information makes it a basic working tool of the library.

- *The library is a teaching and learning system.* The librarian, and whatever staff is available, has a major role as teacher and a minor role as stocker and guardian of the book warehouse. There probably is no better way that a school can deal with the individualization of instruction for talents than by developing a place for individual learning with suitable adult assistance to keep such a center going. The library needs to take on the role of teacher and should become the place where individualized learning takes place. The library needs many spaces in which small groups or individuals can work, and a staff to help students; it needs to connect students with other students or other people, either in or outside the community, who can help. The redeployment of staff so that individuals and small groups can work effectively as an alternative or substitute to group instruction may be the salvation of programs to educate the talented and gifted. The individual or small group work spaces in a library may well involve not only the use of books and audiovisual carriers in conference rooms or carrels, but also music instrument practice in movable "pieces of quiet," science experimentation areas and places with capabilities for practicing design—in effect, the entire range of talent demands.

- *The library is a storehouse for things.* The library must store and make available not only tools to transmit knowledge but also those tools devoted to nurturing talents, whether they be common items such as books and electronic equipment or infrequently used items such as wall partitions, sinks, snakes, and chemicals. Just as the library with its books and audiovisual materials stores less and uses a network more, so the library as a storehouse for things of education stores frequently used items and has a network of sources for infrequently used materials.

- *Question negotiation is an art.* The most sophisticated problem facing a school dealing with talented students exploring wide-ranging areas is to answer questions students do not know how to ask. A formidable problem for the information scientist is to help the student connect what he/she wants to do with the information and tools necessary to accomplish the goal. A subsidiary problem is how to organize both the actual collection of things and the network for the distribution of these tools so that the student can use the materials. It goes beyond merely listing and categorizing. The talented student must understand not only how to use the material but also when and where. The library's role as a learning and information center will be complete when it connects what with what, when it transforms fragile and incomplete thoughts into new thoughts and ideas.

The space occupied by such a library, and one should resist changing the name even though the function may broaden, cannot be predicted. It is larger, much larger, because of the additions of collections of things. Its nature changes with computers and fork-lift trucks. Its components change so that its partitioning must take on great flexibility, and utility services may be required where least expected. There will be a "come in" attitude rather than a "keep out" point of view. The fine art of communication will be used intensively at its entrance, where skilled practitioners of the information science interact with students. The library will be a better, more inclusive, workplace.

Conclusion

The management of a school for gifted/talented students is probably different in its needs for space. The management process will include the entire school community. A substantial space will be devoted to forecasting, planning, and managing the resources of the institution, an admirable workplace for the development of student talents in this area.

There will be enlarged staff places because so many of the faculty will be adjunct teachers drawn from the community in order to increase faculty talents and to better relate the school and its students to the larger community.

With all the planning and thinking in advance, the development of spaces for a school that encourages the gifts and talents of its students should be approached with humility. It is not predictable. The development of a physical environment that continually is able to respond to changes of direction and to new needs is the basic contribution that space can make to program.

Suggested Readings

Ainsworth, M. D. S. *Infancy in Uganda: Infant Care and the Growth of Love.* Baltimore: Johns Hopkins Press, 1967.

―――――― ,and Amatruda, C. S. *Developmental Diagnosis.* New York: Paul B. Hoeber, 1962.

Ashlock, Robert. *Error Patterns in Computation.* Columbus, O.: Merrill Publishing Co., 1976.

Barron, F. The Solitariness of Self and Its Mitigation Through Creative Imagination. In I. A. Taylor and J. W. Getzels (Eds.), *Perspectives in Creativity.* Chicago: Aldine, 1975.

Bayley, N. Comparison of Mental and Motor Test Scores for Ages 1―15 Monthly by Sex, Birth Order, Geographic Location and Education of Parents. *Child Development*, 1965, *36*, 379―411.

Berger, Emil (Ed.). *Instructional Aids in Mathematics.* Reston, Va.: National Council of Teachers of Mathematics, 1973.

Black, H. *They Shall Not Pass.* New York: Morrow, 1963.

Brazelton, T. B., Robey, J. S., and Collier, G. A. Infant Development in the Zinacantico Indians of Southern Mexico. *Pediatrics*, 1969, *44*, 274.

―――――― , Koslowski, B., and Tronick, E. Neonatal Behavior Among Urban Zambians and Americans. Unpublished report presented at the Biennial Meeting of the Society for Research in Child Development, Minneapolis, April 4, 1971.

Burns, Marilyn. *The I Hate Mathematics! Book.* Boston: Little, Brown, 1975.

Callaway, W. R. *Modes of Biological Adaptation and Their Role in Intellectual Development.* PCD Monographs. Vol. 1 (1). Los Angeles, Calif.: Galton Institute, 1970.

Campbell, Roald F., et al. *The Organization and Control of American Schools* (4th ed.). Columbus, O.: Charles E. Merrill Publishing Co., 1980.

Charbonneau, Manon P. *Learning to Think in a Math Lab.* Boston: National Association of Independent Schools, 1971.

Church, J. Techniques for the Differential Study of Cognition in Early Childhood. In Hellmuth (Ed.), *Cognitive Studies.* New York: Brunner/Mazel, 1970, pp. 1-23.

Clark, K. B. *Dark Ghetto: Dilemma of Social Power.* New York: Harper & Row, 1965.

Coleman, James S. The Concept of Equality of Educational Opportunity. *Harvard Educational Review,* 1968, *38,* 7-22. ·

———, et al. *Equality of Educational Opportunity.* Washington, D.C.: U.S. Government Printing Office, 1966.

Connors, C. K. A Teacher Rating Scale for Use in Drug Studies With Children. *American Journal of Psychiatry,* 1969, *126,* 152-156.

———, Eisenberg, L., and Sharpe, L. Effects of Methylphenidate (Ritalin) on Paired-Associate Learning and Porteus Maze Performance in Emotionally Disturbed Children. *Journal of Counseling Psychology,* 1964, *28(1),* 14-22.

Crain, R. L., and Weisman, C. S. *Discrimination, Personality and Achievement: A Survey of Northern Blacks.* New York: Seminar Press, 1972.

Crosswhite, F. Joe (Ed.). *Organizing for Mathematics Instruction.* Reston, Va.: National Council of Teachers of Mathematics, 1977.

Curti, M. W., Marshall, F. B., and Steggerda, M. The Gesell Schedules Applied to 1, 2, and 3 Year Old Negro Children of British West Indies. *Journal of Comparative Neurology,* 1935, *20,* 125.

Davids, A. An Objective Instrument for Assessing Hyperkinesis in Children. *Journal of Learning Disabilities,* 1971, *4,* 499-501.

Denhoff, E., Davids, A., and Hawkins, R. Effects of Extroamphetamine on Hyperkinetic Children: A Controlled Double Blind Study. *Journal of Learning Disabilities,* 1971, *4(9).*

Dewey, J. *Democracy and Education.* New York: Macmillan Publishing Co., Inc., 1916.

Dienes, Z. P. *Building up Mathematics.* London: Hutchinson Educational Ltd., 1960.

———.Mathematics in the Primary School. London: Macmillan, 1964.

Dreger, R. M. Intellectual Functioning. In K. S. Miller and R. M. Dreger (Eds.), *Comparative Studies of Blacks and Whites in the United States.* New York: Seminar Press, 1973, pp. 185-222.

Education of the Gifted and Talented: Report to the Congress of the United States by the U.S. Commissioner of Education. Washington, D.C.: U.S. Government Printing Office, 1972.

Einstein, E. Classroom Dynamos. *Human Behavior,* 1979, *8(4),* 58-59.

Escalona, S. K. Patterns of Infantile Experiences and the Developmental Process. *Psychoanalytic Study of the Child,* 1963, *18,* 197.

Flavell, J. H. *The Developmental Psychology of Jean Piaget.* Princeton, N.J.: Van Nostrand, 1963.

Gagne, Robert M. *The Conditions of Learning*. New York: Holt, Rinehart and Winston, 1970.

––––––, and Briggs, Leslie J. *Principles of Instructional Design*. New York: Holt, Rinehart and Winston, 1974.

Geber, M. Developpement Psychomoteur de l'Enfant Africain. *Courrier*, 1956, *6*, 17-29.

––––––. L'Enfant Africain Occidentalise et de Niveau Social Superior en Uganda. *Courrier*, 1958, *8*, 517-523.

––––––. Problemes Poses par le Developpement du Jeune Enfant Africain en Fonetion de son Milieu Sc Social. *Le Travail Humain*, 1960, *23*, 97-111.

––––––, and Dean, R. F. A. Gesell Tests on African Children. *Pediatrics*, 1957, *6*, 1055-1065.

––––––. The State of Development of Newborn African Children. *Lancet*, 1957 *1*, 1216-1219.

Gesell, A., and Amatruda, C. S. *Developmental Diagnosis*. New York: Paul B. Hoeber, 1962.

––––––, and Ames, L. B. Early Evidences of Individuality in the Human Infant. *Journal of Genetic Psychology*, 1937, *47*, 339.

Goren, C. C., Sarty, M., and Wu, P. Y. K. Visual Following and Pattern Discrimination of Face-Like Stimuli by Newborn Infants. *Pediatrics*, 1975, *56(4)*, 544-549.

Gottfried, N. W. Effects of Early Interaction Programs. In K. S. Miller and R. M. Dreger (Eds.), *Comparative Studies of Blacks and Whites in the United States*. New York: Seminar Press, 1973, 274-292.

Graubard, A. The Free School Movement. *Harvard Educational Review*, 1972, *42(3)*, 351-373.

Greenes, Carole E., Willcutt, Robert E., and Spikell, Mark A. *Problem Solving in the Mathematics Laboratory*. Boston: Prindle, Weber and Schmidt, 1972.

Griffiths, R. *The Abilities of Babies*. London: University of London Press, 1954.

Gross, M. B., and Wilson, W. C. *Minimal Brain Dysfunction*. New York: Brunner/Mazel, Publishers, 1974.

Guilford, J. P. *The Nature of Human Intelligence*. New York: McGraw Hill, 1967.

––––––. *Way Beyond the IQ*. Buffalo, N.Y.: Creative Education Foundation, 1977.

Hirsch, J. Behavior-Genetic Analysis and Its Biosocial Consequences. In K. S. Miller and R. M. Dreger (Eds.), *Comparative Studies of Blacks and Whites in the United States*. New York: Seminar Press, 1973, pp. 34-50.

Hunt, J. McV. The Implications of the Changing Ideas on How Children Develop Intellectually. In J. L. Frost and G. R. Hawkes (Eds.), *The Disadvantaged Child: Issues and Innovations*. Boston: Houghton Mifflin Co., 1970.

Jackson, J. J. Family Organization and Technology. In K. S. Miller and R. M. Dreger

(Eds.), *Comparative Studies of Blacks and Whites in the United States*. New York: Seminar Press, 1973, pp. 408-440.

Jencks, Christopher, et al. *Inequality: A Reassessment of the Effects of Family and Schooling in America*, New York: Basic Books, 1972.

Jensen, A. R. How Much Can We Boost I.Q. and Scholastic Achievement? *Harvard Educational Review*, 1969, *39*, 1-123.

Kaplan, J. D., and Cohen, S. Alan. *High Intensity Learning Systems—Mathematics*. New York: Random House: 1974.

Karnes, M. B., et al. *A Comparative Study of Pre-school Programs for Culturally Disadvantaged Children: A Highly Structured and Traditional Final Report*. Urbana, Ill.: University of Illinois, E6-10-235, U.S. Office of Education, 1966.

Katz, Michael B. *Class, Bureaucracy, and Schools*, New York: Praeger Publishers, 1971.

Kennedy, Leonard M. *Experiences for Teaching Children Mathematics*. Belmont, Calif.: Wadsworth Publishing Co., 1973.

Kirkpatrick, J. J. Occupational Aspirations, Opportunities and Barriers. In K. S. Miller and R. M. Dreger (Eds.), *Comparative Studies of Blacks and Whites in the United States*. New York: Seminar Press, 1973, pp. 357-370.

Klatskin, E. H., Jackson, E. B., and Wilkin, L. C. The Influence of Degree of Flexibility in Maternal Child Care Practices in Early Child Behavior. *American Journal of Orthopsychiatry*, 1956, *26*, 79.

Klaus, M. H., Kennel, J. H., Plumb, N., and Zvehlke, S. Human Maternal Behavior at the First Contact with Her Young. *Pediatrics*, 1970, *46*, 187.

Kogan, Nathan. Cognitive Styles in Infancy and Early Childhood. *LEA*, 1976.

————, Koslowski, B., and Tronick, E. Neonatal Behavior Among Urban Zambians and Americans. Unpublished report presented at the Biennial Meeting of the Society for Research in Child Development, Minneapolis, April 4, 1971.

Kvaraceus, W. C., et al. *Negro Self Concept*. New York: McGraw-Hill, 1965.

Lamkins, A. *A Model: Planning, Designing and Evaluating Identification and Instructional Programs for Gifted, Talented and/or Potentially Gifted Children*. Albany, N.Y.: New York State Department of Education, 1977.

Laycock, Mary, and Watson, Gene. *The Fabric of Mathematics*. Hayward, Calif.: Activity Resources, 1975.

Lesser, G. S., Fifer, G., and Clark, D. H. Mental Abilities of Children from Different Social Class and Cultural Groups. *Monograph Social Research Child Development*, 1965, *30(4)*, 102.

Levine, Donald, and Bane, Mary Jo (Eds.). *The "Inequality" Controversy*. New York: Basic Books, 1975.

Levitan, S. A., Johnston, W. B., and Taggert, R. *Still a Dream*. Cambridge, Mass.: Harvard University Press, 1975.

Lewis, M., and Wilson, C. D. Infant Development in Lower Class American Families. *Human Development*, 1972, *15*, 112-127.

MacKinnon, D. W. IPAR's Contribution to the Conceptualization and Study of Creativity. In I. A. Taylor and J. W. Getzels (Eds.), *Perspectives in Creativity*. Chicago: Aldine, 1975.

McClelland, D. C. Managing Motivation to Expand Human Freedom. *American Psychologist*, 1978, *33*, 201-210.

Meeker, M. N. *The Structure of Intellect and Its Interpretation and Use*. Columbus, O.: Merrill, 1969.

Morgan, H. Demands for Recognition—and Beyond. *Educational Leadership: Journal of the Association for Supervision and Curriculum Development*, 1969, *27(3)*, 229-231.

———. Myth and Reality of I.Q. Scores. *The Black Scholar*, 1973, *4(8-9)*.

Moss, H. Sex, Age and State as Determinants of Mother-Infant Interaction. *Merrill-Palmer Quarterly*, 1967, *13*, 10-35.

———, and O'Connell, E. J. Parent-Child Interaction: Daughters' Effects Upon Mothers' and Fathers' Behaviors. *Developmental Psychology*, 1972, *7*, 157-168.

Orlansky, H. Infant Care and Personality. *Psychological Bulletin*, 1949, *46*, 1.

Osofsky, J. D. Children's Influences Upon Parental Behavior: An Attempt to Define the Relationship with the Use of Laboratory Tasks. *Genetic Psychology Monographs*, 1971, *83*, 147-169.

———, and O'Connell, E. J. Parent-Child Interaction: Daughters' Effects Upon Mothers' and Fathers' Behaviors. *Developmental Psychology*, 1972, *7*, 157-168.

Pasamanick, B. A. A Comparative Study of the Behavioral Development of Negro Infants. *Journal of Genetic Psychology*, 1946, *69*, 3-44.

Payne, Joseph N. (Ed.). *Mathematics Learning in Early Childhood*. Reston, Va.: National Council of Teachers of Mathematics, 1975.

Pedersen, Eigel, and Foucher, Theresa Annell, with William W. Eaton. A New Perspective on the Effects of First-Grade Teachers on Children's Subsequent Adult States. *Harvard Educational Review*, 1978, *48*, 1-31.

Pezzullo, T. R., Thorsen, E. E., and Madaus, G. F. The Heritability of Jensen's Level I and II and Divergent Thinking. *American Educational Research Journal*, 1972, *9*, 539-546.

Pope, L. Motor Activity in Brain-Injured Children. *American Journal of Orthopsychiatry*, 1970, *40*, 783-793.

Rainwater, L., and Dean, R. F. A. Gesell Tests on African Children. *Pediatrics*, 1957, *6*, 1055-1065.

———. The State of Development of Newborn African Children. *Lancet*, 1957, *1*, 1216-1219.

———, and Yancey, W. L. (Eds.). *The Moynihan Report and the Politics of Controversy.* Cambridge, Mass.: MIT Press, 1967.

Rich, C. J. The Difference at Birth (quote of T. Berry Brazelton). *Race Relations Reporter,* 1973, *4(17).*

Rie, H. E. Therapeutic Tutoring. *Professional Psychology,* 1974, *5(1),* 70-75.

———. Hyperactivity in Children. *American Journal Diseases in Children,* 1975, *129,* 783-789.

Rist, R. C. The Milieu of a Ghetto School as a Precipitator of Educational Failure. *Phylon,* 1970 *43(4),* 348-360.

Robson, K. The Role of Eye-to-Eye Contact in Maternal Infant Attachment. *Journal of Child Psychology and Psychiatry,* 1967, *8,* 13.

Ryan, W. *Blaming the Victim.* New York: Random House, 1971.

Scott, R. B., Jenkins, M. E., and Crawford, R. P. Growth Development of Negro Infants: Analysis of Birth Weights of 11,818 Newly Born Infants. *Pediatrics,* 1950, *6.*

Serrano v. Priest. 5 Cal. 3d 584, 787, p.2d, 1241, 1971.

Shirley, M. *The First Two Years: A Study of Twenty-five Babies.* Minneapolis: University of Minnesota Press, 1933.

Sigel, Irving E., and Hooper, Frank H. (Eds.). *Logical Thinking in Children.* New York: Holt, Rinehart and Winston, 1968.

Silver, R. A. *Shout in Silence; Visual Arts and the Deaf.* New York; Metropolitan Museum of Art, 1976.

Skeels, H. M. *Adult Status of Children with Contrasting Early Life Experiences.* Chicago; Society for Research in Child Development, University of Chicago Press, 1966.

Skinner, B. F. *The Behavior of Organisms.* New York: Appelton-Century-Crofts, 1938.

Smith, Seaton E., and Backman, Carl A. (Eds.). *Games and Puzzles for Elementary and Middle School Mathematics.* Reston, Va.: National Council of Teachers of Mathematics, 1975.

Spitz, R. A., and Wolf, K. M. The Smiling Response; A Contribution to the Ontogenesis of Social Relations. *Genetic Psychological Monograph,* 1946, *34,* 57.

Stein. A. Strategies for Failure. *Harvard Educational Review,* 1971, *41(2),* 137-157.

Stevenson, I. Is the Human Personality More Plastic in Infancy and Childhood? *American Journal of Psychiatry,* 1957, *114,* 152.

Strickland, Dorothy. Preschool Programs Should Balance Cognitive, Affective Learning. *Right to Read '77,* 1977, *3(4).*

———. Pre-elementary School Reading. In *Projections for Reading Preschool*

Through Adulthood. B. Calkins, F. Hesser, Schiffman, and R. Staiger. (Eds.), Washington, D.C.; HEW, 1978.

Taylor, C. W., and Ellison, R. L. *Alpha Biographical Inventory.* Salt Lake City: Institute for Behavioral Research in Creativity, 1968.

_____ . Moving Toward Working Models in Creativity: Utah Creativity Experiences and Insights. In I. A. Taylor and J. W. Getzels (Eds.), *Perspectives in Creativity.* Chicago: Aldine, 1975.

_____ Predictors and Criteria of Creativity. In C. W. Taylor (Ed.), *Climate for Creativity.* New York: Pergamon Press, 1972.

Thomas, A., Chess, S., and Birch, H. G. *Temperment and Behavior Disorders in Children.* New York: New York University Press, 1968.

Thomas, E., Leiderman, P., and Olson, J. Neonate—Mother Interaction During Breast Feeding. *Developmental Psychology,* 1972, 6, 110-118.

Torrance, E. P. *Guiding Creative Talent.* Englewood Cliffs, N.J.: Prentice-Hall, 1962.

_____ . Broadening Concepts of Giftedness in the 70's. *Gifted Child Quarterly,* 1970, 14, 199-208.

_____ . Creativity Research in Education: Still Alive. In I. A. Taylor and J. W. Getzels (Eds.), *Perspectives in Creativity.* Chicago: Aldine, 1975.

_____ . Creativity Testing in Education. *Creative Child and Adult Quarterly,* 1976, 1(3), 136-148.

_____ . *Education and the Creative Potential.* Minneapolis: University of Minnesota Press, 1963.

_____ . *Rewarding Creative Behavior.* Englewood Cliffs, N.J.: Prentice-Hall, 1965.

_____ . Some Guiding Principles in Evaluating Excellence. *Creativity Newsletter* (Aligarh Muslim University, India), 1974, 4(1), 1-10.

_____ . *The Torrance Tests of Creative Thinking; Norms—Technical Manual.* Lexington, Mass.: Personnel Press/Ginn and Co., 1966, 1974.

_____ , and Myers, R. E. *Creative Learning and Teaching.* New York: Harper & Row, 1970.

Tulkin, S. and Kagan, J. Mother—Child Interaction in the First Year of Life. *Child Development,* 1972, 43, 31-41.

Tyack, David B. *The One Best System.* Cambridge, Mass.: Harvard University Press, 1974.

Valentine, C. A. It's Either Brain Damage or No Father. In Robert Buckout, (Ed.), *Toward A Social Change: A Handbook for Those Who Will.* New York: Harper & Row, 1971.

Washington Research Project. *Children out of School in America.* Children's Defense Fund, Cambridge, Mass.: 1975.

White, B. L. The Initial Coordination of Sensorimotor Schemas in Human Infants: Piaget's Ideas and the Role of Experience. In B. Elkind and J. H. Flavell *Studies in Cognitive Development.* New York: Oxford University Press, 1969.

———— , and Held, R. Plasticity of Sensorimotor Development in the Human Infant. In J. F. Rosenblith and W. Allinsmith, (Eds.), *Causes of Behavior: Readings in Child Development and Educational Psychology.* 2nd ed. Boston: Allyn and Bacon, 1966, pp. 60-71.

Wilcox, P. The Thrust Toward Community Control of the Schools in Black Communities. In R. L. Green (Ed.), *Racial Crisis in American Education.* Chicago: Follet, 1969.

Williams, J. R., and Scott, R. B. Growth and Development of Negro Infants. IV. Motor Development and Its Relationship to Child Rearing Practices in Two Groups of Negro Infants. *Child Development,* 1953, *24,* 103-121.

Wilson, T. L. Notes Toward a Process of Afro-American Education. *Harvard Educational Review,* 1972, *42(3),* 374-389.

Yarrow, L. J., and Goodwin, M. Some Conceptual Issues in the Study of Mother— Child Interaction. *American Journal of Orthopsychiatry,* 1965, *35,* 473-481.

Yarrow, M. R., Waxler, C. Z., and Scott, P. M. Child Effects on Adult Behavior. *Developmental Psychology,* 1971, *5,* 300-311.

Zeigler, L. Harmon, and Jennings, M. Kent. *Governing American Schools.* North Scituate, Mass.: Duxbury Press, 1974.

Zuckerman, C. B., and Rock, I. An Appraisal of the Roles of Past Experience and Innate Organizing Processes in Visual Perception. *Psychological Bulletin,* 1957, *54,* 269.

Index

Minuteman Vocational High School
(Concord, Massachusetts), 343
Model Cities/Chicago Committee on
Urban Opportunity (CSA), 329
Montclair, New Jersey, 41, 314
desegregation in, 48
Montclair Gifted/Talented Program,
2–4, 5, 34, 44–48, 116–21, 248–49
aesthetics component of, 117, 119, 120
basics component of, 117, 119
creative I component of, 117, 120–21
Montclair Public Schools, 2, 48
Montclair School of Performing Arts, 46
Montessori schools, 36, 39
Moral/ethical guidelines for evaluating
education, 295, 301–302
Moral responsibility, 115
Motivation, giftedness and, 15
Mousetrap, The (play), 230–31
Multicultural Environment Survey
(MES), 155
Multiple Talents Model, 13
Museums
student work experience in, 68
as teachers, 41
Music, 98
in school curricula today, 270
Musicians as teachers, 41

N

Names, study of, 263–64
National Association of Secondary School
Principals bulletin (Sept. 1973), 216
National Defense Education Act, 23
National Education Association (NEA),
322
National Foundation for the Arts and
Humanities, 328–30
Navajo Indians, 162–66
Neighborhood schools, 22–23
Neill, A. S., 36, 37
Netsilik Eskimos, 166
Networking, 65–66
New York, alternative schools in, 40
New York City, 39
New York State Department of
Education, 13
Nisbet, Robert, 28
Nonsymbolic mathematics for early
childhood, 236–39
North Carolina School of the Arts,
323–24
Nursing homes, student work experience
in, 68

O

Occupations, fresh ways of thinking and
acting on, 65
Office of Alternative Education
(Philadelphia), 39
Olson, David, 278
"Open classroom" experiments, 37
Oral cultural tradition of Afro-Americans,
53–60
Oral grammar, 54

P

Parent education program, 130–32
Parent task forces, 130
Parents
desegregation and, 134-35
involvement in schools, 127–34
relationship with children, 133–34,
141–42
Parent-Teachers Association (PTA), 135
Parkway Project (Philadelphia), 39
Pasadena, California, 40
Perception, cognition and, 276
Performing arts, 11, 89
facilities for, 343
Persona maxima, 125
Personality inventories, 150
Person-to-person relationships, 83–84
Phenomenal absolutism, 57
Philadelphia, 39, 41
Philosophers as teachers, 67
Philosophy, 87, 99–100
Photographers as teachers, 67
Photography, 343
Physical arts, 99
Physical environment in the classrooms,
189–90
Piaget, Jean, 153, 236, 237
on conceptual ordering in children, 249
Planning Flexible Learning Places
(Legett et al.), 342
Planning talents, facilities for, 343
Plato, 245, 269–70, 274
Plowman, P. D., 246–47
Pluralism, 34
emergence of, 29
Poe, Edgar Allan, 45, 231
Police Woman (TV program), 229
Political actions, 26–27
Polyculturation, 51
Pre-elementary grades, educational
models for, 181–92
Prereading skills, direct and incidental
teaching of, 188